Psychological Processes in Early Education

EDUCATIONAL PSYCHOLOGY

Allen J. Edwards, Series Editor
Department of Psychology
Southwest Missouri State University
Springfield, Missouri

Phillip S. Strain, Thomas P. Cooke, and Tony Apolloni. Teaching Exceptional Children: Assessing and Modifying Social Behavior

Donald E. P. Smith and others. A Technology of Reading and Writing (in four volumes).

　　Vol. 1. Learning to Read and Write: A Task Analysis (by Donald E. P. Smith)

　　Vol. 2. Criterion-Referenced Tests for Reading and Writing (by Judith M. Smith, Donald E. P. Smith, and James R. Brink)

　　Vol. 3. The Adaptive Classroom (by Donald E. P. Smith)

Joel R. Levin and Vernon L. Allen (eds.). Cognitive Learning in Children: Theories and Strategies

Vernon L. Allen (ed.). Children as Teachers: Theory and Research on Tutoring

Gilbert R. Austin. Early Childhood Education: An International Perspective

António Simões (ed.). The Bilingual Child: Research and Analysis of Existing Educational Themes

Erness Bright Brody and Nathan Brody. Intelligence: Nature, Determinants, and Consequences

Samuel Ball (ed.). Motivation in Education

J. Nina Lieberman. Playfulness: Its Relationship to Imagination and Creativity

Harry L. Hom, Jr. and Paul A. Robinson (eds.). Psychological Processes in Early Education

In preparation:

Donald E. P. Smith and others. A Technology of Reading and Writing (in four volumes).

　　Vol. 4. Preparing Instructional Tasks (by Judith M. Smith)

Harvey Lesser. Television and the Preschool Child: A Psychological Theory of Instruction and Curriculum Development

Donald J. Treffinger, J. Kent Davis, and Richard E. Ripple (eds.). Handbook on Teaching Educational Psychology

Kay Pomerance Torshen. The Mastery Approach to Competency-Based Education

Psychological Processes in Early Education

EDITED BY

HARRY L. HOM, JR.

PAUL A. ROBINSON

Department of Psychology
Southwest Missouri State University
Springfield, Missouri

Academic Press NEW YORK   SAN FRANCISCO   LONDON   1977

A Subsidiary of Harcourt Brace Jovanovich, Publishers

ACADEMIC PRESS, INC.
111 Fifth Avenue, New York, New York 10003

United Kingdom Edition published by
ACADEMIC PRESS, INC. (LONDON) LTD.
24/28 Oval Road, London NW1

Library of Congress Cataloging in Publication Data

Main entry under title:

Psychological processes in early education.

    (Educational psychology series)
    Bibliography: p.
    1.   Education, Preschool—Addresses, essays,
lectures.   2.   Child psychology—Addresses, essays,
lectures.   I.   Hom, Harry L.   II.   Robinson, Paul A.,
Date
LB1140.2.P82   372.21'01'9   76-42972
ISBN 0–12–354450–5

PRINTED IN THE UNITED STATES OF AMERICA

To Brian and Andrew

                H.L.H., Jr.

To Dru, Becky, and Eric

                P. A. R.

Contents

40233

PART 2
SOCIALIZATION PROCESSES

PART 3
ASPECTS OF CHILD BEHAVIOR AND COGNITION

7 Cognitive Development and Early Childhood Education: Piagetian and Neo-Piagetian Theories   *157*

PAUL R. AMMON

8 Language, the Child, and the Teacher: A Proposed Assessment Model   *203*

MARION BLANK

9 Prosocial Behavior   *233*

JAMES H. BRYAN

10 Behavior Disorders in Preschool Children   *261*

THOMAS M. ACHENBACH

11 Individual Differences: A Perspective for Understanding Intellectual Development

295

IRVING E. SIGEL

DAVID M. BRODZINSKY

List of Contributors

Numbers in parentheses indicate the page on which the authors' contributions begin.

Thomas M. Achenbach (261), Laboratory of Developmental Psychology, National Institute of Mental Health, Bethesda, Maryland

Paul R. Ammon (157), Department of Education, University of California, Berkeley, Berkeley, California

Marion Blank (203), Department of Psychiatry, College of Medicine and Dentistry of New Jersey, Rutgers Medical School, Piscataway, New Jersey

David M. Brodzinsky (295), Department of Psychology, Douglass College, Rutgers The State University of New Jersey, New Brunswick, New Jersey

James H. Bryan (233), Department of Psychology, Northwestern University, Evanston, Illinois

Ronald S. Drabman (133), Department of Psychiatry and Human Behavior, University of Mississippi Medical Center, Jackson, Mississippi

David Hammer (133), Department of Psychiatry and Human Behavior, University of Mississippi Medical Center, Jackson, Mississippi

Robert P. Hawkins (99), Department of Psychology, West Virginia University, Morgantown, West Virginia

Harry L. Hom, Jr (23), Department of Psychology, Southwest Missouri State University, Springfield, Missouri

Ross D. Parke (71), Department of Psychology, University of Illinois, Champaign, Illinois

Donald L. Peters (1), College of Human Development, The Pennsylvania State University, University Park, Pennsylvania

Paul A. Robinson (23), Department of Psychology, Southwest Missouri State University, Springfield, Missouri

Irving E. Sigel (295), Institute for Research in Human Development, Educational Testing Service, Princeton, New Jersey

Barry J. Zimmerman (37), Department of Education, The Graduate School and University Center, The City University of New York, New York, New York

Preface

This book presents research-based information about the development and modification of young children's behavior. Our goals are: (*1*) to extend relevant psychological theory and research into early childhood settings, whether they be day-care centers, nursery schools, compensatory education programs, kindergartens, or home situations, and (*2*) to communicate effectively to students, paraprofessionals, professionals, and parents involved in the education of the young. Currently special emphasis is being placed by both education and child psychology on the important role of parents in early education. It is our hope that this book will be of value to parents as well as those more readily recognized as educators.

The extension of psychological theory and research into an applied setting such as early education is obviously a difficult task. On the one hand, the psychological research literature is likely to be foreboding to the practitioner in early education. On the other hand, the practical problems and conditions which exist in applied settings are likely to be foreign to the laboratory researcher. Some principles that are isolated in laboratory research may be inapplicable or impractical in applied settings. For example, laboratory studies have shown that intense punishment is more effective than milder punishment in eliminating undesired behavior in both animals and children. But this finding is of little value to preschool teachers because of ethical and legal considerations and the teachers' concern for the child's emotional well-being. Conversely, knowledge of other research findings can be very useful. Research shows that even mild punishment, for instance, can be very effective if the agent of punishment provides the child with an appropriate rationale for the punishment and reinforces behavior which is incompatible with the punished behavior.

Some child and educational psychologists have combined an interest in basic psychological research and theory with an interest in applied research and practice in early education. It was the purpose of this book to bring together such individuals to review psychological research data from both laboratory and field studies and to suggest the applicability and relevance of this information to early education. The volume is not intended to be either a "cookbook" or curriculum book for professionals in early education, nor is it intended to offer a comprehensive survey of child psychology or early education. In selecting topics for the book the editors focused on productive areas of psychological research that were of particular relevance to early education. The authors were given considerable leeway to emphasize those aspects of their area in which they had the greatest interest and expertise. The editors encouraged some degree of speculation and encouraged suggestions as to new approaches that might be taken to research and to application in early education.

The book is organized into three sections. The first section provides an overview of early education and its relationship to child psychology. In Chapter 1, Don Peters reviews the major developments that have taken place in early education in recent years. He offers a lucid and succinct survey of what has been achieved so far in the field and points out several basic questions that remain to be answered. In Chapter 2, Paul Robinson and Harry Hom evaluate the relationship between child psychology and early education. They discuss advances in research methodology, cognitive theory, and learning theory, and evaluate the implications of these advances for early education.

The second section deals with a variety of socialization processes. Of all the areas of recent research in child psychology, one of the most productive and significant has been the study of modeling. Barry Zimmerman, in Chapter 3, offers a comprehensive survey of modeling research with young children. He shows how modeling processes influence many important social behaviors in children and he also illustrates the power of modeling processes in teaching cognitive skills and concepts to children. As Zimmerman notes in discussing the relevance of modeling research to education, the root meaning of the word *teach* is *to show*. In Chapter 4, Ross Parke reviews research (much of it his own) on punishment. He argues convincingly for a shift from physical punishment to control of young children's behavior through nonphysical and cognitive means. The research that Parke cites on the importance of reasoning as an adjunct to punishment is of particular relevance to those who exercise control over young children. Robert Hawkins, dealing with behavioral analysis in Chapter 5, reviews the literature and shows how this sometimes maligned approach can be used effectively in early education. In arguing for this approach, Hawkins notes that "no other approach to human behavior has had nearly the breadth of applicability or obtained nearly as much scientific evidence of its effectiveness." In Chapter 6, Ronald Drabman and David Hammer show how incentives are a powerful force for motivating children to learn an amazingly wide variety of social and academic behaviors.

The third section of the book includes chapters dealing with several basic aspects of child behavior and cognition, including Piagetian and neo-Piagetian theory, language, prosocial behavior, behavior disorders, and individual differences. Chapter 7 deals with Piagetian and neo-Piagetian theory. Paul Ammon critically evaluates Piaget's theory in terms of its implications for education. He then describes a promising neo-Piagetian theory, that of Pascual-Leone. Ammon points out how Pascual-Leone's theory attempts to overcome some of the deficiencies of Piaget's theory, and he discusses the potential value of this new theory for early education. As noted by Marion Blank in Chapter 8, "Language, the Child, and the Teacher," there has been an absence of relevant research and theoretical analysis in the role of language in the teacher—child interaction. In this chapter, Blank "offers a new model for the exploration of the language interaction between teachers and young children." The model examines the major processes that occur in the language interaction of the teacher and the child and provides a system for evaluating the strengths and weaknesses of the interaction.

Historically, psychology has emphasized the study of agressive and antisocial behaviors more than the study of prosocial behaviors such as generosity and helping. In recent years, this imbalance has been rectified to some extent by an increase in research on prosocial behaviors. James H. Bryan, in Chapter 9, reviews what we have learned about the development of prosocial behavior in children, and discusses the relevance of this information to the educator.

In virtually every educational setting with a group of young children, the educator will confront children with behavior disorders of some sort, and will face a decision as to how to cope with these problems. In Chapter 10, Thomas Achenbach reviews what we know (and do not know) about behavioral disorders in young children. Achenbach examines the contributions of different theoretical perspectives in this area and evaluates the problems of diagnosing disorders. He then discusses the characteristics, causes, and treatments available for a number of specific behavior disorders found among preschool-age children. Finally, Irving Sigel and David Brodzinsky (Chapter 11) focus on the topic of individual differences in the "cognitive styles" of field independence–dependence, reflectivity–impulsivity, and style of categorization. For each of these topics, they evaluate implications for the field of early education.

Editing responsibilities for this book were shared equally by the coeditors. Senior and junior editorship were determined by a flip of the coin.

Acknowledgments

As editors, we owe a debt of gratitude to the many people who contributed to this book. The major part of the work was done by the authors who contributed the individual chapters. We are also indebted to our wives and children who provided encouragement and emotional support during this project. Special acknowledgement is given to Susan Hom for her constructive criticism concerning grammar and readability of the book and for preparing the index. We appreciate the feedback provided by Beth Cates and A. J. Edwards, who read the entire manuscript, and to Dale Range and Don Peters, who read portions of the manuscript. We also wish to thank Beth Cates, Kathy Kemper and her clerical staff, and Dorothy Randolph for their efforts in preparing parts of the manuscript. We wish to acknowledge the editor of this series, A. J. Edwards, for his encouragement and support in initiating as well as completing this project.

Appreciation is expressed to the following institutions and publishers who gave permission to use their material.

pp. 90–91: Bandura, A. The role of modeling processes. In W. W. Hartup and Nancy L. Smothergill (Eds.), *The young child: Reviews of research.* National Association for the Education of Young Children, 1834 Connecticut Ave., N.W., Washington, D.C. 20009, 1967.

pp. 26–27: Bandura, A. *Aggression: A social learning analysis.* Englewood Cliffs, N. J.: Prentice-Hall, 1973.

p. 209: Barnes, D. Language in the secondary classroom. In D. Barnes, J. Britten, and H. Rosen (Eds.), *Language, the learner and the school.* Harmondsworth, England: Penguin Books, 1969. (Revised edition, 1971). Pp. 160, 161–162. Copyright © Douglas Barnes, James Britton, Harold Rosen, and the London Association of Teachers of English, 1969, 1970. Reprinted by permission of Penguin Books, Ltd.

p. 218: Blank, M. and Solomon, F. How shall the disadvantaged child be taught? *Child Development,* 1969, 40, 47–61.

p. 208: Bellack, Arno A., Kliebard, Hyman, R. H. M., Hyman, R. T., and Smith, F. L., Jr. *The language of the classroom.* New York: Teachers College Press, 1966.

p. 16: Reprinted from Bronfenbrenner, U., A Report on Longitudinal Evaluations of Preschool Programs, Volume II—Is Early Intervention Effective? DHEW Publication No. (OHD) 75–25, 1974, p. 3. Washington, D.C.: U.S. Department of Health, Education, and Welfare Office of Human Development, Office of Child Development Children's Bureau.

p. 255: Bryan, J. H. Why children help: A review. *Journal of Social Issues,* 1972, 28, 3, 87–104.

pp. 233–234: Bryan, J. H. Children's cooperation and helping behaviors. In M. Hetherington (Ed.), *Review of Child Developmental Research.* Chicago: © 1975 The University of Chicago Press, 1975.

p. 27: Caldwell, B. M. Seeking protection against early childhood mythology. *Young Children,* 1974, 26, 385–396. National Association for the Education of Young Children, 1834 Connecticut Ave., N.W., Washington, D.C., 20009.

pp. 197–198: Case, R. Structures and strictures: Some functional limitations on the course of cognitive growth. *Cognitive Psychology,* 1974, 6, 544–573.

p. 207: Criper, C. and Davies, A. Research on spoken language in the primary school. A report to the Scottish Education Department, Department of Linguistics, University of Edinburgh, 1974.

p. 127: Hawkins, R. P., Axelrod, S., and Hall, R. V. Teachers as behavior analysts: Precisely monitoring student performance. In T. A. Brigham, R. P. Hawkins, J. Scott, and T. F. McLaughlin (Eds.), *Behavior analysis in education: Self-control and reading.* Dubuque, Ia.: Kendall-Hunt Publishing Co., in press.

p. 114: Kazdin, A. E., and Bootzin, R. R. The token economy: An evaluative review. *Journal of Applied Behavior Analysis,* 1972, 5, 342–372. Copyright 1972 by the Society for the Experimental Analysis of Behavior, Inc.

p. 74: Reprinted with permission from *Behavior Modification* by A. E. Kazdin. Homewood, Ill.: The Dorsey Press, 1975, pp. 16–17.

p. 278: Macfarlane, J. W., Allen, L., and Honzik, M. P. A developmental study of the behavior problems of normal children between twenty-one months and fourteen years. Berkeley, Calif.: University of California Press, 1954. Published in 1954 by the Regents of the University of California; reprinted by permission of the University of California Press.

p. 28: Neisser, U. Changing conceptions of imagery. In P. W. Sheehan (ed.), *The function and nature of imagery.* New York: Academic Press, 1972.

p. 77: O'Leary, K. D., Kaufman, K. F., Kass, R. E., and Drabman, R. S. The effects of loud and soft reprimands on the behavior of disruptive students. *Exceptional Children,* 1970, 37, 145–155. Copyrighted by the Council for Exceptional Children 1970. Reproduced with permission.

p. 93: Parke, R. D. Socialization into child abuse: A social interactional perspective. In J. L. Tapp and F. J. Levine (Eds.), *Law, justice and the individual in society: Psychological and legal issues.* New York: Holt, Rinehart & Winston, 1976.

p. 8: Verma, S. and Peters, D. L. Day care teacher practices and beliefs. *The Alberta Journal of Educational Research.* 1975, 21, 46–55.

p. 279: Werry, J. S., and Quay, H. D. The prevalence of behavior symptoms in younger elementary school children. *American Journal of Orthopsychiatry,* 1971, 41, 136–143. Copyright © 1971 by the American Orthopsychiatric Association, Inc. Reproduced by permission.

p. 302: Kogan, N. Educational implications of cognitive styles. In G. L. Lesser (Ed.), *Psychology and educational practice.* Glenview, Ill.: Scott, Foresman & Co., 1971.

p. 299: Lowentin, R. C. The fallacy of biological determinism. *The Sciences,* 1976, 16, 6–10.

Part 1

OVERVIEW
OF PSYCHOLOGY
AND EARLY
CHILDHOOD EDUCATION

1

Early Childhood Education: An Overview and Evaluation

DONALD L. PETERS

The Pennsylvania State University

Early childhood education is not new. It has been part of man's history for thousands of years. Each generation has been concerned with the socialization of its children and with their enculturation into the norms, values, and attitudes of the group (King & Kerber, 1968, p. 13). How best to educate society's children has been the concern of the best thinkers throughout time. Philosophers such as Plato, Aristotle, Comenius, Locke, and Rousseau, and educators like Pestalozzi and Froebel addressed central questions of early education long before there was a separate discipline of psychology.

Yet there is something new in early education. What is new is governmentally legislated, large-scale, systematic intervention into the lives of young children with the explicit intention of accomplishing broad social goals, for example, counteracting the destructive effects of poverty or optimizing human development. This phenomenon, beginning in the 1960s, was both the product of political, economic, and social change within society *and* a reflection of increasing knowledge about human development. The latter was, in great part, the contribution of the field of psychology.

Changes in psychological theory and research provided the necessary foundation for broad early childhood education efforts. Included were:

1. convincing evidence of the importance of early development for later life,
2. a conviction that children are highly malleable and that growth and development can be modified extensively through environmental intervention,
3. the hypothesis that critical periods exist early in life and that early intervention is necessary both for the prevention and remediation of later developmental dysfunctions [Evans, 1975].

1

Based upon these convictions, and with reasonable confidence that presently on hand or soon to be discovered knowledge and skills could be applied to bring about the desired changes in behavior and development, educators, psychologists and others moved ahead and early childhood education became a major component of the American scene.

EARLY CHILDHOOD EDUCATION: THE EXPANDED DEFINITION

For a number of sometimes logical and sometimes serendipitous reasons early childhood education is a multidisciplinary field. Because early education encompassed many children who were "preschool" age, traditional school subject curricula did not apply. Since, for political reasons, Head Start was not originally housed within the formal education governmental structure, traditional education channels and educators were bypassed as it was designed and implemented. Reliance was placed on psychologists, sociologists, and child development experts. Since day-care services were funded through welfare channels, it became defined as a family service and concern was directed toward enriching the entire family environment. Since public schools had difficulty assimilating school-age handicapped and retarded children, the care of younger children with developmental dysfunctions was left to health and welfare agencies or to private foundations and citizen groups. Since most programs were for the poor or "disadvantaged," it was necessary to incorporate health care and nutrition programs. The net result has been that as early education grew, so did its multidisciplinary nature: a fact that both suggests its strength as a field and the cause of frequent confusion in the evaluation of its results.

Definition

A look at contemporary early childhood education, then, suggests the adoption of a broad definition. Early childhood education may be assumed to be a programmatic effort in which an *agent,* operating within a *context,* uses some *means,* according to some *plan* to bring about changes in the behavior of children between birth and age 8 in terms of some definable *criteria* (Peters, 1973). This definition suggests a range of global variables available for study and manipulation in research on early childhood education. It also provides a preliminary handle for grasping program differences that exist in the field today.

Potential Independent Variables

Within the above definition the agents, contexts, means, and plans may all be construed as independent variables—variables which, in their application, could conceivably bring about changes in the behavior and development of children. Indeed, contemporary early education efforts employ the full range of possible variations.

Agents

The agents of change within early childhood education include professionals (usually but not exclusively teachers), paraprofessionals, parents, siblings, peers, and other adults and children. Each comes to the situation with differential skill, background, and personality characteristics.

Contexts

Early education programs vary in both their physical and social contexts.

Physical Contexts. Physical contexts are defined by settings (home, school, day-care center, hospital, playground), by the organization of space within settings (open, closed), and by atmosphere (warm, austere, bright, gloomy).

Social Contexts. Social contexts may be defined by such variables as group size (dyad, small group, large group), group composition (heterogeneous or homogeneous on age, ability, socioeconomic status), or by the type and quantity of interaction patterns that exist (teacher–child, child–child, child–materials).

Means

The means employed within early childhood education vary most widely. They include variations in the reliance on verbal interaction with the teacher, the central importance of the materials provided, variations in the timing, duration, and mode of presentation, and a host of other variations designed to directly change the behavior of the child. They also include a wide range of indirect means which alter the environment (both physical and social) to yield changes in the child's learning and development. The latter would include parent education programs, community development projects, and health screening programs.

Plans

Included within plans are such things as sequences of learning, curriculum models, prescriptions for action, and intervention strategies. Each usually has a basis in some rationale, theory, or philosophy which dictates answers to such questions as:

1. Who will intervene?
2. When will they do it?
3. Where and under what conditions will it occur?
4. How will it be accomplished?
5. What are the goals of the effort?

In other words, the plan provides a rationale and structure which includes the preceding three elements of the definition. It also directs attention to the desired outcomes of the early education process.

Potential Dependent Variables

Potentially, the outcomes of early childhood education could include any change in behavior or development deemed desirable by the child, the child's parents, educators, or the larger society. The desired outcomes could be defined through survey (cf. Peters & Marcus, 1973), through a search of the child development literature (e.g., Butler, Gotts, Quinsenberry, & Thompson, 1971), through derivation from developmental theory (Willis & Clement, 1973; Kamii, 1971), or through analysis and interpretation of cultural and societal imperatives. Whatever the source, the defined outcomes constitute the child-related criteria for the effectiveness of early childhood education efforts and the dependent variables for research in the area.

In general, no consensus or agreement has yet been reached as to what constitutes the most important potential outcomes for early education. In fact, it is highly debatable whether any universally acceptable answer can ever exist. At issue are such concerns as whether the focus should be on short-term goals or long-range preparation for later life, whether the goals should be individualized and personalized or concerned with basic generic competencies, whether ethnic and cultural pluralism or a "melting pot" conception of social unity should be fostered. These rest heavily on personal philosophy and sociopolitical theory and are not easily addressed by the educator or psychologist.

We shall return to this criterion question later.

PSYCHOLOGICAL THEORY AS A BASE FOR EARLY EDUCATION PRACTICE

It was mentioned previously that there must be a knowledge base that provides the foundation for early childhood programs. Of concern here is the basis provided by psychological theory. Theory permits the derivation of cause and effect relationships and the prediction of outcomes of actions and events. Application of theory increases the probability of specific outcomes in particular situations and under particular circumstances. It permits, therefore, the development of plans for action in the sense we have used the word above.

Kohlberg (1968) conceptualizes three broad streams of educational and psychological thought that vary somewhat from generation to generation and from program to program in their expression, but that represent three continuously evolving program types derived from different theoretical bases. They are the maturationist—socialization stream, the cultural training or behaviorist stream, and the cognitive—developmental or interactional stream.

Maturationist–Socialization Stream

This view holds that what is most important to the development of the child is that which comes from within him. Education should allow inner "goods" to unfold in a warm, social environment. Focus is frequently placed upon affective and social development through dramatic play and creative activities. Of major importance is the establishment of a positive social–emotional classroom climate in which the child receives encouraging interactions with the teacher. The child is free to explore many social roles and to express himself in many different modes of activity. This stream of thought has its philosophical roots in the writings of Rousseau and its psychological derivations from the work of Freud, Erikson, Gesell, and more recently Carl Rogers.

Behaviorist Stream

This stream of thought assumes that what is important in child development is the learning of preacademic and academic skills, moral knowledge, and the rules of the culture. The role of early education is preparation for later education and for integration into the mainstream of life. The obligation of education is to teach such information and skills in the most direct and efficient way. Based upon the philosophy of John Locke and the research of Thorndike, Skinner, and Bandura, programs within this tradition strive to arrange optimal instructional environments by carefully specifying the behaviors deemed desirable; employing structured, sequenced, high-interest materials; employing systematic teaching strategies based upon learning principles (e.g., prompting, fading, errorless learning), by insuring controlled consequences for the child's behavior, and by providing salient models of desired behavior.

Cognitive–Developmental Stream

This view is based upon the premise that the cognitive and affective behaviors which education should nourish are natural emergents from the interaction between the child and the environment under conditions where such interaction is allowed and fostered. Development is seen as occurring in stages; the child's manner of reasoning and interacting with his or her environment will be qualitatively different at different developmental stages. The principal theoretical contributer to the cognitive–developmental point of view is Jean Piaget.

THEORY DERIVATIONS

Not all components in theory are equally important for application. Indeed, some aspects of theory are only remotely relevant to day-to-day program planning for children. Yet some aspects of theory can serve for direct derivations to practical settings. Figure 1.1 provides a framework for viewing the interrelation of psycho-

Theory ——▶ Theory Derivations ——▶ Theory Applications ——▶ Program Components ——▶ Program

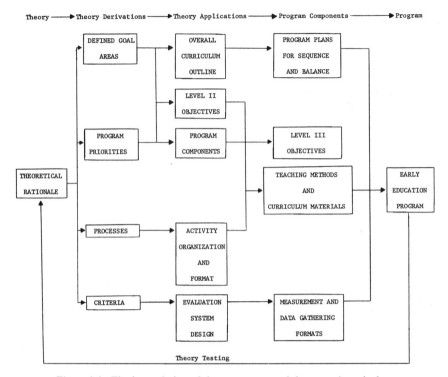

Figure 1.1. The interrelation of the components of theory and curriculum.

logical theory and the resultant early childhood education practices. At an abstract level, the figure describes the contribution of theory to practice and the capability of practice to validate theory. The potential derivations from theory include: program goals, program priorities, processes of learning and development, and the criteria for change.

Goals

Differences in psychological theory focus are related to the presumed importance of some aspects of development to the total development of the child. Hence the adoption of a particular theoretical position limits the scope of concern of the derived program and focuses attention to goal areas of most importance within the theoretical perspective.

Kamii (1971) makes this point clearly. Using a classification system similar to that suggested above to sort out a large number of early childhood programs according to their underlying rationale, she undertook an analysis of their stated or implied objectives. Programs falling within the maturationist–socialization perspective clearly stressed objectives in the socioemotional domain. Such programs emphasize the learning of inner controls of behavior, learning to interact with other children, and learning to get along with adults and children. Such programs deemphasize cognitive development but stress pride in mastery, particularly in the areas of perceptual-motor coordination and creativity.

Programs within the behaviorist stream vary in the range of objects they address, but in all there is a concern for preacademic skills including basic reading and mathematical readiness. There is also a major focus on language development. Indeed, within some programs this focus clearly overshadows all others.

Cognitive-developmental programs generally stress cognitive objectives including classification skills, basic number concepts, spatial relationships, and language. Psychomotor development is stressed to the degree that it facilitates environmental interaction and exploration. Within the interactionist point of view, aspects of social and emotional development are clearly linked with the cognitive domain.

Program Priorities

All psychological theories set priorities for developmental concern. If a "stage" theory is adopted then the assumed or hypothesized developmental sequence will suggest "critical" or "sensitive" periods with specific concerns to be addressed at different stages of development. If a nonstage-related theory is adopted, then task analyses or other analytic or empirical procedures are used to determine which behaviors, singly or in combination, are necessary before others. Theory may also suggest the generalizability of certain behaviors and their interrelationship with other behaviors. So, for example, the child's peer interactions within the classroom may be dependent upon his self-esteem, which may, in turn, be affected by his rate of physical growth.

Processes of Learning and Development

Psychological theories formulate different assumptions about children, development, and learning (Kohlberg, 1968; DeVries, 1974). These assumptions are important for deriving program activities, materials, teacher–child interaction patterns, and the like. For example, the theories of Piaget and Skinner are vastly different and programs derived from their formulations are noticeably different in design and practice. The literature suggests at least 10 dimensions on which the two theories differ and which lead to markedly different practices (Verma & Peters, 1975). Table 1.1 summarizes the dimensions of concern.

Piaget formulates a child that is active, intrinsically motivated, and who passes through invariant stages of development as a result of multisensory general experience in the exploration of his or her environment. The preschool child, being in an early stage of development, behaves and learns differently from the adult. As such, the process of the child's interactions with the environment is more important than the content of his understanding at a particular point in time.

Operant theory, on the other hand, portrays the child as a passive responder to the contingent reinforcers provided by the environment. The child is seen as

TABLE 1.1
Theoretical Assumptions of Two Theories[a]

	Piaget's theory	Operant theory
Children	1. Active	1. Passive
	2. Qualitatively unlike adults	2. Qualitatively like adults (adult miniatures)
Development	3. Qualitative	3. Quantitative
	4. Interaction between child and environment	4. External environment
Learning	5. Intrinsic motivation	5. Extrinsic motivation
	6. Based on sensory education	6. Based on language, and direct tuition labeling
	7. Stage dependent	7. Knowledge and familiarity with task or tasks similar to it
	8. Based on massive general type of experience	8. Based on specific training
	9. Process approach	9. Product approach
	10. Irreversible (invariant)	10. Reversible

[a]From Verma and Peters, 1975.

learning through specific experience, direct instruction, labeling, and modeling. The direct outcomes of the child's actions are important to future performance. Knowledge and skills are acquired in a cumulative fashion as the result of each discrete learning experience. The learning principles involved apply equally well to adults or children. Since learning is cumulative, the content of the child's repertoire of behavior is important as a predictor of future learning.

Criteria

At the abstract level, the criteria for developmental change and learning, as derived from theory, are related to the goals of development (scope and focus) and the processes of development and learning (process versus product). At a more concrete level, theory provides direction for specification of behavioral outcomes of importance and, through theory-testing research, specific indices of theory-derived outcomes. For example, aspects of Piaget's cognitive developmental theory have been tested in a large number of studies. These studies, including those conducted by Piaget and his colleagues, have produced a number of procedures for the measurement of the child's developmental level in the understanding of concepts of number, space, classification, seriation, and the like. Such measures may be used as criteria measures within research or program evaluation designs.

THEORY APPLICATIONS AND PROGRAM COMPONENTS

While theory derivations form the basis for program development, they do not, in themselves, provide the means for application. Another "ingredient" is necessary.

The needed ingredient is the "how to" of program development. This includes curriculum theory, knowledge of program design and packaging, and the like. Through the use of these additional sources of knowledge and skills, the program derivations may be organized into curriculum outlines, specific objectives, practical program components, daily activities and presentation formats. Outcome criteria are organized into an evaluation design and its associated measurement system. Finally, specific program components and evaluation procedures are defined, given temporal order, and placed in use.

INTERRELATION OF THEORY AND PRACTICE

The importance of theory to practice has received much attention in the early childhood education literature (DeVries, 1974; Parker, 1974; Peters, Cohen, & McNichol, 1974; Verma & Peters, 1975; Willis, Cohen, & Clement, 1974; EPIE, 1972). An explicit and solidly based theoretical stance is seen as critical to the improvement of early childhood programming. Theory provides a basis for planning and acting in consistent ways. Through recourse to theory the teacher can derive program goals, set priorities, develop appropriate teaching methods, select materials, deductively arrive at solutions to everyday problems, and predict appropriate responses to future situations.

However, as can be seen from Figure 1.1, the process of moving from theory to practice is essentially one of "operationalizing" theory. In some sense then, the resulting early childhood education program is an operational definition of much of theory. As such it provides an appropriate and legitimate testing ground for theory itself and the result of early intervention efforts feed back into theory to increase our knowledge and improve future application efforts.

THE ERA OF CURRICULUM MODELS AND PLANNED VARIATION

With the introduction of governmentally legislated, large-scale intervention programs like Head Start in 1965, extensive efforts at program development really began. Yet, results were not very encouraging. First of all, the short-term gains often noted after Head Start experience were not found to endure. Perhaps the key study highlighting this was the Westinghouse report (Cicirelli, 1969; Westinghouse Learning Corporation, 1969).

The central focus of the Westinghouse study was the intellectual and personal–social development of primary grade children with and without Head Start experience. The results were interpreted as indicating that Head Start experience yielded no enduring effects in either the cognitive or affective domain. The study did not address the medical or nutritional benefits of the program.

Critics of this study were quick to point out that Head Start, a program that served over a half a million children a year, was not a uniformly administered treatment and that such global comparisons failed to look at the differential effects of alternative program organizations, plans, and implementations. It was felt that poorly designed and carried out programs should not be clumped together with well-designed programs when assessing outcomes. Further, since the children generally showed gains while in Head Start, but their advantage was attenuated after attending the public school, it seemed equally likely that the problem was that of the public schools and not of Head Start. Such reasoning introduced the era of curriculum models, planned variation studies, and Follow Through.

Through a process similar to that described previously in this chapter, and with the input of trial and error, common sense, and federal money, a number of relatively complete early education "packaged" curricula have been developed for both Project Head Start and for Project Follow Through—the extension of early intervention into the primary grades. These models, essentially falling into categories consistent with the three theoretical streams of thought mentioned above, have been described extensively elsewhere and will not be reiterated here. (Readers who desire substantial overviews are referred to Evans, 1975, Chow & Elmore, 1973, or Parker, 1972.)

RESEARCH ON PROGRAM COMPARISONS

When considering research on the comparison of different early education curriculum models two questions immediately come to mind.

1. Are the programs actually different?
2. Do the program differences yield differences in development or learning of the children enrolled?

Program Differences

Conceptually, the 22 Follow Through models and the numerous additional variations available within Head Start and other programs differ in their basic features, theoretical foundations, and program derivations (Maccoby & Zellner, 1970; Gordon, 1972; Parker, 1974). Analyses based upon written materials, curriculum guides, and the like are interesting, but the real question is "Do they differ in actual practice?" The answer would appear to be a qualified "Yes".

Soar and Soar (1972), in an extensive factor analytic study based upon classroom observation, determined that classroom behaviors differed across Follow Through programs on two major factors: free choice versus structured learning in groups and teacher-directed activity versus pupil-selected activity. In a somewhat similar study, Verma and Peters (1975) found that teacher behavior observed within four different, well-implemented preschool model programs differed in significant ways on such items as teacher versus child initiation of activities, provision of reinforcement, structuring of the environment, requiring completion of activities, and teacher provision of information. The results in both cases were similar, and observed program differences were consistent with those expected from the conceptual analysis of programs.

Both studies also point to the problems of implementing program models in the "real" world. Considerable variation is found in the implementation of program models by persons other than the developers (Bissell, 1973). This problem is referred to by Parker and Day (1972) as one of exportability. When curriculum models are highly structured, provide detailed written instructions, and provide explicit prescriptions for teacher behavior, the problem is less acute. When teacher behavior, child activities, and classroom organization are more open-ended and flexibly treated, extensive supervised training is necessary to insure that the program is carried out reliably. In either case the issue of exportability is critical to program comparison research since failure to accurately implement the compared models diminishes differences between programs and increases the difficulty of assessing differential effects.

Program Effects

Since a curriculum model's activities are geared towards specific objectives and priorities derived from the body of knowledge upon which the model is based, commonality of objectives across models is not common. Therefore, general practice in program comparison research has been to use relatively global outcome measures to assess the comparative effects of programs. At times these have been standardized measures (generally of intelligence or achievement, cf. Bronfenbrenner, 1974); at other times they have been derived from generally acceptable early education goal statements (Kirchner & Vondracek, 1972; Kirchner, 1973a). Only rarely has observation of program variations been systematically related to outcome measures for children (Soar & Soar, 1972; Miller & Dyer, 1975; Stallings, 1975). In any event, the results have generally been the same. Summarized they might be stated:

1. Each curriculum model yields specific effects in areas directly related to its objectives and activities. For example, DISTAR-trained children may be able to sound out written words while children in a cognitive–developmental program may be better able to sort and classify objects.

2. When properly implemented, all curriculum models have a general positive (if short-term) impact on child development and learning.

3. Differential effects of curriculum models are negligible when assessed by generally acceptable global measures such as the Standford-Binet or Peabody Picture Vocabulary test [Evans, 1975; Kirchner, 1973b].

4. The dimensions of classroom behavior that most discriminate between curriculum models are not always the ones which most strongly relate to child development and learning. For example, Soar and Soar's factors of pupil talk versus teacher talk did not differentiate among program models but was highly related to child cognitive outcome measures while the factor specific focus of learning differentiated among program models but was not related to the outcome measures used [Soar & Soar, 1972].

OTHER VARIATIONS

The research and development efforts involved in curriculum models and planned variation have all focused primarily upon a teacher–classroom combination of agent and context to deliver, for a few hours per day, an educational experience to children between the ages of 3 and 8. The number of other possible variations within the definition of early education remains great. It is to some of these that we will now turn.

Head Start Options

Project Head Start was initially conceived and launched as a national demonstration of comprehensive developmental services for children of low-income families. At its inception it was primarily a one-shot intensive summer experience for children just prior to their entry in the public schools. During the 10 years of its history, the project has been a continuing experimental effort itself and has spawned a series of major experiments in early childhood development. Summer programs were discontinued in favor of full-year programs. The standard 5-day-per-week, center-based classroom format is gradually giving way to variations involving home teaching and flexible attendance. Locally designed options in program format are being encouraged so that programs may better adapt to community needs and the individual characteristics of their locale and clientele (Head Start Newsletter, 1973). Child and Family Resource programs, by broadening the focus to entire families, provide continuity in meeting developmental needs, concentrating resources to serve children from the prenatal period through preschool (Office of Child Development, 1973). Home Start programs seek to involve the parents as the major means for helping the child and to provide them with the training to make it possible (O'Keefe, 1973). Developmental Continuity programs work with the child and his/her family from infancy through the early school years.

The evolution of Head Start over a brief decade has produced an extraordinarily rich set of options for comprehensive service delivery to young children and their families. Though the formats differ, the options have in common the capability of providing systematic social, educational, health and nutritional services to large numbers of young children. Several million children are now Head Start graduates.

Home-based Programs

Recognizing that parents are the primary and most enduring influences in the life of the child and that the young child spends more time in the home than in the school, a considerable variety of "home-based" programs have been developed. These include Home Visitor programs (Gordon, 1971; Shearer and Shearer, 1972), Parent as Teacher programs (Levenstein, 1973, 1975), Parent Group Meeting programs (Clarizio, 1968; Nimnicht, 1972; Pushaw, 1969; Garcia, 1972), Remote Control Parent Involvement programs (Dudzinski & Peters, 1975; Alford, 1972) and a variety of others. For a detailed review and a complete set of references on home-based alternatives, the reader is referred to Honig (1975).

Several analyses (e.g., Bonfenbrenner, 1974; Dudzinski & Peters, 1977) have suggested the most important elements that go into making successful home-based programming. These include:

1. Structure of the learning situation.
2. Individualization of program activities.
3. Focus on the mother–child dyad rather than on the mother of the child.
4. Shifting of educational responsibility to the mother.
5. Motivation of the parents.
6. Comprehensiveness of the family support system.

Programs that include these elements have been successful in enhancing the cognitive and socioemotional growth of children and in changing the attitudes and behaviors of parents in enduring ways. Children have achieved substantial IQ gains which are still significant 3–5 years after the termination of intervention (Levenstein, 1975). The gains also tend to be cumulative; children continue to improve their scores when enrolled in a program for the second year. (For a more detailed evaluation see Bonfenbrenner, 1974.)

Children enrolled in successful home-based programs have also shown changes in socioemotional development. Infants begin attachment earlier and it is more intense (Lasater, Briggs, Malone, Gillion, & Weisberg, 1975). Such children are more responsive to people (Lambie et al., 1974) and show greater socioemotional maturity (Lally, 1973). When they reach school age, they have fewer school problems (Levenstein, 1975).

Just as parent–child interaction is a two-way process, there is also a two-way effect. Mothers of children enrolled in home-based programs have shown changes in attitude and behavior as well as unintended outcomes in skill acquisition. Such mothers endorse statements of warm reciprocal relationships between mother and child; they emphasize communication and success more (Lasater et al., 1975); they are more accepting (Andrews, Blumenthal, Bache, & Weiner, 1975). Behaviorally, mothers are more accessible to their children, more sensitive and responsive to their children's requests and signals (Lasater et al., 1975); they are warmer, more autonomy granting, and use more reasoning and praise (Leler, Johnson, Kahn, Hines, & Torres, 1975); they show richer and increased verbal interaction with their children (Lambie et al., 1974; Andrews et al., 1975) and provide more appropriate play materials (Leler et al., 1975; Lambie et al., 1974).

Home-based program mothers have also shown an increased concern with their own development. They enroll in high school equivalency and other skill courses (Leler et al., 1975; Lambie et al., 1974); they take an interest in community and school affairs (Karnes, Teska, Hodgins, & Badger, 1970); they open checking and savings accounts (Gilmer, Miller, & Gray, 1970). Members of the experimental group in the Gilmer et al. (1970) study even expressed a desire to move out of the low-income housing project from which they had been drawn as subjects. In general, mothers who participate in the programs gain a sense of environmental mastery. They gain confidence in their own abilities and become hopeful instead of hopeless.

An added benefit of home-based programs is their potential diffusion effects. Klaus and Gray (1968), for example, found that although 5-year-old target children in their program did not make significant IQ gains, their younger siblings did. This, no doubt, could be attributed to the improved parenting skills of the parents.

Educational Television Programs

"Sesame Street," "Mister Rogers' Neighborhood," and a number of other educational programs for young children represent a relatively new phenomenon. Such programs have been conceived with recognition of the fact that television reaches approximately 97% of American homes and that the average child spends more time watching television than he does in formal schooling (Cooney, 1970). Such programs attempt to accomplish a wide range of educational goals in both the affective and cognitive domains. "Sesame Street," for example, is concerned with symbolic representation skills, skills of cognitive organization, reasoning and problem-solving skills, concepts of self, and knowledge of social roles, groups, and institutions. "Mister Rogers' Neighborhood" focuses upon such aspects of development as self-acceptance, understanding fears, and the value of individual differences.

"Sesame Street" has been the most studied of children's television programs. Large-scale studies of its effects have been carried out by the Educational Testing Service, which has had continuing responsibility for assessing and evaluating the impact of the show on children 3–5 years of age (Ball & Bogatz, 1970). Throughout the studies, a positive relationship between children's program viewing time and their test performances in most goal areas was confirmed. These findings appear to hold regardless of the child's socioeconomic, ethnic, sex, or residential status. The ETS reports contain many more comprehensive analyses and interesting findings and the reader is directed there for a complete, systematic presentation of results (Ball & Bogatz, 1970, 1973; Bogatz & Ball, 1971). Several other scholarly reviews of the effects of television of young children are worth noting. These include: Friedrich and Stein (1973); Stein (1972); Bryan and Schwartz (1971); Liefert, Neale, and Davidson (1973).

One finding of particular interest in the "Sesame Street" research is that while learning was not directly dependent upon concurrent formal adult supervision, children who had greater amounts of viewing time also tended to have maternal company and reported more frequent discussions with their mothers about program content (Evans, 1975, p. 349). This finding is supportive of another type of television usage in early education—one which involves both parents and children. The Home-Oriented Preschool Education program (HOPE) (Alford, 1972) has aired 30-minute televised lessons and provided weekly home visits to parents and young children in remote rural areas. The program provides materials and activities which the parents can use with their child to accomplish selected educational goals. Such efforts have the advantage of enlisting parents in the educational effort and focusing their interest on their preschool child's learning, thus combining the effects of television and home-based programming.

EVALUATING THE EFFECTS OF EARLY CHILDHOOD EDUCATION

It was stated earlier that early childhood education is a multidisciplinary field. In such a field the problems of evaluation are numerous and complex. No one study or series of studies can provide the ultimate answers to the questions raised by parents, educators, funding agents, or society as a whole. In this overview, some of the more global findings of current research have been indicated. In this section attention is directed toward some of the troubling problem areas of evaluation.

None of the large-scale early education efforts of today is solely concerned with *child* behavior change. Programs such as Head Start, and federally funded (Title XX) day care seek to bring about changes in children, in families, in institutions, and ultimately in society (Peters, 1973; Williams & Evans, 1969; Cohen, 1970). Adequately assessing the effects of such programs can go well beyond the capability of any one study. Simply defining the target population can become a major problem, particularly if the focus of concern is a cost–benefit analysis.

If one limits concern to child behavior change (a limit that seems questionable when dealing with broad-intent social programs), at least three problems still remain. They involve the availability and selection of measurement techniques, the range of measurement, and the timing for assessing effects.

Availability and Selection of Measures

It seems safe to say that while the number of testing and observational devices appropriate for analysis of the behavior of young children has grown at a staggering rate in recent years, there remain few measurement techniques that are both valid and practical for use in evaluating early education programs (Evans, 1974). Testing procedures for use with very young children are constrained by the necessity for individual administration, nonverbal response potential, and brief administration time. Such constraints limit both the types of behavior that can be measured and the reliability of the measurement. Individual measures with young children also are highly susceptible to tester biases. The problems are compounded as early education programs reach further down the age spectrum and involve younger and younger children. For lower age groupings, standardized measures, particularly in the affective domain, become more and more rare.

One way to compensate for the lack of standardized measures is to utilize criterion-referenced behavior checklists, teacher–parent ratings, and other direct observational techniques. Such measures are capable of providing reliable indices of child behavior change. When directly related to program objectives, they may produce the information most relevant for program improvement (formative evaluation). To date, however, such techniques have not been found to be useful in broad program comparisons nor do they provide the kind of information which permits broad inferences about the effectiveness of early childhood education.

Range of Measurement

Most early childhood education efforts take a "whole child" approach. That is, they hold objectives for the child in psychomotor development, cognitive development including language, social development, and emotional development. Programs also generally have objectives for the child's health and nutritional status. Few if any evaluation efforts include assessment of change in all the potential areas of program impact. It was mentioned earlier that the Westinghouse study did not consider physical health and nutrition. Nor did it consider changes within the family. Yet these were significant goal areas for Head Start. They also were areas where its impact might be most immediately noticeable. The Westinghouse study, like most studies, stressed academic achievement variables. Bronfenbrenner's (1974) analysis of longitudinal studies similarly focused upon intelligence test scores. Available measurement procedures primarily tap the cognitive domain. Until the full range of potential impact areas is adequately assessed, it will not be possible to truly evaluate early education. As Bronfenbrenner (1974) states:

> It is of the utmost importance to recognize that the failure of one or another form of preschool intervention to increase or maintain the levels of performance in objective tests of intelligence or achievement must not be interpreted as evidence that such programs are not contributing in important ways to the development and welfare of the child, and for that matter, of his family, community, or even the society as a whole [p. 3].

Timing

It is a sobering fact that the evidence from longitudinal research and the various follow-up studies on Head Start indicates that the gains made while children are enrolled in the program are lost after a few short years. By and large, few gains are recorded when intervention extends beyond one year. This is true no matter what curriculum model is employed. Only when early education programs bring about enduring changes in the home environment, particularly in parent—child relations, do the benefits of intervention for the child last (at least in terms of IQ test scores) (Bronfenbrenner, 1974).

Such findings clearly indicate the necessity for longitudinal designs in evaluative research and the importance of the timing of the measurement of effects. At the same time, some of the major goals of early education programs are likely to be ones which cannot be realized within a few years. Goals focused upon "breaking the cycle of poverty," decreasing school dropout rates, and developing human beings who are productive contributors to society can only be assessed after many years. Questions of long-range effectiveness of early education await answering.

CONCLUDING REMARKS

In the limited space of one chapter it is impossible to do justice to a complex field such as early childhood education. Yet, even from such a review, some conclusions can be drawn.

First, early childhood education is a diverse, multidisciplinary field. Diversification is the best way to characterize the changes that have occurred since 1965 and this trend will likely carry into the future. New formats, new means, new plans of intervention will continue to be derived and implemented. As a result the definition of what early childhood education is will continue to expand.

Yet, recent history indicates that while political and social forces have provided the incentive, experimentation has provided direction and control for the field's growth. Much of what is new in early education today has been derived from psychological research and theory. This healthy interplay between psychological theory and educational practice, much as advocated by Hilgard (1964), has produced both program improvement and theory refinement. New curriculum organizations and intervention strategies have been suggested by theory at the same time that voids in theory have been uncovered by application attempts in the real world. Such cross-fertilization is mutually enriching.

Secondly, there is an increasing refinement in the kinds of questions that are asked. Global questions are giving way to more precise ones which provide answers of both theoretical and practical importance.

Current findings seem to support several tentative conclusions.

1. Carefully planned and implemented programs, based upon a sound theoretical rationale, are more likely to produce positive outcomes than programs that are intuitively based and inconsistently implemented.

2. In terms of long-term goals or global measures of intelligence or achievement, no one theoretically derived and accurately implemented model has superiority over any other.

3. Theoretically derived curriculum models and intervention strategies which are highly structured and prescriptive are more exportable, that is, they may be more reliably implemented in new settings by new agents.

4. While any carefully planned and implemented early childhood program may have an immediate effect, enduring effects are achieved when the focus of intervention is the parent–child relationship. The greatest and most lasting child changes are achieved when parents are given the responsibility, support, and training to be effective change agents for their child.

5. The effects of intervention are most dramatic when implemented early and sustained over a period of years.

The evidence at this point is too fragmentary and inconclusive to provide even tentative answers to many questions. Are the various curriculum models differentially effective with different kinds of children? Would sequential implementation of different curricula produce broader, more enduring effects on child development? What are the characteristics of the agents of change which most effect child outcomes? What interactive effects are there among agents, settings, and plans? These and a host of other questions remain (Peters, 1971).

Thirdly, the most important need in early education today remains. Continued progress in answering the many questions that can be raised requires further development of appropriate measurement tools. Even the tentative conclusions cited above require hedging because the data on which they are based are frequently incomplete—being based upon only intellectual or achievement measures, or being too global to show program specific impacts. A continued major commitment toward meeting this need is required. The problems are not insurmountable.

Finally, the professionals in the field of early childhood education are increasingly committed to self-evaluation and self-improvement. This commitment is represented in the use of research and systematic evaluation in sorting out the essential from the unessential, in building practice on theory and data, and in amassing additional evidence to fill gaps in the knowledge base. When the people in a field feel free to diversify and experiment, to be creative, and at the same time to subject their creativity to empirical evaluation, the field they represent has a secure and promising future.

REFERENCES

Alford, R. D. (Ed.). *Home oriented preschool education: Curriculum planning guide.* Charleston, West Virginia: Appalachia Educational Laboratory, 1972.

Andrews, S. R., Blumenthal, J. M., Bache, W. L., & Weiner, G. The New Orleans Model: Parents as early childhood educators. Paper presented at the biennial meeting of the Society for Research in Child Development, Denver, Colorado, April, 1975.

Ball, S., & Bogatz, G. *The first year of Sesame Street: An evaluation.* Princeton, New Jersey: Educational Testing Service, 1970.

Ball, S., & Bogatz, G. Research on Sesame Street: Some implications for compensatory education. In J. Stanley (Ed.), *Compensatory education for children, ages 2 to 8.* Baltimore: The John Hopkins Press, 1973, 11–24.

Bissell, J. Planned variation in Head Start and Follow Through. In J. Stanley (Ed.), *Compensatory education for children, ages 2 to 8.* Baltimore: The John Hopkins Press, 1973. Pp. 63–108.

Bogatz, G., & S. Ball. *The second year of Sesame Street: A continuing evaluation.* Princeton, New Jersey: Educational Testing Service, 1971.

Bronfenbrenner, U. *Is early intervention effective?* Washington, D.C.: Office of Child Development, 1974.

Bryan, J., & Schwartz, T. Effects of film material upon children's behavior. *Psychological Bulletin,* 1971, *75,* 50–59.

Butler, A., Gotts, E., Quinsenberry, N., & Thompson, R. *Literature search and development of an evaluation system in early childhood education: Behavioral objectives.* Washington, D.C.: Final Report, Department of Health, Education and Welfare, 1971.

Chow, S., & Elmore, P. *Early childhood information unit: Resource manual and program descriptions.* New York: Educational Products Information Exchange, 1973.

Cicirelli, V. Project Head Start, A national evaluation: Brief of the study. In D. Hays (Ed.), *The britannica review of American education.* Chicago: Encyclopedia Britannica, 1969, Pp. 235–243.

Clarizio, H. F. Maternal attitude change associated with involvement in project Head Start. *The Journal of Negro Education,* 1968, *37,* 106–113.

Cohen, D. Politics and research: Evaluation of social action programs in education. *Review of Educational Research,* 1970, *40,* 213–238

Cooney, J. Sesame Street. *PTA Magazine,* 1970, *64,* 25–26.

DeVries, R. Theory in educational practice. In R. Colvin, & E. Zaffiro (Eds.), *Preschool education: A handbook for the training of early childhood educators.* New York: Springer, 1974, Pp. 3–40.

Dudzinski, D., & Peters, D. Home-based programs: A growing alternative. *Child Care Quarterly.* In press.

Educational Products Information Exchange. *How to select and evaluate educational materials* (No. 42). New York: EPIE, 1972.

Evans, E. Measurement practices in early childhood education. In R. Colvin, & E. Zaffiro (Eds.). *Preschool education: A handbook for the training of early childhood educators.* New York: Springer, 1974, 283–342.

Evans, E. *Contemporary influences in early childhood education,* Second Edition. New York: Holt, Rinehart and Winston, 1975.

Friedrich, L., & Stein, A. Aggressive and prosocial television programs and the natural behavior of preschool children. *Monographs of The Society for Research in Child Development,* 1973, *38.*

Garcia, A. Developing questioning children: A parent program. *Team Exchange,* 1972, *2,* 3–7.

Gilmer, B., Miller, J. O., & Gray, S. *Intervention with mothers and young children: Study of intra-family effects.* Nashville, Tennessee: DARCEE, 1970.

Gordon, I. *Early child stimulation.* Washington, D.C.: Final Report, Children's Bureau, U.S. Department of Health, Education and Welfare, 1971.

Gordon, I. An instructional theory approach to the analysis of selected early childhood programs. In I. Gordon (Ed.), *Early childhood education.* Chicago: National Society for the Study of Education, 1972.

Head Start Newsletter. Vol. 7, No. 2, November, 1973. Washington, D.C.: Office of Child Development.

Hilgard, E. A perspective on the relationship between learning theory and educational practices. In E. Hilgard (Ed.), *Theories of learning and instruction.* Chicago: National Society for the Study of Education, 1964, 402–418.

Honig, A. *Parent involvement in early childhood education.* Washington, D.C.: National Association for the Education of Young Children, 1975.

Kamii, C. Evaluation of learning in preschool education: Socio-emotional, perceptual-motor cognitive development. In B. Bloom, J. Hastings, & G. Madaus (Eds.), *Handbook of formative and summative evaluation of student learning.* New York: McGraw-Hill, 1971.

Karnes, M. D., Teska, J., Hodgins, A., & Badger, E. Educational intervention at home by mothers of disadvantaged infants. *Child Development,* 1970, *41,* 925–935.

King, E., & Kerber, A. *The sociology of early childhood education.* New York: American Book Co., 1968.

Kirchner, E. An assessment inventory for the day care child: Field evaluation and preliminary findings. University Park, Pennsylvania: Center for Human Services Development, The Pennsylvania State University, 1973. (a)

Kirchner, E. The sensitivity of selected measures of the day care inventory to change over time and to nursery school program differences. In D. Peters (Ed.), *A summary of the Pennsylvania Day Care Study.* University Park, Pennsylvania: Center for the Human Services Development, The Pennsylvania State University, 1973. (b)

Kirchner, E., & Vondracek, S. *An assessment inventory for the day care child: Background development and sample.* University Park, Pennsylvania: Center for Human Services Development, The Pennsylvania State University, 1972.

Klaus, R., & Gray, S. The early training project for disadvantaged children: A report after five years. *Monographs of the Society for Research in Child Development,* 1968, *33.*

Kohlberg, L. Early education: A cognitive–developmental view. *Child Development,* 1968, *39,* 1013–1062.

Lally, J. R. *The family development research program—a program for prenatal, infant and early childhood enrichment.* Washington, D.C.: Progress Report, Office of Child Development, 1973.

Lambie, D. Z., Bond, J., & Weikart, D. *Infants, mothers, and teaching: A study of infant education and home visits.* Ypsilanti, Michigan: High/Scope Educational Research Foundation, 1974.

Lasater, T., Briggs, J., Malone, P., Gillion, C., & Weisberg, P. The Birmingham model for parent education. Paper presented at the biennial meeting of the Society for Research in Child Development, Denver, Colorado, April, 1975.

Leler, J., Johnson, D., Kahn, A., Hines, R., & Torres, M. The Houston Model for parent education. Paper presented at the biennial meeting of the Society for Research in Child Development, Denver, Colorado, April, 1975.

Levenstein, P. VIP children reach school: The latest chapter. Paper presented at the biennial meeting of the Society for Research in Child Development, Denver, Colorado, April, 1975.

Levenstein, P., Kochman, A., & Roth, H. From laboratory to real world: Service delivery of the mother–child home program. *American Journal of Orthopsychiatry,* 1973, *43,* 72–78.

Liebert, R., Neale, J., & Davidson, E. *The early window: Effects of television on children and youth.* New York: Pergamon, 1973.

Maccoby, E., & Zellner, M. *Experiments in primary education: Aspects of Project Follow Through.* New York: Harcourt, 1970.

Miller, L. & Dyer, J. Four preschool programs: Their dimensions & effects. *Monographs of The Society for Research in Child Development,* 1975, *40.*

Nimnicht, G. P. A model program for young children that responds to the child. Far West Regional Laboratory for Education and Development, Berkeley, Calif., 1972.

Office of Child Development. *Child and family resource program.* Washington, D.C.: U.S. Department of Health, Education and Welfare, 1973.

O'Keefe, R. The Home-Start demonstration program: An overview. Washington, D.C.: Office of Child Development, 1973.

Parker, R. Theory in early education curricula. In R. Colvin, & E. Zaffiro (Eds.), *Preschool education: A handbook for the training of early childhood educators.* New York: Springer, 1974, 41–74.

Parker, R. (Ed.), *The preschool in action.* Boston: Allyn & Bacon, 1972.

Parker, R., & Day, M. Comparisons of preschool curricula. In R. Parker (Ed.), *The preschool in action.* Boston: Allyn & Bacon, 1972.

Peters, D. The development of self-regulatory mechanisms: Epilog. In D. Walcher, & D. Peters (Eds.), *Early childhood: The development of self-regulatory mechanisms.* New York: Academic Press, 1971.

Peters, D. The decision to intervene: Early childhood. Paper presented at a conference entitled, Human Development: Issues in intervention. The Pennsylvania State University, University Park, Pennsylvania, June, 1973.

Peters, D., Cohen, A., & McNichol, M. The training and certification of early childhood personnel. *Child Care Quarterly,* 1974, *3,* 39–53.

Peters, D., & Marcus, R. Defining day care goals: A preliminary study. *Child Care Quarterly,* 1973, *2,* 270–276.

Pushaw, D. (Ed.), *Teach your child to talk: A parent handbook.* Cincinnati: CDBCO, Standard Publishing Co., 1969.

Shearer, M., & Shearer, D. The Portage Project: A model for early childhood education. *Exceptional Children,* 1972, *38,* 210–217.

Soar, R., & Soar, R. An empirical analysis of selected Follow-Through programs. In I. Gordon (Ed.), *Early childhood education.* Chicago: National Society for the Study of Education, 1972, 229–260.

Stein, A. Mass media and young children's development. In I. Gordon (Ed.), *Early childhood education.* Chicago: National Society for the Study of Education, 1972, 181–202.

Stallings, J. Implimentation and child effects of teaching practices in Follow-Through Classrooms. *Monographs of The Society for Research in Child Development,* 1975, *40.*

Verma, S., & Peters, D. Day-care teacher practices and beliefs. *The Alberta Journal of Educational Research,* 1975, *21,* 46–55.

Westinghouse Learning Corporation. *The impact of Head Start: An evaluation of the effects of Head Start on children's cognitive and affective development.* Columbus, Ohio: Ohio University, 1969.

Williams, W., & Evans, J. The politics of evaluation: The case of Head Start. *The Annals of The American Academy of Political and Social Science,* 1969, *385,* 118–132.

Willis, S., & Clement, J. Goals and objectives for a cognitive developmental early childhood education program. The Pennsylvania State University, 1973. Unpublished manuscript.

Willis, S., Cohen, A., & Clement, J. Formative evaluation in a cognitive developmental program for young children. In *Proceedings of the fourth invitational interdisciplinary seminar: Piagetian theory and its implications for the helping professions.* University of Southern California, 1974.

2

Child Psychology and Early Childhood Education

PAUL A. ROBINSON

HARRY L. HOM, JR.

Southwest Missouri State University

Early education in the United States prior to the 1960s was not strongly influenced by research data and theory from child psychology. As Evans (1975) has noted: "[E]arly nursery school curricula gave no strong evidence of organized theoretical frameworks, save vague and scattered references to Freudian psychoanalysis and Deweyian philosophy ... [p. 29]." The relative detachment of early education from child psychology during this period is not surprising. Child psychology was a very young science. As in any newly emerging field of science, the dominant theories had a relatively weak research basis and were in many respects vague, imprecise, or incorrect. Fortunately, since the middle 1950s there have been impressive advances in child psychology. There has been a dramatic increase in the amount of research. The study of children's cognitive processes and language has emerged as a central focus of research and theory, and the growth of information in these areas has sharply increased the relevance of child psychology to early education. Our knowledge of childrens' learning has increased greatly, and the practical value of this information has been demonstrated repeatedly in many applied settings with children. Underlying the advances in cognitive theory and learning theory have been changes in research strategies: The power of research methodology in the area has increased sharply as a result of greater use of controlled laboratory research methods. With these and other changes, child psychology now provides a much stronger scientific foundation for early education.

This chapter will examine the major changes that have occurred in child psychology in recent years and will discuss the implications of these changes for

23

40233

early childhood education. The discussion will focus on changes in research methodology, cognitive theories, and learning theories.

EARLY THEORIES OF CHILD DEVELOPMENT

The most influential theories of child psychology during the first half of this century—Freudian psychosexual theory, early behavioristic learning theory, and Gesell's normative—maturational theory—each contributed significantly to our understanding of child development. Their usefulness in early education, however, was limited by a number of problems and deficiencies.

Freud's theory of psychosexual development has been widely known and very influential in child psychology for several decades, but it remains very much a speculative theory, lacking both clarity and empirical support. The theory was based not on the direct study of children, but on Freud's analysis of adult neurotic mental patients (Achenback, 1974; White, 1968). Relatively little rigorous research has been carried out in the attempt to clarify, test, or elaborate upon the theory. Moreover, what research has been conducted in recent years has not provided strong support for Freud's psychosexual hypotheses (Achenbach, 1974). The lack of rigorous evaluative research may well be due to the theory's vagueness. Many major concepts (e.g., penis envy, libido) are not clearly defined and the relationship between environmental events (e.g., parental practices) and behavior is often not clearly specified. Aside from the above problems, the value of the theory for early education has been limited because the theory focuses primarily on abnormal personality development. It has relatively little to say about the processes involved in the development of cognitive and social skills in normal children.

Substantial advances were made in the psychology of learning between the 1890s and the 1950s, due to the research efforts of learning psychologists such as Pavlov, Thorndike, Watson, Tolman, Guthrie, Hull, Skinner, Miller, and Mowrer. The bulk of the research by these noted scientists, however, focused primarily on the behavior of rats, pigeons, and other nonhuman animals. Watson (1928), Skinner (1953), and others suggested (and in some cases demonstrated) how learning principles such as classical and instrumental conditioning could be extended to account for and control many aspects of human behavior. But, for the most part, the scope of and power of these learning processes with humans was yet to be determined or demonstrated by the late 1950s. A technology of human learning was yet to be created, thus limiting the usefulness of learning theory in educational practice. The power of early learning theories was also limited by their failure to take account of the role of cognitive processes in modifying and interacting with basic learning processes.

Gesell's normative—maturational theory of child development was more clearly anchored to systematic observation of children than were the psychoanalytic or early learning theories of development. Gesell carefully observed and described various aspects of children's motor, social, and cognitive behavior during development. He formulated age norms describing the behaviors that were typical of children at different stages and he described typical developmental sequences. This normative information was and is of value to many persons interested in child development. However, Gesell is widely, and justifiably (in our view) criticized for overemphasizing the importance of biological maturation as the primary determinant of child development and for underestimating the importance of learning processes (cf. Hunt, 1964). Furthermore, his age norms often fail to take advantage account of individual differences in behavior and development. As his theory has been applied to early childhood education, it has lead to some rather nonspecific notions about the desirability of providing a congenial atmosphere in which the natural unfolding of the child's development can occur (see Spodek, 1973).

Given the limitations of the theories and research data available in child psychology during the first half of the century, it is easy to see why educators of young children did not rely heavily on child psychology for inspiration and guidance. The question may arise, however, as to whether or not early education needed child psychology. That is, in the absence of a firm scientific foundation in child psychology, were educators nonetheless able to develop effective preschool programs? The answer to this question, of course, cannot be simple since it depends, among other things, on how one defines "effective," and what group of children one is talking about. As a source of day care for middle class children, the "traditional" type of preschool program that evolved in the United States between the 1920s and the 1950s may be quite adequate. However, as an effort at accelerating the intellectual development of disadvantaged children, the available data suggests that traditional programs have not been consistently effective (see Evans, 1975). On the whole, early education prior to the 1960s appeared to reflect the inadequacies of the poorly developed science of child psychology. Sigel (1973) has characterized early education during this period as "fragmented, limited in scope, atheoretical [p. 101]."

CHANGES IN RESEARCH STRATEGIES IN CHILD PSYCHOLOGY

A comparison of contemporary research journals in child psychology with those of the 1950s reveals that there has been a great increase in the proportion of research that is experimental in nature or that takes place in a controlled laboratory setting. That is, there has been an increase in research in which the investigator manipulates and controls the environment, as contrasted with research in which the investigator observes the relationship between variables without manipulating and controlling environmental conditions. Progress in physics, chemistry, biology, and most other fields of science has been directly dependent upon the adoption of experimental methods. Despite practical and ethical considerations that restrict or complicate the use of experimental methods with humans, the advantages of these methods have already been amply demonstrated in many areas of child psychology (e.g., see Chapters 3, 4, 5, and 9 in this volume).

Nevertheless, many educators and psychologists question the utility of an experimental approach in child psychology. According to the "phenomenological" point of view that is widely held in the field of early education, "most observations must be made outside the laboratory, in field situations. The relationship between a person's behavior and his environment is so complex, it is felt, that limiting the environment and controlling or eliminating variables creates a distorted view of this relationship [Spodek, 1973, p. 65]." Others have criticized experimentation in child psychology for allegedly leading to trivial findings—findings that are insignificant or already apparent to common sense. These points of view, in our opinion, are fundamentally in error.

The correlational field research methods favored by this phenomenological point of view are, of course, essential in the study of child development. In some areas of child behavior research (e.g., child abuse) they may be the only methods that are practical or ethical. However, a number of difficulties limit their value. Consider, for example, the problems that may be encountered in using a purely observational approach to evaluate the role of imitation (or modeling) in child development. Field observations of parent—child relationships will reveal many similarities between the behavior of children and their parents. For instance, aggressive children tend to have aggressive parents. These observations may be interpreted as an indication that children imitate their parents. However, a number of factors other than imitation may also account for the observed relationship; for example, genetic similarities between parents and children, parental reinforcement patterns, parental reactions to the child's behavior, or the influence of environmental factors (e.g., community, school) common to parents and children. Because so many factors are likely to be confounded in the parent—child relationship or in peer—peer relationships as they occur in everyday life, it will not be possible to determine the relative influence of any one factor. Only by controlling and limiting the overwhelming complexity of the natural environment can an investigator hope to isolate the process of interest and determine the variables that control the process.

It is obviously not easy to study complex behaviors experimentally, but that it can be a very effective and powerful method in the study of children has been demonstrated repeatedly. In the case of research on modeling, for example, a large number of experimental studies over the past few years have succeeded in demonstrating the powerful impact of modeling on many different aspects of child behavior and have determined many of the factors that control the modeling process (see Chapter 3). These research findings have found wide applicability in education and psychotherapy.

The contention that laboratory investigations are "artificial" and create conditions which may never occur spontaneously in the child's natural environment is, of course, correct. But, as Bandura (1973) has noted, this is precisely the strength of the experimental method:

Experiments are not intended to duplicate events as they occur in real life, and they would lose their value if they did. Laws are formulated on the basis of simulated conditions and then evaluated in terms of how well they enable one to predict and to control phenomena as they occur under natural circumstances . . . . This view of experimentation is taken for granted in all other branches of science. Airliners are built on aerodynamic principles developed largely in artificial wind tunnels; bridges and skyscrapers are erected on structural principles derived from experiments that bear little resemblance to the actual constructions; and knowledge about physiological functions is principally gained from artificially induced changes, often in animals. Indeed, preoccupation with matching actual conditions can retard advancement of knowledge—witness the demise of venturesome fliers who tried to remain airborne by flapping wings strapped to their arms in the likeness of soaring birds [p. 63].

Processes of child behavior and development which are observed in controlled laboratory studies may, of course, be altered or obscured by the influence of other variables that operate in an applied setting. In order to assess the practical value of a principle established in the laboratory, it is therefore necessary to conduct further research in the applied setting of interest. Several researchers and practitioners in early education have pointed out the need for careful, step-by-step applied research in attempting to extrapolate findings from relatively controlled research settings to the complex settings of early childhood education. Caldwell (1974) has recommended a sequence of steps "through which every socially relevant idea must pass, without skipping any steps, before we okay the idea for public consumption." This sequence would involve "beginning with an animal study (if relevant), following with a small controlled pilot study done with humans. If results warrant, the next step should involve double-blind field testing and replication by an independent group of investigators [p. 395]."

Fischhoff (1975) has noted a human tendency toward what he calls "creeping determinism", that is, "the tendency to see whatever is reported to have happened as having been relatively inevitable [p. 6]." This creeping determinism is, in our view, sometimes reflected in interpretations of psychological research and in the criticism that laboratory research has led only to trivial findings. With the benefit of hindsight, the results of many significant laboratory research programs may appear to have been obvious or matters of common sense. Research on operant conditioning of child behavior may appear trivial to some because it is "obvious" to everyone that rewards strengthen behavior and punishments weaken behavior; Harlow's finding that parental contact—comfort is essential to healthy emotional development has been dismissed on similar grounds. These findings, however, were by no means apparent to everyone's common sense prior to laboratory research in these areas; and, many of the findings related to these topics were probably not evident to anyone—for example, the effects of schedules of reinforcement or the power of shaping procedures. Moreover, the dictates of common sense and tradition are often misleading, incorrect, or hopelessly oversimplified—evaluate the common sense dictum "Spare the rod and spoil the child," for instance, in light of the complicated body of research findings which Parke discusses in Chapter 4, on punishment.

In sum, a major part of recent progress in our understanding of child development has depended on the adoption of controlled laboratory research methods, and future progress will depend on continued utilization of such methods. Applied research is necessary to determine the practical value of laboratory research findings, but there is no doubt that laboratory research has contributed and will continue to contribute substantially to child psychology and to practical endeavors such as early childhood education.

ADVANCES IN THE PSYCHOLOGY OF COGNITION

Psychology between the 1930s and the late 1950s was dominated by a rather narrow interpretation of behaviorism. The early behavioristic (S–R) approach focused on the study of the relationship between environmental events and behavior, and gave little consideration to the covert "mental" activities and processes which intervened between the environmental events and behavior. This behavioristic approach was an improvement on the earlier introspectionist approach that had dominated psychology, and it led to the establishment of many productive research programs, particularly in the area of learning. However, because of its narrowness and restrictiveness, the S–R approach was ineffective and sterile in some areas of research. Neisser (1972) has noted that under the influence of the early behavioristic orientation

> The study of memory and of thinking . . . became sterile and uninteresting when it was assumed that only stimulus variables (the nature of the material, the number of trials, the rate of presentation, etc.) were important in determining behavior. The subject's own contributions to the outcome were given short shrift. If his mental processes were considered at all, it was in a pitifully limited way: he was given credit for forming associations and nothing more [p. 241].

In recent years, most psychologists have come to acknowledge that one cannot successfully account for a person's interaction with his environment unless one understands the cognitive processes which regulate this interaction. As stated by Neisser, "A host of ingenious experiments demonstrate that what matters [in accounting for human performance in thinking and memory tasks] is not so much what the experimenter does, but what the subject does [p. 241]." Human performance in learning, memory, and problem-solving tasks will depend, for instance, on what the subject attends to, how he uses language and/or visual imagery to represent what he perceives, and on the memory and problem-solving strategies he applies to the task. A child's ability to imitate, learn from punishment, or engage in prosocial behavior will, similarly, depend on his perceptual processes, representational skills, memory strategies, problem-solving activities, and so on. As child psychology has begun to take account of these cognitive processes, it has become more successful in explaining and predicting behavior and has become more relevant to educational endeavors where cognitive development is a primary concern.

Piaget's Delayed Impact in Developmental Psychology

Although a restrictive interpretation of behaviorism dominated psychology from the 1930s through the 1950s, there were exceptions to this orientation—most notably, the cognitive—developmental psychology of Jean Piaget. Contrary to the prevailing zeitgeist, Piaget's research and theoretical efforts focused squarely on the study of cognitive processes and their development. For a number of reasons, however, Piaget's extensive body of research and theory went relatively unappreciated among English-speaking psychologists until the early 1960s. As Brown (1970) has noted, appreciation of Piaget's theory came only after a number of new developments in psychology had led to a new perspective toward the topic of human cognition. "Computer simulation, psycholinguistics, curriculum reform, and mathematical models altered our notion of the scientific enterprise in such a way as to cause us to see Piaget as a very modern psychologist. To see that he was, in fact, the great psychologist of cognitive development [Brown, 1970]." The delay in the assimilation of Piaget's theory resulted also from the complexity of his theory, the abstruseness and occasional obscurity of his writing, and the difficult-to-comprehend nature of the relationship between his research data and his theory. In order for Piaget's theory to make much sense to an experimentally oriented psychologist not familiar with his system, an immense scholarly effort was necessary to interpret and put into perspective his goals, methods, contributions, and limitations. Scholarly efforts by Flavell (1963) and others helped provide this interpretation and perspective.

Piaget's contributions to child psychology are now almost universally acknowledged. More than any other theory, Piaget's theory influences contemporary research and scientific thinking concerned with the development of intelligence. And, despite the fact that Piaget himself has not written extensively on the educational implications of his theory, it has found wide application in educational settings. This has been particularly true in early childhood education, where a number of recent preschool programs have been based on various interpretations of his theory (e.g., Kamii & DeVries, 1974; Lavatelli, 1970; Sigel, 1973).

Limitations of Piaget's Theory in Early Education

Although Piaget's contribution to child psychology and early education has been immense, his research and theory obviously do not comprise a fully comprehensive or adequate account of the nature of cognitive development. His theory remains very much a theory in the making, in need of clarification, testing, revision, and elaboration. As it stands, it is much more adequate as a description of the cognitive changes that occur during development than as an account of how these cognitive changes occur (Flavell & Wohlwill, 1969). The theory is somewhat vague and imprecise as to the conditions that prompt cognitive change (see Chapter 7).

Many of the processes of cognitive change stressed in Piaget's theory are no doubt correct in a general sense: for example, that children learn through activity (physical or mental) in which they attempt to organize and interpret new experiences in terms of what they already know; that each child's interests and ability to learn new cognitive skills will depend on his current cognitive structures; that new cognitive skills and information emerge through the gradual elaboration and modification of existing skills and information; and that social interaction with peers promotes cognitive development. But these are very abstract, general principles, and there is considerable confusion as to how these principles can be translated into effective educational practice.

Since educational practice is concerned primarily with the process of inducing cognitive change in children, Piaget's theory leaves much to be desired as a conceptual basis for educational practice. Those who have sought to apply Piagetian theory to early education have not always been in agreement with each other as to the educational implications of his theory. Different investigators have sometimes drawn different conclusions as to how, or whether, one should go about trying to promote intellectual development in young children, and some bickering and debate has developed as to what the "correct" interpretation of Piaget may be in this respect (see Evans, 1975).

Given the present lack of knowledge concerning the processes that account for and can modify the course of intellectual development, the need for careful evaluative research in early education is clear. The educational value of any hypothesis concerning development—whether based on Piaget's theory, social learning theory, or some other theory—can be established only by careful research. In the area of early education, this implies the construction of experimental preschool programs in which: (1) the theoretical assumptions on which the program is based are clearly specified; (2) these assumptions are translated into explicit teaching methods and curricula; (3) the effect of the program on the children's behavior is carefully assessed (Sigel, 1973). At present, there are research data suggesting that some Piaget-based programs have been effective in promoting children's cognitive development (e.g., Sigel, 1973; Weikart, Rogers, Adcock, & McClelland, 1971). However, the development and evaluation of such programs is still in its early stages. Based on the research now available, it is not yet known how one Piagetian program compares with another or how Piagetian-based programs compare with programs based on other theories, such as social learning theory (see Chapter 1, this volume, and Evans, 1975, for extended discussions of the complex issues involved in program evaluation).

Other Contributions to the Psychology of Cognition

Although Piaget's theory is the single most influential theory of intellectual development, it is a mistake to equate the psychology of cognitive development with Piagetian theory. There has been an enormous body of cognitive–developmental research and theory that has not been directly dependent upon or related to Piaget's theory. Much of this "non-Piagetian" research and theory has already had an impact in early education (e.g., Blank, 1973; Karnes, Zehrbach, & Teska, 1972).

It seems likely that the impact of this research will be greater in future years, since there is often a lag of several years between research discoveries and their practical application.

Research concerning social class differences in cognition has suggested that the intellectual deficiencies of disadvantaged children are largely due to language deficiencies (cf. Hess & Shipman, 1965); accordingly, a number of early education programs have focused on compensatory language training as the core of their program. Our knowledge of language development in general has been increased immensely by researchers utilizing a number of different theoretical models and research methods. Psycholinguistic theory has exerted a particularly strong influence in this research area (see Brown, 1973).

An information processing model of human cognition (see, for example, Farnham-Diggory, 1972; Nelson, 1973) has become increasingly influential as a theoretical model guiding research on children's perception, memory, language, and other cognitive processes; however, this research has not yet been applied to any significant degree in early education.

A partial listing of other significant contributions to cognitive–developmental psychology would include: research and theory concerning individual differences in cognitive style (see Chapter 11); research on social learning influences in cognitive development (see chapters 4 and 9); research on moral reasoning and development (Kohlberg, 1964); Bruner's theory and research on cognitive development (Bruner, Olver, & Greenfield, 1966); White's (White & Watts, 1973) studies of the development of competence; and studies of children's memory development (Flavell, 1970).

ADVANCES IN THE PSYCHOLOGY OF LEARNING

The scope and power of learning processes such as classical and instrumental conditioning have been demonstrated in a plethora of scientific research studies with children since 1960. Scientific journals such as the *Journal of Applied Behavior Analysis* are replete with examples of the practical applicability of basic learning procedures. Areas of application include the following: decreasing the frequency of aggression, hyperactivity, impulsivity, and social isolation in children; increasing cooperative peer interactions, prosocial behaviors (helping, sharing, generosity), compliance with teachers' demands, self-regulation of behavior and attention span, decreasing fearfulness and increasing assertiveness, teaching various intellectual concepts and skills such as letter discrimination, reading, and writing, and modifying social and intellectual behaviors of psychotic, retarded, and delinquent children (see chapters 5, 6, and 10).

Many of the basic learning principles used in applied behavior analysis, such as the principles of classical and instrumental conditioning, were originally formulated in the early behaviorists' research with animals. Advances in the psychology of learning have by no means, however, been restricted to the development of a technology for applying animal learning principles to humans. Many processes which are central to human learning may be much less important (or absent altogether) in many animal species; for example, observational learning, language processes, visual imagery, and logical reasoning. Perhaps the area of greatest progress in learning psychology in recent years has been in the study of observational learning (modeling) processes (see Chapter 3).

Gains have also been made in the study of how learning processes interact with various cognitive processes to determine behavior. To an increasing degree, accounts of human learning processes such as punishment, classical and instrumental conditioning, and modeling take into account the role of the subject's cognitive activities and capacities in modifying and controlling these learning processes. Bandura (1973), for instance, in his exposition of social learning theory, explicitly acknowledges the fundamental role of cognitive processes in regulating the modeling process. Whether children will imitate a model's actions will be influenced by what the children attend to, how they describe or represent the model's actions, whether they rehearse their representation of the model's action, and by other conceptual processes. Similarly, Parke (Chapter 4) notes that the effects of punishment are dependent upon children's cognitive activities and abilities. The effect of delayed punishment on children's behavior, for example, will depend on whether or not the children are induced to recall or imagine their misdeeds immediately prior to the administration of the punishment.

By describing some of the basic intellectual processes that characterize human thinking, cognitive psychologists have provided learning psychologists with a number of important and fundamental questions to work on. How are these processes learned? To what extent can learning processes such as modeling and shaping be used to teach young children cognitive skills such as classification, ordering, conservation, combinatorial logic, rehearsal, memory retrieval strategies, planning, and self-regulation of behavior? To what extent can learning procedures modify individual differences in cognitive styles such as field dependence and impulsivity? Are Piaget's stages of development invariant? Can progress through these stages be accelerated? Are the processes which are responsible for language acquisition fundamentally different from the processes that account for other types of learning? Although the answers to many of these questions remain to be determined, it is clear that many basic cognitive skills can be effectively taught to young children using social learning procedures (see chapters 3, 5, and 6).

Applications of Learning Theory in Early Education

Several early education programs have applied learning and behavior analysis principles to teach social and cognitive skills to preschool children (Bereiter & Engelmann, 1966; Bushell, 1973; Engelmann, Osborn, & Engelmann, 1972; Risley, 1972). These programs differ from traditional preschool programs in a number of ways. Behavior analysis programs typically set very specific behavioral objectives. They attempt to achieve these objectives through carefully programmed teaching sessions; the teacher exercises a high degree of control and direction, carefully managing the conditions of learning and the child's behavior. Complex intellectual skills are reduced to simpler component skills, which are then taught through the use of modeling, verbal instruction, shaping, prompting, fading, and other learning processes. Behavior analysis programs have been exemplary in their attempts to evaluate carefully the results of their programs by careful testing and measurement. Program assessments have shown that these programs can be successful in accelerating many aspects of cognitive development in disadvantaged and non-disadvantaged children. As is the case with all early education programs, however, fundamental questions concerning timing, content, and methodology remain to be resolved—questions that will be settled only through continued research and not by polemics. For instance, it remains to be determined to what extent the frequent use of material and social reinforcers in the teaching process may affect the child's "intrinsic motivation" to learn.

As is the case with some Piagetian-based programs in early education, behavior analysis programs in this area have sometimes suffered from a scientific myopia or "tunnel vision" of sorts, that is, a failure to make use of relevant scientific information generated from other theoretical perspectives. Beilin (1972), in discussing one behavior analysis program that attempts to promote language development in preschool children, notes that the program is based on an outdated model of language structure and acquisition—a model which has been "largely discredited" by psycholinguistic analysis and research in language development. As Beilin further points out, a behavior modification program that sets language goals "not related to an adequate theory of language, cognition, or learning may lead to behavior modification that is in no way meaningful or significant. On the other hand, a behavior modification technology that is tied to a meaningful theory can be a powerful educational device [p. 179]."

AN ARGUMENT FOR ECLECTICISM IN EARLY EDUCATION

The science of psychology has outgrown the age in which it could be dominated by one or another "school" or theory. No single theory or system in psychology—whether Freudian psychoanalysis, Skinnerian behaviorism, Piagetian theory, or whatever—can begin to encompass more than a small part of the available scientific information concerning such diverse topics as sensation, perception, memory, language, problem solving, learning, motivation, social behavior, and behavior disorders. Within child psychology as a subfield of psychology, no single theory or system can encompass more than a fraction of the developmental information available concerning these and other aspects of development. For a given psychological topic there are likely to be a number of theoretical perspectives and research programs that can contribute to an understanding of that topic. For instance, contributions to our understanding of behavior disorders have come from behavior therapy, cognitive theory, psychophysiology, psychoanalytic theory, and sociological theories (see Chapter 10). Different theories may, in some respects, contain contradictory implications for education, but they are also likely to be complementary, in part, in the sense that they may deal with different problems or different aspects of the same problem.

Many recent programs in early education have been based predominantly on a single theory or orientation in child psychology, such as Piagetian theory or behavior analysis, and have essentially ignored the contribution of other theories. This may, at present, be a useful research strategy in attempting to evaluate the possible applications of the theory, but in the long run, it seems likely that more effective preschool programs will be developed by taking a more eclectic approach— that is, by utilizing scientific information from more than one theoretical perspective (as Achenbach does in Chapter 10). Just as it seems desirable for a language training program based on operant learning theory to make use of the information that psycholinguists and other developmental psychologists have acquired concerning language and cognitive development in normal and disadvantaged children, so it seems advisable for Piaget-based program to take account of what is known about the influence of modeling and reinforcement processes on cognitive and social development. In cases in which different theories lead to incompatible implications, it will be necessary to base a program on one theory or the other. But any preschool program will deal with a number of problems and aspects of development for which information from many theoretical perspectives and research areas can be of value.

REFERENCES

Achenbach, T. M. *Developmental psychopathology.* New York: Ronald, 1974.
Bandura, A. *Aggression: A social learning analysis.* Englewood Cliffs, New Jersey: Prentice-Hall, 1973.
Beilin, H. The status and future of preschool compensatory education. In J. C. Stanley (Ed.), *Preschool programs for the disadvantaged.* Baltimore: The Johns Hopkins University Press, 1972.
Bereiter, C., & Engelmann. *Teaching the culturally disadvantaged child in the preschool.* Englewood Cliffs, N. J.: Prentice-Hall, 1966.
Blank, M. *Teaching learning in the preschool: A dialogue approach.* Columbus, Ohio: Charles E. Merrill, 1973.
Bloom, L. Language development. In F. D. Horowitz (Ed.), *Review of child development research,* (Vol. 4). Chicago: University of Chicago Press, 1975.
Brown, R. Introduction. In *Cognitive development in children.* Chicago: University of Chicago Press, 1970.
Brown, R. *A first language: The early stages.* Cambridge, Massachusetts: Harvard University Press, 1973.
Bruner, J. S., Olver, R. R., & Greenfield, P. M. *Studies in cognitive growth.* New York: Wiley, 1966.
Bushell, D., Jr. The behavior analysis classroom. In B. Spodek (Ed.), *Early childhood education.* Englewood Cliffs, New Jersey: Prentice-Hall, 1973.

Caldwell, B. M. Seeking protection against early childhood mythology. *Young Children*, 1974, *26*, 385–396.

Engelmann, S., Osborn, J., & Engelmann, T. *Distar language program*. Chicago: Science Research Associates, 1972.

Evans, E. D. *Contemporary influences in early childhood education*. New York: Holt, Rinehart, & Winston, 1975.

Farnham-Diggory, S. (Ed.), *Information processing in children*. New York: Academic Press, 1972.

Fischoff, B. Hindsight: Thinking backward? *Oregon Research Institute Monograph, 14*, Number 1, 1975.

Flavell, J. H. *The developmental psychology of Jean Piaget*. New York: D. Van Nostrand, 1963.

Flavell, J. H. Developmental studies of mediated memory. In H. W. Reese & L. P. Lipsitt (Eds.), *Advances in child development and behavior* (Vol. 5). New York: Academic Press, 1970.

Flavell, J. H., & Wohlwill, J. F. Formal and functional aspects of cognitive development. In D. Elkind & J. H. Flavell (Eds.), *Studies in cognitive development: Essays in honor of Jean Piaget*. New York: Oxford University Press, 1969.

Hess, R., & Shipman, V. Early experience and socialization of cognitive modes in children. *Child Development,* 1965, *36,* 869–886.

Hunt, J. McVicker. The implications of changing ideas on how children develop intellectually. *Children,* 1964, May–June. Reprinted in J. L. Frost (Ed.), *Early childhood education rediscovered*. New York: Holt, Rinehart, & Winston, 1968.

Kamii, C., & DeVries, R. Piaget for early education. In R. Parker (Ed.), *The preschool in action*. Boston: Allyn and Bacon, 1974.

Karnes, M. B., Zehrbach, R. R., & Teska, J. A. An ameliorative approach in the development of curriculum. In R. K. Parker (Ed.), *The preschool in action*. Boston: Allyn and Bacon, 1972.

Kohlberg, L. Development of moral character and ideology. In M. L. Hoffman (Ed.), *Review of child development research* (Vol. 1). New York: Russell Sage, 1964.

Lavatelli, C. *Piaget's theory applied to an early childhood curriculum*. Boston: American Science and Engineering, 1970.

Neisser, U. Changing conceptions of imagery. In P. W. Sheehan (Ed.), *The function and nature of imagery*. New York: Academic Press, 1972.

Nelson, K. Structure and strategy in learning to talk. *Monographs of the Society for Research in Child Development,* 1973, 38, No. 149.

Risley, T. Spontaneous language and the preschool environment. In J. C. Stanley (Ed.), *Preschool programs for the disadvantaged*. Baltimore: The Johns Hopkins University Press, 1972.

Sigel, I. E. Where is preschool education going: Or are we en route without a road map? *Proceedings of the 1972 Invitational Conference on Testing Problems—Assessment in a Pluralistic Society,* Educational Testing Service, 1973.

Skinner, B. F. *Science and human behavior*. New York: Macmillan, 1953.

Spodek, B. *Early childhood education*. Englewood Cliffs, New Jersey: Prentice-Hall, 1973.

Watson, J. B. *Psychological care of infant and child*. New York: Norton, 1928.

Weikart, D., Rogers, L., Adcock, C., & McClelland, D. *The cognitively oriented curriculum: A framework for preschool teachers*. Washington, D. C.: National Association for the Education of Young Children, 1971.

White, B. L. Informal education during the first months of life. In R. D. Hess & R. M. Bear (Eds.), *Early education: Current theory, research, and action*. Chicago, Aldine, 1968.

White, B. W., & Watts, J. C. Experience and environment: *Major influences on the development of the young child*. (Vol. I). Englewood Cliffs, New Jersey: Prentice-Hall, 1973.

Part 2

SOCIALIZATION PROCESSES

3

Modeling

BARRY J. ZIMMERMAN

The Graduate School and University Center of
The City University of New York

It has been observed that man is basically a social creature. Early in life, he begins to seek the presence of others for support and information. This chapter will survey research on how children learn through observation of other poeple. Any keen observer of young children is immediately struck by the exquisite detail exhibited when a young child imitates a model, but recent research indicates that this sort of exact copying or mimicry constitutes only a small portion of what a child learns by observing others (Zimmerman & Rosenthal, 1974b). But before explaining just how selective this learning process can be, let us consider some of the developmental changes that a child typically goes through when learning to observe and imitate others.

DEVELOPMENTAL CHANGES IN A CHILD'S IMITATION AND THEORETICAL EXPLANATIONS

Neonate Attention to Movement and Rapid Learning to Attend to Humans

From the moment of birth, children are attracted to people around them. Of all the characteristics of stimuli which attract a newborn's attention, movement appears to be one of the most important. There is evidence that neonates will track a moving series of dots (Dayton & Jones, 1964). One measure of discrimination in very young infants is whether or not any other habitual actions are altered during exposure to a particular stimulus. Haith (1966) found that babies between 3 and 5 days old stopped sucking when a light moved before them but not when it remained stationary. Interestingly, this characteristic of movement inheres in the human stimuli in a child's environment as well.

Within a few hours of birth, social stimuli such as faces begin to attract a child's attention. For example, newborns prefer looking at a schematic drawing of a face rather than at a picture having the same component lines arranged in a random pattern (Stechler, 1964). Frantz (1963) found that infants varying in age between 5 hours and 10 days already showed a preference for watching a face to looking at newsprint. It could be argued that perhaps some other property of the stimuli attracted the child, such as the complexity of faces rather than their human form. However, Haaf and Bell (1967) presented four stimuli varying along a dimension of "faceness" and along a dimension of complexity to 4-month-old infants. Each child's preferences were inferred from his duration of looking at the pictures. These fixation patterns were perfectly correlated with the amount of facial detail. Thus social stimuli rapidly become major factors controlling children's attention and behavior.

Unfortunately, relatively little is known about developmental changes in children's skill in imitating. Practically no experimental research has been conducted on children younger than 2 years of age. Piaget's (1962) observations of his own children are perhaps the most detailed descriptive evidence presently available. Piaget has described changes in children's patterns of imitation in six separate stages which parallel stages he noted in general intellectual development. Many of the observations made by Piaget have been also reported by other psychologists on the basis of their informal experience with children. From these observations, other psychologists have constructed theories of how imitation occurs just as Piaget did.

Early psychologists and social philosophers (James, 1890; Morgan, 1896; Ross, 1908; Tarde, 1903) attributed imitation to instinctual origins because of the pervasiveness of imitation within vastly different cultures. *Instinct* theory was particularly prominent around the turn of the century. In general it assumed that imitation was a reflexive sort of action that few could resist when exposed to social stimuli. James (1890) felt imitation usually occurred without any conscious intention and was manifested in the behavior of large masses of people in mobs, orgies, or gatherings of any sort. Instinct explanations could explain the presence of imitation reasonably well but were generally unable to predict the absence or developmental character of imitation. Evidence subsequently emerged that learning influenced the occurrence and form of people's behavior, and these findings conflicted with instinct theory's emphasis on reflexive causation of behavior. As a result, instinct positions fell into disrepute by the 1930's.

Prompting Imitation by Copying an Infant's Ongoing Behavior

The first evidence of imitation in young children appears to involve direct prompting by adults. It has been widely observed that a young child can be induced to imitate if another person would contingently mimic a particular action of the child. Many adults—parents, visiting relatives, or other aficionados of preschool-age children such as politicians looking for a few votes—have been known to try to establish rapport with an infant by mimicking one of the child's utterances, for example, saying "dada" immediately after the child said it. Typically the youngster will give a startled look and suddenly blurt out a slightly longer string of "dadas," and the game is on.

Piaget (1962) found that an infant responded to prompted imitation between the ages of 1 and 4 months, and he termed this phenomenon a "circular reaction." According to Piaget, a child learns to discriminate a response by producing it over and over to himself. In this way, primitive concepts are formed. *Piaget* theorizes that a child imitates mimicked actions because his intellect is acting upon the environment. He feels that the intellect has the inherent capacity to develop itself, and he suggests that this occurs as a result of two complementary mental tendencies termed "assimilation" and "accommodation." Assimilation refers to a process in which information is ingested without requiring any changes in the mental structure; whereas accommodation refers to the process in which the mental structure is altered in order for new information to be comprehended. Assimilation and accommodation are properties of a child's intellect, and they direct and sustain overt action such as imitation. According to Piaget, a child's initial concepts or schemata center on motoric action and resulting sensory feedback. These action-concepts must be repeated many times before they become fully differentiated from other actions. Piaget interpreted the fact that a child increasingly makes a particular sound as a result of an adult's mimicking as indicating that the child is actively attempting to form a primitive sensorimotor concept. Thus prompted imitation is viewed as overt behavioral evidence of an inherent capacity of each person's intellect to develop itself.

Other psychologists have explained this same phenomenon according to a classical conditioning model (Allport, 1924; Humphrey, 1921; Smith & Guthrie, 1921). These *associationists* believed that contingent copying influences a child's behavior because the model's actions were positively valued as a result of prior conditioning. The model's presence and responses have been associated with pleasurable outcomes for the child such as being diapered, fed, or held. During prompted imitation, a model's actions are paired with the child's response of the same form. Through classical conditioning, the child's actions also become positively valenced, and this property leads the child to repeat them or imitate. This formulation not only accounted for why the child would repeat the responses that the model copied, but also could explain why the child would repeat the responses outside the model's presence. One difficulty with the associationist position is that it does not explain why responding eventually stops. Associationists do not believe that novel responses can be learned through observation alone. They assume that the child has to behave before an adult's copying can bring the response under the control of modeling cues.

Imitating Known Responses without
Direct Mimicking by the Model

Another development in a child's skill in imitating occurs when he can emulate the actions of another person that are unrelated to his own momentary behavior. Piaget (1962) reported that this occurs when a child is approximately 4 or 5 months of age. This accomplishment indicated to Piaget that the child was capable of reacting mentally to the model. However, Piaget believes that novel responses cannot be imitated at this age and that actions which are imitated constitute relatively complete response chains. From this nonselective quality of a child's imitation, he concluded that the child was unable to reorganize knowledge internally during observation of another person's actions.

Mowrer (1960) are more recently Aronfreed (1968) have advanced an *affective feedback* explanation for imitation. Mowrer has suggested that vicarious learning occurs in one of two ways. One type of learning, which he termed "imitation," occurs when a child observes a model display a response, and then he receives rewards for duplicating the model's performance. For example, a preschool-age child who attempts to dress himself in the morning "like Daddy does" will probably receive social approval from mother. The actions of the model are copied because they are directly rewarded. Mowrer recognized another type of vicarious learning which he termed "empathy." In this case, the model not only performs but also receives consequences for his actions. The observer must intuit the model's satisfactions (or dissatisfactions) in order to learn empathically. Aronfreed (1968) suggested that vicarious rewards create emotional reactions within the observer because a model's responses have been previously associated with direct rewards and punishment to the observer as well. Therefore the reason a younger child will cry when his older brother is spanked is because his sibling's spankings have been previously associated with his own punishment. The most important assumptions of the affective feedback position is that imitative responses are acquired and sustained by the emotional cues that are elicited within the observer when he executes the behavior.

We are all aware that we receive sensations from muscles and other visceral tissue as we respond. Mowrer and Aronfreed are suggesting that these sensations become emotionally charged as a result of their association with rewards or punishment. Consequently human action is directed by and reflects a person's attempts to repeat responses that create positive affective states. This theory is a sort of second generation associationist position that has been expanded to include instrumental as well as classical conditioning. Aronfreed has included a "cognitive template" or mental component in his version. Thus he assumes that affective experience can be mentally registered or evoked. This assumption permits his theory to account for the occurrence of vicarious learning with little overt performance. However, Aronfreed does not appear to believe that cognitive processes can directly trigger imitation but that an intervening stage must occur wherein affective cues are elicited.

While there is ample evidence that changes in affect can accompany vicarious learning, there is research that such learning can occur mentally without any somatic feedback from response execution (e.g., Black, 1958; Taub, Bacon, & Berman, 1965). In addition, research on involuntary muscle groups that are involved in affective reactions, such as blood pressure or heart rate, has found that these reactions are slow to activate and inhibit and are poorly correlated with changes in overt response (Hodgson & Rachman, 1974). It appears that additional clarification is needed concerning the nature and functioning of the cognitive template construct before definitive judgments can be made about Aronfreed's version of this theory. Clearly substantial evidence conflicts with any simple affective feedback explanations for imitation.

Another theoretical explanation for imitation has been offered which stresses *reinforcement* or feedback but refrains from offering any hypotheses about internal states which mediate actions (e.g., Gewirtz & Stingle, 1968). This model is an instrumental or operant conditioning paradigm in which rewards that follow imitation are given primary importance. According to this account, imitative behavior is a *general* response class which is acquired early in development when a child's responses that are similar to those of a model's are selectively reinforced. Thus imitation is learned through successive approximations or shaping. Once a child learns that rewards follow those of his actions which are like those of a model, he has learned to imitate. For example, a preschool-aged child might be induced to smile if he sees his mother smile and perhaps is also tickled. The child's reaction will be typically rewarded by behaviors such as hugging. Verbal responses such as saying "ma ma" might also be learned the same way. After several such experiences, a child can learn the general imitation rule: Behaving like mother produces rewards. It is assumed that a child's efforts to imitate will be rewarded on an intermittent basis. Intermittent reinforcement for imitation makes the response more likely to persist for long periods of time without any rewards. According to this account, the child will copy unfamiliar people because they share human and behavioral properties with models whose action when imitated was directly rewarded. There is evidence that atypical children (often mentally retarded) who don't spontaneously imitate can be taught to imitate using an instrumental conditioning procedure (Baer & Sherman, 1964). Reinforcement psychologists believe that they need not consider cognitive activity within an observer to explain imitation.

While there is little doubt that children can be taught to imitate using reinforcement procedures, this formulation does not explain how a child can learn a completely new response from watching a model. Remember that according to this account, the child must be able to display responses like the model's before he can be reinforced for imitating.

Imitating New Responses, Particularly after Delay

Piaget (1962) observed that his children began imitating new responses about 1 year of age. He attributed this accomplishment to his children's general intellectual development. He observed a considerable amount of trial and error responding as they attempted to imitate unfamiliar responses. He believed that the children were attempting to deal mentally with two concepts at the same time. By approximately 16 months of age, Piaget's children were able to imitate novel actions without any trial and error gropings. He also observed that the children could imitate after long delays in time even when the model was not present. Piaget believed that the latter developments indicated covert or mental images had supplanted the need to imitate overtly in order to learn vicariously. These images could later be recalled to guide overt imitation in different environments. Thus images were assumed to be covert imitative responses.

Piaget did not systematically observe changes in his children's imitation beyond the age of approximately 2. He made several rather general summary conclusions without offering any specific anecdotal evidence. It seems fair to infer that since he believed that vicarious learning had become a covert mental process by the time the child was 2 years of age, he no longer felt any need to treat this phenomenon separately from general intellectual development.

A SOCIAL LEARNING ANALYSIS OF HUMAN BEHAVIOR

The most sophisticated theory that has been advanced to explain vicarious learning has been proposed by Bandura (Bandura & Walters, 1963; Bandura, 1969, 1971). This formulation, termed *social learning theory*, sought to explain the more complex aspects of observational learning as well as the simple. This theory has guided a prodigious amount of research on observational learning, and it represents a wedding between behavioral and informational processing explanations for human functioning.

Bandura (1969) accepted evidence that people can acquire novel responses from observation alone. There are a number of studies (e.g., Rosenthal, Alford, & Rasp, 1972; Zimmerman & Rosenthal, 1972a) which have reported that completely unfamiliar responses were learned through observation without any practice or direct reinforcement. Bandura suggested that learning occurs through observation of stimuli being paired contiguously together in time or space. This learning can occur mentally, and the observer is generally aware of it. Information obtained through observation is then assumed to be transformed and stored as a cognitive representation. Bandura feels that these representations are either verbal or imagistic. He found evidence (e.g., Bandura & Jeffery, 1973; Gerst, 1971) that an observer's cognitive activities during observation played a large role in determining what was remembered and displayed during imitation. These effects were particularly pronounced if there were long delays in time between observation and the opportunity to imitate. Thus according to this social learning formulation, observational learning is primarily a cognitive, representational process where stimuli that are observed together (such as a model's actions and their environmental consequences) become associated. These representations are then mentally transformed, stored, and retrieved before being manifested in overt imitation.

Bandura (1971) has concluded that each observer, even a child, plays a major role in selecting who he imitates, what portions of each modeling sequence will be emulated, and to what settings a vicariously learned skill can be legitimately transferred. However, while he views each person's decisions as playing a major role in influencing his responding, the cognitive bases for making these decisions are attributable to previous social experience.

Social learning psychologists (e.g., Rosenthal & Zimmerman, 1972b; Siegler & Liebert, 1972) differ in position from Piaget (1952) in that they believe that a person's cognitive structures and modes for processing information are learned inductively from direct and vicarious experience. In contrast, Piaget believes that while experience may provoke a structure to emerge, the form of a child's structures are genetically endowed (see Furth, 1969, Pp. 75–76). Social learning theory assumes that similarities in children's cognitive structures can be explained on the basis of common social experiences. The social learning formulation has the added advantage of explaining differences in cognitive functioning between children or by a child in two different settings on the basis of a person's own particular social experience (Mischel, 1968, 1973). Thus inaccurate or idiosyncratic concepts as well as other less abstract forms of deviant behavior can be described and justified by the same set of principles that are used to account for normal developmental patterns. Because of the emphasis of this theory on the role of social experience in children's development, it is possible for teachers to use these principles to organize classroom demonstrations to teach concepts as well as less abstract skills to children.

Components of Observational Learning

Bandura (1971) has suggested that there are four basic subprocesses underlying human behavior in general and vicarious learning in particular: attention, retention, motoric enactments, and motivation. Each of these subprocesses plays a role during observational learning as well as other forms of human behavior. Attention refers to the fact that a learner must observe a model before he can learn from him. Retention processes refer to the fact that a model's behavior must be represented before an observer can imitate. In addition, coding, storage, and retrieval processes are given a prominent role in explaining imitation, particularly selective observational learning, transfer, and recall of modeled acts after delays in time. Bandura suggested that some analysis of the motoric requirements in responding is also important. This distinction suggests that what one *can do* and what one *knows* may differ. Finally, motivation is designated as a separate subprocess in order to explain the observation that what an observer *does* imitate and what he *can* imitate often differ. Bandura (1965) describes this discrepancy as *performance* versus *acquisition.*

Factors Influencing Observational Learning

Bandura (1971) isolated three classes of events that control human behavior: stimulus, reinforcement, and cognitive or mental factors. He believes that theories which exclude cognitive events from consideration can not adequately explain observational learning, particularly the more complex varieties. At the same time, cognitive activities are assumed to be influenced by stimuli impinging directly or vicariously on the observer. Thought processes during observation are affected by what was seen and heard from models (stimulus control) and by what happened to the observer after he imitated (reinforcement control). Thus an observer's thought patterns are influenced by the behavior patterns of models he sees or by traces of a model's actions on the physical environment. For example, when traveling in a snowstorm, one's conception of where a road lies beneath a deep mantle of snow is affected by the tire tracks of the preceding car. However, this conception will be altered if those tracks lead you into the ditch! Social learning psychologists believe that a child learns most concepts about the world in much the same way. Basic concepts such as number (e.g., Rosenthal & Zimmerman, 1972b) or equivalence (Zimmerman, 1974) can be gleaned from the actions of people around a child. Once these concepts are formed, they influence the form and frequency of a number of other behaviors. If these concepts assist an observer in obtaining control of and rewards from his environment, they will be retained. If not, they will be altered. Thus these three classes of events (preceding stimuli, cognitive activities, and consequent reactions of the environment) interact together to determine human behavior.

Effects of a Model's Performance on an Observer

Three types of modeling effects have been found: inhibition–disinhibition, facilitation, and learning new responses (Bandura, 1969). A model can *inhibit* an observer by purposely avoiding making a particular action. For example, a new child in school may be inhibited in his choice of a place to play with blocks by observing other children who all use this toy on a rug in the corner of the classroom. These inhibition effects become particularly pronounced if the observer sees a model punished. Teachers often punish one child in the presence of others to deter them from the same misdeeds. Vicarious punishment can be symbolically modeled through oral and written accounts. One common example of this practice are stories with a moral, such as "The Boy Who Cried Wolf."

It is also possible to *disinhibit* particular actions by watching a model. When a child sees another youngster violate a social norm or school rule, he is more likely to follow suit. Policing the halls of public schools has been a time-honored teacher duty. Teachers will readily attest to what ensues if one child gets away with running down the hall, particularly if the floors are slippery enough to permit sliding. If the child receives rewards in addition, such as being the first in line at the cafeteria, this effect will be enhanced.

A second major effect of modeling is that it *facilitates* responding. People usually have certain types of responses available to them that they do not use. When they see someone else use a skill, it encourages them to recall it and use it when appropriate. We have found this effect to operate on creativity tasks. Many times people do not mention the "wilder" ideas they have when solving problems because they are unconventional. There is evidence (e.g., Harris & Evans, 1973;

Zimmerman & Dialessi, 1973) that a model's uninhibited "brainstorming" or throwing out ideas on a creativity task facilitated the production of creative ideas by observing youngsters. Disinhibition is not the same as facilitation; disinhibition can only occur if a response has not been inhibited (usually through punishment). Facilitation occurs when a response that an observer was unlikely to make becomes more probable after seeing the model perform.

Both facilitation and inhibition–disinhibition deal with changes in an observer's display of known responses after being exposed to a model. It is also possible to learn *new* responses through modeling. There are many examples of this type of learning in both children and adults. With children, the process is often quite obvious; with adults, it is generally quite subtle. A boy watches his father nail two boards together to use as a frame to cover garden vegetables. Later the child may use the same nailing strategy to make a frame to use as a tepee. He has acquired a new response pattern by simply watching his father perform.

With older children and adults, this type of learning is often overlooked because it is less obvious. Such learning is often highly selective and typically only certain features of a model's actions are imitated. For example, novice artists are encouraged to emulate certain aspects of a master's techniques but would be chastised for copying an entire painting.

It is assumed by social learning researchers that the vast majority of people's responses are learned through observation and imitation. Often observers witness the actual responses being displayed by the model. This is particularly true for preschool-age children. Another form of social learning can occur from exposure to the products or traces of a model's actions on the physical environment without actually seeing the response being executed. A child can learn to write by tracing the outline of another person's letters. This type of social learning is more abstract and usually requires some previous experience with overt behavior before it can occur. According to this account, an adult's learning from books, symbols, and explanations is seen as a socially mediated process.

RESPONSES INFLUENCED BY VICARIOUS EXPERIENCE

Promoting Desirable Behavior

It is useful when examining modeling studies to distinguish between associative responses and those involving rule learning. Associative responses refer to situations where two or more stimuli are related: a word and its referent, several words, or two events, for example. Often one of the stimuli is familiar or has meaning before being associated with another, such as the sight of the family dog and learning that he is a cocker spaniel. Many times emotional or affective reactions are involved in this associative process, such as when a new girl in class is called a crybaby by a peer. Thus during associative learning, two or more stimuli become related.

One class of associative–affective responses that has been found to be affected by vicarious experience is human *values* or *preferences.* We are all familiar with the situation where a child refuses to touch his bicycle until a visiting cousin expresses an interest in it. Simply put, we form and change our preferences on the basis of the opinions of others, particularly if they share some characteristics with us. For example, children were found to change their toy preferences after being informed of the preferences of most children of the same or different sex (Liebert, McCall, & Hanratty, 1971). The youngsters imitated the indicated preferences of children of the same sex. Zimmerman and Koussa (1975a) found that children changed their ratings and use of toys after seeing a model's choice and use of toys during his play. In addition, it was found that the presence of positive emotional cues by the model tended to enhance this vicarious change in values. When the model appeared enthusiastic instead of passive, significantly greater changes occurred. In subsequent research (Zimmerman & Koussa, 1975b), it was established that a model's use of toys in a storylike sequence of actions (flying an airplane or cleaning house) also enhanced the children's opinion and use of the model's toy. It was observed that when a child was really involved with and interested in a toy, he would use the toy while "making believe." Thus three playacting cues indicated to the observer that the model highly valued the toy.

Modeling procedures have been used to increase children's liking of food. Harris and Baudin (1972) studied the effects of viewing a Popeye cartoon alone or in conjunction with observing a live model eat spinach on children's consumption of this vegetable. Both groups of children ate more spinach than youngsters in a no-model control group. Thus there is evidence that children will increase the value they ascribe to various objects in their environment on the basis of another person's behavior.

Another class of associative responses that has been found to be affected by social experience are children's *play* patterns. As discussed above, the choice of toys that a child selects to use during play was affected by the actions of models that he observes. There is evidence that many other aspects of children's play is similarly affected by models. In recent research, Zimmerman and Brody (1975) studied the play patterns of fifth grade boys who met each other for the first time. The boys played together in dyads, one boy was black and the other was white in race. Each dyad then watched a brief televised episode in which an older black and a white boy played together in a very friendly manner or in a distant but nonhostile fashion. After viewing this tape, each pair of boys was observed during play again. Two marked patterns of interaction were found during play depending upon which taped episode was observed. Pairs of boys who watched the friendly tape sat significantly closer together, faced each other more directly, gave each other more eye contact, talked and cooperated together more often. Thus the manner that children play together is affected by the play patterns that they observed others display. The implication of these results for teachers is that the quality of children's interaction in the classroom not only influences the actual participants, but also any other children that might be watching.

Vicarious experience has also been found to play a significant role in a child's development of self-control. One aspect of self-control that has been studied involves a child's ability to *delay gratification*. As children get older, they appear to be more able to put off immediated smaller rewards in favor of larger rewards that are delayed in time (Mischel, 1966). This capacity was tested by giving the youngster the choice of a small toy or candy bar at the time or waiting for a larger one a few days later. There is evidence that a child's willingness to wait for larger rewards is affected by vicarious experience (Bandura & Mischel, 1965). Children who witnessed a model abstain from immediate gratification in preference for the larger eventual reward displayed similar delays in self-gratification. The effects of this one modeling experience were even detected after 1 month.

Another aspect of self-control that has been studied are *standards of achievement*. Early in a child's life, he or she begins to adopt standards by which to judge his or her performance. Once these standards for judging one's performance are formed by a child, they are used as a basis for self-reward or self-punishment. This author had the moving yet frightening experience of seeing his younger 3-year-old daughter suddenly begin screaming during her solitary play. She was frustrated because she could not draw a sufficiently round head on her picture as her older sister did. One of the interesting findings that has emerged from research on children's achievement is that children with poor records of achievement set unreasonable or nonproductive goals for themselves (McClelland, 1958). Their goals are usually too easy or too difficult; whereas, consistent achievers set their goals slightly above present skill levels. Obviously setting unattainable goals for oneself can make life a bitter and frustrating experience. Setting easily attained goals does not permit a person to develop himself to his capacity.

Models have been found to play a prominent role in influencing a child's *self-reward* patterns. Bandura and Kupers (1964) found that children tended to imitate the self-reward patterns of models they observed. If a model adopted lax standards for himself, so did the child observer. Self-reward patterns were studied using a bowling game in which the score was prominently displayed and could be easily manipulated without making the child suspicious. In subsequent research (Mischel & Liebert, 1966), it was found that if the model verbally set one standard for himself (a score that would appear on the machine) and then rewarded the child more leniently (from a box of chips that were present), lower standards of self-reward were followed when the child played the game by himself. The use of the same high standard of performance by both the model and the observer led the latter to adopt and maintain the most stringent levels of self-reward. Consistent with conventional wisdom, the model who rewarded himself more leniently than he rewarded the child during the game was less effective than the model who adhered to the same standard that he imposed on the child. It appears that models must practice what they preach if they want to be optimally effective.

Another important aspect of children's performance on complex tasks is their *cognitive tempo* or *style* (Kagan, 1965). It has been observed that some young children appear to perform poorly on conceptual tasks because they don't take time to consider all the alternatives. They seize one of the answers very quickly in the problem-solving process, and the answer is generally incorrect. These youngsters have been labeled as *impulsive.* Children who do well on this cognitive task are generally more *reflective* although there is a significant number of children who don't fit either category. The test used to determine children's conceptual tempo involves making complex discriminations. The child must select the figure that correctly matches a standard figure from an array of others having missing parts. Several studies have been conducted that found that a child's conceptual tempo was influenced by a model's performance (Debus, 1970; Ridberg, Parke, & Hetherington, 1971). Impulsive observers became more reflective (made fewer errors and increased the time used for decision making) after watching a reflective model perform. Reflective youngsters became more impulsive after viewing an impulsive model perform. The latter finding indicates that adverse models can also influence a child's conceptual behavior. This finding should serve as a caution to teachers that maladaptive responses can also be increased through modeling. Children can be encouraged to rush through a task as a result of social experience, and thus the speed at which conceptual tasks are demonstrated for a child should be appropriate to the complexity of the task. There is evidence that the speed of a model's performance affects creative responding as well (Zimmerman & Dialessi, 1973).

Recent research on modeling has focused on another class of responses that are of particular relevance to educators. These responses are termed *rule governed* (Zimmerman & Rosenthal, 1974b) and are unique in that abstraction and transfer are involved. Children can learn to abstract rules by watching another person demonstrate a common conceptual strategy on a variety of different tasks. Through this vicarious experience the child can gradually separate the general aspects of the model's strategy from those actions that are related to each specific task. Once this abstraction occurs, it is possible for the youngsters to transfer the skill to new, unfamiliar tasks.

Let's consider a concrete example of this process. A child can learn a plural morpheme rule of adding an *s* to words used to describe multiple objects by watching a model label objects depicted on cards (Guess, Sailor, Rutherford, & Baer, 1968). In this study, the model used *s* on the end of words that described multiple objects and dropped this suffix when labeling single objects. The child learned to label correctly objects on cards that the model used and was able to transfer the plural rule to new stimulus cards.

There is evidence that both a child's acquisition and use of *language* are influenced by the utterances of models around him. For example, it was found that a child's use of verb tense, prepositional phrases, and sentence structure changes when a youngster comes into contact with the speech of another person. These changes occurred when a child was asked and rewarded for imitating (Bandura & Harris, 1966; Odom, Liebert, & Hill, 1968). Changes also occurred when a child was just told to watch the model (Carroll, Rosenthal, & Brysch, 1972; Rosenthal & Whitebook, 1970) or when the child was given no orienting instructions (Harris & Hassemer, 1972). In the latter study, the child was simply told to make up sentences about pictures while taking turns with a model on alternative cards. The model's sentences varied in length and linguistic complexity. Changes in these same grammatical structures were noted in the child's subsequent speech patterns.

New and unfamiliar language rules can also be learned from models by children with reasonably well-developed speech skills. In one study, a new word sequence rule was learned (Liebert, Odom, Hill, & Huff, 1969), and in another an artificial grammatical rule was learned (Marlouf & Dodd, 1972) through observation.

Psychologists working with atypical children such as the mentally retarded have also used modeling procedures along with rewards to teach regular grammatical rules. These children were typically older and had generally shown no evidence of the particular language structure in their normal speech. Speech rules such as the plural morpheme (Guess *et al.*, 1968), verb tense (Shumaker & Sherman, 1970), and the comparative (*-er*) and superlative (*-est*) suffix endings were effectively taught using modeling and reinforcement. Whitehurst (1971, 1972) has found that very young children can also learn language rules by watching a model perform and receiving reinforcement. It can be expected from this modeling research on children's language that if parents and teachers know how to use modeling and reinforcement techniques, they could accelerate their children's language development. Whitehurst, Novak, and Zorn (1972) have found that parents could improve their child's language through systematic use of these procedures. Zimmerman and Pike (1972) found that the use of modeling procedures by a teacher figure enhanced her effectiveness in teaching question-asking skills to bilingual disadvantaged children. In conclusion, there is a substantial amount of evidence that the social environment plays a major role in children's acquisition and use of both the semantic content and the grammatical structure of language.

A child's *conceptual* distinctions about the world are influenced by the reactions of other people he sees. For example, a child's notion of "same" and "different" can be influenced by an adult's overt comparison of two or more stimuli. Zimmerman (1974) found that children changed the criterion by which they group "same" pictures together after viewing a model perform using another criterion. Rosenthal *et al.* (1972) also found that a novel rule for grouping concrete objects together could be learned through observation.

One conceptual rule that has attracted a considerable amount of study is Piaget's notion of conservation. Piaget (1952) has observed that young children fail to appreciate the idea that the stimulus property of amount is separable from overt shape or configuration. Thus young children will judge two equal amounts of clay to be unequal if they don't have the same shape. This judgment is rendered even though the child is aware that both amounts were equal when initially presented in identical form. Piaget has attributed this inability to a young child's deficient logical structure. Modeling procedures have been found effective in teaching children to conserve precociously (e.g., Rosenthal & Zimmerman, 1972b; Zimmerman & Lanaro, 1974; Zimmerman & Rosenthal, 1974a). In these studies, the model overtly disregarded shape and configuration cues to instead respond to initial cues of equality and inequality when the stimuli were presented in similar formats or shapes. Transfer and retention of the conservation rule was found in these studies.

Not only are a child's concepts influenced by the actions of models, but a youngster's strategies for gathering information or methods of *problem solving* are also affected by vicarious experience. There are several studies (Rosenthal & Zimmerman, 1972a; Rosenthal, Zimmerman, & Durning, 1970) which found that the kinds of questions children ask are influenced by the questioning strategies they see other people use. For example, Rosenthal, Zimmerman, and Durning (1970) found that when a model asked causal questions about some pictures that were presented, observing children asked more of this type of question even though their questions generally differed from those of the model in word content. A series of studies have been devoted to teaching question-asking strategies on a "twenty questions" game using modeling procedures (Denny, 1975; Lamal, 1971; Laughlin, Moss, & Miller, 1969). This game is a variant of the game played on radio a number of years ago. In this version, pictures are presented, and the child must ask any question that can be answered by "Yes" or "No" and try to guess the correct picture in the fewest number of attempts. The superior strategy—consistently used by older children (above the age of 10)—is to ask questions which eliminate more than one picture. This strategy is termed "constraint seeking" questions. Random questioning directed at eliminating only one picture per question is an inferior strategy. In general, this research indicated that children as young as 6 could vicariously learn the superior strategy. Eight- and nine-year-olds learned constraint seeking strategy just by watching a model ask this type of question. However, the 6-year-old children did not completely learn and comprehend this strategy unless the model mentioned the rule he used to formulated questions, visually removed the pictures that were eliminated by each question from the array, and described how he was going to use the information derived from the answer to each question (Denny, 1975). This procedure apparently made the logical implications of the model's superior questioning strategy more evident to these young children. The implication of this study for teachers is that sometimes it is necessary to incorporate additional cues in their normal modeling demonstrations to instruct successfully children with highly deficient backgrounds. It appears that the effect of these additional supports is to make some of the covert aspects of the problem-solving performance more overt and therefore more readily observable. This issue will be discussed in detail later.

Another general type of problem-solving strategy involved in the scientific method has been taught by demonstration. Piaget devised a pendulum task to measure hypothetical deductive reasoning, and he found that children cannot usually solve this problem until they reach adolescence. The task requires the learner to determine which factors influence the speed at which a pendulum swings. There are a number of potential hypotheses that are readily evident that must be tested, such as the initial force used to start the weight swinging, the size of the weight, and the location of the weight on the pendulum. In a study by Siegler, Liebert, and Liebert (1973), the children learned this strategy by watching the model perform and by practicing on analogous problems. The training tasks differed in stimulus properties from that used during training, but a similar number of factors had to be systematically tested in order to achieve a correct solution. These children were able to learn the hypothetical deductive strategy of holding all remaining dimensions constant while testing one dimension at a time and were able to solve the pendulum problem without ever being trained on it. These findings were obtained with 10- and 11-year-old preadolescents who were younger than the age at which the skill generally appears.

Closely associated with problem solving is the generation of creative products such as a new tool or a novel work of art. *Creativity* has been traditionally treated as an individual difference trait that each person is assumed to have to some degree and can apply when needed. Recent social learning research has indicated that the quality and quantity of creative response a youngster displays is greatly affected by models he observes (Harris & Evans, 1973; Zimmerman & Dialessi, 1973). One task that has been used in creativity studies in an "unusual uses" test. The child is asked to think of as many different uses for an object as he can. In these studies, some sort of general rule for producing novel and creative responses was displayed by the model, such as shifting categories or responding in a rapid, uninhibited, brainstorming manner. Observers displayed similar qualitative shifts in their performance on subsequent transfer tasks.

Another class of rule-governed behavior that has been studied by psychologists are children's *moral judgments*. Piaget (1948) has observed his children make moral judgments for misdeeds such as lying, accidents, and stealing. He found that young children (of less than approximately 8 years) generally failed to consider the intentions of a person when determining culpability for misdeeds (subjective moral criterion) and instead focused on the amount of damage that occurs (objective moral criterion). Thus a protagonist in a story who intentionally breaks a dish is viewed as less blameworthy than another figure who accidentlly breaks a number of dishes. There are a number of studies (e.g., Bandura & McDonald, 1963; Cowan, Langer, Heavenrich, & Nathanson, 1969) that have reported that children can abstract the criterial rule used by a model to make moral judgments concerning brief stories, and that these youngsters used the same criteria to guide their own moral judgments on new unfamiliar stories. Children who were initially subjective as well as those who adhered to an objective model criterion altered their judgmental rule when confronted by a model using the opposite moral rule. There was evidence that these changes were maintained over time (Cowan *et al.*, 1969).

Thus a wide variety of rule-governed behaviors have been found to be influenced by a model's performance. Clearly children can abstract important dimensions, rules, and strategies just from watching other people perform.

Eliminating Undesirable Behavior

Models are influential in eliminating or reducing maladaptive behavior in children as well. For example, there is a substantial amount of evidence (Bandura, 1973) that children will become more *aggressive* after watching aggressive films or television programs. Recently, psychologists have used modeling procedures to increase prosocial behavior such as altruism (e.g., Rosenhan & White, 1967) and cooperation (e.g., Zimmerman & Brody, 1975). Liefert and his colleagues (Liefert, Neale, & Davidson, 1973) have created short films that can be shown on televison that exemplify important prosocial skills. One film shows two youngsters running to a single swing, beginning to fight for it, and then deciding to cooperate and take turns. This brief exposure to a modeling experience was highly effective in influencing children to play cooperatively together.

Other forms of maladaptive behavior have been reduced through exposure to a model. O'Connor (1969) treated a group of socially *withdrawn* preschool children using filmed models. These youngsters where shown films of other children who sought the attention and cooperation of their peers. These approach responses were responded to favorably by the peers in the film. After viewing the film, the withdrawn children displayed significant increases in their number of social interactions with other children in their classroom. Children in a control group who watched an irrelevant film remained withdrawn. While this study was modest in scope, involved only brief training, and no attempts were made to reinforce the child for changing his behavior patterns in the classroom, it did indicate that models can assist children to overcome social inhibitions in a school setting.

Modeling procedures have proven highly successful in eliminating and reducing *fears* or phobias in both children and adults. A child's fears have been difficult to treat with traditional forms of psychotherapy because children have often been unresponsive to verbal instructions and reasoning. Of course it is a terrifying experience to attempt to rid children of fears by directly exposing them to the object or event that is feared. There is evidence that fears can be greatly reduced or eliminated by exposing an observer to a model who fearlessly approaches the feared stimulus such as a snake or dog (Bandura, Blanchard, & Ritter, 1969; Bandura & Menlove, 1968). For example, people with fears of dogs viewed a model approach the dog, pet him, put his chain on, and even get inside the pen with the animal. The observers were encouraged to approach a tame, live dog when they felt they could do so comfortably. Thus the vicarious experience of seeing the dog handled successfully without adverse consequences reduced the fears to the point that approach responses could be undertaken without undue stress. Some children's television programs have employed modeling techniques to reduce fears. "Mr. Rogers' Neighborhood" is notable in this regard. For example, Mr. Rogers has been shown fearlessly going to the hospital for a checkup to help youngsters overcome this common fear. There is also evidence that test-taking anxiety can be reduced by observing another person relax while having testing events vividly described to him (Mann & Rosenthal, 1969). Thus there is a considerable amount of research that fears can be reduced by exposure to a model. Conversely, fears can be created vicariously by seeing injurious consequences befall a model for particular actions (Bandura & Rosenthal, 1966). These studies not only indicate another important educational use for modeling procedures, but they serve as a sober reminder that children's reactions to events such as seeing blood oozing from an open cut are greatly affected by the reactions of others, perhaps even more so than from the pain of the event itself.

VARIABLES AFFECTING A MODEL'S EFFECTIVENESS

It is quite apparent that people differ in their effectiveness as models. In addition, children will copy some aspects of a model's performance and not other aspects. What factors account for this differential effectiveness?

Consequences to a Model and an Observer

Perhaps the most significant factor controlling whether a model is watched and imitated involves the consequences he or the observer receives. It is clear that a model's actions that produce rewards are more likely to be imitated than those that produce no results or are punished. Bandura (1965) studied the effects of a model who behaved aggressively. In one case, the model was rewarded with praise and treats, in another he was severely punished, and in a third condition, his actions were ignored. Children were then observed playing alone. The highest degree of imitation was displayed by children who were exposed to the rewarded model; an intermediate level was exhibited by those who did not see any consequences to the model, and the lowest level of imitation was shown by children who witnessed the model being punished for his actions. In a post experimental session, all children were offered large rewards for repeating any of the model's responses that they could remember. It was found that the children in all consequence groups displayed *equal* levels of learning. Thus consequences received by a model appear to influence imitative *performance* rather than vicarious *acquisition,* per se. However, there were no competing stimuli in this study that could have detracted from watching the model in the no-consequence condition. Under such circumstances rewarding alternatives might have attracted the observer's attention.

Model Characteristics

Another factor that has been assumed to influence a model's effectiveness is his (or her) personal characteristics. These characteristics can be divided into at least two classes: (*1*) physical properties of the model such as age, sex, or racial group, and (*2*) acquired characteristics such as competence, purported expertise, or status. There is some evidence that models who are similar to an observer in ethnicity (Epstein, 1966), sex (Bandura, Ross, & Ross, 1963; Maccoby & Wilson, 1957), or age (Bandura & Kupers, 1964; Hicks, 1965; Jakubczak & Walters, 1959) are imitated more often. Similarly models who are higher in socially desirable qualities such as competence (e.g., Gelfand, 1962, Mausner & Block, 1957; Rosenbaum & Tucker, 1962), being a celebrity (Hovland, Janis, & Kelley, 1953), purported expertise (Mausner, 1953), and rewardingness or nurturance (Bandura & Huston, 1961; Mischel & Grusec, 1966) tend to be more effective models. These findings have prompted many casual readers of modeling research to conclude that models are not effective unless they possess these characteristics.

However, a careful analysis of these studies reveals that this conclusion is inaccurate. For the most part, differences in imitation that are attributable to a model's characteristics have been relatively small and often occur inconsistently. For example, one of the most studied characteristics of a model is his valence or nurturance. While there is evidence that children are more likely to imitate nurturant models than nonnurturant ones (e.g., Bandura & Huston, 1961; Mischel & Grusec, 1966), there are a large number of studies that failed to find any model nurturance effects (Aronfreed, 1964; Grusec & Skubiski, 1970; Rosenhan & White, 1967; Stein & Wright, 1964). In the studies that reported model nurturance effects, however, these differences were not usually substantial and were often delimited to a subset of the response classes studied such as incidental responses (Bandura & Huston, 1961; Mussen & Parker, 1965) or emotionally laden responses such as aversive behavior (Mischel & Grusec, 1966; Paskal, 1969). Aronfreed (1968) has concluded that while model nurturance may determine imitation to some degree, it certainly is not a unique determinant of it. It is clear from this research that other events interact with and qualify the impact of a model's rewardingness. To clarify this issue, it will be necessary to specify the relative attractiveness of other stimuli in each study. It is not possible to ascertain the relative obviousness of these cues from the brief descriptions of procedures given in most studies conducted to date. For example, certain constraints of different experimental designs can influence the importance a particular characteristic such as nurturance plays in affecting imitation. In designs where the observer was exposed to only one model who either is nurturant or is not, the importance of this characteristics may be masked by the overall salience of the model. The model may be observed because he (or she) was the most attractive stimulus in the situation regardless of whether or not he (or she) was nurturant. On the other hand, in designs where the observer was simultaneously exposed to a model who was nurturant and another model who was not under conditions where viewing one model precluded viewing the other (e.g., Yussen & Levy, 1975), the model salience factor would be controlled. Then a direct determination of the importance of nurturance could be made. Another problem in this research is whether a model's nurturance affects vicarious acquisition without always being manifested in overt imitative performance. In research that has been conducted on model characteristics thus far, little attempt has been made to distinguish between acquisition and performance despite Bandura's (1965) evidence concerning the importance of this distinction. It is likely that different variables influence acquisition versus performance. For example, a person's initial feeling about a particular response (e.g., stealing) before it was modeled might affect whether it would be performed imitatively but not necessarily determine whether or not it would be vicariously learned. Perhaps this is why model nurturance effects were found on certain response classes and not on others.

In summary, a model's characteristics appear to affect his effectiveness in eliciting imitation. These effects are not generally huge and are qualified by other factors that are not yet well understood. It is certainly true that observers are influenced by models who do not possess optimal characteristics.

Observer Characteristics

Closely associated with the study of model characteristics are those of an observer. This joint study has often occurred since it has been assumed that observers will be more likely to imitate models who are similar to them. The observer characteristic literature parallels the model characteristic findings in that strong effects have not consistently emerged.

There is some evidence that the personality traits of the observers influence vicarious learning. A greater amount of imitation has been found for youngsters with a high need for social approval (Lipton, 1971), with greater dependency (Bandura & Huston, 1961; Ross, 1966), and who are less personally competent (Gelfand, 1962; Kanareff & Lanzetta, 1960; Mausner, 1953). In this literature also, a fairly sizable number of studies have failed to obtain effects on some subset of the response classes studied (e.g., Barber, 1967; Henker, 1964; Jacobson, 1969).

Studies of demographic characteristics of observers have also revealed an inconsistent pattern of findings. For example, several studies have been conducted on the effects of a child's race on imitation (Thelen, 1971; Thelen & Fryrear, 1971a, 1971b), and no consistent evidence of increased imitation was found for observers who were of the same race as the model.

The age of a child appears to be one characteristic that has had a more consistent relationship with the type and quality of imitation than any other observer characteristic. In general older children appear to be more influenced by a model's performance than younger children (Elliot & Vasta, 1970; Midlarsky & Bryan, 1967). The complexity of the behaviors modeled appears to be a factor that determines whether the age of observing children is relevant or not. There are several studies indicating that complex responses can be acquired observationally by 4-year-olds if they are broken into smaller units (e.g., Rosenthal & Zimmerman, 1972b, Experiment 4; Zimmerman & Lanaro, 1974). There is also evidence that young children are more affected by any incompleteness occurring in a model's performance (Zimmerman, 1974). These studies will be discussed in more detail later. Although research on the influence of an observer's age on vicarious learning is far from complete, age appears to be one of the more important observer characteristics associated with differences in imitation, particularly on complex and abstract tasks. While knowing a child's age does not tell us *why* he can or cannot imitate, it is useful for teachers to consider this variable when exploring other factors that they can control to some degree in the classroom.

The sex of the observer is another characteristic that has received considerable attention. Here again, inconsistent findings have been reported. Several studies have attempted to determine whether the sex of a model differentially influences boy and girl observers. No interactions between observer and model sex have been reported in several studies (Breyer & May, 1970; Richard, Ellis, Barnhart, & Holt, 1970). However, there is some evidence that boys and girls do imitate differentially (Fryrear & Thelen, 1969; Zimmerman & Koussa, 1975a). Careful analysis of these studies indicates that interactions between a model's and an observer's sex occurred mainly on tasks which were sex-role-linked. For example, Fryrear and Thelen (1969) found that girls imitated a female model's affection responses more than boys did. Zimmerman and Koussa (1975a) found that boys imitated a highly exuberant model more than girls on a highly masculine play task. Zimmerman and Koussa (1975b) hypothesized that the interaction between the sex of a model and that of an observer does not occur universally irrespective of the type of behavior being modeled but does occur on certain sex-role-linked responses. In the latter study, the influence of the masculine or feminine character of the task was varied as well as the sex of the model and child. The results indicated that interactions between the sex of the model and observer did not occur directly but both interacted with the sex role content of the behavior that was modeled. Thus all three factors must be considered to make accurate predictions about an observer's imitation based on his sex.

These findings on the importance of task characteristics in determining whether an observer's sex will influence imitation may be generalizable to research on other observer characteristics. In reviewing the entire literature on observer characteristics, Akamatsu and Thelen (1974) concluded that the effects of observer traits in general are ambiguous, equivocal, and appear to depend on the type of imitative task employed. Does this lack of generality mean these variables are unimportant? I believe the answer is no. Mischel (1968, 1973) has examined the personality literature and has concluded that situation-specific factors play a much larger role in determining human response than previously expected. He suggested that variations in response from one situation to another often reflect highly discriminant rather than capricious functioning by an observer. Copying a male model on a type of task that is masculine and not on one that is feminine would be a case in point. It thus appears that future research on observer characteristics might be more interpretable if more attention is given to situational factors.

Information-Conveying Aspects of a Model's Performance

In recent research, social learning psychologists have become interested in how children acquire abstract conceptual rules from a model's actions. It has been found that differences in the *degree* and *type* of *organization* of a modeling sequence had a significant impact on the type and amount of vicarious learning that occurred. As previously mentioned, if the model's actions follow a rule, this will influence the observer's performance in predictable ways such as improving retention (Liebert & Swenson, 1971b), enhancing transfer (e.g., Zimmerman & Bell, 1972), and permitting the observer to predict future actions of the model (Liebert & Swenson, 1971a). Research on concept formation indicates that a concept such as *red* can be abstracted from a series of pictures by varying all other aspects of the pictures such as shape, size, or the object depicted. When using modeling procedures to teach concepts, the common aspects of the model's reactions to the critical stimulus dimension must also be abstracted such as saying "red" or pointing to the word. Thus both task stimuli and consistent response elements in the model's performance must be abstracted. Research on nonsocial concept attainment indicates that the greater the number of different instances of a concept that are presented, the better the quality of abstraction and the more appropriate the transfer (Hull, 1920).

There is evidence that imitation is affected by the amount of sequential organization in a model's performance. Rosenthal and Zimmerman (1973) studied children's vicarious learning of a complex rule for associating the arrow-hand of a clocklike stimulus with the selection of colored spools. In this task, four arrow positions (up, right, down, left) were related to picking spools (one, two, three, or four respectively). The color of the arrow-hand designated the correct color of the spools. They found that children learned the rule faster if the arrow moved in a systematic clockwise direction (which was concordant with the rule) over successive examples rather than in an unpredictable manner. Surprisingly, however, this increased level of imitation was not maintained on a transfer task. The effects of high organization in the model's performance failed to transfer in subsequent research as well (Rosenthal & Zimmerman, 1976). From these studies, it appears that high levels of organization in a model's performance assist performance on highly comparable tasks but may not transfer to altered tasks.

Most teachers have experienced occasions when a child has difficulty imitating certain complex actions after viewing an accomplished model perform. Often this occurs on tasks which require high levels of abstraction. There is evidence that complex skills can be imitated and learned if the model's actions can be broken down into smaller behavioral units. For example, Rosenthal and Zimmerman (1972b) reported that a model's performance on a series of Piagetian conservation tasks have to be subdivided into separate tasks (of weight, number, etc.) in order to permit very young, 4-year-old children to imitate. Zimmerman and Lanaro (1974) found that even further subdivisions in conservation tasks had to be made in order to teach disadvantaged 4-year-old minority children to conserve. In both studies, the child was encouraged to imitate the model's rule-governed performances immediately after they were modeled. This appeared to assist acquisition, and it provided the teacher—experimenter with evidence of how much was being learned.

Another important factor controlling the impact of a model's action is *adjunctive language*. In general, explanations accompanying a model's performance enhance observational learning. These verbalizations range from simple descriptions of the model's actions to rule statements or codes that call attention only to certain key aspects of the model's performance. When a parsimonious statement of the exemplified rule accompanies the model's actions, the highest levels of acquisition, generalization, and retention have been consistently reported (e.g., Zimmerman & Rosenthal, 1972a, 1972b). Verbal codes have been found to enhance vicarious learning whether they were provided by the model (Rosenthal *et al.*, 1972), by the experimenter (Zimmerman & Rosenthal, 1972a), or by the observer himself (Gerst, 1971).

There is reason to believe that the informative qualities of adjunctive explanations must be given prime consideration. Complete descriptions of a model's actions that fail to draw attention to the conceptually relevant portion of the performance do not appear to aid discrimination nor do they reduce the amount of information that needs to be cognitively processed. For example, Rosenthal *et al.*, (1972) found greater observational learning and recall occurred when a model offered a brief statement of the underlying rule rather than simply describing his actions. Gerst (1971) reported similar findings with observer-produced explanations. The observers were taught to react verbally or nonverbally to the model's performance in one of several different ways. Exact verbal descriptions of the model's behavior by the observer assisted learning but were not nearly as effective as a summary coding procedure. The superiority of the summary code was even more pronounced after an extraneous task was introduced. Thus the effects of verbal rule statements are greater when imitation is delayed in time or after intervening experiences occur. From Bandura's (1969) point of view, either of these factors should put greater stress on cognitive functioning, and thus cognitive aids such as rule statements could be expected to be particularly effective.

Two other aspects of a model's actions have been found to affect observational learning: *speed* and *completeness.* Borden and White (1973) found that the speed of responding that a model displayed as he performed was highly influential in affecting an observer's subsequent rate of response. Speed of performance can be expected to be a highly important consideration when teaching by demonstration. Many complex tasks require careful and deliberate responding in order for any accuracy to be achieved—such as perceptual discrimination tasks in which a hidden figure must be recognized or in which a figure in an array must be selected that exactly matches a standard figure. It may be recalled that this was the type of task used in research on cognitive tempo, and that models who reacted to this task quickly and impulsively influenced a child's speed of performance and degree of accuracy (Ridberg *et al.*, 1971). Impulsive children's speech of performance could be slowed down by exposure to a more contemplative model (see also Debus, 1970).

Zimmerman and Dialessi (1973) found that a model's speed of "idea" production on a creativity task had a vicarious impact on observers. Research on creativity has generally found that fast, uninhibited generation of ideas, or brainstorming without regard to idea merit is an important quality of creative people (e.g., Parnes & Meadow, 1959). This research has found that the quality of ideas is highly correlated with the quantity of ideas that are generated. Zimmerman and Dialessi found that children who were exposed to a model who rapidly produced ideas thought of significantly more ideas on another task than youngsters who were exposed to a more lethargic model. As was expected from previous research, the quality of ideas (the distinctiveness) was also greater.

The completeness of a model's performance is an important factor. Not all actions of a model are imitated with equal frequency. It is very clear from the research discussed thus far that observers are constantly making inferences that extend well beyond what is being observed. For example, Alford and Rosenthal (1973) found that a child could learn rules vicariously from the effects of a model's actions on the physical environment without actually seeing him perform. In this study, children learned a complex toy clustering rule by seeing the toys grouped together or by watching the model actually go through the clustering motions as well. The children who just viewed the toy clusters displayed a substantial amount of learning. However, significantly more learning occurred when the child saw the model create the clusters. This indicates that children can and usually do learn more than what they actually see during a modeling demonstration. A child apparently draws upon his previous experience with toys to "fill in" or infer which actions were required to create the clusters. The occurrence of inference during observational learning by children is so pervasive that teachers often take it for granted, but not without some hazards. Vicarious learning may not occur or may be incomplete if children lack prerequisite experiences to make accurate inferences. Hence individual differences in experience or age can be expected to be related to the kind of information extracted from a modeling sequence if any important details are left out. Conversely, individual differences in vicarious learning will be reduced to the degree that a model's behavior is completely informative.

For example, Zimmerman (1974) taught young children a new way to group pictures together that differed from the rule the youngsters spontaneously used. After training on the new rule, the older children, who were 5 years of age, could use either the new or old rule to group pictures, but the younger children, who were 3 or 4, could not shift back to the old rule without specific training. So a modeling sequence was created which showed the model flexibly shifting between both rules. This procedure was effective, and the younger children then were also able to use both grouping rules. Individual differences based on age or experience occurred only when part of the terminal behavior (the new rule) was modeled. However, these differences were eliminated when the modeling episode depicted the entire shifting strategy. This study emphasizes an important point for teachers. Often a demonstration of a complex skill as it is typically performed by an accomplished model will be incomplete from the standpoint of a naive child observer. Under these circumstances, observational learning will be attenuated and will occur differentially between children. This same problem of incompleteness has been noted in modeling research on teaching children to seriate.

APPLICATION OF MODELING PROCEDURES IN TEACHING A CHILD TO SERIATE

In practice, teaching a complex conceptual rule using modeling procedures to a child, especially the preschool child, is more difficult than it sounds. Often the logical structure of the task can be fairly readily deduced by teachers or content specialists. However, converting this structure, which is usually hierarchical in organization, to a horizontal sequence of actions is not always readily apparent or deducible from logical bases alone. Knowledge of research on modeling is helpful in making this translation.

You might be asking yourself, Why is this translation difficult? Aren't you proposing that a child learns abstract rules by observing the behavior of people around him who are responding according to these rules? The answer is that on simple tasks it is not difficult. You can simply ask an adult or another peer to name letters or numbers, and the child can learn them without additional programming. But with complex tasks that involve abstraction, adults are often covert about many steps in a problem-solving sequence, and thus overt action often abridges the underlying logical sequence in the performance of accomplished models. For example, an adult doing an addition problem might not write the numbers carried from one column to the top of the next. In addition, accomplished adults often inadvertently violate the natural order of operations because of their ability to store information or to short-circuit normal deductive processes; they may write the solution to an addition problem from left to right instead of in the natural order. Thus I am suggesting that observational learning of complex cognitive skills in the natural environment often leaves a lot to be desired. One of the reasons that this author believes that social learning researchers have been successful in teaching complex skills precociously is that they have been able to rectify many of the deficiencies limiting observational learning in the natural environment.

Let me be a bit more detailed about how to use modeling principles and procedures to teach the conceptual skill of seriation. This Piagetian task involves ordering things according to some property like length or size, for example, putting five pencils of different lengths in order from the longest to the shortest. We began to analyze this task by watching an adult seriate. We were immediately impressed with the complexity of this skill. The adults seldom explained their actions unless they were told to teach the child. Even whey they did verbalize, the adult's actions tended to be highly inconsistent with regard to sequence from the viewpoint of a naive observer, even though these actions did produce correct end-state solutions to each problem. Each time the adult model rearranged a scrambled array, he would start at a different beginning point and would move different stimuli in different directions. The whole visual experience was a confusing mess despite the model's explanations. As one perplexed youngster deftly put it, "I knew a magician once who could do this trick."

So we went back to the drawing board and decided to take a dii rent task. We decided to create our modeling sequences on the basis of the simple structure of the task and on the basis of prior social learning research. We wanted to devise a single procedure that could be used consistently to solve all tasks. Our analysis and pilot testing revealed the following: the seriation task was composed of two separable components, (1) discriminating if an array was properly ordered, and (2) learning to reorder an array when it was disordered. From pilot testing, we found that teaching the discrimination skill did not discernably assist the child to correct disordered arrays. So we concluded that it was necessary to teach two rules. In teaching the discrimination component, we invented a verbal mnemonic to accompany the model's discrimination responses. Starting from the largest outside stimulus in the array, the model would ask himself, "Do they go down like stairs?" Then he would "walk" his finger across the top of the stimuli saying "down" each time he walked down to the next stimulus and "up" when his fingers walked up. The moment his finger went up, he knew the array was not lined up properly because "they didn't go down like stairs." After teaching a number of children to correctly discriminate disordered arrays, we also watched them attempt to reorder scrambled arrays. We saw a number of manipulative problems that interfered with successful solutions, such as failing to put the bottoms of the stimuli together and keep them there, keeping more than one stimulus in the hand at a time, and mixing the corrected parts of the array with the scrambled portion because the child didn't leave enough space before them. In order to minimize the problems of lining up the ends of the stimuli, we used a sort of music stand device which had an edge that could be used to line up the ends and could hold the stimuli in place. We made this stand large enough so that the child could set up a new array away from the scrambled array. We also devised a *consistent* method for reordering the stimuli in all cases. This involved lining up the stimuli, then selecting the largest from the group, and then moving that stimulus to the other end of the music stand. Next the child returned to the scrambled array and selected the largest remaining stimulus and placed it beside the extracted one. This procedure was continued until all stimuli were lined up. Then the model would check the new array by using the discrimination rule sequence. If the array passed the test, it was declared correct; if it did not, the reorganization rule sequence was begun again.

This procedure satisfied the criteria for rule learning deduced from prior social learning research. The task was analyzed into component rules. These rules were exemplified using a consistent pattern of responses, and this consistency was made as obvious as possible through the model's actions and words. Covert aspects of the process were made as overt as possible. The stimuli used by the model in his performance were varied as much as possible to insure generalization. We found these procedures to be effective in pilot testing and they were later used by scriptwriters in developing a televised teaching sequence. This televised teaching sequence was shown to young 4-year-old American Indian children and was found to be successful in imparting the seriation skill (Henderson, Swanson, & Zimmerman, 1975).

IMPLICATIONS OF MODELING RESEARCH FOR EDUCATING YOUNG CHILDREN

Most scientific research on how children and adults learn from models has occurred since 1960. Educational psychologists are just beginning to utilize this research in educational settings. Initial attempts to utilize these techniques in prototypic classrooms (e.g., Zimmerman & Pike, 1972) or in educational television programming (e.g., Henderson, Swanson, & Zimmerman, 1975; Liebert, Neale, & Davidson, 1973) have been highly encouraging. When carefully examining the results and conclusions of research on modeling, a number of traditional assumptions about educating young children appear to be in need of reexamination. Let us consider some of these assumptions.

It has often been asserted and debated that *the best type of learning occurs by discovery*. Advocates have claimed that discovery learning is inherently more meaningful, is retained longer, and motivates further learning more effectively than receptive learning approaches (cf. Shulman & Keisler, 1966). Critics of this notion (Skinner, 1968) have pointed out that discovery learning is highly inefficient because it involves a relatively high degree of trial and error responding. Modeling procedures avoid this liability. Watching the performance of a model who knows the target response is an extremely efficient way of conveying information. Trial and error gropings can often be reduced if not eliminated since only correct responses are displayed. However, highly probable incorrect responses can also be modeled and vicariously corrected.

Critics (Ausubel, 1961) have also argued that meaningful learning and discovery learning are separate entities, contrary to assumptions made by adherents. This claim of meaningfulness has always been difficult to prove or disprove since the term has seldom been clearly defined. It would seem that if a skill that is learned can be transferred and retained, it must have been meaningfully learned. The criterion of transfer has been used to indicate the benefits of meaningful learning in much past research on this topic (e.g., Katona, 1940). Since children who have learned complex cognitive skills through modeling have consistently been able to generalize and retain vicariously learned rules, it would appear that such learning qualifies as meaningful.

It should be also noted that there have been several attempts to review the entire literature on discovery learning (e.g., Wittrock, 1966), and *no* conclusive evidence was found for assuming any advantages for discovery approaches. In modeling research, discovery learning procedures were found to be highly inferior to modeling and explanation techniques (Zimmerman & Rosenthal, 1972a). These results were obtained with a task that was extremely complex and guessing the correct answer for each problem did not make the underlying rule obvious. Under these demanding conditions, modeling procedures can be expected to be greatly superior to a discovery approach.

Another assumption that has been espoused by many educators, particularly those of progressive education vintage, is *the need for a child to learn by doing*. Few psychologists would discount the important of direct personal experience on a task in assisting learning. On the other hand, it is another thing to insist that a child must be engaged in direct performance before any real learning can occur. Modeling research has indicated that learning of a novel sort can occur vicariously without any direct task performance by the observer.

There are other problems with stressing learning by doing. Evidence is available (Zimmerman & Rosenthal, 1974b) that overt performance can sometimes interfere with learning. A number of years ago, two psychologists (Hillix & Marx, 1960) conducted a study in which they taught a complex rule for operating an electronic apparatus. One group of children experimented by pushing switches and watching a display of lights to determine the correct pattern. Each child in another group learned by watching the experimenter push the switches in the same order as one child in the first group. Thus both groups were exposed to the same information, but one group did not have to actively respond. Much to the researchers' surprise, the passive observers displayed more learning of the rule than the active participants. They repeated the experiment and obtained the same results. Thus it appears that overt responding can interfere with learning under certain conditions. Under these circumstances, vicarious learning procedures have a decided advantage over methods requiring direct responding.

In another study, Rosenthal and Zimmerman (1973) compared vicarious learning procedures with direct guidance of a child's actions in learning a complex conceptual rule. In the direct learning procedure, children had their hands guided by the experimenter and thus never had the opportunity to behave erroneously. Both modeling and guided practice techniques created significant learning, however the modeling procedure was nearly twice as effective even under these *optimal* conditions for learning by doing. Clearly these data suggest that any unrestricted generalizations about the importance of overt responding in learning must be questioned. Undoubtedly motoric performance will assist learning of many tasks where the response components are unfamiliar, but educators must be cautious about generalizing to learning of abstract rules.

There is another practical problem involved in requiring a child to directly participate during instruction. Often teachers are faced with children who are reluctant to perform on a particular task, particularly if it is unfamiliar. One intuitive explanation for this common occurrence is that the child fears that he will fail. This author has seen attempts to overcome these fears with attractive incentives fail. An effective procedure that many experienced teachers use is simply to have the recalcitrant child watch another child participate first. Generally after a few demonstrations, the observing child will "assert" his right to take a turn. This procedure thus avoids the need to force the child to participate to learn and offers an alternative to postponing instruction until some future time when the child is "ready."

The *readiness* assumption is another widely held belief by educators of young children. Readiness notions stem primarily from the assumption that biological maturation plays a large role in influencing a child's learning. This author has on numerous occasions seen teachers refer to stage theories of development such as Piaget's to justify their decision to terminate or delay instruction of a child who doesn't readily learn complex skills such as mathematics or reading. Some sort of readiness notion appears implicit in stage theories of development. Many psychologists and educators have been bothered by this assumption (Bruner, 1966; Siegler &

Liebert, 1972; Zimmerman & Lanaro, 1974) because it is used to justify terminating attempts to teach a child. Some psychologists have suggested that readiness
notions should be stripped of the underlying assumptions of the preeminence of
maturation and could be profitably recast in terms of specific learning experiences
that set the stage for more complex learning. For example, Gagne (1968) performed a task analysis of Piaget's test for conservation of liquid quantity. He
suggested that being able to learn to conserve presupposed certain underlying skills,
such as knowing that containers vary in three dimensions. The child also needs to
know how these dimensions are interrelated, that is, how changes in one or more
dimensions affect the container's volume and thus level of a fixed amount of liquid.
By teaching each underlying skill, which he depicted in a hierarchy, children can be
taught to conserve. He concluded that this procedure obviates the need to make
assumptions about a child's state of readiness and provides a practical procedure for
instituting remedial instruction. Bruner (1966, p. 29) came to similar conclusions
on the basis of his research, "any subject can be taught effectively in some
intellectually honest form to any child at any stage of development." He labeled
the assumption of readiness "a mischevious half-truth."

Research on modeling has led to similar conclusions. Through demonstration
and imitation, children have been taught many complex skills precociously, such as
learning to conserve (e.g., Rosenthal & Zimmerman, 1972b), to seriate (Henderson
et al., 1975), to reason hypothetically (Siegler et al., 1973), to make sophisticated
moral judgments (Bandura & McDonald, 1963) and many other complex skills.
These findings were obtained with children who showed little evidence of "readiness." Normal developmental patterns were even reversed in several studies (e.g.,
Bandura & McDonald, 1963; Rosenthal & Zimmerman, 1972b).

Readiness assumptions are very tempting to assert as conclusions. This author
(Zimmerman & Lanaro, 1974) attempted to teach a conservation rule to preschool-
age disadvantaged minority group children using the same modeling procedures that
worked with children from middle class families (Rosenthal & Zimmerman, 1972b,
Experiment 4). The minority group youngsters could not initially imitate the
model. It would have been easy to conclude at this point that these youngsters were
not ready to learn since an obviously successful procedure that worked with other
children of the same age failed with this disadvantaged group. Yet when the task
was broken down into smaller units, these children were able to imitate and acquire
the conservation rule.

A final assumption that is commonly made is that *a teacher cannot teach a child
who doesn't want to learn.* Many educators, from Dewey (1916) to contemporary
advocates of open education (e.g., Gordon, 1970), have emphasized the need to
gear instruction to the interests of the child. As a general procedure, few would
quarrel with this recommendation. However, difficulty is encountered with this
procedure if a child prefers not to participate in needed learning activities such as
reading. Educators who accept a child's interests as an unalterable premise on
which instruction must be based are left with the choice of changing the form of
instruction or waiting until the child is ready. Behavioristic educators (Engelman,

1970) have argued that incentives be used to motivate recalcitrant children to engage in these learning activities. Social learning research indicates that another approach is viable (Bandura & Huston, 1960; O'Connor, 1969; Zimmerman & Koussa, 1975a). Children can be exposed to models who display preferences for particular activity or object such as reading or books. The model's choices will change the value the child gives to these activities or objects, particularly if the model is a rewarding person or displays great relish (positive emotional cues) for the activity in question. This procedure is not only highly effective, but it is, in my experience, seldom viewed as being coercive by children or teachers.

In conclusion, educators have often been critical of psychologists' suggestions because they are based on learning theories that seem so far removed from the practical considerations with which teachers must deal. Bruner (1966) has cogently argued that most theories of learning cannot be readily translated into theories of instruction because they don't describe the behavior of the instructional agent such as a parent or teacher. In most traditional research on learning, information is not presented socially, but rather through some sort of nonsocial feedback. Social learning theory, on the other hand, offers an important break in this tradition. In each modeling study, whether it was conducted in a laboratory or in the natural environment, a human was directly (or infrequently indirectly) involved in conveying information to the observer, either through explanation or demonstration. From these studies, it is possible to draw relevant conclusions concerning how a particular skill can be optimally taught. Thus social learning theory appears to be uniquely suited for guiding practical and usable research for teachers. The direct relationship between modeling research and teaching is evident in the very definition of the word *teach*; Webster defines the root meaning as *to show*.

REFERENCES

Akamatsu, T. J., & Thelen, M. H. A review of the literature on observer characteristics and imitation. *Developmental Psychology,* 1974, *10,* 38–47.

Alford, G. S., & Rosenthal, T. L. Process and products of modeling in observational concept development. *Child Development,* 1973, *44,* 714–720.

Allport, F. H. *Social psychology.* Boston: Houghton–Mifflin, 1924.

Aronfreed, J. The origin of self criticism. *Psychological Review,* 1964, *71,* 193–218.

Aronfreed, J. The concept of internalization. In D. A. Goslin (Ed.), *Handbook of socialization theory and research.* Chicago: Rand McNally, 1968. Pp. 263–323.

Ausubel, D. P. In defense of verbal learning. *Educational Theory,* 1961, *11,* 15–25.

Baer, D. M., & Sherman, J. A. Reinforcement control of generalized imitation in young children. *Journal of Experimental Child Psychology,* 1964, *1,* 37–49.

Bandura, A. Influence of a model's reinforcement contingencies on the acquisition of imitative responses. *Journal of Personality and Social Psychology,* 1965, *11,* 589–595.

Bandura, A. *Principles of behavior modification.* New York: Holt, Rinehart and Winston, 1969.

Bandura, A. *Social learning theory.* New York: General Learning Press, 1971.

Bandura, A. *Aggression: A social learning analysis.* Englewood Cliffs, New Jersey: Prentice-Hall, 1973.

Bandura, A., Blanchard, E. B., & Ritter, B. The relative efficacy of desensitization and modeling approaches for inducing behavioral, affective, and attitudinal changes. *Journal of Personality and Social Psychology*, 1969, *13*, 173–199.

Bandura, A., & Harris, M. B. Modification of syntactic style. *Journal of Experimental Child Psychology*, 1966, *4*, 341–352.

Bandura, A., & Huston, A. C. Identification as a process of incidental learning. *Journal of Abnormal and Social Psychology*, 1961, *63*, 311–318.

Bandura, A., & Jeffery, R. W. Role of symbolic coding and rehearsal processes in observational learning. *Journal of Personality and Social Psychology*, 1973, *26*, 122–130.

Bandura, A., & Kupers, C. J. The transmission of patterns of self reinforcement through modeling. *Journal of Abnormal and Social Psychology*, 1964, *69*, 1–9.

Bandura, A., & McDonald, F. J. Influence of social reinforcement and the behavior of models in shaping children's moral judgments. *Journal of Abnormal and Social Psychology*, 1963, *67*, 274–281.

Bandura, A., & Menlove, F. L. Factors determining vicarious extinction of avoidance behavior through symbolic modeling. *Journal of Personality and Social Psychology*, 1968, *8*, 99–108.

Bandura, A., & Mischel, W. Modification of self-imposed delay of reward through exposure to live and symbolic models. *Journal of Personality and Social Psychology*, 1965, *2*, 698–705.

Bandura, A., & Rosenthal, T. L. Vicarious classical conditioning as a function of arousal level. *Journal of Personality and Social Psychology*, 1966, *3*, 54–62.

Bandura, A., Ross, D., & Ross, S. A. Imitation of film mediated aggressive models. *Journal of Abnormal and Social Psychology*, 1963, *66*, 3–11.

Bandura, A., & Walters, R. H. *Social learning and personality development.* New York: Holt, Rinehart, and Winston, 1963.

Barber, K. J. Imitative behavior as a function of task reinforcement, need for social approval, and simulated interpersonal compatibility. *Dissertation Abstracts*, 1967, *27*, 3510.

Black, A. H. The extinction of avoidance responses under curare. *Journal of Comparative and Physiological Psychology*, 1958, *51*, 519–524.

Borden, B. L., & White, G. M. Some effects of observing a model's reinforcement schedule and rate of responding on extinction and response rate. *Journal of Experimental Psychology*, 1973, *97*, 41–45.

Breyer, N. L., & May, J. G., Jr. Effect of sex and race of the observer and model in imitation learning. *Psychological Reports*, 1970, *27*, 639–646.

Bruner, J. S. *Toward a theory of instruction.* Cambridge, Massachusetts: Belknap Press of Harvard University Press, 1966.

Carroll, W. R., Rosenthal, T. L., & Brysh, C. G. Social transmission of grammatical parameters. *Journal of Educational Psychology*, 1972, *63*, 589–596.

Cowan, P. H., Langer, J., Heavenrich, J., & Nathanson, M. Social learning and Piaget's cognitive theory of moral development. *Journal of Personality and Social Psychology*, 1969, *11*, 261–274.

Dayton, G. O., Jr., & Jones, M. H. Analysis of characteristics of fixation reflexes in infants by use of direct current electrooculography. *Neurology*, 1964, *14*, 1152–1156.

Debus, R. L. Effects of brief observation and model behavior on conceptual tempo of impulsive children. *Developmental Psychology*, 1970, *2*, 22–32.

Denny, D. R. The effects of exemplary and cognitive models and self rehearsal on children's interrogative strategies. *Journal of Experimental Child Psychology*, 1975, *19*, 476–488.

Dewey, J. A. *Democracy and education.* New York: Macmillan, 1916.

Elliot, R., & Vasta, R. The modeling of sharing: Effects associated with vicarious reinforcement, symbolization, age, and generalization. *Journal of Experimental Child Psychology*, 1970, *10*, 8–15.

Engelman, S. Comments in E. E. Maccoby & M. Zellner (Eds.), *Experiments in primary education.* New York: Harcourt, Brace, and Jovanovich, 1970. P. 65.

Epstein, R. Aggression toward outgroups as a function of authoritarianism and imitation of aggressive models. *Journal of Personality and Social Psychology*, 1966, *3*, 574–579.

Frantz, R. L. Pattern vision in newborn infants. *Science*, 1963, *140*, 296–297.

Fryrear, J. L., & Thelen, M. H. Effects of sex of model and sex of observer on the imitation of affectionate behavior. *Developmental Psychology*, 1969, *1*, 298.

Furth, H. G. *Piaget and knowledge: Theoretical foundations*. Englewood Cliffs, N. J.: Prentice-Hall, 1969.

Gagne, R. M. Contributions of learning to human development. *Psychological Review*, 1968, *75*, 177–191.

Gelfand, D. M. The influence of self-esteem on rate of verbal conditioning and social matching behavior. *Journal of abnormal and social psychology*, 1962, *65*, 259–265.

Gerst, M. D. Symbolic coding processes in observational learning. *Journal of Personality and Social Psychology*, 1971, *19*, 7–17.

Gewirtz, J. L., & Stingle, K. G. Learning of generalized imitation as a basis for identification. *Psychological Review*, 1968, *75*, 374–397.

Gordon, I. Comments in E. E. Maccoby and M. Zellner *Experiments in primary education*. New York: Harcourt, Brace, and Jovanovich, 1970. P. 61.

Grusec, J., & Skubiski, S. L. Model nurturance, demand characteristics and altruism. *Journal of Personality and Social Psychology*, 1970, *14*, 353–359.

Guess, D., Sailor, W., Rutherford, G., & Baer, D. M. An experimental analysis of linguistic development: The productive use of the plural morpheme. *Journal of Applied Behavior Analysis*, 1968, *1*, 297–306.

Haaf, R. A., & Bell, R. Q. A facial dimension in visual discrimination by human infants. *Child Development*, 1967, *38*, 893–899.

Haith, M. M. The response of the human newborn to visual movement. *Journal of Experimental Child Psychology*, 1966, *3*, 235–243.

Harris, M. B., & Baudin, H. Models and vegetable eating: The power of popeye. *Psychological Reports*, 1972, *31*, 570.

Harris, M. B., & Evans, R. C. Models and creativity. *Psychological Reports*, 1973, *33*, 763–769.

Harris, M. B., & Hassemer, W. G. Some factors affecting the complexity of children's sentences: the effects of modeling, age, sex, and bilingualism. *Journal of Experimental Child Psychology*, 1972, *13*, 447–455.

Henderson, R. W., Swanson, R., & Zimmerman, B. J. Training seriation responses in young children through televised modeling of hierarchically sequenced rule components. *American Educational Research Journal*, 1975, *12*, 479–489.

Henker, B. The effect of adult model relationships on children's play and task imitation. *Dissertation Abstracts*, 1964, *24*, 4797.

Hicks, D. J. Imitation and retention of film mediated aggressive peer and adult models. *Journal of Personality and Social Psychology*, 1965, *2*, 97–100.

Hillix, W. A., & Marx, M. H. Response strengthening by information and effect in human learning. *Journal of Experimental Psychology*, 1960, *60*, 97–102.

Hodgson, R., & Rachman, S. Desynchrony in measures of fear. *Behaviour Research and Therapy*, 1974, *12*, 319–326.

Hovland, C. I., Janis, I. L., & Kelley, H. H. *Communication and persuasion*. New Haven, Connecticut: Yale University Press, 1953.

Hull, C. E. Quantitative aspects of the evolution of concepts. *Psychological Monographs*, 1920, *28*, No. 123.

Humphrey, G. Imitation and the conditioned reflex. *Pedagogical Seminary* (now *Journal of Genetic Psychology*), 1921, *28*, 1–21.

Jacobson, E. A. A comparison of the effects of instruction and models upon interview behavior of high dependent and low dependent subjects. *Dissertation Abstracts*, 1969, *29*, 3485.

Jakubczak, L. F., & Walters, R. A. Suggestibility as dependency behavior. *Journal of Abnormal and Social Psychology*, 1959, *59*, 102–107.

James, W. *The principles of psychology*. 2 Vols. New York: Henry Holt, 1890.

Kagan, J. Impulsive and reflective children: Significance of conceptual tempo. In J. D. Krumboltz (Ed.), *Learning and the educational process*. Chicago: Rand McNally, 1965.

Kanareff, V., & Lanzetta, J. T. Effects of success–failure experiences and the probability of reinforcement upon acquisition and extinction of an imitative response. *Psychological Reports*, 1960, *7*, 151–166.

Katona, G. *Organizing and memorizing*. New York: Columbia University Press, 1940.

Lamal, P. A. Imitation learning of information processing. *Journal of Experimental Child Psychology*, 1971, *12*, 223–227.

Laughlin, P. R., Moss, I. L., & Miller, S. M. Information-processing in children as a function of adult model, stimulus display, school grade, and sex. *Journal of Educational Psychology*, 1969, *60*, 188–193.

Liefert, R. M., Neale, J. M., & Davidson, E. S. *The early window: effects of television on children and youth*. New York: Pergamon Press, 1973.

Liefert, R. M., McCall, R. B., & Hanratty, M. A. Effects of sex-typed information on children's toy preferences. *Journal of Genetic Psychology*, 1971, *119*, 133–136.

Liefert, R. M., Odom, R. D., Hill, J. H., & Huff, R. L. The effects of age and rule familiarity on the production of modeled language constructions. *Developmental Psychology*, 1969, *1*, 108–112.

Liefert, R. M., & Swenson, S. A. Abstraction, inference, and the process of observational learning. *Developmental Psychology*, 1971, *5*, 500–504. (a)

Liefert, R. M., & Swenson, S. A. Association and abstraction as mechanisms of imitative learning. *Developmental Psychology*, 1971, *4*, 289–294. (b)

Lipton, M. B. Individual differences in the imitation of models. *Dissertation Abstracts International*, 1971, *31*, 5624.

Maccoby, E. E., & Wilson, W. C. Identification and observational learning from films. *Journal of Abnormal and Social Psychology*, 1957, *55*, 76–87.

Mann, J., & Rosenthal, T. L. Vicarious and direct counterconditioning of test anxiety through individual and group desensitization. *Behaviour Research and Therapy*, 1969, *7*, 359–367.

Marlouf, R. E., & Dodd, D. H. Role of exposure, imitation, and expansion in the acquisition of artificial grammatical rule. *Developmental Psychology*, 1972, *7*, 195–203.

Mausner, B. Studies in social interaction: III. Effect of variation in one partner's prestige on the interaction of observer pairs. *Journal of Applied Psychology*, 1953, *37*, 391–393.

Mausner, B., & Block, B. L. A study of the additivity of variables affecting social interaction. *Journal of Abnormal and Social Psychology*, 1957, *54*, 250–256.

McClelland, D. C. Risk taking in children with high and low need for achievement. In J. W. Atkinson (Ed.), *Motives in fantasy, action and society*. Princeton, New Jersey: Van Nostrand, 1958. Pp. 306–321.

Midlarsky, E., & Bryan, J. H. Training charity in children. *Journal of Personality and Social Psychology*, 1967, *5*, 408–415.

Mischel, W. Theory and research on the antecedents of self-imposed delay of reward. In B. A. Maher (Ed.), *Progress in experimental personality research*. New York: Academic Press, 1966, *3*. Pp. 85–132.

Mischel, W. *Personality and assessment*. New York: Wiley, 1968.

Mischel, W. Toward a cognitive social learning reconceptualization of personality. *Psychological Review*, 1973, *80*, 252–283.

Mischel, W., & Grusec, J. Determinants of the rehearsal and transmission of neutral and aversive behaviors. *Journal of Personality and Social Psychology*, 1966, *3*, 45–53.

Mischel, W., & Liebert, R. M. Effects of discrepancies between observed and imposed reward criteria on their acquisition and transmission. *Journal of Personality and Social Psychology*, 1966, *3*, 45–53.

Morgan, C. L. *Habit and instinct*. London: E. Arnold, 1896.

Mowrer, O. H. *Learning theory and the symbolic processes*. New York: Wiley, 1960.

Mussen, P., & Parker, A. L. Mother nurturance and girls' incidental imitative learning. *Journal of Personality and Social Psychology*, 1965, *2*, 94–97.

O'Connor, R. D. Modification of social withdrawal through symbolic modeling. *Journal of Applied Behavior Analysis*, 1969, *2*, 15–22.

Odom, R. D., Liebert, R. M., & Hill, J. H. The effects of modeling, cues, reward, and attention set on the production of grammatical and ungrammatical syntactic construction. *Journal of Experimental Child Psychology*, 1968, *6*, 131–140.

Parnes, S. J., & Meadow, A. Effects of "brain storming" on creative problem solving by trained and untrained subjects. *Journal of Educational Psychology*, 1959, *50*, 171–176.

Paskal, V. The value of imitative behavior. *Developmental psychology*, 1969, *1*, 463–469.

Piaget, J. *The moral judgment of the child*. Glenncoe, Illinois: Free Press, 1948.

Piaget, J. *The origins of intelligence in children*. New York: Norton, 1952.

Piaget, J. *Play, dreams, and imitation in childhood*. New York: Norton, 1962.

Richard, H. C., Ellis, N. R., Barnhart, S., & Holt, M. Subject–model sexual status and verbal imitative performance in kindergarten children. *Developmental Psychology*, 1970, *3*, 405.

Ridberg, E. H., Parke, R. D., & Hetherington, E. M. Modification of impulsive and reflective cognitive style through observation of film mediated models. *Developmental Psychology*, 1971, *5*, 185–190.

Rosenbaum, M. E., & Tucker, I. F. The competence of the model and the learning of imitation and nonimitation. *Journal of Experimental Psychology*, 1962, *63*, 183–190.

Rosenhan, D., & White, G. M. Observation and rehearsal as determinants of prosocial behavior. *Journal of Personality and Social Psychology*, 1967, *5*, 424–431.

Rosenthal, T. L., Alford, G. S., & Rasp, L. M. Concept attainment, generalization, and retention through observation and verbal coding. *Journal of Experimental Child Psychology*, 1972, *13*, 183–194.

Rosenthal, T. L., & Whitebook, J. S. Incentives versus instructions in transmitting grammatical parameters with experimenter as model. *Behaviour Research and Therapy*, 1970, *8*, 189–196.

Rosenthal, T. L., & Zimmerman, B. J. Instructional specificity and outcome expectation in observationally-induced question formulation. *Journal of Educational Psychology*, 1972, *63*, 500–504. (a)

Rosenthal, T. L., & Zimmerman, B. J. Modeling by exemplification and instruction in training conservation. *Developmental Psychology*, 1972, *6*, 392–401. (b)

Rosenthal, T. L., & Zimmerman, B. J. Organization, observation, and guided practice in concept attainment and generalization. *Child Development*, 1973, *44*, 606–613.

Rosenthal, T. L., & Zimmerman, B. J. Organization and stability of transfer in vicarious concept attainment. *Child Development*, 1976, *47*, 110–117.

Rosenthal, T. L., Zimmerman, B. J., & Durning, K. Observationally-induced changes in children's interrogative classes. *Journal of Personality and Social Psychology*, 1970, *16*, 681–688.

Ross, D. Relationship between dependency, intentional learning, and incidental learning in preschool children. *Journal of Personality and Social Psychology*, 1966, *4*, 374–381.

Ross, E. A. *Social psychology: An outline and source book*. New York: Macmillan, 1908.

Shulman, L. S., & Keisler, E. R. *Learning by discovery*. Chicago: Rand McNally, 1966.

Shumaker, J., & Sherman, J. A. Training generative verb usage by imitation and reinforcement procedures. *Journal of Applied Behavior Analysis*, 1970, *3*, 273–287.

Siegler, R. S., & Liebert, R. M. Effects of presenting relevant rules and complete feedback on the conservation of liquid quantity task. *Developmental Psychology*, 1972, *7*, 133–138.

Siegler, R. S., Liebert, D. E., & Liebert, R. M. Inhelder and Piaget's pendulum problem: Teaching preadolescents to act as scientists. *Developmental Psychology*, 1973, *9*, 97–101.

Skinner, B. F. *The technology of teaching*. New York: Appleton–Century–Crofts, 1968.

Smith, S., & Guthrie, E. R. *General psychology in terms of behavior*. New York: Appleton, 1921.

Stechler, G. Newborn attention as affected by medication during labor. *Science*, 1964, *144*, 315–317.

Stein, A. H., & Wright, J. G. Imitative learning under conditions of nurturance and nurturance withdrawal. *Child Development*, 1964, *35*, 927–938.

Tarde, G. *The laws of imitation* (2nd Ed.). New York: Henry Holt, 1903.

Taub, E., Bacon, R. C., & Berman, A. J. Acquisition of a trace conditioned avoidance response after deafferentation of the responding limb. *Journal of Comparative and Physiological Psychology,* 1965, *59,* 275–279.

Thelen, M. H. The effect of subject race, model race, and vicarious praise on vicarious learning. *Child Development,* 1971, *42,* 972–977.

Thelen, M. H., & Fryrear, J. L. The effects of model race on the imitation of self-reward. *Developmental Psychology,* 1971, *5,* 133–135. (a)

Thelen, M. H., & Fryrear, J. L. Imitation of self-reward standards by black and white female delinquents. *Psychological Reports,* 1971, *29,* 667–671. (b)

Whitehurst, G. J. Generalized labeling on the basis of structural response classes by two young children. *Journal of Experimental Child Psychology,* 1971, *12,* 59–71.

Whitehurst, G. J. Production of novel and grammatical utterances by young children. *Journal of Experimental Child Psychology,* 1972, *13,* 502–515.

Whitehurst, G. J., Novak, G., & Zorn, G. A. Delayed speech studies in the home. *Developmental Psychology,* 1972, *7,* 160–177.

Wittrock, M. C. The learning by discovery hypothesis. In L. S. Shulman and E. R. Keislar (Eds.), *Learning by discovery.* Chicago: Rand McNally, 1966.

Yussen, S. R., & Levy, V. M., Jr. Effects of warm and neutral models on the attention of observational learners. *Journal of Experimental Child Psychology,* 1975, *20,* 66–72.

Zimmerman, B. J. Modification of young children's grouping strategies: The effects of modeling, verbalization, incentives, and age. *Child Development,* 1974, *45,* 1032–1041.

Zimmerman, B. J., & Bell, J. A. Observer verbalization and abstraction in vicarious rule learning, generalization, and retention. *Developmental Psychology,* 1972, *7,* 227–231.

Zimmerman, B. J., & Brody, G. H. Race and modeling influences on the interpersonal play patterns of boys. *Journal of Educational Psychology,* 1975, *67,* 591–598.

Zimmerman, B. J., & Dialessi, F. Modeling influences on children's creative behavior. *Journal of Educational Psychology,* 1973, *65,* 127–134.

Zimmerman, B. J., & Koussa, R. Social influences on children's toy preferences: Effects of model valence and affectivity. Unpublished manuscript, Graduate School and University Center, City University of New York, 1975. (a)

Zimmerman, B. J., & Koussa, R. Sex factors in children's observational learning of value judgments of toys. *Sex Roles: A Journal of Research,* 1975, *1,* 120–133. (b)

Zimmerman, B. J., & Lanaro, P. Acquiring and retaining conservation of length through modeling and reversibility cues. *Merrill-Palmer Quarterly,* 1974, *20,* 145–161.

Zimmerman, B. J., & Pike, E. O. Effects of modeling and reinforcement on the acquisition and generalization of question-asking behavior. *Child Development,* 1972, *43,* 892–907.

Zimmerman, B. J., & Rosenthal, T. L. Concept attainment, transfer, and retention observation and rule provision. *Journal of Experimental Child Psychology,* 1972, *14,* 139–150. (a)

Zimmerman, B. J., & Rosenthal, T. L. Observation, repetition, and ethnic background in concept attainment and generalization. *Child Development,* 1972, *43,* 605–613. (b)

Zimmerman, B. J., & Rosenthal, T. L. Conserving and retaining equalities and inequalities through observation and correction. *Developmental Psychology,* 1974, *10,* 260–268. (a)

Zimmerman, B. J., & Rosenthal, T. L. Observational learning of rule governed behavior by children. *Psychological Bulletin,* 1974, *81,* 29–42. (b)

4

Punishment in Children: Effects, Side Effects, and Alternative Strategies

ROSS D. PARKE

University of Illinois

INTRODUCTION

Few topics have generated as much debate in recent years as the impact of punishment on children's behavior. In this chapter, recent scientific findings will be reviewed in order to provide some guidelines concerning the effects and side effects of punishment. Punishment effectiveness is dependent on a variety of factors including the timing, intensity, and consistency of the punishment, as well as the nature of the relationship between the agent and recipient of punishment and the type of cognitive structuring that accompanies the punishment. The factors that control the selection and utilization of different disciplinary tactics will be examined. In addition, the negative and undesirable side effects that often accompany punishment will be detailed. Finally, the relationship between our increasing recognition of children's rights and our continued use of physical punishment as a socialization technique will be critically evaluated. It will be argued that physical punishment is generally unjustified and alternative techniques are both more humane and more effective.

Preparation of this chapter and the research by Parke that is reported here was supported in part by National Science Foundation Grant GS-31885X to the author.

TYPES OF PUNISHMENT

Definition

Punishment involves the presentation of a noxious or aversive stimulus with the aim of suppressing some undesirable behavior. Although theorists vary in their explanations of punishment, many assume that the noxious stimulus generates fear or anxiety in the recipient. In turn, by being associated with the unpleasant emotions of fear or anxiety, the punished response is less likely to be emitted by the child.

The term *punishment* refers to a wide range of procedures and tactics available to the socializing agent. In this section, we will outline some of the common forms of punishment that are used in real life environments, as well as the types typically employed in laboratory studies.

Physical Punishment

Perhaps the best known, least understood, and most undesirable form of discipline is physical punishment. In fact, laymen often make the error of equating physical punishment with all forms of punitive tactics. The principal characteristic of physical punishment is the use of physical force directed toward another individual in order to achieve compliance or suppression of an undesirable behavior. Physical punishment can, of course, include a wide range of actions from a gentle tap on the hand or buttocks to more extreme forms such as physical restraint, or hitting the child with an object such as a belt or brush. In extreme forms, it is often no longer labeled punishment; rather it is legitimately relabeled physical abuse. Some have argued that physical punishment is not a preferred technique of discipline among North American parents (Sears, Maccoby, & Levin, 1957) and others (Bronfenbrenner, 1958) note that it is largely limited to lower class parents. However, recent surveys have questioned both of these assumptions. First, as Gil (1970) notes, physical punishment is probably much more prevalent than we have previously recognized, with a surprisingly high percentage of our population actively utilizing physically punitive tactics. Second, there is little evidence that either physical punishment or physical abuse is restricted to lower class families (Erlanger, 1974; Parke & Collmer, 1975). In spite of its prevalence in naturalistic situations, it will be argued in this chapter that the use of physical punishment is neither justified, desirable, nor necessary.

Due to the ethical limitations governing the conduct of research with children, there have been no laboratory studies of the effectiveness of physical punishment on children's social behavior. The exception is Lovaas (Bucher & Lovaas, 1968), who utilized electric shock as a therapeutic technique in a treatment setting for modifying the self-destructive behavior of autistic children. In laboratory studies of normal children, the nearest approximation to traditional physical punishment is probably the loud unpleasant sounds employed by a number of researchers (e.g., Aronfreed & Leff, 1963; LaVoie, 1974a; Parke, 1969). The usefulness of noise as an analogue to physical punishment in social situations stems from the possibility of investigating under controlled conditions certain parameters, such as intensity, which are important for understanding the manner in which punishment may change behavior. However, generalization from laboratory studies of noise, buzzers, and other noxious auditory stimuli to real life situations must be undertaken with great caution; detailed understanding of the impact of physical punishment must rely on naturalistic observational investigations.

Verbal Punishment

The most common form of punishment in naturalistic contexts such as homes, schools, and playgrounds is probably some form of verbal punishment. Verbal, as well as physical, punishment can assume a variety of forms, including shouting or yelling, threatening, verbal rebukes, labeling an action as "incorrect" or wrong, ridicule, criticism, scolding, and nagging. Unfortunately, little systematic research has been devoted to carefully examining the relative effectiveness of different forms of verbal punishment.

In contrast to physical and verbal punitive tactics, which involve a direct assault upon the victim, there are other forms of punishment, such as withholding and withdrawal of rewards, which rely on the loss of some valued event, object, or opportunity rather than the direct induction of painful or unpleasant stimulation.

Loss of Positive Reinforcement

In naturalistic situations, a common form of punishment involves withdrawal of positive reinforcers, such as loss of material rewards (e.g., the loss of a favorite toy or withholding of allowance). The effectiveness of this type of punishment has been clearly demonstrated in both field and laboratory studies. For example, Baer (1961, 1962) demonstrated that children's motor behavior or thumb sucking could be depressed by withdrawal of reward, in the form of interruption of a movie. Numerous other studies have found that loss of pennies, marbles, tokens, and toys can suppress children's behavior (LaVoie, 1974a).

Withdrawal or Withholding of Affection

Loss of reinforcement as a control technique need not be restricted to the loss of material or tangible rewards. Parents and teachers often attempt to exert control over others by manipulating the availability of nontangible reinforcers such as attention and affection.

Sears et al. (1957) list a variety of forms that withdrawal or withholding of affection may take; these include refusing attention, accusing the child of hurting the parents' feelings, shutting him off from contact with the family (isolation), and other devices to indicate that the parent's affection is conditional on the child's conforming to parental demands. Laboratory analogues of such forms of discipline include withholding or withdrawal of affectional interaction and brief isolation (Parke, 1967).

Some have argued that in real life situations, the efficacy of all disciplinary

practices, including physical and verbal punishment and the withdrawal or withholding of material rewards, is "undoubtedly due, at least in part, to the child's
perception of the loss of material rewards as symbolizing the loss, or threat of loss,
of parental love and affection [Walters & Parke, 1967, p. 203]."

A particularly popular form of attention withdrawal that has been utilized in
behavior modification programs in recent years is "time-out." As Kazdin notes:

> Time-out refers to the removal of all positive reinforcers for a specific time
> interval. During time-out the individual does not have access to the reinforcers
> normally available in the setting for the entire time interval. For example, a child
> in a classroom may be isolated from his peers for a few minutes. During the time
> interval, the child will have no interaction with others nor engage in privileges or
> activities. Time-out only requires a few minutes to be effective rather than a long
> interval of time. Undesirable eating behaviors, stuttering, bizarre speech, antisocial
> and aggressive behaviors, thumb sucking and toileting accidents have been sup-
> pressed with time-out [Kazdin, 1975, p. 16–17].

At present, there is little comparative data concerning the relative effectiveness
of different types of punishment techniques. In one exception, LaVoie (1974a)
compared a variety of techniques, including withdrawal of affection, an aversive
stimulus (loud noise), a verbal rationale, and withholding of resources (pennies). In
this study, first and second grade children were first punished by one of these
techniques for touching prohibited toys. The children were then left alone with the
toys, and the extent to which they touched the toys was recorded as a measure of
their resistance to deviation. Although the aversive stimulus was the most effective
suppressor in the early phases of the test period, by the end of the 12-min
resistance-to-deviation test period there were few differences across the different
types of punishment. In spite of the similarity in effectiveness of various techniques, there are clear disadvantages associated with some tactics, such as physical
punishment, which undermine their usefulness. The undesirable side effects of some
types of punishment will be reviewed in a later section. Now we turn to an
examination of the variables that control the effectiveness of punishment.

DETERMINANTS OF PUNISHMENT EFFECTIVENESS

The effectiveness of punishment is dependent on a variety of factors. The aim of
this section is to review these variables, including the timing and the intensity of
punishment, the nature of the relationship between the agent and the recipient of
punishment, the consistency with which punishment is administered and the
amount and type of verbal explanation that accompanies the punishment. Only by
considering this diverse set of variables can the impact of punishment be understood.

Timing of Punishment

A factor of considerable importance in naturalistic socialization contexts is the
timing of punishment. By timing, we refer to the amount of time between the

initiation of an action and the administration of punishment by the socialization agent. In home and school situations punishment is often delayed beyond the completion of the deviant behavior. For example, a teacher may delay punishing a child until the end of a class or even the end of the school day. Or a parent may delay punishment until the other parent, usually the father, returns home. Does the timing of the administration of a punishment alter its effectiveness as a means of inhibiting undesirable behavior? To answer this question, consider a study by Walters, Parke, and Cane (1965), who tested the effects of timing of punishment on resistance to deviation in 6- to 8-year-old boys. These investigators presented their subjects with pairs of toys—one attractive and one unattractive—on a series of nine trials. The 6- to 8-year-old boys were punished by a verbal rebuke, "No, that's for the other boy," when they chose the attractive toy. One group of children was punished as they approached the attractive toy, but before they actually touched it. For the remaining boys, punishment was delivered only after they had picked up the critical toy and held it for 2 sec. Following the punishment training session, the subjects were seated before a display of toys similar to those used in the training period and were reminded not to touch the toys. The resistance-to-deviation test consisted of a 15-min period during which the boy was left alone with an unattractive German–English dictionary and, of course, the prohibited toys. The extent to which the subject touched the toys in the absence of the external agent was recorded by an observer located behind a one-way screen. The early punished children touched the taboo toys less than did the boys punished late in the response sequence. This timing of punishment effect has been replicated by a number of investigators (Aronfreed & Reber, 1965; Parke & Walters, 1967; Cheyne & Walters, 1969).

Extensions of this experimental model indicate that this finding is merely one aspect of a general relation: the longer the delay between the initiation of the act and the onset of punishment, the less effective the punishment for producing response inhibition. This proposition is based on a study in which the effects of four different delay-of-punishment intervals were examined (Aronfreed, 1965). Using a design similar to Walters, Parke, and Cane (1965), Aronfreed punished one group of children as they reached for the attractive toy. Under a second condition, the subject was permitted to pick up the attractive toy and was punished at the apex of the lifting movement. Under a third condition, 6 sec elapsed after the child picked up the toy before punishment was delivered. In the final group, 6 sec after the child picked up the toy he was asked to describe the toy and only then was punishment administered. The time elapsing between the experimenter's departure until the child made the first deviation steadily decreased as the time between the initiation of the act and the delivery of punishment increased.

Punishment may be less effective in facilitating learning as well as less effective in facilitating resistance to temptation if the punishment is delayed. Using a learning task in which errors were punished by the presentation of a loud noise combined with the loss of a token, Walters (1964) found that punishment delivered immediately after the error speeded learning more than did punishment which was delayed 10 sec or 30 sec.

Since it is often difficult to detect and punish a response in the approach phase of a transgression sequence, the practical implications of these studies may be questioned. However, Aronfreed (1968) has noted one feature of naturalistic socialization that may dilute the importance of punishing the act in the execution phase. "Parents frequently punish a child when he is about to repeat an act which they dislike [p. 180]." In this case, punishment may be delivered in the early stages of the next execution of the act, even though it is delayed in relation to the previous commission of the act.

In addition, the importance of timing of punishment may be contingent on a variety of other features of punishment administration, such as the intensity of the punishment, the nature of the agent—child relationship, and the kind of verbal rationale accompanying the punishment. The effects of these variables will be examined in the following sections.

Intensity of Punishment

It is generally assumed that as the intensity of punishment increases, the amount of inhibition will similarly increase. It is difficult to study severity of punishment in the laboratory due to the obvious ethical limitations upon using potentially harmful stimuli in experimentation with children. Until recently most of the evidence concerning the relative effectiveness of different intensities of punishment derived either from animal studies or from child-rearing interview studies.

The animal studies (e.g., Church, 1963), in which electric shock is most often used as the punishing stimulus, have supported the conclusion that more complete suppression of the punished response results as the intensity of the punishment increases. On the other hand, the child-rearing data relating to the effects of intensity on children's behavior have not yielded clear-cut conclusions. It is difficult, however, to assess the operation of specific punishment variables using rating scales of parent behavior because most of these scales confound several aspects of punishment, such as frequency, intensity, and consistency (Walters & Parke, 1967). Differences between scale points may, therefore, be due to the impact of any of these variables, either alone or in combination.

Recent laboratory studies have avoided some of these shortcomings and have yielded less equivocal conclusions concerning the effects of punishment intensity on children's behavior. Using the resistance-to-deviation approach already described, Parke and Walters (1967) punished one group of boys with a soft tone (65 db) when they chose a prohibited toy. A second group heard a loud tone (96 db) when they chose the toy. In the subsequent temptation test, children who were exposed to the loud punisher were less likely to touch the prohibited toys in the experimenter's absence than were boys exposed to a less intense version of the tone. This finding has been confirmed using a noxious buzzer as the punishing stimulus (Cheyne & Walters, 1969; Parke, 1969).

This research has also yielded some suggestive evidence concerning the impact of intensity variations on other aspects of punishment, such as timing (Parke, 1969).

Under conditions of high-intensity punishment, the degree of inhibition produced by early and late punishment was similar. Under low-intensity conditions, however, the early punished subjects showed significantly greater inhibition than did subjects punished late in the response sequence. Thus, timing of punishment may be less important under conditions of high-intensity punishment. However, the generality of this conclusion is limited by the narrow range of delay-of-punishment intervals that have been investigated. Perhaps when punishment is delayed over a number of hours, for example, this relationship would not hold. Further research is clearly required.

However, high-intensity punishment is not always superior to less intense forms in controlling children's behavior. Aronfreed and Leff (1963), for example, found that in learning situations that involve subtle discriminations, children benefit more from low-intensity punishment than high-intensity punishment. Intense punishment may sometimes create a level of anxiety too high to permit adaptive learning to occur and therefore may retard the inhibition of undesirable behaviors.

Moreover, high-intensity punishment is not more effective than low-intensity discipline in all settings. In a typical classroom setting, a child who receives a loud reprimand from his teacher is often noticed by his peers; in turn, this peer group attention may be rewarding and therefore undermine the effectiveness of the punisher. In an interesting classroom experiment, O'Leary and his colleagues (O'Leary, Kaufman, Kass, & Drabman, 1970) examined the effects of loud and soft reprimands on the behavior of disruptive second grade children. Their observations indicated that teacher reprimands were nearly always loud and could be heard by many other children in the class. To compare the impact of loud and soft reprimands, teachers were asked to use primarily soft reprimands which were audible only to the child being reprimanded. With the institution of the soft reprimands, the frequency of disruptive behavior declined in most children. As the authors note:

> Soft reprimands offer several interesting advantages over loud ones. First of all, a soft reprimand does not single out the child so that his disruptive behavior is made noticeable to others. Second, a soft reprimand is presumably different from the reprimands that disruptive children ordinarily receive at home or in school, and consequently, it should minimize the possibility of triggering conditioned emotional reactions to reprimands. Third, teachers consider soft reprimands a viable alternative to the usual methods of dealing with disruptive behavior [O'Leary et al., 1970, p. 146].

Punishment intensity is an important determinant of punishment effectiveness, but the nature of the social setting needs to be considered in evaluating the effectiveness of high and low intensities of punishment on children's behavior.

Nature of the Relationship between the Agent and Recipient of Punishment

The nature of the relationship between the socializing agent and the child is a significant determinant of the effectiveness of punishment. It is generally assumed that punishment will be a more effective means of controlling behavior when this relationship is close and affectional than when it is relatively impersonal. This argument assumes that any disciplinary act may involve in varying degrees at least two operations—the presentation of an aversive stimulus and the withdrawal or withholding of a positive reinforcer (Bandura & Walters, 1963). Physical punishment may, in fact, achieve its effect partly because it symbolizes the withdrawal of approval of affection. Hence, punishment should be a more potent controlling technique when used by a nurturant parent or teacher.

Sears et al. (1957) provided some evidence in favor of this proposition. Mothers who were rated as warm and affectionate and who made relatively frequent use of physical punishment were more likely to report that they found spanking to be an effective means of discipline. In contrast, cold, hostile parents who made frequent use of physical punishment were more likely to report that spanking was more effective when it was administered by the warmer of the two parents.

A study by Parke and Walters (1967) confirmed these child-rearing findings in a controlled laboratory situation. In this investigation, the nature of the experimenter–child relationship was varied in two interaction sessions prior to the administration of punishment. One group of boys experienced a 10-min period of positive interaction with a female experimenter on two successive days. Attractive constructional materials were provided for the children and, as they played with the materials, the female experimenters provided encouragement and help and warmly expressed approval of their efforts. A second group of boys played with relatively unattractive materials in two 10-min sessions while the experimenter sat in the room without interacting with the children. Following these interaction sessions, the children underwent punishment training involving verbal rebuke and a noxious noise for choosing incorrect toys. In the subsequent test for response inhibition, children who had experienced positive interaction with the agent of punishment showed significantly greater resistance to deviation than boys who had only impersonal contact.

The implication of the study is clear: The nature of the relationship between the agent and recipient of punishment is an important determinant of punishment effectiveness.

Reasoning and Punishment

In all of the studies discussed, punishment was presented in a relatively barren cognitive context. Very often, however, parents and teachers provide the child with a rationale for the punishment they administer. Is punishment more effective when accompanied by a set of reasons for nondeviation? Field studies of child rearing suggest that the answer is positive. For example, Sears et al. (1957), in their interview investigation of child-rearing practices, found that mothers who combine physical punishment with extensive use of reasoning reported greater success in controlling their children's behavior than mothers who used punishment alone. Field investigations, however, have yielded little information concerning the relative effectiveness of different aspects of reasoning. In the child-training literature, reasoning may include not only descriptions of untoward consequences that the child's behavior may have for others, but also the provision of examples of incompatible socially acceptable behaviors, explicit instructions on how to behave in specific situations, and explanations of motives for placing restraints on the child's behavior. Moreover, these child-training studies do not indicate the manner in which the provision of reasons in combination with punishment can alter the operation of specific punishment parameters such as those already discussed— timing, intensity, and the nature of the agent–child relationship.

It is necessary to turn again to experimental studies for answers to these questions. First, laboratory investigations have confirmed the field results in that punishment is more effective when accompanied by a rationale. Parke (1969), for example, found that when children, in addition to being punished, were told that a toy was fragile and might break, greater inhibition occurred than when children were punished without an accompanying rationale. In a later experiment, Parke and Murray (1971) found that a rationale alone is more effective than punishment alone. However, comparison of the results of the two studies indicates that the combination of punishment and a rationale is the most thoroughly effective procedure.

These results are highly consistent with the findings of a study of LaVoie (1973). He compared the effectiveness of punishment alone, punishment ac-companied by a rationale, and rationale alone for producing response inhibition in adolescent boys. The training procedure used in our other studies with children (Parke, 1969; Parke & Murray, 1971) was altered for LaVoie's study to insure that the objects were of interest to boys of this age. Instead of using "professional" experimenters, the subject's mother or father was used as the training agent. A 2 X 2 X 2 design was employed involving three independent variables: (1) sex of parent—mother or father; (2) punishment (104-db noise) versus no punishment; and (3) presence or absence of a rationale. The no-noise, no-rationale group served as a control condition. The rationale used was a property rationale: "You don't handle other people's property without their permission." As predicted, the rationale plus punishment combination produced the most response inhibition. The subjects who received neither punishment nor rationale training exhibited the greatest amount of deviant behavior. Punishment alone and rationale alone were of intermediate effectiveness. As with the earlier comparisons involving child subjects (Parke, 1969; Parke & Murray, 1971), the rationale alone produced more inhibition than did the punishment alone; however, the difference between these two groups was not significant. The consistency of these results across subjects of different ages clearly suggests that the provision of a rationale is an effective technique for achieving response inhibition in children. However, these experiments suggest that punish-ment and the provision of an accompanying rationale operate additively to produce a degree of response inhibition that is greater than that resulting from either a rationale alone or from punishment alone.

To understand the impact of reasoning on the timing of punishment effect, let us examine, a pioneering set of studies by Aronfreed (1965). In the earlier timing experiments, cognitive structure was minimized and no verbal rationale was given for the constraints placed on the child's behavior. In contrast, children in a second group of experiments were provided, in the initial instructions, with a brief explanation for not handling some of the toys. In one variation, for example, the cognitive structuring focused on the child's intentions. When punished, the child was told" "No, you should not have wanted to pick up that thing." The important finding here was that the addition of reasoning to a late-timed punishment markedly increased its effectiveness. In fact, when a verbal rationale accompanied the punishment, the usual timing of punishment effect was absent; early- and late-timed punishments were equally effective inhibitors of the child's behavior. Other investigators have reported a similar relation between reasoning operations and timing of punishment (Cheyne & Walters, 1969; Parke, 1969). In the latter studies, the reasoning procedures presented in conjunction with punishment did not stress intentions but focused on the consequences of violation of the experimenter's prohibition.

The delay periods used in all of these studies were relatively short. In everyday life, detection of a deviant act is often delayed many hours, or the punishment may be postponed, for example, until the father returns home. An experiment reported by Walters and Andres (1967) addressed itself directly to this issue. Their aim was to determine the conditions under which a punishment delivered 4 hours after the commission of a deviant act could be made an effective inhibitor. By verbally describing the earlier deviation at the time that the punishment was administered, the effectiveness of the punishment was considerably increased in comparison to a punishment that was delivered without an accompanying restatement. An equally effective procedure involved exposing the children to a videotape recording of themselves committing the deviant act just prior to the long-delayed punishment. A partially analogous situation, not studied by these investigators, involves parental demonstration of the deviant behavior just before delivering the punishing blow. In any case, symbolic reinstatement of the deviant act, according to these data, seems to be a potent way of increasing the effectiveness of delayed punishment.

A question remains. Do reasoning manipulations alter the operation of any other parameters besides the timing of the punishment? Parke (1969) examined the modifying impact of reasoning on the intensity and nurturance variables. When no rationale was provided, the expected intensity of punishment effect was present: High-intensity punishment produced significantly greater inhibition than low-intensity punishment. However, when a rationale accompanied the punishment, the difference between high and low intensity of punishment was not present.

As noted earlier, children who experience nurturant interaction with the punishing agent prior to punishment training deviate less often than subjects in the low-nurturance condition. However, this effect was present in the Parke (1969) study only when no rationale accompanied the noxious buzzer. When the children were provided with a rationale for not touching certain toys, the children who had experienced the friendly interaction and the children who had only impersonal contact with the agent were equally inhibited during the resistance-to-deviation test period. Taken together, these experiments constitute impressive evidence of the important role played by cognitive variables in modifying the operation of punishment.

A common yardstick employed to gauge the success of a disciplinary procedure is the permanence of the inhibition produced. It is somewhat surprising, therefore, that little attention has been paid to the stability of inhibition over time as a consequence of various punishment training operations. One approach to this issue involves calculating changes in deviant activity occurring during the resistance-to-deviation test session in experimental studies. Does the amount of deviant behavior increase at different rates, for example, in response to different training procedures? As a first step in answering this question, Parke (1969) divided the 15-min resistance-to-deviation test session into three 5-min periods. The low cognitive structure subjects (no rationale) increased their degree of illicit toy touching over the three time periods, while the degree of deviation over the three intervals did not significantly change for the high cognitive structure (rationale provided) subjects. Cheyne and Walters (1969) have reported a similar finding. These data clearly indicate that the stability of inhibition over time was affected by the reasoning or cognitive structuring procedures. The most interesting implication of this finding is that long-term inhibition may require the use of cognitively oriented training procedures. Punishment techniques that rely solely on anxiety induction, such as the noxious noises employed in many of the experiments discussed or the more extreme forms of physical punishment sometimes used by parents, may be effective mainly in securing only short-term inhibition.

However, children often forget a rationale or may not remember that a prohibition is still in force after a lengthy time lapse. A brief reminder or reinstatement of the original punisher or rationale may be necessary to insure continued inhibition. To investigate the impact of such reinstatement on the stability of inhibition was the aim of an experiment by Parke and Murray (1971). In this study, following the typical punishment training procedure, the 7- to 9-year-old boys were tested immediately for resistance-to-deviation and then retested in the same situation 1 week later. Half of the children were "reminded" of the earlier training by the experimenter. For example, in the case of the boys who were punished by a buzzer during the training session, the experimenter sounded the buzzer a single time and reminded the children that it signaled that they should not touch the toys ("You shouldn't touch the toys"). For children who received rationales unaccompanied by any punishment, the experimenter merely restated the rationale ("Remember those toys belong to another boy" or "They are fragile and may break") before leaving the children alone with the toys. For the remaining children, no reminder or reinstatement of the earlier training was provided. As Figure 4.1 indicates, reinstatement of the original training clearly increased the persistence of the response inhibition.

However, the effectiveness of different types of reasoning procedures for producing inhibition varies with the developmental level of the child. Cheyne (1972),

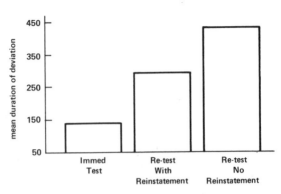

Figure 4.1. Stability of inhibition over 1 week with and without reinstatement.

for example, found that third grade children increased their resistance to deviation in response to a prohibitory rationale stressing the norm of ownership, while first graders responded equally to both a rationale and a simple verbal prohibition. As Parke and Murray (1971) have demonstrated, the type of rationale is important for achieving optimal inhibition with children of different ages. It is necessary to match the type and complexity of the rationale with the level of the child's cognitive development. Only if children can readily comprehend the bases of the rationale will it be an effective inhibitor. To test this proposition, Parke and Murray exposed 4- and 7-year-old children to two types of rationales that varied in degree of abstractness. The first—an object-oriented appeal—was relatively concrete and focused on the physical consequences of handling the toy ("The toy is fragile and might break"). This emphasis on the physical consequences of an action is similar to the types of justificatory rationales that young children use in their moral judgments (Kohlberg, 1964). The second rationale was a property rule which stressed the ethical norm of ownership. This person-oriented rationale was more abstract and assumed that children understand the rights of other individuals. In Kohlberg's moral judgment system this understanding represents a more sophisti- cated level of moral development. It was predicted that the property rationale would be most effective with the older children and that the concrete rationale would be more effective with the younger children. The results were consistent with this prediction. The concrete rationale was significantly more effective than was the property rationale in producing response inhibition in the younger children. At the older age level the effectiveness of the two rationales was approximately equal, the property rule being slightly more effective. In a more recent study (Parke, 1974) with boys and girls of nursery school age, a similar interaction of Age X Type of rationale was found. The children in the younger age group (3–4.5 years) were more inhibited by the object-oriented rationale than by the property ratio- nale; children in the older age group (4.5–6 years) were inhibited equally by the two types of rationales, although the property rationale was, again, slightly more effective. As in the earlier study, the children at the two age levels differed in their response to the property rationale. The replication increases our confidence in this relationship; moreover, the finding suggests that during the latter half of the fourth year the child is showing a significant shift in response to abstract rationales.

Rationales do not vary only in terms of their object- versus person-oriented qualities. As a number of writers (Aronfreed, 1968; Hoffman, 1970; LaVoie, 1974a) have stressed, rationales vary in terms of their focus on either (*1*) the consequences or outcomes of the rule violation, or (*2*) the motivation or intention underlying the deviation. Since children utilize consequences as the basis for judging rule infractions at an earlier age than they utilize the actors' intentions, it is likely that appeals that focus on the consequences of misbehavior would be more effective for producing response inhibition than appeals that focus on the child's intentions. In fact, LaVoie (1974b) recently evaluated this proposition; 7-, 9-, and 11-year-old children heard either a consequence-focused rationale ("That toy might get broken or worn out from you playing with it") or an intention-focused rationale ("It is wrong for you to *want* to play with that toy or think about playing with that toy"). As expected, the consequence rationale was equally effective at all ages, but the intention-focused rationale increased in effectiveness across age. For older children, focusing on intentions yields more effective control than focusing on the consequences of the act.

Other types of rationales have been investigated as well. For example, Parke and Sawin (1975a) examined the relative effectiveness of different types of emotional appeals on response inhibition in children at different ages. Children at three ages, 3–4, 5–6, 7–8, were exposed to either a fear-based rationale or an empathy-based rationale. The fear rationale focused on expression of adult anger directed toward the child (i.e., "I will be angry if you touch the toys") while the empathy rationale focused on the negative affect that rule violation would generate in the adult ("I will be sad if you touch the toys"). The effectiveness of these two types of rationales in producing resistance to deviation in the toy-touching situation varied with the age of the child. The provision of the fear-invoking (angry) rationale was an effective prohibition of children at all age levels. However, the empathy-invoking consequences were less effective for the young children than for the older children. These findings suggest that empathetic appeals are relatively ineffective with young children.

Another factor to be considered is the length of the explanation; since young children have shorter attention spans than older children, lengthy explanations may simply not be very effective with young children. Hetherington (1975), in fact, found that parents who used brief explanations gained better control over their children than parents who used long and involved explanations.

Together the findings emphasize the importance of considering developmental factors in studies of different types of control tactics. Finally, by using cognitively based control tactics, age changes in behavioral aspects of moral development are clearly demonstrated. The task of charting in more detail age changes in relation to specific types of prohibitory rationales would appear to be worthwhile.

The use of reasoning not only produces better subsequent self control, but also may transform the child into a rule transmitter who may enforce adult-established rules on his peers. In other words, reasoning may have second-order effects beyond merely producing immediate response inhibition. Parke (1973) altered the usual resistance-to-deviation paradigm used in earlier punishment studies in order to investigate this issue. In addition to the training phase in which the prohibition is established, a test phase was added to examine the extent to which the trained children would transmit the prohibitory rule to a second child. During this phase, a peer who was given permission to touch the "prohibited" toys was introduced into the test setting. By recording the trained child's attempts to influence the peer, the effect of various training tactics for producing rule transmission was evaluated. The results indicated that the children who had been originally trained with the rationale more frequently attempted to inhibit the second child's rule-breaking-toy-touching activities than children trained with punishment. These findings suggest that the use of rationales as a socializing technique may not only produce a greater degree of inhibition, but may also result in greater rule transmission. Subsequent studies (Bosserman & Parke, 1973) reveal that the rule transmission experience itself can increase self-control. Children who were given responsibility for assuming the role of rule enforcer for the behavior of another child showed greater subsequent self-control than children who were not given this responsibility. Affording children responsibility for enforcing rules, in short, increases their own rule-following behavior.

Consistency of Punishment

In naturalistic contexts, punishment is often intermittently and erratically employed. Two types of inconsistent punishment merit distinction. Intraagent inconsistency refers to the extent to which a single agent treats violations in the same manner each time they occur or to the extent to which a parent, teacher or other socializing agent follows through on their threats of punishment. Interagent inconsistency, on the other hand, refers to the degree to which different socializing agents, such as two parents, respond in a similar fashion to rule violations. Do they react with the same type and level of punishment? Do they agree on the occasions on which punishment should be employed?

Information concerning the effects of inconsistent punishment comes from both field and laboratory studies. The field studies of the antecedents of delinquency have yielded some suggestive leads concerning the consequences of inconsistent discipline. Glueck and Glueck (1950) found that parents of delinquent boys were more "erratic" in their disciplinary practices than were parents of nondelinquent boys. Similarly, McCord, McCord, & Howard (1961) found that erratic disciplinary procedures were correlated with high degrees of criminality. Inconsistent patterns involving a combination of love, laxity, and punitiveness, or a mixture of punitiveness and laxity alone were particularly likely to be found in the background of their delinquent sample. However, the definition of inconsistency has shifted from study to study in delinquency research, making evaluation and meaningful conclusions difficult (Walters & Parke, 1967).

To clarify the effects of inconsistent punishment on children's aggressive behavior, Parke and Deur (Parke & Deur, 1972, Deur & Parke, 1970) conducted a series of laboratory studies. Aggression was selected as the response measure in order to relate the findings to previous studies of inconsistent discipline and aggressive delinquency. An automated Bobo doll was used to measure aggression. The child punched the large, padded stomach of the clown-shaped doll, and the frequency of hitting was automatically recorded. In principle, the apparatus is similar to the inflated punch toys commonly found in children's homes. To familiarize themselves with the doll, the boys participating in the first study (Parke & Deur, 1972) punched freely for 2 min. Then the children were rewarded with marbles each time they punched the Bobo doll, for a total of 10 trials. Following this baseline session, the subject experienced one of three different outcomes for punching: termination of reward (no outcome), a noxious buzzer on half of the trials and no reward on the other half, or consistent punishment by the buzzer on every trial. All the boys had been informed that they could terminate the punching game whenever they wished. The main index of persistence was the number of hitting responses that the child delivered before voluntarily ending the game. The results were clear: subjects in the no-outcome group made the greatest number of punches, while the continuously punished children delivered the fewest punches; the inconsistently punished children were in the intermediate position. This laboratory demonstration confirms the common child-rearing dictum that intraagent intermittent punishment is less effective than continuous punishment.

Parents and other disciplinary agents often use consistent punishment only after inconsistent punishment has failed to change the child's behavior. To investigate the effectiveness of consistent punishment after the child has been treated in an inconsistent fashion was the aim of the next study (Deur & Parke, 1970). Following the baseline period, subjects underwent one of three different training conditions. One group of boys were rewarded for 18 trials, while a second group of children received marbles on 9 trials and no reward on the remaining trials. A final group of boys was rewarded on half of the trials but heard a noxious buzzer on the other 9 trials. The children were informed that the buzzer indicated that they were playing the game "badly." To determine the effects of these training schedules on resistance to extinction (where both rewards and punishers were discontinued) and on resistance to continuous punishment (where every punch was punished) was the purpose of the next phase of the study. Therefore, half of the children in each of the three groups were neither rewarded nor punished for hitting the Bobo doll, and the remaining subjects heard the noxious buzzer each time they punched. The number of hitting responses that the child made before voluntarily quitting was, again, the principal measure. The punished subjects made fewer hitting responses than did subjects in the extinction condition, which suggests that the punishment was effective in inhibiting the aggressive behavior. The training schedules produced particularly interesting results. The inconsistently punished subjects showed the greatest resistance to extinction. Moreover, these previously punished children tended to persist longer in the face of consistent punishment than the boys in the other training groups. The effects were most marked in comparison to the consistently rewarded subjects. The implication is clear: the socializing agent using inconsistent punishment builds up resistance to future attempts to either extinguish deviant behavior or suppress it by consistently administered punishment.

What are the effects of interagent inconsistent punishment? Parke and Sawin (1975b) recently investigated this issue. Employing the Bobo doll paradigm, 8-year-old boys were exposed to two female socializing agents who reacted in one of the following ways to the boys' punching behavior: (1) the two agents were both rewarding ("That's good, great, terrific.") (2) the two agents were both punitive ("That's bad, awful, terrible.") or (3) one agent was rewarding, while the other agent was punishing. The results revealed that the boys persisted longer in punching when the agents were inconsistent that when the two agents were consistently punitive. Nor are the effects of interagent inconsistency restricted to aggression. In an earlier study, Stouwie (1972) demonstrated that inconsistent instructions between two agents in a resistance-to-deviation situation lessened the amount of subject control. Unfortunately, little is known concerning the impact of interagent inconsistency on the persistence of the behavior under extinction or consistent punishment. Nor do we know about the generalizability of these effects. Do inconsistent parents make it more difficult for teachers to gain control over children's behavior?

THE CHILD'S ROLE IN SPARING THE ROD

Research and theories of childhood socialization have traditionally been based on a undirectional model of effects; it was assumed that the rewarding and punishing activities of socializing agents serve to shape the behavior patterns of children. In fact, the research that we have discussed so far in this chapter reflects this orientation. The child, it implies, is acted upon by adults; the child is a passive recipient of adult-controlled input. However, this model is inadequate and a bidirectional model is necessary in which the child is explicitly recognized as an active participant and modifier of adult behavior. As Bell (1968) has so persuasively argued, children shape adults just as adults shape children. Moreover, this general principle has recently been shown to operate in important ways in disciplinary contexts (Parke, 1974). Specifically, children can modify the degree and amount of punitiveness by their reactions after violation of a rule or by their behavior following the administration of discipline by an adult. The following studies by Parke and Sawin (1975c) will illustrate the role of the child in modifying adult disciplinary tactics.

In one study, adult females were given the opportunity to administer rewards and punishments to a 7-year-old boy. They were first shown a videotape of two boys sitting at desks in a schoollike context. They were asked to assist in assessing "how adults and children can interact by means of a remote closed-circuit television monitoring and control system that might be used in understaffed day-care facilities to supplement regular person-to-person contacts." The adult was asked to evaluate the boys' behavior by delivering or removing points that could be later traded in for varying amounts of free play time. In fact, the children's behavior on the videotapes was prerecorded and the adult's feedback to the child was surreptitiously recorded by the experimenter. To evaluate the impact of children's behavior on adult disciplinary actions, adults saw one of four videotaped sequences, which were similar except for one section of the tape. All tapes showed one boy pushing a second child's workbook off his desk. Prior to the adult's opportunity to discipline or reward the child, the deviant child gave one of four reactions: (*1*) reparation— offered to pick up the book (*2*) pleading—pleaded for leniency (*3*) ignoring—turned his back to the adult (*4*) defiance—acted in a defiant fashion by saying "It was a dumb book anyway." Although all of the children were punished, the amount of punishment varied. The adults who saw the reparative child, who offered to correct his misbehavior, delivered the least amount of punishment, while the adults who saw the child ignore the adult or behave in a defiant fashion delivered the harshest punishment. The way that a child reacts after misbehaving but before the adult administers punishment can significantly modify the severity of the adult's disciplinary behavior.

In a related study, (Sawin, Parke, Kreling, & Harrison, 1975) the impact of the child's reaction *after* being disciplined on the adults' later disciplinary actions was examined. As in the earlier study, an adult monitored children on a videotape. Again, one of the children misbehaved, but this time the adult was allowed to finish punishing the child before viewing the child's reaction to being punished. One of four reactions followed: (*1*) reparation (*2*) pleading (*3*) ignoring or (*4*) defiance. Immediately following the target child's reaction to being punished, the adult was signaled to respond again; this was the crucial test trial since it followed immediately on the child's reaction to the prior discipline. As Figure 4.2 illustrates, the subsequent discipline was significantly affected by the child's reaction to the earlier adult discipline. In fact, the adults who witnessed the child make reparation were *not* even punitive, but were mildly rewarding. As in the earlier study, the defiance and ignoring reactions elicited the most severe punitive reactions from the adults. The study clearly demonstrates that children's reactions to discipline serve as determinants of how severely they will be dealt with on future occasions. Children can play a role in sparing the rod!

A question remains, namely the extent to which children are aware of their potential impact on the behavior of adults in disciplinary encounters. To answer this question, a series of social perception studies was conducted (Parke, Sebastian, Collmer, & Sawin, 1974). Specifically, we asked children to predict how an adult agent would respond to different reactions of a child either after discipline or after rule violation but prior to the administration of discipline. To assess developmental changes in children's perceptions of the effectiveness of different reactions for modifying adult behavior, children ranging from 4 to 12 years of age, as well as adults, were used as judges. All viewers saw a single 2-min videotape in which a child misbehaved (deliberately knocked a book off a peer's desk) and a

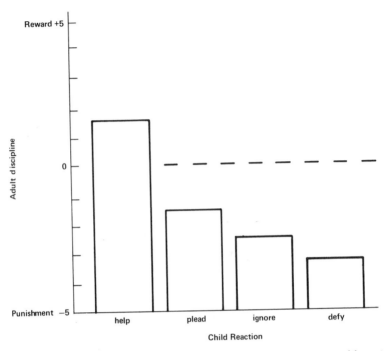

Figure 4.2. Adult discipline in response to children's reactions to prior punishment.

female teacher verbally reprimanded the misbehaving child ("That was bad; you shouldn't have done that. You won't be able to go out for recess."). The child's reaction to being disciplined was varied in one of the following ways: reparation— the child offered to pick up the book; defiance—the child told the teacher, "I don't like recess anyway"; pleading—the child protested the punishment, "I wasn't that bad; I really want to go out for recess"; ignoring—the child showed no verbal reaction but turned away from the teacher.

Each viewer saw a single film and then rated on a five-point scale the probability that the teacher would show different positive and negative behaviors. Positive reactions were smiling ("respond positively by smiling") and consolation ("tell the child not to worry, he can go out another day"). The negative reactions were anger ("become angry with the child") and threat ("tell the child if he doesn't behave, he'll have to stay in tomorrow").

Children and adults who saw the child make reparation (offer to pick up the book) were significantly more likely to predict that the teacher would respond positively by "smiling" than were adults who saw the child react defiantly or ignore the disciplinary agent. Pleading elicited more predictions that the teacher would console the child than did either ignoring or defiance. If the child reacted defiantly after being reprimanded, most adults predicted that this would increase the probability that the teacher would react with anger or threat. It is particularly noteworthy that there were no age differences; as early as 4 years of age, children have well-defined and accurate notions about how adults will respond to the reactions of children to being disciplined.

A related question concerns the impact of children's reactions that occur after misbehaving, but before discipline is administered, on the type or severity of discipline that an adult will select. The same videotape technique that was used in the earlier studies was employed. Children from 4 to 7 years of age saw a short videotape of a child model of the same age and sex as themselves misbehaving (pushing a peer's books off his desk) and then immediately exhibiting one of the four reactions that were examined in the previous studies. On a five-point scale of punitiveness, the children rated the adults' choice of discipline. The results indicated that ignoring the teacher or behaving defiantly led to predictions of more severe discipline than did either pleading or making reparation. There were no age effects.

In summary, children expect defiant reactions to lead to more severe discipline and more negative responses from adults; reparative reactions are expected to elicit more positive responses and less severe discipline.

What are the implications of these findings? First, children's awareness of the impact of their reactions on adult disciplinary choices and postdisciplinary behaviors suggests that children probably play an important controlling role in modifying adult discipline. Second, child reactions may contribute to inconsistency in the selection and administration of discipline. Moreover, it is possible that positive reactions following a disciplinary procedure may dilute the inhibitory value of the discipline. In other words, by reacting positively shortly after administering a reprimand, an adult may undermine the effectiveness of the discipline. Not only is such inconsistency ineffective in achieving suppression of unacceptable behavior in the immediate situation (Parke & Deur, 1972), but it may also make it more difficult to control the child with this kind of discipline on future occasions. In fact, other findings (Deur & Parke, 1970) have indicated that the combination of inconsistent reward and punishment increases resistance to subsequent control either by extinction or by consistent punishment. Possibly a better understanding of the tactics used by children that promote inconsistent discipline will suggest techniques for training socializing agents to increase their consistency.

While the focus of our research has been on the behavior patterns that may elicit different degrees of punitiveness, there are certain characteristics of the child, such as age, sex, or even physical appearance that may determine adult disciplinary patterns. Clifford (1959), in a surprisingly rare examination of the manner in which parents and other socializing agents alter their disciplinary tactics as the child becomes older, studied the types of discipline that mothers used with children at 3, 6 and 9 years of age. Noncognitive tactics, such as spanking and forcibly removing the child from a situation, are used more frequently with younger children than they are with older children; cognitive techniques, such as appeals to humor and self-esteem, are used more often with older children. Reasoning, according to Clifford, is used frequently at all ages, but many types of reasoning are hidden under this blanket label. For our purposes it is necessary that we have more information concerning the shifts in the specific types of prohibitory rationales used by parents and other socializing adults in order to elucidate the direct role that shifts in adult input may play in the developmental effectivness of different types of rationales.

Another modifier of adult disciplinary behavior is the sex of the child. A number of interview and observational studies of child-rearing indicate that boys receive more physical punishment than girls (Sears *et al.,* 1957; Bronfenbrenner, 1960; Siegelman, 1965; Newson & Newson, 1968). Similarly, Feshbach (1973) observed maternal punitiveness in a mother–child teaching situation; the 4-year-old boys received more "negative reinforcement" than girls. Of particular relevance is the recent study of nursery school teachers' treatment of boys and girls (Serbin, O'Leary, Kent, & Tonick, 1973). They found that boys receive more negative sanctions, particularly loud reprimands, and were more likely to be physically restrained than girls. These findings were present even after controlling for the frequency of the child's deviant behavior. Experimental studies have confirmed these general findings: Dion (1972), for example, asked adults to decide on the amount of punishment that either a boy or girl should receive for committing a similar severe offense (stealing); the adults advocated less punishment for females than for males. Cross-sex effects are present as well; while fathers are more lenient with their daughters, mothers are more lenient with their sons (Rothbart & Maccoby, 1966). Recently, Gurwitz and Dodge (1975) reported a similar cross-sex effect: Adults were more permissive with the opposite-sex child.

Not only are age and sex of the child important, but the physical attractiveness of the child is also an important determinant of adult punitiveness. Dion (1974) found that female adults were less punitive toward an attractive boy in an experimental learning situation than toward either an attractive girl or an unattractive child of either sex. Whether men are sensitive to children's appearance remains to be determined. Physical appearance, in short, is another child characteristic that may play a role in the determination of adult disciplinary practices.

Finally, these findings concerning the child's behavior and characteristics provide strong support for a bidirectional model of adult–child interaction in which the role of the child in controlling adult behavior is recognized.

UNDESIRABLE CONSEQUENCES OF PUNISHMENT

Although punishment can be effective in producing response suppression, punishment may have undesirable side effects which limit its usefulness as a socializing technique. In the first place, the teacher or parent who employs physical punishment to inhibit undesirable behaviors may also serve as an aggressive model. Bandura (1967) has summarized this viewpoint as follows: "When a parent punishes his child physically for having aggressed toward peers, for example, the intended outcome of this training is that the child should refrain from hitting others. The child, however, is also learning from parental demonstration how to aggress physically. And the imitative learning may provide the direction for the child's behavior when he is similarly frustrated in subsequent social interactions [p. 43]."

Until recently, evidence supporting this position was, at best, indirect. There is a sizable body of data indicating a relation between the frequent use of physical punishment by parents and aggressive behavior in their children (Becker, 1964). However, the increases in aggression could possibly be due to the direct encouragement that punitive parents often provide for behaving aggressively outside the home situation. Alternatively, highly aggressive children may require strong, physically punitive techniques to control them. Thus, even if it is assumed that the punitive parent acts as an aggressive model, there is no evidence demonstrating that children imitate the aggressive behaviors the disciplinarian displays while punishing the child. It is recognized that exposure to aggressive models increases aggressive behavior in young children (Bandura, 1967). It is of questionable legitimacy, however, to generalize from Bobo doll studies to children imitating a physically punitive adult who is often carrying out a justified spanking in line with his role as parent or teacher.

Fortunately, a direct test of the modeling hypothesis has recently been reported (Gelfand, Hartmann, Lamb, Smith, Mahan, & Paul, 1974). These investigators exposed 6- to 8-year-old children to rewarding, punishing or unresponsive adults in a marble drop game. When each child was later given the opportunity to train another child to play the game, he employed techniques strikingly similar to those he had previously experienced himself. Of particular importance was the finding that children who themselves had been punished by the adult used punitive techniques in interactions with another child.

Another negative side effect is the avoidance of the punishing agent. This is illustrated in a recent study by Redd, Morris, and Martin (1975) in which 5-year-old children interacted with three different adults who employed various control strategies. One adult behaved in a positive manner and smiled and made positive comments ("Good," "Nice boy," "Tremendous") while the child performed a color-sorting task. A second adult dispensed mild verbal reprimands whenever the child deviated from the sorting task (for example, "Stop throwing the tokens around," "Don't play with the chair"). A third adult was present but didn't comment on the child's behavior. While the results indicated that the punitive adult was most effective in keeping the child working on the task, the children tended to prefer the positive and neutral agents to the punitive adult. When asked to indicate which adult they wished to work with a little longer, the children always chose the positive adult. Similarly, the children always avoided the punitive adult as their partner on other tasks or as a playmate. The implication is clear: Punishment may be an effective modification technique, but the use of punishment by an adult may lead the child to avoid that socializing agent and therefore undermine the adult's effectiveness as a future influence on the child's behavior.

Conditions such as the classroom often prevent the child from physically escaping the presence of the agent. Continued use of punishment in an inescapable context, however, may lead to passivity and withdrawal (Seligman, Maier, & Solomon, 1969) or adaptation to the punishing stimuli themselves. In any case, whether escape is possible or not, the quality of the agent–child relationship may deteriorate if punishment is used with high frequency; punishment administered by such an agent will, therefore, be less effective in inhibiting the child.

The undesirable effects of punishment mentioned here probably occur mainly in situations where the disciplinary agents are indiscriminately punitive. In child-training contexts where the agent rewards and encourages a large proportion of the child's behavior, even though selectively and occasionally punishing certain kinds of behavior, these side effects are less likely to be found (Walters & Parke, 1967).

REINFORCEMENT OF INCOMPATIBLE BEHAVIOR: AN ALTERNATIVE TO PUNISHMENT

In light of these undesirable side effects, other ways of controlling behavior should be considered. One technique involves increasing the availability of alternative, prosocial responses. For example, Perry and Parke (1975) found that resistance to touching a prohibited toy could be enhanced by making an alternative toy available. Specifically, 6- to 8-year-old boys were left alone with either only a prohibited toy or with *both* a prohibited toy and a less attractive, but nonprohibited alternative toy. Touching of the prohibited toy was reduced when the alternative toy was available. Control can be increased by the provision of prosocial alternative behaviors.

However, not only should alternatives be available, but children should be reinforced for engaging in alternative behaviors which are incompatible with the prohibited behavior. Brown and Elliot (1965) asked several nursery school teachers to ignore aggressive acts and only encourage behaviors that were inconsistent with aggression, such as cooperation and helpfulness. Encouraging these alternative behaviors resulted in a marked decrease in classroom aggression. Similarly, Parke, Ewall, and Slaby (1972) have found that encouraging college subjects for speaking helpful words also led to a decrease in subsequent aggression. In an extension of this work, Slaby (1974) found a similar effect for 8- to 12-year-old children. The lesson is clear: Speaking in a manner that is incompatible with aggression may actually inhibit hostile actions. Words, as well as deeds, can alter our physical behaviors. The advantage of the incompatible response technique for controlling behavior is that the unwanted side effects associated with punishment can be avoided.

THE RIGHTS OF CHILDREN

It is not simply the side effects associated with the use of punishment that weakens the case for physical punishment as a control tactic. The problem of punishment cannot be evaluated merely in cost-efficiency terms; the decision to use a particular control tactic is inevitably intertwined with the broader sociopolitical and moral issue of children's rights. The historical view of children as property not only has been used to justify our use of punishment, but may have set the stage for child abuse (Zalba, 1971). If so, control and decline of the use of physical punishment as a control tactic can only come about as rapidly as individuals in society reconceptualize and redefine the status and rights of children.

Too often the use of physical disciplinary tactics in controlling children and the limitations on children's rights are justified in terms of children's limited cognitive abilities. However, research has clearly shown that children are cognitively capable of understanding the sociolegal and moral basis of social rights, and of articulating their ideas about law and justice at a much earlier age than generally has been assumed. (Tapp & Kohlberg, 1971; Tapp & Levine, 1974).

Moreover, the evidence presented in this chapter suggests a parallel increase in children's responsivity to nonphysical control tactics in the form of cognitive rationales (Parke, 1974). Clearly, children can both understand and effectively utilize rationally based social rules to govern their own behavior early in development. Justifying physical punishment as a control tactic in terms of the child's limited capacity for appreciating more humane, cognitively derived procedures is no longer tenable. Moreover, a shift toward more nonpunitive control tactics is consistent with a more profound shift in thought and action concerning the rights of children. This formulation, which has been recently championed by both legal and social science scholars (Rawls, 1971; Tapp & Levine, 1974; Worsfold, 1974) suggests that the rights of children as individuals are not limited by their status but only by their capacity to participate competently in the formulation of social rules. In light of these arguments, the recent 1975 Supreme Court ruling (*Baker* v. *Owen*) which has legalized the rights of schools to use physical punishment as a disciplinary control tactic can only be viewed as unfortunate and regressive.

It should be stressed that advocating children's rights does not imply or justify dismissing adult responsibility.

> Socialization involves a responsibility on the part of socializing agents, such as teachers and parents, to provide children with the opportunity to learn the rules and norms of their society and culture and at the same time to realize their full social and cognitive potential. While it is very unlikely that physical punishment is either necessary or useful in this process, a shift away from physically punitive control tactics does not imply a shift to unsupervised freedom. Socialization implies control, but a view of the child as a self-respecting and self-determining human needs to be given primary recognition in evaluating the goals and types of regulation [Parke, 1977, p. 37].

In the final analysis, the primary purpose of socialization is the teaching of new appropriate behaviors in addition to teaching suppression of unacceptable forms of behavior. "In fact, in real-life situations the suppressive value of punishment is usually only of value if alternative prosocial responses are elicited and strengthened while the undesirable behavior is held in check [Walters and Parke, 1967, p. 217]."

By focusing on the task of promoting acceptable behavior patterns, the necessity of using punishment in the socialization of young children will lessen.

REFERENCES

Aronfreed, J. Punishment learning and internalization: Some parameters of reinforcement and cognition. Paper read at biennial meeting of Society for Research in Child Development, Minneapolis, 1965.

Aronfreed, J. *Conduct and conscience.* New York: Academic Press, 1968.

Aronfreed, J. & Leff, R. The effects of intensity of punishment and complexity of discrimination upon the learning of an internalized inhibition. Unpublished manuscript, University of Pennsylvania, 1963.

Aronfreed, J., & Reber, A. Internalized behavioral suppression and the timing of social punishment. *Journal of Personality and Social Psychology,* 1965, *1,* 3–16.

Baer, D. M. Effect of withdrawal of positive reinforcement on extinguishing a response in young children. *Child Development,* 1961, *32,* 67–74.

Baer, D. M. Laboratory control of thumbsucking by withdrawal and representation of reinforcement. *Journal of Experimental Analysis of Behavior,* 1962, *5,* 525–528.

Bandura, A. The role of modeling processes in personality development. In W. W. Hartup and Nancy L. Smothergill (Eds.), *The young child: Reviews of research.* Washington: National Association for the Education of Young Children, 1967, Pp. 42–58.

Bandura, A., & Walters, R. H. *Social learning and personality development.* New York: Holt, Rinehart and Winston, 1963.

Becker, W. C. Consequences of different kinds of parental discipline. In M. L. Hoffman and L. W. Hoffman (Eds.), *Review of child development research* (Vol. 1). New York: Russell Sage Foundation, 1964. Pp. 169–208.

Bell, R. Q. A reinterpretation of the direction of effects of socialization. *Psychological Review,* 1968, *75,* 81–95.

Bosserman, R., & Parke, R. D. The effects of assuming the role of rule enforcer on self-control in children. Paper presented at the Biennial meeting of the Society for Research in Child Development, Philadelphia, 1973.

Bronfenbrenner, U. Socialization and social class through time and space. In E. E. Maccoby, T. M. Newcomb, and E. L. Hartley (Eds.), *Readings in social psychology.* New York: Holt, Rinehart, and Winston, 1958.

Bronfenbrenner, U. Some familial antecedents of responsibility and leadership in adolescents. In L. Petrullo and B. M. Bass (Eds.), *Studies in leadership.* New York: Holt, Rinehart, and Winston, 1960.

Brown, P., & Elliot, R. Control of aggression in a nursery school class. *Journal of Experimental Child Psychology,* 1965, *2,* 102–107.

Bucher, B., & Lovaas, I. Use of aversive stimulation in behavior modification. In M. R. Jones (Ed.), *Miami Symposium on the prediction of behavior 1967: Aversive stimulation.* Miami: University of Miami Press, 1968.

Cheyne, A. Punishment and reasoning in the development of self-control. In R. D. Parke (Ed.), *Recent trends in social learning theory.* New York: Academic Press, 1972.

Cheyne, J. A., & Walters, R. H. Intensity of punishment, timing of punishment and cognitive structure as determinants of response inhibition. *Journal of Experimental Child Psychology,* 1969, *7,* 231–244.

Church, R. M. The varied effects of punishment on behavior. *Psychological Review,* 1963, *70,* 369–402.

Clifford, E. Discipline in the home: A controlled observational study of parental practices. *Journal of Genetic Psychology,* 1959, *95,* 45–82.

Deur, J. L., & Parke, R. D. The effects of inconsistent punishment on aggression in children. *Developmental Psychology, 1970, 2,* 403–411.

Dion, K. Physical attractiveness and evaluation of children's transgressions. *Journal of Personality and Social Psychology, 1972, 24,* 207–213.

Dion, K. K. Children's physical attractiveness and sex as determinants of adult punitiveness. *Developmental Psychology, 1974, 10,* 772–778.

Erlanger, H. S. Social class differences in parents' use of physical punishment. In S. K. Steinmetz and M. S. Straus (Eds.), *Violence in the family.* New York: Dodd, Mead and Co., 1974.

Feshbach, N. D. Reinforcement patterns of children. In A. Pick (Ed.), *Minnesota Symposium on child psychology* (Vol. 7). Minneapolis: The University Minnesota Press, 1973, Pp. 87–116.

Gelfand, D. F., Hartmann, D. P., Lamb, A. K., Smith, C. L., Mahan, M. A., & Paul, S. C. The effects of adult models and described alternatives on children's choice of behavior management techniques. *Child Development, 1974, 45,* 585–593.

Gil, D. G. *Violence against children: Physical child abuse in the United States.* Cambridge, Massachusetts: Harvard University Press, 1970.

Glueck, S., & Glueck, E. *Unraveling juvenile delinquency.* Cambridge: Harvard University Press, 1950.

Gurwitz, S. B., & Dodge, K. A. Adults' evaluations of a child as a function of sex of adult and sex of child. *Journal of Personality and Social Psychology, 1975, 32,* 822–828.

Hetherington, E. M. Children of divorce. Paper presented at the Biennial Meeting of the Society for Research in Child Development, Denver, 1975.

Hoffman, M. L. Moral development. In P. Mussen (Ed.), *Manual of child psychology.* New York: Wiley, 1970.

Kazdin, A. E. *Behavior modification.* Homewood, Illinois: Richard Irwin, 1975.

Kohlberg, L. Development of moral character and moral ideology. In M. L. Hoffman and Lois W. Hoffman (Eds.), *Review of child development research.* (Vol. 1). New York: Russell Sage Foundation, 1964, Pp. 383–431.

LaVoie, J. C. Punishment and adolescent self-control. *Developmental Psychology,* 1973, *8,* 16–24.

LaVoie, J. C. Type of punishment as a determinant of resistance to deviation. *Developmental Psychology, 1974, 10,* 181–189. (a)

LaVoie, J. C. Cognitive determinants of resistance to deviation in seven, nine and eleven year old children of low and high maturity of moral judgment. *Developmental Psychology, 1974, 10,* 393–403. (b)

McCord, W., McCord, J., & Howard, A. Familial correlates of aggression in non-delinquent male children. *Journal of Abnormal and Social Psychology, 1961, 62,* 79–93.

Newson, J., & Newson, E. *Four years old in an urban community.* Harmondworth, England: Pelican Books, 1968.

O'Leary, K. D., Kaufman, K. F., Kass, R. E., & Drabman, R. S. The effects of loud and soft reprimands on the behavior of disruptive students. *Exceptional Children, 1970, 37,* 145–155.

Parke, R. D. Nurturance, nurturance withdrawal and resistance to deviation. *Child Development, 1967, 38,* 1101–1110.

Parke, R. D. Effectiveness of punishment as an interaction of intensity, timing, agent nurturance and cognitive structuring. *Child Development, 1969, 40,* 213–236.

Parke, R. D. The role of punishment in the socialization process. In R. A. Hoppe, G. A. Milton, and E. C. Simmel (Eds.), *Early experiences and the processes of socialization.* New York: Academic Press, 1970, Pp. 81–108.

Parke, R. D. Explorations in punishment, discipline and self-control. In P. Elich (Ed.), *Social learning.* Bellingham, Washington: Western Washington State Press, 1973.

Parke, R. D. Rules, roles and resistance to deviation in children: Explorations in punishment,

96 Ross D. Parke

discipline and self control. In A. Pick (Ed.), *Minnesota Symposia on child psychology,* Vol. 8. Minneapolis: University of Minnesota Press, 1974.

Parke, R. D. Socialization into child abuse: A social interactional perspective. In J. L. Tapp and F. J. Levine (Eds.), *Law, justice and the individual in society: Psychological and legal issues.* New York: Holt, Rinehart and Winston, 1977.

Parke, R. D., & Collmer, C. W. Child abuse: An interdisciplinary analysis. In E. M. Hetherington (Ed.), *Review of child development research,* (Vol. 5). Chicago: University of Chicago Press, 1975.

Parke, R. D., & Deur, J. L. Schedule of punishment and inhibition of aggression in children. *Developmental Psychology,* 1972, *7,* 266–269.

Parke, R. D., Ewall, W., & Slaby, R. G. Hostile and helpful verbalizations as regulators of nonverbal aggression. *Journal of Personality and Social Psychology,* 1972, *23,* 243–248.

Parke, R. D., & Murray, S. Reinstatement: A technique for increasing stability of inhibition in children. Unpublished manuscript, University of Wisconsin, 1971.

Parke, R. D., & Sawin, D. B. The impact of fear and empathy-based rationales on children's response inhibition. Unpublished manuscript, Fels Research Institute, 1975. (a)

Parke, R. D., & Sawin, D. B. The effects of inter-agent inconsistent discipline on aggression in children. Unpublished manuscript, Fels Research Institute, 1975. (b)

Parke, R. D., & Sawin, D. B. The impact of children's reactions to discipline on adult disciplinary choices. Unpublished manuscript, Fels Research Institute, 1975. (c)

Parke, R. D., Sebastian, R., Collmer, C., & Sawin, D. Child and adult perceptions of the impact of reactions to discipline on adult behavior. Unpublished research, Fels Research Institute, 1974.

Parke, R. D., & Walters, R. H. Some factors determining the efficacy of punishment for inducing response inhibition. *Monographs of Society and Research in Child Development,* 1967, *32* (Serial No. 109).

Perry, D. G., & Parke, R. D. Punishment and alternative response training as determinants of response inhibition in children. *Genetic Psychology Monographs,* 1975, *91,* 257–279.

Rawls, J. *A theory of justice.* Cambridge, Massachusetts: Belknap Press of Harvard University, 1971.

Redd, W. H., Morris, E. K., & Martin, J. A. Effects of positive and negative adult-child interaction on children's social preferences. *Journal of Experimental Child Psychology,* 1975, *19,* 153–164.

Rothbart, M. K., & Maccoby, E. E. Parents' differential reactions to sons and daughters. *Journal of Personality and Social Psychology,* 1966, *4,* 237–243.

Sawin, D. B., Parke, R. D., Kreling, B., & Harrison, N. The child's role in sparing the rod. Paper presented the Annual Meeting of the American Psychological Association, Chicago, 1975.

Sears, R. R., Maccoby, E. E., & Levin, H. *Patterns of child rearing.* Evanston, Illinois: Row, Peterson, 1957.

Seligman, M. E. P., Maier, S. F., & Solomon, R. L. Unpredictable and uncontrollable aversive events. In F. R. Brush (Ed.), *Aversive conditioning and learning.* New York: Academic Press, 1969.

Siegelman, M. Evaluation of Bronfenbrenner's questionnaire for children concerning parental behavior. *Child Development,* 1965, *36,* 163–174.

Serbin, L. A., O'Leary, D. K., Kent, R. N., & Tonick, I. J. A comparison of teacher response to the preacademic and problem behavior of boys and girls. *Child Development,* 1973, *44,* 796–804.

Slaby, R. G. Verbal regulation of aggression and altruism. In J. deWit and W. W. Hartup (Eds.), *Determinants and origins of aggression.* The Hague: Mouton, 1974, Pp. 209–216.

Stouwie, R. J. An experimental study of adult dominance and warmth, conflicting verbal instruction, and children's moral behavior. *Child Development,* 1972, *43,* 959–972.

Tapp, J. L., & Kohlberg, L. Developing senses of law and legal justice. *Journal of Social Issues,* 1971, *27,* 65–92.

Tapp, J. L., & Levine, F. J. Legal socialization: Strategies for an ethical legality. *Stanford Law Review*, 1974, *27*, 1–72.

Walters, R. H. Delay-of-reinforcement effects in children's learning. *Psychonomic Science*, 1964, *1*, 307–308.

Walters, R. H., & Andres, D. Punishment procedures and self-control. Paper read at the Annual Meeting of the American Psychological Association, Washington, D.C., September, 1967.

Walters, R. H., & Parke, R. D. The influence of punishment and related disciplinary techniques on the social behavior of children: theory and empirical findings. In B. Maher (Ed.), *Progress in experimental personality research*. Vol. 4. New York: Academic, 1967, pp. 179–228.

Walters, R. H., Parke, R. D., & Cane, V. A. Timing of punishment and the observation of consequences to others as determinants of response inhibition. *Journal of Experimental Child Psychology*, 1965, *2*, 10–30.

Worsfold, V. L. A philosophical justification for children's rights. *Harvard Educational Review*, 1974, *44*, 142–157.

Zalba, S. Battered children. *Trans-action*, 1971, *8*, 9–10, 58–61.

5

Behavior Analysis and Early Childhood Education: Engineering Children's Learning

ROBERT P. HAWKINS

West Virginia University

Behavior analysis is a relatively new approach to any area of human behavior, including early childhood education. Most of the dominant values and concepts stem from the writings of B. F. Skinner (1950, 1953, 1968, 1969, 1974), though others were primarily responsible for discovering the principles that Skinner organized and applied to human problems. The behavior analytic approach to understanding and dealing with human behavior differs in several respects from other approaches. It puts great emphasis on learning and on scientific principles describing how learning (and maintenance of learned performance) takes place. It soft-pedals the contribution of physiological, genetic, and biochemical variables to behavior, not because they play no role but because their role has been so overemphasized in the past that our culture tends to be pessimistic and defeatist about solving or even ameliorating such problems as retardation, schizophrenia, learning disabilities, and senile behavior. It tends to question the value of complex theories that go far beyond the objective data, especially such loosely founded theories as Freud's, but also including theories that have partial scientific bases, such as Piaget's theory of cognitive development, Chomsky's theory of language development, and the Hull-Spence theory of learning. It has immense appreciation for objective, precise, quantitative data. It prefers research methods that keep the scientist in very close touch with what is happening to the behavior of the "subject" (pigeon, rat, child, client, student, etc.) of any research. It sees Homo sapiens as one species of primate; and though it recognizes that the remarkable complexities of human behavior (especially those introduced by a language that is much more complex and flexible than the languages of other species) make analysis difficult, it is quite willing to apply principles and techniques discovered with lower animals to human behavior. And, finally, it includes both basic scientists, who are primarily interested in the discovery of general principles describing "how behavior works," and applied scientists and practitioners, who are primarily interested in improving "the human condition" in some way.

The behavior analytic approach is often characterized as being appealing because of its simplicity, but that simplicity is partly illusion. It is fairly simple to teach someone *about* behavior analysis (or at least about the portion known better as behavior modification), so that the person can verbalize a few key principles and techniques, such as reinforcement, extinction, shaping, and prompting. But it is very difficult to train someone to *do* competent behavior analysis or even behavior modification. Although the skills needed to be a competent behavior analyst have themselves been subjected to a task analysis (Sulzer-Azaroff, Thaw, & Thomas, 1975), much remains to be done in determining the component skills and how they can be developed efficiently and reliably.

Whatever the skills of the behavior analyst are, several outstanding scientists seem to have developed these skills and applied them to a remarkably wide variety of human problems. For example, this approach has been applied to reducing litter in a prison yard (Hayes, Johnson, & Cone, 1975), to teaching language to autistic children (Lovaas, 1973), to remedying multiple problems of delinquent youth (Phillips, Phillips, Fixsen, & Wolf, 1973), to treatment of transexualism (Barlow, Reynolds, & Agras, 1973), to severe stuttering (Webster, 1970), to teenage "self-consciousness" (Schwarz & Hawkins, 1970), to numerous problems of the retarded (Lent, LeBlanc, & Spradlin, 1970; Wolf, Birnbrauer, Lawler, & Williams, 1970; Foxx & Azrin, 1973), to various problems of psychotic adult patients (Liberman, Teigen, Patterson, & Baker, 1973; Kale, Zlutnick, & Hopkins, 1970; Schaefer & Martin, 1970), and to many aspects of education at all levels (Ramp & Semb, 1975; Daniels, 1974; Ulrich, Stachnik, & Mabry, 1974; MacMillan, 1973; O'Leary & O'Leary, 1972; Sulzer & Mayer, 1972). No other approach to understanding human behavior has had nearly the breadth of application or obtained nearly as much scientific evidence of its effectiveness.

The terms *behavior analysis* and *behavior modification* are each used with two distinct meanings. The more common meaning has to do with a reliance upon experimentally discovered *principles* of behavior, and educators using the term "behavior modification" usually mean only this. The second meaning has to do with the *methodology* by which behavior is to be studied. These two meanings of behavior analysis will be discussed separately.

BEHAVIOR ANALYSIS AS A RELIANCE ON BASIC BEHAVIOR "THEORY" AND TECHNOLOGY

One of the more basic assumptions of the typical behavior analyst is that if we are to make decisions about human behavior, it will generally be wisest to make them on the basis of scientific information. One type of scientific information is the basic principles that have been discovered and elaborated through thousands of well-controlled studies with several species, including humans, and that simply describe "how behavior works" in a fashion that is objective and relatively unbiased by preconceived theory.

We all are taught many theoretical assumptions about human behavior as a part of our acculturation from infancy on. These assumptions are vague, ill-founded, and conflicting; but they are so ingrained that we not only are hampered in solving many problems of human behavior, we even create many of the problems ourselves. Skinner (1950, 1953) proposed that scientists take an unbiased, atheoretical approach to studying behavior, and inductively arrive at principles describing how behavior is influenced (controlled, learned, conditioned). This approach is like that which a scientific being from outer space might take, were it to come to Earth and study Homo sapiens, and it has proven quite effective.

When studying behavior from an atheoretical viewpoint one is likely to attend more carefully to the behavior one is studying and develop techniques for producing particular patterns of behavior. This results in a powerful technology for the "engineering" of behavior and in a great deal of optimism about the maleability of behavior. This engineering skill and optimism are characteristic of behavior analysts.

Now let us consider briefly some of the more basic principles and techniques that have been discovered thus far. Many of the principles were discovered by persons outside the behavior analysis movement, so it is important not to attribute all of this knowledge to the research of behavior analysts, of whom there have been significant numbers only since the late 1950s.

Control Exerted by Consequences

The principles most familiar to educators and others as being used by behavior analysts are those involving the consequences of behavior. Skinner emphasizes consequences, and novice behavior analysts often focus exclusively on the effects of consequences. It may well be that the influence of consequences on behavior is the most profound single area of contribution behavior analysts are making thus far to our culture's understanding of behavior. Only the main principles of consequence control will be presented here, not their extensive elaboration; and the terms and definitions used for them here are not necessarily accepted by all behavior analysts.

Operant versus Respondent Behavior

First, it appears that there are two general classes of behavior, *operant* and *respondent*. Operant (or instrumental) behavior is controlled in strength by its consequences, by how it *operates* on (thus its name) or effects changes in the environment. This is the kind of behavior we are most often interested in as educators. Respondent behavior occurs in reaction to preceeding stimuli and is controlled in strength by those stimuli. Respondent behavior is reflexive and includes such responses as the contraction of the pupil of the eye following increases in brightness of light, or an increase in heart rate when startled. These reflexes can be learned (elicited by a new stimulus) by the pairing of *antecedent stimuli,* while operant behavior is only learned (occasioned by a new stimulus) if the right kind of *consequent stimuli* follow when the behavior occurs (in the presence of the new stimulus).

It should be evident that as educators our primary interest is in operant behavior, not reflexes; thus the principles of operant behavior are of greatest interest, and only these will be presented. The presentation will be brief, because full exposition is lengthy, and excellent books are available that are particularly appropriate to education and child development (Sulzer & Mayer, 1972; Bijou & Baer, 1961).

Defining Internal States in Terms of Observable Behavior

Before presenting the principles it may be important to clarify one further point that often proves a source of confusion to educators. The term "behavior" has already been used several times and will be used often throughout this chapter. Some educators respond to discussions such as the present one by saying such things as "That's fine for dealing with *behavior,* but I'm also interested in developing favorable *attitudes* and assuring that the child has healthy *feelings* and *self-concept*; don't behavior analysts have any interest in such things?" The answer is a resounding Yes, and a careful look at the behavior analytic literature will reveal this to the interested person. As you might suspect, the problem is semantic; the educator quoted above is differentiating attitudes, feelings, and self-concept from behavior, while the behavior analyst does not. For example, a behavior analyst is likely to define an attitude such as "appreciation for books and reading" in terms of observable components such as frequency of looking at books, frequency of asking that a story be read, frequency of talking about the content of stories, effectiveness of access to books as a reinforcing consequence for other behavior, and the like. Such specification is characteristic of a highly objective approach to the study and modification of behavior, and it has been one of the reasons why behavior analysts have been so successful, because their efforts are focused on clear objectives and they can readily measure the outcome (Hawkins, Axelrod & Hall, 1976).

The Principle of Reinforcement

To proceed with principles of operant behavior, the principle of *reinforcement* is doubtless the most familiar of these. When a particular consequence occurs immediately contingent upon a response and that response becomes more frequent or reliable (stronger) as a result, we call that effect reinforcement and we call the consequence a *reinforcer.* It may be experienced as pleasant by the learner and thus be a fairly obvious reinforcer, such as delicious smells, certain social activities, sweet foods, and kind words. It may be experienced as neutral, such as the feel of one's foot touching the next step when descending stairs, the sight of flame when striking a match, or the sound $\overline{oo}$ when one's mouth is formed appropriately to make such a sound. It is possible that under some circumstances a consequence that is experienced as unpleasant by the learner still serves to strengthen or maintain the response upon which it is contingent, as may be the case with the pain accompanying injections in the arm of a heroin addict, the pain resulting immediately from head-banging in a severely retarded child, or even the embarrassment we experience when being profusely flattered.

Thus, a reinforcer is defined by its *actual* effect, over time, on the reliability of the behavior it *follows,* not by the emotional response it brings from the learner, by the learner's verbal report of pleasure or dismay, or by the expectation of someone who may be responsible for the consequence's occurrence (such as a parent, teacher, boss, or peer). One of the reasons why behavior analysts have been so successful in engineering the learning and maintenance of selected behavior is that they do not usually persist at applying consequences that are not having the intended effect; they quickly conclude that either the consequence is not a reinforcer or it is being inadquately applied (in too small quantites, too slowly, too irregularly, etc.).

The Principle of Punishment

At present the simplest statement of the principle of punishment is that some events, when they immediately follow a response, weaken that response (more rapidly than does the absence of a consequence).[1] Again, an event is defined as a *punisher,* or aversive consequence only if it has the effect of weakening the behavior upon which it is contingent.

The Principle of Extinction

A response that has been strengthened and maintained through reinforcement will weaken if that reinforcing consequence simply stops occurring. Such response-weakening due to neutral consequences (neither reinforcing nor punishing) or the absence of consequences is called *extinction.*[2] Although the term *extinction* is used for the behavioral *phenomenon* of a response weakening when followed by a neutral consequence or none at all, it is also used for the *procedures* used to produce such a phenomenon. Therefore, this term will appear again later in the chapter, under the heading of basic behavioral engineering techniques.

Principles of Consequence Schedules

A fourth principle or set of principles has to do with the "scheduling" of consequences. The occurrence of a reinforcer for every occurrence of a particular

---

[1] Ultimately this may be inaccurate in the sense that it only strengthens other responses, avoidance and escape responses. It may be that animals can only have behavior strengthened, that the concept of weakening behavior will prove inadequate. It should also be mentioned that many behavior analysts prefer terms like "escape conditioning" to "punishment."

[2] It is uncertain whether or not the extinction phenomenon would be better considered a punishment phenomenon, but this kind of questioning and revision of scientific principles is inevitable and healthy, so long as revisions simplify the principles or are made necessary by the weight of experimental evidence. For practical purposes, the concept of extinction is useful at present.

response is called *continuous reinforcement*. A response will be strengthened more rapidly if reinforced on every occurrence than if reinforced less consistently. Similarly, a response will be weakened more rapidly if punished on every occurrence.

While constant consequences thus produce more rapid *changes* in behavior than do variable ones, the maintenance of behavior is another matter. For the educator's purposes, the most useful information at this time appears to be the fact that *intermittent reinforcement* is often quite adequate for maintaining performance, once that performance has been learned. Thus a teacher may arrange for continuous reinforcement of accurate responding until such responding becomes reliable; then the teacher may shift to a leaner and leaner schedule of reinforcement and still be able to maintain perfect performance. This can often save the teacher time, energy, or other resources. In addition, intermittent reinforcement can make the appropriate behavior more resistant to extinction, so that the child continues to respond accurately even when several consecutive responses typically go unreinforced.

Another aspect of the schedules or timing of consequences has to do with their *immediacy*. A consequence affects most the response that is occurring at the moment of the consequence. Its next most powerful effect is on the response that occurred immediately before that one, and as one moves back in time from the occurrence of the consequence one finds a continuously diminishing effect. Let us look at a preschool example of the principle of immediacy. Suppose that play with peers and play with toy trucks are both reinforcers for Johnny. Johnny may learn to grab toy trucks from playmates because that behavior is immediately reinforced by toy trucks even though this *eventually* leads to an aversive state of affairs: reduced play with peers. Even if the punisher is of greater magnitude than the reinforcer, the behavior may be strengthened because the reinforcer is more immediate.[3]

Control Exerted by Antecedent Stimuli and Past Experiences

Generalization and Discrimination

When we speak of learning, we mean that a certain response comes more reliably under the control of certain cues or antecedent stimuli, such as a child's learning to say "Thank you" when someone is helpful. As discussed earlier, the probability of such stimulus–response relations is increased through the process called reinforcement, and if reinforcing events consistently fail to follow this stimulus–response sequence, the stimulus will lose its control over the behavior.

However in strengthening the control exerted by a particular stimulus, one is also strengthening the control exerted by other, similar stimuli over that same response. Thus, when a toddler learns to say "dog" in the presence of the

---

[3] This kind of phenomenon accounts for a wide variety of adjustment problems experienced by children and adults, probably including such profound problems as psychotic behavior, suicide, and many criminal behaviors.

neighbor's collie, the toddler's parents may find that the same response is occasioned by the sight of a horse, a cat, and several other four-footed mammals. This universal type of phenomenon is called *stimulus generalization,* and it is the source of many common and sometimes embarrassing errors made by children, such as calling the postman "Daddy" or speaking of bodily functions too openly in public. Stimulus generalization is not restricted to children, of course; it occurs in all learning by all animals of any age.

When children do make errors of overgeneralization, adults are likely to initiate *stimulus discrimination* training. The child is taught to make the response to only the appropriate stimuli. This can be done through several mechanisms, such as extinction (nonreinforcement) of all errors, punishing of errors, prompting correct responses (to be discussed later) and modeling (to be discussed also). A child's learning to make the sound "b" when presented the letter *b* and to make the sound "k" when presented the letters *k* or *c* are also a result of discrimination training. A common error among children learning to read is to say "saw" for *was,* and vice versa; and a common error among educators is to label that child "perceptually handicapped" instead of simply arranging more effective discrimination training for the child.

Errors of overdiscrimination are also common, such as a child's learning to say "please" only under a few of the appropriate conditions and not under others, or learning to read a certain letter of the alphabet only when it is printed in a particular style or size. Then the teaching task is one of generalization training. A form of generalization training needed by many preschool children is to behave in socially constructive ways (e.g., share playthings, help someone needing it, avoid physical aggression, etc.) in the absence of adult surveillance.

Motivating Operations

The concept of motivation has been a source of much controversy in psychological theory. Educators training teachers tend to use the term in a very limited and theoretically vague sense. They describe, as methods to "motivate" children, such teacher activities as "relating the to-be-taught material or skills to material, skills, and values the child already knows or has." From a practical standpoint there is no question that this is an extremely important part of teaching methodology, whether one calls it "motivation" or not. But educators tend to leave out an aspect of motivation that has a firmer base in scientific research: the processes of *deprivation* and *satiation.* Another, less documented but practically useful, phenomenon has to do with the long-term motivational effects of various learning experiences, and this issue will also be discussed as it relates to education.

The behavior analyst in early childhood education, when addressing issues of "motivation," is likely to think in terms of questions such as. "How effective is this reinforcer likely to be for these children or this child, and how can I increase its effectiveness?" A wealth of research has shown that certain reinforcers become more effective the longer the learner is deprived of them. This is easily demonstrated with certain biological reinforcers, such as food and water. Though the picture is probably more complicated with many of the reinforcers important in education, the *deprivation* concept can be useful in teaching. For example, in a preschool setting, certain toys and games can be reserved as special treats to be used only when a certain child or group has performed particularly well at some task. Thus permission to play with that toy or game would tend to be a more powerful reinforcer the longer the children are deprived of it, other things being equal.

Satiation is the opposite of deprivation. The more recently, and continuously, a learner has experienced a reinforcer, the less effective it is as a reinforcer. Thus, while the opportunity to play a certain game will strengthen whatever behavior preceeds that opportunity, after the game has been played for a period of time, it loses more and more of its potential as a reinforcer, until eventually the behaviors of engaging in that game are no longer prepotent over other behaviors and the child leaves that game for other activities. The reinforcing power of all events is constantly shifting in this way, becoming greater as the learner is deprived of them for a time, and temporarily decreasing as the learner experiences them continuously for a period.

Given that a child receives at least a modicum of the biological reinforcers (e.g., air, food, water, warmth) the most important reinforcers for the child's behavioral development are complex, learned reinforcers. Learned or *conditioned reinforcers* depend on a child's experience for their long-term effectiveness. A child's behavior is probably reinforced by such events as mastery of a teacher-presented task, praise, recognition, or play with peers, only if the child has had certain kinds of complex learning experiences that establish these events as reinforcers. Likewise, activities such as playing hide-and-seek, hearing a story, or playing dominoes are reinforcers only because of previous learning experiences; and some such events lose most of their reinforcing value later in childhood because of other learning experiences. One thing a teacher can do to increase the effectiveness of his or her praise and recognition as a reinforcer is to take a few moments each week to exchange a few pleasant, personal words with each child about a topic unrelated to the child's school work.

Basic Behavioral Engineering Techniques

In addition to discovering basic laws or principles that describe how behavior works, behavioral science has developed some basic techniques for the modification of behavior that are proving very useful in virtually any setting with any learner and any learning objective. The individual-subject style of research used by behavior analysts has been a major circumstance promoting the development of behavioral engineering techniques, because the behavior analyst gets continuous feedback from the learner's behavior that tells whether the technique being used is effective. Research designs comparing the performance of an experimental group, after a procedure has been employed, with the performance of a control group that did not experience the procedure are much less useful in developing techniques for behavior change or maintenance.

Shaping

Given a particular set of stimuli, a learner's response to them is not perfectly constant. Even a well-practiced response will vary from one occurrence to the next. Because of this fact, and because of the fact that a response does not extinguish when only a few occurrences go unreinforced, it is possible to mold or shape a response gradually, through successive approximations. This is a way to teach totally new behavior to a child, behavior the child has never emitted before. Or it can extend existing behavior.

An excellent preschool example of shaping was described by Harris, Wolf, and Baer (1964). The study involved teaching a very passive preschool boy to play on a climbing apparatus. The child's approaching the apparatus was reinforced at first, then only his touching the apparatus, then only his climbing it a little, and finally only his extended climbing. Reinforcement was then made increasingly intermittent. As a result, vigorous climbing activity became a stable part of the boy's repertoire.

Shaping can also be used to reestablish behavior that the person previously learned but has stopped emitting. For example Harris, Johnston, Kelly, and Wolf (1964) worked with a 3-year-old girl who had regressed to crawling. At first they reinforced the child's simply pulling herself to an upright position, regardless of how long that position was maintained, while they avoided reinforcing crawling. Then they waited for longer and longer periods of upright behavior before dispensing reinforcers. Gradually they succeeded in reestablishing a normal pattern of upright behavior. In this example, the normal behavior was already occurring, and in this sense a new response was not being established. But the behavior was inadequate in duration, and it was this aspect that was shaped. Similarly, a teacher can shape longer and longer occurrence of attention to learning tasks (both teacher-presented and child-initiated), thus developing a child's "attention span," persistence, and task completion (e.g., Allen, Henke, Harris, Baer, & Reynolds, 1967).

The notion of making a task easy for the young learner is often basically a shaping approach. Thus a child learning to write is first expected only to write large letters, a child learning to throw a ball is praised for throwing it in the right general direction, and a child learning to speak is acknowledged and responded to even if many of the sounds are crude approximations to adult performances. Unfortunately, if a child fails to get shaping experiences adequate to teach more advanced performance and therefore falls far behind peers, we often eventually stop trying to provide those particular experiences for that child, label the child as defective (perceptually handicapped, lazy, minimally brain damaged, stubborn, learning disabled, emotionally disturbed, etc.), and place the child in special programs that may or may not provide the relevant training adequately.

Extinction Procedures

Earlier, the behavioral phenomenon of extinction was described. As a behavioral engineering technique, extinction refers to procedures in which one arranges to prevent the reinforcement of a response. For example, Wright and Hawkins (1970) eliminated the tattling behavior of a school child by arranging for teachers and the school secretary to simply ignore the child when he began tattling, on the assumption (which proved correct, since the behavior decreased) that the behavior was being maintained by these persons' responses to it. Similarly, Wolf, *et al.* (1970) found that a retarded child's vomiting behavior was being reinforced by her release from the classroom whenever she became nauseous, for termination of this contingency eliminated the nauseous responses and reinstatement of the contingency produced reinstatement of the response.

Sometimes the reinforcers maintaining undesired behavior are not so readily eliminated. In that case the teacher has other options, including powerful reinforcement of incompatible behavior, eliminating opportunities for the behavior, or punishment. However, if the reinforcers are coming from peers, the teacher should consider strengthening peer behaviors that would be incompatible with those behaviors that reinforce the undesired responses.

Prompting and Fading

If a child never makes the correct response to a stimulus, the response cannot be reinforced. Though shaping is one way to produce the correct response, it tends to be a slow process, and it is simply inapplicable to some tasks. An alternative is prompting.

The notion of prompting is that if one provides sufficient "stimulus support" for the desired behavior it can be made to occur and can thus be reinforced. A prompt can be thought of as a "hint," except that this term tends to imply only a limited type of stimulus support.

There are several different types of prompts. For example, an adult trying to teach a child to say "Thank you" when others do something pleasant for the child may provide a *verbal prompt* by saying "What do you say?" The wise adult will then praise the child's appropriate response, of course, or else the response may never be occasioned by the desired cue, the favor from someone.

Tangentially, it should be pointed out that it is perfectly appropriate to provide a child with the complete answer to a question or other task, if that is what is likely to be needed in order to get an accurate response. That is called a "full prompt." An example would be for a teacher to say "What color is this, Johnny? Say red." Johnny's saying "Red" would then be met with enthusiastic praise by the teacher, so that it would become a more probable response in the presence of the color red.

Verbal prompts are really of two kinds, oral and written. With persons who can read, correct responses can be prompted with written words or letters. For example, a child learning basic science might be given text saying "Plants need water, soil, light, and air. What four things do plants need?"

Manual prompts are often needed by small children and severely retarded persons. In manual prompting one physically guides the person through the correct response. A child learning to cut with scissors, to line up, to button a coat, or to cut food with a knife is likely to need manual prompting. Teachers and parents should not hesitate to provide manual prompts when a child is likely to have difficulty with a new skill. As children become linguistically developed to the point that verbal explanations are effective in producing accurate motor responses from them, manual prompting is infrequently needed. Thus, a 6-year-old learning to print the letter *n* may be told "Come straight down, then pick up your pencil," and an 8-year-old learning to use a wrench to loosen nuts can be told "Turn it to the left."

Pictorial prompts are useful in teaching reading and other skills. A child learning to read the word "dog" can be shown a picture of a dog beside the word. *Color prompts* are sometimes used to teach a difficult discrimination, as when a child's left boot and shoe are given a red dot to make correct placement easier.

Several other types of prompts can be devised, and one additional type will be discussed shortly, but the point of prompting should be clear: It is to provide extra, temporary, stimulus support for accurate responding so that correct responses can occur immediately and be reinforced. The stimulus support is "extra" in the sense that it contains more stimulus components than will eventually be required to produce the behavior; and it is "temporary" in the sense that it will eventually be removed. Extensive prompting is one aspect of assuring success and thus making learning a very positive experience for children (or anyone).

The removing of prompts without loss of the correct behavior is sometimes a delicate art. Generally it is best to accomplish the process in successive steps, sometimes quite gradually. This gradual or stepwise removal of prompts is called *fading,* and researchers have shown that totally new discriminations can be taught to even subhuman species without error, if the process is gradual enough (Terrace, 1963). Using some of the previous examples of prompting, the following would be possible fading procedures:

1. The teacher training Johnny to name colors would, after having given full prompts several times (and reinforced correct answers), shift to saying, for the color red, "Say re_." The next step might be, "Say r___." If the child still needs any prompting after several such trials, the next step might be "Say (teacher then forms mouth to pronounce r but makes no sound)."

2. A teacher prompting correct lining up may at first point to the place to stand, say "Stand behind the last person," and gently push the child toward that position. The push may then be reduced to a hand on the shoulder, and then dropped altogether, while the pointing and verbalization might remain in effect. Then the pointing component might be dropped, and finally the verbal explanation, leaving only the normal cue "Line up" as the antecedent stimulus for the response.

3. The child with a red dot painted (e.g., with fingernail polish) on each left shoe and boot, may automatically receive fading as the paint wears off, perhaps too rapidly. It would be best to paint these dots at points on the apparel where the

child will eventually need to look in order to discriminate left from right shoes that are not specially marked, so that the observing response (looking at the dot) being used temporarily to get the correct response is as close as possible to the observing response needed later, when there is no prompt.

One of the keys to successful fading is a general rule used by good behavior analysts and, in fact, by good teachers of all kinds; namely, "Let the learner's performance be your guide." If the performance becomes very unreliable when a prompt is faded or dropped, despite the continued availability of effective reinforcers, the teacher returns to a fuller level of stimulus support temporarily. As teachers we are sometimes inclined to say, "I already taught him that"; but a skill has not been adequately *taught* until it has been adequately *learned* by the learner. The person who arranges that learning occurs is a *teacher*; the person who merely goes through teaching rituals is not.

Modeling

One of the more profound and exciting areas of behavior research since the early 1960s has dealt with the phenomena of modeling and imitation. Very early in life we, like other primates, learn to imitate behavior modeled by those around us. This is not a totally new discovery, of course, but the pervasiveness of the phenomenon, its role in the development of complex behavior patterns such as language and sex roles, the mechanisms through which it develops, and the mechanisms by which it works have only recently received extensive attention, and this research is described by Zimmerman in Chapter 3.

Modeling is useful to the teacher as a form of prompt to be subsequently faded or dropped. Teachers can often be seen modeling (demonstrating) removal of caps from paint jars, buttoning, washing play tables, and the like. They also point out another child's competent performance of a task, thus facilitating use of a peer as a model. Teachers can also use modeling and role playing to teach courteous behaviors, conversation skills, dealing with aggression from a peer, cooperating, sharing of playthings, reasoning with others, and many other social skills. It is important that the modeling be followed immediately by practice and reinforcement.

Chaining

We do not respond with discrete, isolated responses most of the time. Our more intelligent behavior usually consists of long chains of responses, such as the utterance of a sentence, the whole recounting of an event, driving to work, washing the dishes, or painting a picture. Stimuli produced by completion of one step or link in the chain act as reinforcers for that step and cues for the next.

The phenomenon leads to two useful techniques: *backward chaining* and *forward chaining.* In backward chaining, one teaches the last link of the chain first, then the next-to-last, and so on. For example, a method of beginning the teaching of shoe tying, suggested by Jacobson (1970), is to complete all steps but the final tightening of the bow and teach the child to make that response (through manual and verbal prompting). Once that is mastered, the pulling through of the bow is taught, so the child is then performing the last two links in the chain. This process is continued until the child is performing the whole chain.

Forward chaining is simply the reverse; it begins by teaching the first link. Some chains seem to be easier to teach one way than the other, and the "right" way is whichever way proves fastest, requires least effort, and is most error-proof.

It is important that errors not be allowed to creep into the chain, because if they are practiced a few times they may be very hard to extirpate from the chain. Thus, a child who holds a pencil the wrong way when first learning to write will likely continue that behavior for life, because it became part of a tightly linked chain. Similarly, a girl who repeatedly enters the house, drops her coat over a chair, then proceeds about other matters will be hard to retrain. The girl's mother may later find the coat, reprimand the girl, and hang it up for her, but that is unlikely to produce the desired chain. The solution is to get the correct sequence to occur repeatedly (Homme, C'de Basca, Cottingham, & Homme, 1968), always with reinforcement of the first several correct performances (later correct performance will be adequately reinforced by the uncontrived events that naturally follow it).

Where there are certain chains to be learned in early childhood education settings—getting out materials for a certain activity, cleaning up materials when an activity is over, washing hands, or getting ready to go outside—it is advisable for teachers to arrange a very orderly practice of them initially, with many prompts. Perhaps only a few children would practice at a time, so that errors can be easily prevented, or at least detected before they are completed. Gradually, prompts can be reduced and groups can be increased in size, until everyone performs the chain without error and with minimal supervision.

Time-out

One form of punisher is called time-out. It consists of removal of the opportunity to gain the reinforcers available in a certain environment, or sometimes it can better be described as termination of ongoing reinforcers, like the turning off of a television set. Time-out can be accomplished by *removing the learner* from the environment where reinforcers are richly available, as when a disturbing child is placed outside the room or outside a group activity for 10 minutes. It can also be accomplished by *terminating the task* so that the learner is prevented from responding, as when a teacher stops a game, story, or discussion group in which the children have many opportunities to participate. Finally, time-out can be accomplished by simply *"shutting off the flow"* of reinforcers, as when a teacher who wishes to decrease "tattling" behavior simply turns away without comment as soon as it is apparent that a child has come to tattle. These are very useful, usually effective forms of punishment if the time-out is immediately contingent on the response to be weakened and if the terminated stimuli or situation is truly rich with reinforcers. If the teacher does not let it become a form of humiliation, it is one of the most humane forms of punishment.

BEHAVIOR ANALYSIS AS METHODOLOGY FOR
ACCOUNTABILITY AND DISCOVERY

Early in this chapter it was pointed out that behavior analysts have a great appreciation for strong scientific evidence. They like to have data that are objective and quantitative, not just impressionistic. They prefer to avoid unnecessary assumptions. They are reluctant to rely on the opinion of "experts," perhaps because they have seen much of this opinion prove to be ill-founded dogma. They like to see experimental demonstration of the relationships between variables, not just correlational evidence. And they prefer a style of research in which they can directly see the effects of variables on the behavior of individuals, as opposed to experiments in which the performance of one group is compared (through inferential statistics) with the average performance of another group, without ever knowing which individuals were affected and how much (Baer, Wolf, & Risley, 1968; Skinner, 1966; Sidman, 1960). Risley (1970) has even gone so far as to *define* behavior analysis (he used the term "behavior modification" at the time) as the reliance on precise, objective data and direct experimental evidence; he omits the reliance on basic behavior theory and technology (a major portion of this chapter) as necessarily a part of behavior analysis.

Full description of methodologies for discovery and scientific documentation of the effects of environmental variables, including teaching techniques, on behavior would be far beyond the scope of this chapter. However, such information is now available in forms appropriate to early childhood educators. First, there are descriptions of the measurement methods used in behavior analysis in Hawkins, *et al.,* 1976, in McLaughlin (1975), in Sulzer and Mayer (1972) and in Hall (1971). These methods alone provide the basis for a level of accountability heretofore unknown in education; because a teacher, principal, school psychologist, counselor, or any other school personnel can use these methods to provide objective data (for themselves or for their peers, students, administrators, parents or the general public) as to the performance of either individual students or groups. Second, there are descriptions of the methods by which school personnel can objectively evaluated the *effects* of procedures they use on the performance of students. These very readable, brief expositions can be found in Sulzer and Mayer, (1972), in Hall (1971) and in Risley and Wolf (1972). Finally, there are numerous examples of behavior analysis efforts described in the published literature, including efforts directed at single responses or a wide range of behaviors; efforts directed at single individuals, whole classes, and even whole schools; and efforts directed at maintaining orderly conduct or at accelerating development of academic and preacademic skills. These descriptions can be found in journals such as *Journal of Applied Behavior Analysis, Behaviour Research and Therapy, Behavior Therapy, and School Applications of Learning Theory.* They can be found in such books as Brigham, Hawkins, Scott, and McLaughlin (1976); Ramp and Semb (1975); Daniels (1974); Ulrich *et al.* (1974); and O'Leary and O'Leary (1972). Many of the studies were carried out by teachers or other school personnel (especially those in Daniels and in *School Applications of Learning Theory*).

SOME MAJOR FINDINGS OF APPLIED BEHAVIOR ANALYSIS APPLICABLE TO EARLY CHILDHOOD EDUCATION

The Power of Attention

One of the most profound outcomes of behavior analysis research has been discovery of the power exerted by the simple act of attending to a learner. While the power of material reinforcers and tokens exchangeable for them has received a certain amount of recognition among educators, and the power of (the more readily accepted) teacher praise has had wide recognition, the power of attention as a reinforcer has been little appreciated, and its implications little understood.

A few studies will illustrate the importance of attention. Hawkins and Hayes (1974) studied the high frequency of wrong, often bizarre, answers given by an emotionally disturbed girl to reading comprehension questions that were being presented orally to the child by a tutor. They noted that when the child gave correct answers the teacher praised her briefly and moved on to the next question, but when the child gave a wrong answer the teacher engaged in relatively lengthy explanations as to why that answer was wrong; in fact it is awkward not to respond this way. The authors persuaded the teacher to reverse these contingencies, making long responses to correct answers and brief responses to errors, thus testing the hypothesis that the teacher's attention alone was such a powerful reinforcer that it would strengthen whichever response could produce more of it. Indeed, that is exactly what happened; when the teacher gave a lengthy response to errors, errors predominated; when the teacher responded at length to correct answers, they predominated. By responding the most natural way, the teacher was actually interfering with the child's performance, apparently because attention was a more powerful reinforcer for this child than was praise or finding out that she was correct.

Madsen, Becker, Thomas, Koser, and Plager (1968) suspected that a teacher whose pupils were often out of their seats at inappropriate times was defeating her own purpose by asking them to sit down, because in so doing she was also giving them her attention and drawing the attention of classmates to them. Their research showed that, indeed, for the class as a whole (not necessarily for each individual) the command "Sit down" served as a reinforcer for getting out of their seats! Similarly, Lovaas and his colleagues (Lovaas, 1973) have shown that autistic children's self-injurious behaviors can be maintained by attention, Williams (1965) showed that a young child's bedtime tantrums were maintained by parental attention; and results obtained by Allen, Hart, Buell, Harris, and Wolf (1964) suggested that isolate behavior of a nursery school child was maintained by the attention it produced. Clearly it is very important for teachers and parents to be alert to what child behaviors obtain their attention and to dispense this reinforcer discriminantly.

Token Economies

Any event or object consistently associated with a reinforcer takes on reinforcing properties itself for the person who has experienced this pairing. This is the principle of conditioned reinforcement (Holland & Skinner, 1961). This principle has led to the development of a wide variety of systems called "token economies," in which tangible objects or symbols are given relatively immediately contingent upon desired behavior and are later exchanged for other objects, symbols, or activities that are of reinforcing value to the learner. Just as with money in national economies, the immediate or "token" reinforcers are worthless in themselves; yet they serve as effective reinforcers because they are the key to other events that already have reinforcing function. These events may be special activities, privileges, edibles, or playthings.

Token economies can be extremely effective in solving one of the primary problems in education: motivation. This is particularly true when they are applied by an enthusiastic, imaginative teacher. Kazdin and Bootzin, (1972) in a review of token economies, indicate that token economies:

> (1) bridge the delay between the target response and back-up reinforcement; (2) permit the reinforcement of a response at any time; (3) may be used to maintain performance over extended periods of time when the back-up reinforcer cannot be parcelled out; (4) allow sequences of responses to be reinforced without interruption; (5) maintain their reinforcing properties because of their relative independence of deprivation states; (6) are less subject to satiation effects; (7) provide the same reinforcement for individuals who have different preferences in back-up reinforcers; and (8) may take on greater incentive values than a single primary reinforcer since, according to Ferster and DeMyer (1962), the effects resulting from association with each primary reinforcer may summate [p. 343].

Another advantage is that tokens can be withdrawn as a form of relatively impersonal, unemotional, punishment called "response cost"; however, it is important that each child's earnings are usually far greater than these losses, otherwise the tokens will rapidly lose their effectiveness because they do not actually lead to the back-up reinforcers reliably.

Many classroom studies have been done employing token economies, and these have been reviewed by O'Leary and Drabman (1971). In addition, a large number of ongoing classroom programs include token economies (e.g., Hawkins & Hayes, 1974; Walker & Buckley, 1972; Miller & Schneider, 1970). A teacher wishing to install a token system can use these for ideas or can obtain material designed specifically to assist in setting up an economy, such as Walker & Buckley's (1974) programmed text, a booklet by Bushell (1974), or a book by Ayllon & Azrin (1968).

Numerous educators objects to the notion of using token reinforcers, particularly if exchanged for material goods. They feel that this is "bribing" the child; but a bribe is payment for unethical or illegal behavior, as Green and Stachnik (1974) have pointed out. It seems curious that adults, who *insist* upon being paid for much of the work they do, can object to the payment of children for the work they do, particularly when that work is not the "job" the child would have chosen, it must be performed under very repressive circumstances (silence, sitting for long periods, etc.), and the child has had fewer years of preparation for the task. Perhaps education is now undergoing a change from the naive notion that children will learn the vast quantity and variety of skills expected of them just "for the love of learning," or "because it is their responsibility." There are many aspects to the issue of motivating learning, and though token economies do not guarantee adequate motivation (Kuypers, Becker, & O'Leary, 1968), they have made remarkable changes in classrooms and can probably change the effectiveness of even the best teacher.

CONDUCTING A BEHAVIOR ANALYTIC EARLY CHILDHOOD EDUCATION PROGRAM

The basic principles, basic behavioral engineering techniques, and major findings from applied behavior analysis presented thus far in this chapter constitute the basis for planning a behavior analysis program for young children. The planning and execution of such a program will now be described.

Planning the Program

Setting Goals and Behavioral Objectives

Not only behavior analysts, but most educational leaders today appear to agree that specification of general goals and specific behavioral objectives is a very important aspect of educational planning. It is the mechanism through which our teaching efforts become focused or directed. The setting of goals and objectives is a complex process that cannot be described here, particularly since there is excellent guidance elsewhere (e.g., Vargas, 1972; Gronland, 1970; Lindvall, 1964; Mager, 1972), but two comments may help make the task easier: First, the term *goals* is here meant to indicate rather general, vague statements of what the program should accomplish; and these do not specify observable behavior.[4] Their purpose is to list the general areas toward which the program is aimed and guide subsequent statement of behavioral objectives. While some authors (e.g., Mager, 1972) soft-pedal or ignore the statement of goals, such statements may play an important role in guiding the development of more precise objectives. Second, textbook authors and

[4] Vargas (1972) uses the term "overall objective" for the most general level and "general objective" for the next level of specificity. Neither of these refer to the precise, overt behavior the learner is to show; that level of specification is a "behavioral objective."

others are increasingly taking seriously the job of stating objectives. Thus there may be excellent material already available that states objectives for at least part of the curriculum.

Selecting and Devising Antecedent Stimuli: Materials and Activities

At least two questions must be asked in weighing the value of any particular teaching activities or materials: (1) How relevant are they for the behavioral objectives of the program? and (2) How efficient are they likely to be in achieving those objectives? The fact that certain activities or materials are traditionally included as part of, say, a nursery school or a second grade does not indicate that they have been carefully evaluated for their relevance and efficiency in achieving certain objectives. Some activities will offer very frequent opportunities for the child to make a desired response, while others require that each child wait idly for long periods between opportunities. Some activities provide modeling naturally or make it easy for a teacher to prompt correct responses, while other activities include no prompts and even make efficient prompting difficult.

Bushell, Jackson, and Weis (1975) described their five criteria for selection of commercially produced teaching materials for use in the behavior analysis model Follow Through classrooms thus: "In making our selection we have given priority to materials that clearly describe the behavior they will develop, allow individual initial placement; require frequent observable student responses; contain regular imbedded criterion-referenced tests; and permit different rates of individual progress [p. 110]."

These are excellent criteria. One might add three more: (1) the criterion that the material be well sequenced in small steps; (2) the criterion that adequate prompts be provided within the material or in the directions to the teacher, and (3) the criterion that the material contain some form of reinforcers, such as feedback to the student on the accuracy of some responses, interesting stories (which inevitably reinforce reading accurately), or freedom to skip certain work when an answer is accurate. A programmed text about behavior analysis by Liberman (1972) exemplifies this last form of reinforcement. The Sullivan *Programmed Reading* series (1973) uses feedback on accuracy. This series also appears to be particularly well sequenced, has interesting humor in the material, and has the advantage of being appropriate and acceptable to a very wide range of ages.

Another aspect of materials selection is that of choosing play materials. As most nursery school and kindergarten experts have long suspected, when only toys designed for isolate play are available, isolate play predominates; when only toys designed for social play are available, social play predominates (Quilitch & Risley, 1973).

Scheduling Across the Day, Week and Year

The business of coordinating a series of learning experiences for a large group of children such that most of them are engaged in activities efficiently directed toward one's teaching objectives is extremely complex. While only a small quantity of behavior analytic research has been done in this area, brief description of one study may be worthwhile.

Doke and Risley (1972) compared an "options" schedule, in which children had two or more activities available to choose from at all times, with a "no-options" schedule in which all children were required to engage in the same activity at the same time. The effects of these two arrangements on children's participation in the ongoing activities was their interest, because obviously children can only learn from an activity by some form of participation. They found that the "no-options" arrangement was capable of producing as high level of participation as the "options" arrangement, but only under certain conditions: At transitions children had to be allowed to begin the next activity individually, as soon as they were ready, rather than wait for the whole group to be ready; and there had to be enough materials for all children to engage in the same activity. This is an important finding because the "no-options" arrangement ensures that all children are exposed to all activities and is much more economical of staff time. The study is also interesting because it illustrates how behavior analysis research may have very little to do with behavior theory or technology. Much more research of this type will be needed before teachers have good scientific bases for their planning of daily schedules.

Scheduling across the week and year must also be determined by the teaching objectives. A behavior analysis classroom, like any well-planned teaching program, builds skills sequentially. The more basic skills are taught earlier, and these are integrated in a cumulative fashion so that they are being used as components of later activities.

Manpower

When one accepts full responsibility for children's learning, as the behavior analyst must (because of the basic principle that learning is a function of the environment, and the environment is what the teacher arranges), the problem of manpower is soon recognized as crucial. If children's time is to be efficiently spent in learning, they must be actively engaged with a teaching environment a very high percentage of the time. In addition, the teaching tasks and prompts must be adapted to the precise level at which the child's skills are developing, so that tasks are neither too hard nor too easy. Finally, reinforcement for a large percentage of correct responses should occur, often including such responses as cooperation or ignoring misbehavior of peers. If all this is to happen, one teacher will frequently be insufficient. Sometimes even two teachers are insufficient.

A supplementary source of manpower that has had increasing use recently is the pupils themselves. Harris, Sherman, Henderson, and Harris (1972) showed that spelling test performance of elementary school children could be consistently increased by the use of peer tutors. Conlon, Hall, and Hanley (1972) showed that simply having a peer mark those answers that were correct on a pupil's paper while that pupil was working (immediate consequences) produced a higher level of accuracy. Johnson and Bailey (1974) showed that fifth grade pupils effectively taught kindergarten pupils arithmetic skills after 1.5-hr training and did so in a very positive manner.

Another source of manpower is parents. If parents are provided some systematic training and monitoring, they can not only help in the education of a group of children but also become better parents for their own children. The behavior analysis Follow Through classrooms involve two parents and two teachers in each classroom (Bushell *et al.*, 1975).

As more persons become involved in the teaching role, the teacher's position as manager of a small educational *system* becomes more evident. This is a legitimate role, and teachers should neither feel that they must do all the teaching themselves or that they must be teaching pupils at all times. Training and monitoring others who are teaching is a legitimate role.

Designing the Motivation System

A number of considerations and technologies for providing motivation will be described shortly. At this point it should suffice to say that the decisions as to what systems will be used should be made in advance. Adjustments will doubtless be made during the year, and the system may call for pupils to determine certain aspects, but most of the details should be set well in advance if the system is to work smoothly.

Accountability

Assessing Entry Skills. The measure of how much a child has learned is the difference in skill between Time A and Time B. Thus, if a classroom environment is to be accountable for its effectiveness, it will be necessary to know what level of skill the children have when they enter. Clearly all skills cannot be assessed, but a number of significant areas that relate to the program's objectives can be assessed within the first few days of school. Some can even be assessed before school begins, through systematic parent interviews.

Routine Monitoring and Charting of Individual Progress. Each child's progress and performance should be systematically monitored in a behavior analysis classroom. Hawkins *et al.* (1976) describe ways that performance can be measured; Kubany and Sloggett (1973) show how little time can be spent in such measurement; and the journals mentioned earlier provide numerous examples of the graphing of such performance. Most of this material is oriented toward such daily *academic* performance measures as words read correctly per minute, percentage of arithmetic problems completed, and number of colors identified correctly, or at such *nonacademic* performance measures as time taken to get work out of desk, number of times tattling, or frequency of interrupting.

It is crucial that the monitoring of such performance be done regularly and frequently. Depending on the nature of the behavior and its importance, this might mean as often as three times a day or as seldom as once a week (even less if the opportunities for the behavior occur less than weekly). If the benefits of monitoring are to be gained, the data will be plotted on graphs the same day they are obtained (Hawkins *et al.*, 1976).

Another aspect of monitoring that is probably as important as measuring such things as accuracy or interrupting, but has not yet been developed extensively, is the assessment and charting of *progress* through a series of tasks. For example, a teacher might chart the successive letter names mastered by a kindergarten child, the number of successive sight words mastered by a first grader, or the number of successive addition procedures mastered by a second grader. If it is difficult to determine what constitutes one unit of progress, such as one addition fact, the teacher can even use simply the pages in a text as the units.

It is necessary to define what constitutes "mastery" of a unit of skill. For example, the teacher might decide that a child will be considered to have mastered a sight word when the child names the word correctly on the first attempt and without prompts on three successive days. The teacher would then either check that item as "mastered" on a chart for the child or, in order for the chart to contain more information (and more reinforcement value, perhaps), write the word itself on the chart (or let the child do so).

The chart would consist simply of squared (graph) paper with successive, equally spaced dates (on which the child's skill is assessed) listed from left to right across the bottom and successive numbers written up the left side. Each time the child mastered another word the teacher would write that word above the date on which it was mastered and one step above the row on which the last word was entered. The result is a cumulative record of the words mastered, and it will appear like stair steps, each word being a step. The steeper the steps the faster the progress being shown by the child. This kind of record provides excellent feedback to children, teacher, and parents, because it shows the actual rate of progress (the slope of the steps), and even the slowest child can be seen to be making progress. On it can be marked a "target number of words" to be learned by a specified date, and the child's rate of progress (slope of steps) toward that target can easily be assessed at any time. It also is very useful to the next teacher who receives the child.

Bushell *et al.* (1975) provide a progress record for a whole class of Follow Through children. They also use a system whereby each individual's rate of progress in each major academic area can be monitored continuously, to see whether it is "on target," and appropriate adjustments made in the time spent on various areas or in the teaching procedures used.

Experimental Evaluation of Teaching Methods and Materials. While the first criterion for accountability is probably the simple demonstration that performance improved over time (or, in some instances, was maintained at a desirable level) and new skills were acquired, this does not demonstrate that the early childhood education program was responsible for this improvement. Many skills improve under the influence of television; through informal teaching by parents, siblings, and friends; and with physiological changes. The fact that a child's skill or performance increases from September to June does not prove that the *schools* are producing change.

While it would be unreasonable to expect teachers (and perhaps even school districts) to carry the responsibility of proving that the environment they create is responsible for children's growth in certain areas, it is quite possible for teachers to test experimentally the effects of at least some of their procedures on at least some behaviors of all or part of their class. For example, Struble (1974) devised a simple method for getting her fourth grade class to prepare for class work quickly upon return from activities outside the room. She tested its effect by measuring the time taken to prepare for class work before she applied the method (baseline), while the method was in regular use, and when she returned to her original procedures. She clearly demonstrated the effectivensss of the technique. Similarly, Axelrod, Whitaker, and Hall (1972) tested the effectiveness of two procedures for improving the learning of spelling words by a class of special education students; Pigeon and Egner (1972) demonstrated the effectiveness of a method for increasing assignment completion and accuracy of a hyperactive first grade child; and Goetz and Baer (1973) evaluated a technique for increasing the creativity of block-building by three 4-year-olds.

The relative effectiveness of various teaching materials can also be tested scientifically in a classroom setting. For example, Whitehurst, Domasch, and Di Gennaro (1976) inserted active responding requirements in a storybook and found it increased participation. Massad and Etzel (1972) showed that the Montessori sandpaper letters used for tracing with the child's finger while the child makes the letter's sound were more effective in teaching the sounds than were identical letters that had no sandpaper.

Studies such as those cited can be conducted routinely by the behavior analysis teaching staff. The first result is that they continuously increase the effectiveness of their own teaching by, in a sense, holding themselves accountable. But in addition they can better justify their methods to others (especially important when they are unusual), and, if they publish their research, they can add to the knowledge of educators everywhere.

Teaching in the Program

Assessing Entry Behavior

The behavior analysis teacher would avoid the common practice of starting each child's education at the same level, as exemplified by having all third graders reading the same material at the same time. Although some teaching must be done in groups and therefore must sometimes ignore individual differences, the most demanding skills can best be taught in a manner that allows each child to move at his or her own pace. But this requires that the teacher begin the teaching by finding out what level of skill each child has achieved. This is referred to as assessing entry behavior.

The traditional devices for assessing entry behavior in academic skills have been achievement tests or informal evaluation of the child's performance on samples of tasks differing in difficulty. An example of the latter is the teacher's listening to each child read aloud from each of three or four readers of different levels.

There is no general approach to such individual evaluation that typifies behavior analysts, only an insistence on the importance of the evaluation. However, Lovitt and Hansen (1976) offer an interesting approach to reading assessment. They place each child in a text according to the child's correct words read orally per minute (that is, "rate correct") from several texts differing in difficulty. If such an approach to placement results in more rapid progress in reading than do other approaches, it is certainly to be preferred. At present it can be considered a very promising, systematic, individualized approach.

Frequent Opportunity for Practice and Reinforcement

For a response to become well established in a child's repertoire, it is important that the response occur many times in the presence of the appropriate antecedent stimuli (cues, problem situations, tasks) and that reinforcing events accompany this pairing. In terms of daily teaching, this seems to imply several things.

First, the children should be *actively involved* in the sense of making the correct response themselves. This may seem obvious, but if one observes in several classrooms one finds that a practice common among teachers, at least in regard to the teaching of certain behaviors, is to *tell* the child what should be done and assume that the child will then emit the appropriate behavior at the appropriate time. The teacher will not have even modeled the behavior motorically, only described it verbally, and the child will have done neither. This type of procedure seems to be especially common when attempting to teach children such nonacademic behaviors as following playground rules, walking quietly in the hall, selecting a book from the library, or being considerate of others. Such procedures are unlikely to be effective teaching.

A second implication is that there should be *frequent opportunities* for the child to respond. Thus, if one is teaching certain skills orally, for example, one would probably pose questions or tasks in relatively rapid fashion and repeat the same or similar questions many times, both within a lesson and through subsequent reviews. In addition, one would see that each child answered each type of question rather than assume that all members of the group have learned a skill on the basis of a few children's having demonstrated it. Bereiter and Engleman have developed an approach to teaching language skills that involves rapid-fire practice and reinforcement in a context where prompts assure success (Evans, 1971). This approach, by the way, has evolved and been applied as a major model of Follow Through known as the Engleman-Becker Model. The Engleman-Becker Model and the behavior analysis model of Follow Through appear to be achieving the largest gains in academic skills of the several (between five and nine, depending on the comparisons made) models involved in a nationwide experiment described by McDaniels (1975). Of course it should be remembered that certain social behaviors are also important behavioral objectives in education, and frequent opportunities for practice of these behaviors is a part of the curriculum to be given the same serious attention as those parts oriented toward development of academic skills.

A third implication is that the child's performance must be *monitored,* so that differential consequences and guiding or corrective prompts can be provided. While a certain amount of such monitoring and prompting can be built into programmed material, particularly reading material for older children and adults, most of the monitoring of young children's practice will have to be done by persons in the role of teachers. As pointed out earlier, this can include other children and parents; the burden need not fall completely on one person.

The fourth implication has to do with the treatment of errors. Probably the most common practice regarding errors is that the teacher indicates to the child that the response was wrong and then moves on to other children or other tasks. This is probably effective in weakening that *particular* error (except that when used in class recitation it provides the child escape from further task presentations, which will be a reinforcer for some), but it does not teach the correct response. A more promising approach is to have the child re-do any task that was done incorrectly, so that the experience always ends with a correct response and a reinforcer. In this way the correct response is strengthened specifically, the child and teacher feel less frsutrated, and the child is learning the general positive attitude, "I can master almost anything if I keep trying." Such *error-contingent remediation* is particularly helpful in areas where full mastery is important, such as arithmetic, basic reading skills, following certain safety rules, and basic handwriting. Some of the Positive Practice Overcorrection procedures designed by Foxx and Azrin (1973) for eliminating such behaviors as head-weaving and perseverative hand-clapping in a severely retarded child are basically this same method for establishing desired behaviors.

The fifth and last implication is that effective *prompts and consequences* must be at hand constantly, their specific nature depending on the skill being learned and the particular situation. Prompting was discussed earlier and will not be presented again here except to reiterate the generalization that the goal of teaching is to *get correct responses* to occur and then to *strengthen them*, not to find out who was smart enough to learn the response with minimal input. Consequences were also discussed earlier, but more detailed and practical considerations are now appropriate.

Managing Consequences

Judicious Use of Attention. Perhaps the first consideration in consequence management is use of control exerted by attention as a reinforcer. The teacher who is consistently careful to attend to appropriate, constructive, productive behavior and generally avoids attending to inappropriate behavior (except to take immediate, effective steps to stop it and perhaps prompt appropriate behavior) is likely to have a relatively orderly, constructive class, other things being equal.

Extensive Use of Praise. Attention alone, however, is insufficient for motivating performance of the difficult tasks and "self-control" (response inhibition) demanded by many school activities, particularly after kindergarten. The next element to consider is praise. Praise or approval from teachers has been shown repeatedly to affect conduct and achievement (Hughes, 1973; Hanley, 1970), and behavior analysis classrooms utilize praise as a reinforcer extensively (e.g., Bushell *et al.,* 1975; O'Leary & Becker, 1967). No data are available yet as to what range of praise frequency is optimal—given certain tasks, skill levels, other motivating techniques, and so on—but Hawkins and Hayes (1974) report an average frequency of one praise per minute in a behavior analysis program for emotionally disturbed children (defining praise conservatively). White (1975) reports rates (actually 20 sec intervals showing praise, which is a crude index of rate) ranging from .06 per minute to 1.3 per minute, based on observations of 104 teachers (presumably not behavior analysts) in grades 1–12, with only first and second grade teachers showing rates over .4 per min.[5] Probably rates averaging (across activities and pupils) in the range of .5 to 1.5 will prove optimal, if typical teaching materials are used, a token economy is in effect for most activities, and disapproval is infrequent.

Use of Feedback. A third important component of the motivation system is the feedback children get on their accuracy. Any response that is not yet well established in the repertoire will require consistent reinforcement, and one form this reinforcement can take is simply the information as to whether it was or was not correct.

This feedback is given tangible form when a child's paperwork is marked in some way. Unfortunately, the practice that is most economical of time is to mark only errors; but a more positive approach is to mark only correct productions, and this integrates well with an earlier recommendation, the reworking of tasks done incorrectly; for when the errors are remedied all answers can be marked correct.

Providing Consequences Immediately. Another consideration is how immediately the feedback is given. Harrison (1973) found that delaying until the child has finished a multistep task (response chain) that takes only a few minutes may still be too long. If he gave the child feedback immediately when a step was done wrong, the child progressed much more rapidly. This should not be surprising in light of the earlier discussion involving response chains, and it is quite possible that the success of the peer tutoring described by Conlon, Hall, and Hanley (1972) was due to the fact that arithmetic answers were scored as soon as they were written.

Graphing Performance and Progress. An extension of the notion of tangible feedback is the use of performance and progress charts not only for teacher accountability, as discussed earlier, but also for pupil accountability. These charts can even be maintained by the pupil, with a small amount of training and monitoring. A student for whom academic (or social) achievement is a reinforcer is likely to benefit from this method alone.

Another technique is to have pupils actually collect the data to be plotted by evaluating their own performance. While this seems to be effective in some cases (e.g., Santogrossi, O'Leary, Romanczyk, & Kaufman, 1973), it fails in others (e.g., Bolstad & Johnson, 1972). More research is needed before it will be evident where the technique can be relied upon.

---

[5] Interestingly, White also reports a declining rate (intervals) of praise after second grade and a predominance of disapproval over approval in every grade thereafter. She suggests that this may be significantly responsible for the "disenchantment," "loss of trust," and "loss of sense of joy in school" often observed around third and fourth grades.

Use of Token Economies. Praise and various forms of feedback are likely to be a moderately powerful motivation system for nearly all well-adjusted, middle class children and for a sizable percentage of other children. But if a teacher wishes to optimize motivation, a token economy is probably essential. Lahey and Drabman (1974) found that second grade children learned a sight-word reading vocabulary significantly faster and retained better when tokens were given for each correct answer than when only the feedback "Right" was given. Miller and Schneider (1974) found that tokens improved the writing response rate of Head Start children, when a token economy condition was compared with a condition in which tokens were not response-contingent; and they found that a token economy class showed a much greater improvement in accuracy than a control class.

What characteristics should the token systems have? For example, what back-up reinforcers should the tokens be exchangeable for? The most effective and flexible systems seem to be those using a whole "menu" of different reinforcers from which the children may select individually or as a group. The children can be very helpful in selecting items for the menu, and the menu can be changed periodically, thus assuring that the contents will include highly effective reinforcers for everyone. Each item on the menu has a listed "price" or token cost, and these can be adjusted by the teacher when it is noted that some items are never selected or are especially popular. The items will vary greatly, depending on the imagination of those constructing the menu. The menu might include class activities, such as a special trip, a walk, a "white elephant" sale, a story, permission to play music during work period, or a game. It might also include individually consumed items such as the use of a table game, early dismissal to recess, use of special playground equipment, a toy to keep, the privilege of running errands for the week, or simply "free time" during which a wide range of activities is acceptable.

Another consideration is what form the tokens are to take. They may consist of poker chips, coupons, marks on a "point card," foreign coins, plastic strips, or any other item that can readily be carried and dispensed by the teacher, stored by the child, counted, and exchanged. There may be different colors of tokens that have different backup reinforcers, as when Wolf, Giles, and Hall (1968), in a special program for underachieving poor children, had one color exchangeable for small items in a classroom "store," another color exchangeable for daily snacks, and a third color exchangeable for weekly field trips. Tokens should not be easy to counterfeit. They can even be predittoed notes to the child's parents telling what good work the child did in some subject (Hawkins, Sluyter, & Smith, 1972). The exchanging of tokens can take place at fixed, convenient times, and these may be several times a day or as seldom as, say, twice a week. In early childhood education it is probably wise to make the exchanges at least one or two times a day.

In delivering tokens the teacher (or whoever is serving the teaching role) should typically deliver praise at the same time. In this way, whichever reinforcer is more effective for that child will tend to add strength to the other reinforcer, so that it gradually becomes more powerful through the principle of conditioned reinforcement. In the behavior analysis model of Follow Through, this pairing of praise with token delivery is one of the performance criteria of a competent teacher (Bushell *et al.*, 1975). It is probably best if this and other praise is "descriptive" in the sense that the teacher's statement indicates clearly what behavior, or what quality of the work product, is praiseworthy; because research is beginning to indicate that descriptive praise is more effective than general statements like "You did a good job!" or "The class has been very well behaved" (e.g., Goetz & Baer, 1973; Goetz & Salmonson, 1972).

If token removal is to be used as a punisher, it should be used consistently yet infrequently. For example, Hawkins and Hayes (1974) report a token withdrawal rate of approximately 2.0 per hour in the same program where token delivery was 62.1 per hour. If a teacher finds that being consistent in a punishment contingency is resulting in a child's losing a significant percentage of the tokens earned, the teacher should reevaluate the whole contingency system, at least for that child. There are always revisions that will assure better success, such as breaking up a task into smaller units (each followed by feedback, remediation, tokens, etc.), lowering the general difficulty of the task, prompting and reinforcing specific behaviors that are incompatible with the behavior being punished, or reducing opportunity for the punished behavior. In this way the whole environment can be kept almost continuously positive and productive for every child.

LIMITATIONS, RESERVATIONS AND PROMISES

Many questions and criticisms have been leveled at behaviorism and behavior analysis.[6] These will not be reviewed here, however. It is to be expected that an approach and technology so different from tradition will be subjected to special scrutiny; and any technology that is highly effective at influencing behavior probably requires an extra degree of caution. A book by a behavior analyst (Wood, 1975) and a 1975 conference on ethics conducted by behavior analysts[7] demonstrate that behavior analysts themselves are concerned about safeguarding society from the potential ill effects that could be wrought under the name of behavior analysis or behavior modification. What will be discussed briefly here are a few cautions relevant for educators; and this will be followed by a prediction regarding the future of behavior analysis.

First, the educator should realize that behavior analysis does not "have all the answers." Behavior analysis contains a theoretical framework from which educational strategies and techniques can be very profitably developed; but these strategies and techniques are often found inadequate when experimentally evaluated, just as the strategies and techniques developed from other approaches would no doubt be found inadequate if subjected to the same evaluation. In addition, behavior analysis is developing methodology by which educational strategies and techniques

---

[6] A number of these have been cogently answered by Skinner (1974).

[7] This conference, chaired by Jon E. Krapfl, was held at West Virginia University in 1975.

can be routinely evaluated in the field, not just by grant-funded, university-based research projects. This potential for accountability is heretofore unheard of, and it can be used to evaluate methods arising from any theoretical base. ·

If behavior analysis does not "have all the answers," where else should school personnel look for guidance? The design and conduct of an early childhood education program involves innumerable decisions, and behavior analytic efforts have addressed only a limited number of these thus far. The wise behavioral analytic educator probably looks to educational tradition and to other theoretical frameworks for suggestions, evaluates the alternatives on the basis of known behavioral principles, and adopts those methods that then seem most promising. If alternatives are then compared experimentally, educated guesswork can be replaced by scientific evidence.

Another issue that educators need to be aware of was raised by Winett and Winkler (1972). They pointed out that the great majority of behavior analytic efforts in education up to that time were directed at getting children to "be still, be quiet, be docile." While O'Leary (1972) showed that Winett and Winkler's observations may have been overstated, he agreed that "their general message should be taken very seriously, *viz*, if the behavior modifier is to have maximal impact in institutional settings such as schools and hospitals, he must seriously question whether the behavior he is being asked to help change should really be changed [p. 509]." Initial behavior analytic efforts in the schools were primarily designed by outsiders called in to help with a problem child or problem classroom. It is not surprising that these outsiders accepted educators' statement of the problem as "Johnny is always out of his seat," "Susan talks out of turn incessantly," or "Bobby is a bully." Increasingly the emphasis of behavior analysts' work is turning toward positive goals such as acquisition of constructive academic and social skills, rather than focusing so exclusively on teaching children to conform to unquestioned rules.

A final issue is that this chapter no doubt makes it seem that conducting a behavior analytic program in early childhood education would be more difficult than conducting a program based on another model. This is the conclusion drawn by Evans (1971) in presenting the behavior analysis approach. This difficulty is probably to be expected from any approach in which the responsibility for children's learning is taken so seriously. Perhaps the best attitude for those planning a behavior analytic program in early child education would be something like this: "We will include the essential characteristics as extensively and intensively as wisdom, energy, and other resources permit; we will see what our data say about our effectiveness; and we will make adjustments until that effectiveness seems to be the best we can do." The resulting program is likely to be outstanding, both in its effectiveness and in the excitement experienced by those involved in it.

This relates to a prediction regarding the future of behavior analysis. Education, like several other fields, is subject to a continuous parade of fads, each suggesting a new set of changes in educational procedures. As has been stated elsewhere,

Some of these changes are to the benefit of the "learners" . . . , some are to their detriment. Unless a procedure produces an immediate and obvious improvement in the learner's performance (achievement, conduct, attitude, adjustment, etc.), the professional cannot objectively judge whether the procedure is helping or harming the learner . . . , the helping professions cannot be confident that their methods will improve year after year; one fad may produce more favorable effects than unfavorable ones, and the next fad may produce more unfavorable effects than favorable ones [Hawkins et al., 1976].

Because of the accountability aspect of behavior analysis, the potential for a cumulative development of educational methodology is greatly increased. If each new proposal is evaluated not only logically (especially in terms of its relationship to basic principles of behavior) but also experimentally, it can be rejected or accepted on the basis of how its documented effects compare with the documented effects of existing procedures. Thus new developments will more consistently be improvements over previous practice, and a cumulative development is attained.

REFERENCES

Allen, K. E., Henke, L. B., Harris, F. R., Baer, D. M., & Reynolds, N. J. Control of hyperactivity by social reinforcement of attending behavior. *Journal of Educational Psychology*, 1967, *58*, 231–237.

Allen, K. E., Hart, B. M., Buell, J. C., Harris, F. R., & Wolf, M. M. Effects of adult social reinforcement on isolate behavior of a nursery school child. *Child Development*, 1964, *35*, 511–518.

Axelrod, S., Whitaker, D., & Hall, R. V. Effects of social and tangible reinforcers on the spelling accuracy of special education students. *School Applications of Learning Theory*, 1972, *4*, 4–14.

Ayllon, T., & Azrin, N. H. *The token economy: A motivational system for therapy and rehabilitation.* New York: Appleton-Century-Crofts, 1968.

Baer, D. M., Wolf, M. M., & Risley, T. R. Some current dimensions of applied behavior analysis. *Journal of Applied Behavior Analysis*, 1968, *1*, 91–97.

Barlow, D. H., Reynolds, E. G., & Agras, W. S. Gender identity change in a transsexual. *Archives of General Psychiatry*, 1973, *28*, 569–579.

Bijou, S. W., & Baer, D. M. *Child Development, Vol. 1: A systematic and empirical theory.* New York: Appleton-Century-Crofts, 1961.

Bolstad, O. D., & Johnson, S. M. Self-regulation in the modification of disruptive behavior. *Journal of Applied Behavior Analysis*, 1972, *5*, 443–454.

Brigham, T. A., Hawkins, R. P., Scott, J., & McLaughlin, T. F. (Eds.), *Behavior analysis in education: Self-control and reading.* Dubuque, Iowa: Kendall-Hunt, 1976.

Bushell, D., Jr. *Tokens for the Behavior Analysis classroom: A teaching guide.* Lawrence, Kansas: University of Kansas Support and Development Center for Follow Through, 1974.

Bushell, D., Jr., Jackson, D. A., & Weis, L. C. Quality control in the Behavior Analysis approach to Project Follow Through. In W. S. Wood (Ed.), *Issues in evaluating behavior modification.* Champaign, Illinois: Research Press, 1975.

Conlon, M. F., Hall, C., & Hanley, E. M. The effects of a peer correction procedure on the arithmetic accuracy of two elementary school children. In G. Semb, D. R. Green, R. P. Hawkins, J. Michael, E. L. Phillips, J. A. Sherman, H. Sloane, D. R. Thomas (Eds.),

Behavior analysis and education, 1972. Lawrence, Kansas: University of Kansas Support and Development Center for Follow Through, 1972.

Daniels, L. K. (Ed.), *The management of childhood behavior problems in school and at home.* Springfield, Illinois: Charles C Thomas, 1974.

Doke, L. A., & Risley, T. R. The organization of day-care environments: Required vs. optional activities. *Journal of Applied Behavior Analysis,* 1972, *5,* 405–420.

Evans, E. D. *Contemporary influences in early childhood education.* New York: Holt, Rinehart and Winston, 1971.

Ferster, C. B., & DeMyer, M. K. A method of experimental analysis of the behavior of autistic children. *American Journal of Orthopsychiatry,* 1962, *32,* 89–98.

Foxx, R. M., & Azrin, N. H. Dry pants: A rapid method of toilet training children. *Behaviour Research and Therapy,* 1973, *11,* 435–442.

Foxx, R. M., & Azrin, N. H. The elimination of autistic self-stimulatory behavior by overcorrection. *Journal of Applied Behavior Analysis,* 1973, *6,* 1–14.

Goetz, E. M., & Baer, D. M. Social control of form diversity and the emergence of new forms in children's blockbuilding. *Journal of Applied Behavior Analysis,* 1973, *6,* 209–217.

Goetz, E. M., & Salmonson, M. M. The effect of general and descriptive reinforcement on "creativity" in easel painting. In Semb, *et al.* (Eds.), *Behavior analysis and education, 1972.* Lawrence, Kansas: University of Kansas Support and Development Center for Follow Through, 1972.

Green, R. L., & Stachnik, R. J. Money, motivation and academic achievement. Phi Delta Kappan, December, 1968, 228–230. Reprinted in L. K. Daniels (Ed.), *The management of childhood behavior problems in school and at home.* Springfield, Illinois: Charles C Thomas, 1974.

Gronlund, N. E. *Starting behavioral objectives for classroom instruction.* New York: Macmillan, 1970.

Hall, R. V. *Behavior modification, Vol. 1: The measurement of behavior.* Lawrence, Kansas: H & H Enterprises, 1971.

Hanley, E. M. Review of research involving applied behavior analysis in the classroom. *Review of Educational Research,* 1970, *40,* 595–625.

Harris, F. R., Johnston, M. K., Kelley, C. S., & Wolf, M. M. Effects of positive social reinforcement on regressed crawling of a nursery-school child. *Journal of Educational Psychology,* 1964, *55,* 35–41.

Harris, F. R., Wolf, M. M., & Baer, D. M. Effects of adult social reinforcement on child behavior. *Young Children,* 1964, *20,* 8–17.

Harris, V. W., Sherman, J. A., Henderson, D. G., & Harris, M. S. Effects of peer tutoring on the spelling performance of elementary classroom students. In G. Semb, *et al.* (Eds.), *Behavior analysis and education, 1972.* Lawrence, Kansas: University of Kansas Support and Development Center for Follow Through, 1972.

Harrison, D. R. Immediacy of feedback: Its effects on academic performance. *School Applications of Learning Theory,* 1973, *5,* 4–14.

Hawkins, R. P., Axelrod, S., & Hall, R. V. Teachers as behavior analysts: Precisely monitoring student performance. In T. A. Brigham, R. P. Hawkins, J. Scott, and T. F. McLaughlin (Eds.), *Behavior analysis in education: Self-control and reading.* Dubuque, Iowa: Kendall-Hunt, 1976.

Hawkins, R. P., & Hayes, J. E. The School Adjustment Program: A model program for treatment of severely maladjusted children in the public schools. In R. Ulrich, T. Stachnik, and J. Mabry (Eds.), *Control of human behavior, Vol. 3: Behavior modification in education.* Glenview, Illinois: Scott, Foresman & Co., 1974.

Hawkins, R. P., Sluyter, D. J., & Smith, C. D. Modification of achievement by a simple technique involving parents and teacher. In M. B. Harris (Ed.), *Classroom uses of behavior modification.* Columbus, Ohio: Charles E. Merrill, 1972.

Hayes, S. C., Johnson, V. S., & Cone, J. D. The marked item technique: A practical procedure for litter control. *Journal of Applied Behavior Analysis*, 1975, *8*, 381–386.

Holland, J. G., & Skinner, B. F. *The analysis of behavior: A program for self-instruction.* New York, McGraw-Hill, 1961.

Homme, L., C'deBaca, P., Cottingham, L., & Homme, A. What behavioral engineering is. *The Psychological Record*, 1968, *18*, 425–434.

Hughes, D. C. An experimental investigation of the effects of pupil responding and teacher reacting on pupil achievement. *American Educational Research Journal*, 1973, *10*, 21–37.

Jacobson, B. Teaching children to tie their shoes. *School Applications of Learning Theory*, 1970, *3*, 47–48.

Johnson, M., & Bailey, J. S. Cross-age tutoring: Fifth graders as arithmetic tutors for kindergarten children. *Journal of Applied Behavior Analysis*, 1974, *7*, 223–232.

Kale, R. J., Zlutnik, S., & Hopkins, B. L. Patient contributions to a therapeutic environment. In R. Ulrich, T. Stachnik, and J. Mabry (Eds.), *Control of human behavior, Vol. 2: From cure to prevention.* Glenview, Illinois: Scott, Foresman & Co., 1970.

Kazdin, A. E., & Bootzin, R. R. The token economy: An evaluative review. *Journal of Applied Behavior Analysis*, 1972, *5*, 343–372.

Kubany, E. S., & Sloggett, B. B. A coding procedure for teachers. *Journal of Applied Behavior Analysis*, 1973, *6*, 339–344.

Kuypers, D. S., Becker, W. C., & O'Leary, K. D. How to make a token system fail. *Exceptional Children*, 1968, *11*, 101–108.

Lahey, B. B., & Drabman, R. S. Facilitation of the acquisition and retention of sight-word vocabulary through token reinforcement. *Journal of Applied Behavior Analysis*, 1974, *7*, 307–312.

Lent, J. R., LeBlanc, J., & Spradlin, J. E. Designing a rehabilitative culture for moderately retarded, adolescent girls. In R. Ulrich, T. Stachnik, and J. Mabry (Eds.), *Control of human behavior, Vol. 2: From cure to prevention.* Glenview, Illinois: Scott, Foresman & Co., 1970.

Liberman, R. P. *A guide to behavioral analysis and therapy.* New York: Pergamon Press, 1972.

Liberman, R. P., Teigen, J., Patterson, R., & Baker, V. Reducing delusional speech in chronic schizophrenics. *Journal of Applied Behavior Analysis*, 1973, *6*, 57–64.

Lindvall, C. M. (Ed.), *Defining educational objectives.* Pittsburgh: University of Pittsburgh Press, 1964.

Lovaas, O. I. *Behavioral treatment of autistic children.* Morristown, New Jersey: General Learning Press, 1973.

Lovitt, T. C., & Hansen, C. L. Round one–placing the child in the right reader. In T. A. Brigham, R. P. Hawkins, J. Scott, & T. F. McLaughlin (Eds.), *Behavior analysis in education: Self-control and reading.* Dubuque, Iowa: Kendall-Hunt, 1976.

MacMillan, D. L. *Behavior modification in education.* New York: Macmillan, 1973.

Madsen, C. M., Becker, W. C., Thomas, D. R., Koser, L., & Plager, E. An analysis of the reinforcing function of "Sit down" commands. In R. K. Parker (Ed.), *Readings in educational psychology.* Boston: Allyn & Bacon, 1968.

Mager, R. F. *Preparing instructional objectives.* Palo Alto, California: Fearon Publishers, 1962.

Massad, V. I., & Etzel, B. C. Acquisition of phonetic sounds by preschool children. In G. Semb, et al. (Eds.), *Behavior analysis and education, 1972.* Lawrence, Kansas: University of Kansas Support and Development Center for Follow Through, 1972.

McDaniels, G. Evaluation problems in Follow Through. In A. M. Rivlin and P. M. Timpane (Eds.), *Planned variation in education: Should we give up or try harder?* Washington, D.C.: The Brookings Institution, 1975.

McLaughlin, T. F. An analysis of the scientific rigor and practicality of the observational and recording techniques used in behavior modification research in public schools. *Corrective and Social Psychiatry and Journal of Behavior Technology Methods and Therapy*, 1975, *21*, 13–16.

Miller, L. K., & Schneider, R. The use of a token system in project Head Start. *Journal of Applied Behavior Analysis*, 1970, *3*, 213–220.

O'Leary, K. D. Behavior modification in the classroom: A rejoinder to Winett and Winkler. *Journal of Applied Behavior Analysis*, 1972, *5*, 505–511.

O'Leary, K. D., & Becker, W. C. Behavior modification of an adjustment class: A token reinforcement program. *Exceptional Children*, 1967, *33*, 637–642.

O'Leary, K. D., & Drabman, R. Token reinforcement programs in the classroom. *Psychological Bulletin*, 1971, *75*, 379–398.

O'Leary, K. D., & O'Leary, S. G. *Classroom management: The successful use of behavior modification.* New York: Pergamon, 1972.

Phillips, E. L., Phillips, E. A., Fixsen, D. L., & Wolf, M. M. Achievement Place: Behavior shaping works for delinquents. *Psychology Today*, June, 1973.

Pigeon, G., & Egner, A. Increasing assignment completion and accuracy in a hyperactive first-grade student. *School Applications of Learning Theory*, 1972, *4*, 24–30.

Programmed reading. New York: Buchanan & Sullivan Associates, McGraw-Hill, 1973.

Quilitch, H. R., & Risley, T. R. The effects of play materials on social play. *Journal of Applied Behavior Analysis*, 1973, *6*, 573–578.

Ramp, E., & Semb, G. (Eds.). *Behavior analysis: Areas of research and application.* Englewood Cliffs, New Jersey: Prentice-Hall, 1975.

Risley, T. R. Behavior modification: An experimental-therapeutic endeavor. In L. A. Hamerlynck, P. O. Davidson, and L. E. Acker (Eds.), *Behavior modification and ideal mental health services.* Calgary, Alberta: University of Calgary Press, 1970.

Risley, T. R., & Wolf, M. M. Strategies for analyzing behavioral change over time. In J. Nesselroade and H. Reese (Eds.), *Life-span developmental psychology: Methodological issues.* New York: Academic Press, 1972.

Santogrossi, D. A., O'Leary, K. D. Romanczyk, R. G., & Kaufman, K. F. Self-evaluation by adolescents in a psychiatric hospital school token program. *Journal of Applied Behavior Analysis*, 1973, *6*, 277–287.

Schwarz, M. L., & Hawkins, R. P. Application of delayed reinforcement procedures to the behavior of an elementary school child. *Journal of Applied Behavior Analysis*, 1970, *3*, 85–96.

Schaefer, H. H., & Martin, P. L. Behavior therapy for "apathy" of hospitalized schizophrenics. In R. Ulrich, T. Stachnik, and J. Mabry (Eds.), *Control of human behavior, Vol. 2: From cure to prevention.* Glenview, Illinois: Scott, Foresman & Co., 1970.

Sidman, M. *Tactics of scientific research.* New York: Basic Books, 1960.

Skinner, B. F. Are learning theories necessary? *Psychological Review*, 1950, *57*, 193–216.

Skinner, B. F. *Science and human behavior.* New York: Macmillan, 1953.

Skinner, B. F. Teaching machines. *Science*, 1958, *128*, 969–977.

Skinner, B. F. What is the experimental analysis of behavior? *Journal of the Experimental Analysis of Behavior*, 1966, *9*, 213–218.

Skinner, B. F. *The technology of teaching.* New York: Appleton-Century-Crofts, 1968.

Skinner, B. F. *Contingencies of reinforcement.* New York: Appleton-Century-Crofts, 1969.

Skinner, B. F. *About behaviorism.* New York: Knopf, 1974.

Struble, J. B. The application of positive social reinforcement to the behaviors of getting ready to work. In L. K. Daniels (Ed.), *The management of childhood behavior problems in school and at home.* Springfield, Illinois: Charles C Thomas, 1974.

Sulzer-Azaroff, B., Thaw, J., & Thomas, C. Behavioral competencies for the evaluation of behavior modifiers. In W. S. Wood (Ed.), *Issues in evaluating behavior modification.* Champaign, Illinois: Research Press, 1975.

Sulzer, B., & Mayer, G. R. *Behavior modification procedures for school personnel.* Hinsdale, Illinois: Dryden, 1972.

Terrace, H. S. Discrimination learning with and without "errors." *Journal of the Experimental Analysis of Behavior*, 1963, *6*, 1–27.

Ulrich, R., Stachnik, T., & Mabry (Eds.). *Control of human behavior, Vol. 3: Behavior modification in education.* Glenview, Illinois: Scott, Foresman & Co., 1974.

Vargas, J. S. *Writing worthwhile behavioral objectives.* New York: Harper & Row, 1972.

Walker, H. M., & Buckley, N. K. Programming generalization and maintenance of treatment effects across time and across setting. *Journal of Applied Behavior Analysis,* 1972, *5,* 209–224.

Walker, H. M., & Buckley, N. K. *Token reinforcement techniques.* Eugene, Oregon: E-B Press, 1974.

Webster, R. L. Stuttering: A way to eliminate it and a way to explain it. In R. Ulrich, T. Stachnik, and J. Mabry (Eds.), *Control of human behavior, Vol. 2: From cure to prevention.* Glenview, Illinois: Scott, Foresman & Co., 1970.

White, M. A. Natural rates of teacher approval and disapproval in the classroom. *Journal of Applied Behavior Analysis,* 1975, *8,* 367–372.

Whitehurst, C., Domash, M., & Di Gennaro, C. The effect of storybook design on attention and story relevant verbalizations in preschool children. In T. A. Brigham, R. P. Hawkins, J. Scott, and T. F. McLaughlin (Eds.), *Behavior analysis in education: Self-control and reading.* Dubuque, Iowa: Kendall-Hunt, 1976.

Williams, C. D. The elimination of tantrum behavior by extinction procedures. In L. P. Ullman and L. Krasner (Eds.), *Case studies in behavior modification.* New York: Holt, Rinehart, and Winston, 1965.

Winett, R. A., & Winkler, R. C. Current behavior modification in the classroom. Be still, be quiet, be docile. *Journal of Applied Behavior Analysis,* 1972, *5,* 499–504.

Wolf, M., Birnbrauer, J., Lawler, J., & Williams, T. The operant extinction, reinstatement and re-extinction of vomiting behavior in a retarded child. In R. Ulrich, T. Stachnik, and J. Mabry (Eds.), *Control of human behavior, Vol. 2: From cure to prevention.* Glenview, Illinois: Scott, Foresman & Co., 1970.

Wolf, M. M., Giles, D. K., & Hall, R. V. Experiments with token reinforcement in a remedial classroom. *Behaviour Research and Therapy,* 1968, *6,* 51–64.

Wood, W. S. (Ed.). Issues in evaluating behavior modification. Champaign, Illinois: Research Press, 1975.

Wright, J. H., & Hawkins, R. P. The elimination of tattling behavior through the use of an operant conditioning technique. *School Applications of Learning Theory,* 1970, *2,* 9–13.

6

Using Incentives in Early Childhood Education

RONALD S. DRABMAN

DAVID HAMMER

University of Mississippi Medical Center

A wealth of evidence for the general effectiveness of the use of reinforcers can be found by examining any of the various psychological and educational journals. This chapter will deal with the use of incentives to improve the social and academic behaviors of preschool children in both classroom and experimental settings. As Baer and Wolf (1968) point out, the preschool classroom is a setting in which the behavior of the children is intentionally or unintentionally changed by what goes on around them. In order for the teacher to be in control of these changes in behavior, she must study and thoroughly understand the nature of incentives and engineer their administration so that the results will be the most benefit. The teacher cannot decide not to use incentives, since they are inherent in the preschooler's environment; she can apply them either in a systematic manner to obtain specific goals or in a random, haphazard manner, resulting in the children's learning random and often inappropriate behaviors.

DEFINITIONS

Throughout the remainder of this chapter, the terms *reward, incentive,* and *reinforcement* will be used interchangeably. They will be used only when the procedure they describe conforms to the following definitions of reinforcement. Incentives or reinforcers occur under two basic classifications. Positive reinforcement can be defined as the *presentation* of a stimulus *contingent* upon a specific response with the *consequence* that the probability of that response is *increased*. Consider the situation where a child performs a behavior, such as complying with a request, and the teacher responds with positive attention and praise. If the child then complies more often, we can say that this attention is positively reinforcing. The critical elements are that the stimulus must be presented contingently and that it results in an increase in the frequency, duration, or intensity of a specific behavior.

Negative reinforcement, on the other hand, is defined as the *removal or delay* of a stimulus *contingent* upon a response with the *consequence* that the probability of that response is *increased*. An example would be when a child learns that by avoiding the living room heater (response) he can avoid being burned. It is important to note that in both classifications of reinforcers or incentives an increase in behavior is involved.

What is important to the preschool instructor is that an effective reinforcer is anything that has been demonstrated to be effective in increasing the desired behavior. In short, it is anything that works. If a given behavior is followed by a reward as a consequence, then the probability that the behavior will occur again is increased. This is the basic rule in the procedure of using incentives to facilitate learning. However, there are a number of different theories which attempt to explain how the reward actually functions to brings about these effects.

THEORIES OF REINFORCEMENT

Three hypotheses each emphasize different factors as the controlling process in reinforcement. The first of these, the drive-reduction hypothesis, suggested by Hull (1943), stresses the state of the person's internal drives and physiological needs. This theory assumes that pain or deprivation causes a physiological need, producing a drive which initiates behavior. The reinforcement occurs when the incentive reduces the drive by satisfying the need. Miller and Dollard (1941) presented a similar stimulus-reduction explanation of how incentives work. Basically, they suggested that any stimulation experienced by the person, regardless of whether or not it is rooted in a need, can result in a drive if it is strong enough. The reinforcement effect results from the reduction of the stimulation.

The second theory on why incentives are effective deals with behaviors such as approaching, attending, and manipulating, which have no function in reducing physiological needs or eliminating aversive stimuli. This explanation emphasizes the nature of the stimulus itself as being critical to the incentive value. The theory is based on numerous studies that demonstrate that sensory feedback, both auditory and visual, can effectively change and maintain behavior. Reinforcement is thought to be the result of the novelty of the stimulation, and studies have in fact shown that novel and complex stimuli can be more effective than simple and more familiar stimuli as reinforcers (Bandura, 1969).

The third theory of incentives emphasizes the response itself. It is based on the

Premack principle. According to this principle, if a person is allowed to perform a frequent activity only after he performs an activity which he normally engages in less often, then the frequency of the less often performed activity will increase. More technically, this means any more-probable behavior will effectively reinforce a less-probable behavior. Premack suggests that, under appropriate conditions, practically any behavior can be an effective incentive. This principle stresses the importance of the response relationships as reinforcement rather than any absolute property of the response. It is based on a number of experiments performed by Premack (1965) and is more an inductive description of his findings than a deductive theoretical explanation of reinforcement.

There is no reinforcement theory that integrates these three divergent theories into one comprehensive explanation of why incentives work. However, investigative research has furnished persons who apply these reinforcement principles a wealth of valuable information. It has demonstrated the wide range of incentives available to the practitioner and it has demonstrated the effectiveness of incentives in a large variety of experimental and applied situations.

TYPES OF INCENTIVES

Although there is no clear-cut system for categorizing the various types of incentives, four general classifications are most common. These are material incentives, token incentives, social or verbal incentives, and activity incentives.

Material Incentives

Material incentives are tangible or concrete items such as edibles, toys, various colored stars, or money. There are some who criticize the use of such tangible reinforcers as being "no less than a bribe." To the contrary, the important distinction between a reinforcer and a bribe is that bribes are generally given *before* the desire behavior while reinforcers are given only *after* the desired behavior. For example, when a parent says, "I will give you an ice cream cone *now* if you promise to be good at the grocery store," the parent is not reinforcing anything except what the child was doing before the bribe was offered, which was most likely misbehaving. An example of reinforcement would be offering the ice cream to the child in the following manner, "I will get you an ice cream cone *when we get home* if you behave here at the grocery store." The reinforcer would be the ice cream cone delivered contingently after the family arrived home.

Material reinforcers may be effective when social or activity forms of reinforcement are not possible or do not have the desired effect. For example, Staats and his associates (Staats, Staats, Schultz, & Wolf, 1962) have demonstrated the efficacy of material incentives in a situation where social incentives failed to maintain performance. Preschool children were given programmed materials designed to help teach them to read. At first, social praise was used as an incentive. Unfortunately, it was found that after 15–20 min, the children did not remain on the reading task. At this point, tangible incentives were introduced in the form of candy, trinkets, and tokens which could be traded for back-up toys. There was a sudden increase in the children's attending to the task. The children began working for 45-min periods and even actively participated in extra sessions. Ideally, as a reinforcement program using material incentives progresses, there should be a gradual shift to the types of incentives that occur more naturally in the normal environment.

Token Incentives

There are special groups of material incentives used in many of the studies involving preschool and older children, and these are called tokens. A token is some form of symbolic representation of the actual back-up incentive. Tokens may be poker chips, marks on a tally sheet, or punches in a card. The procedure involves the teacher giving the child a token every time he or she exhibits the desired behavior; and when the child has collected a designated number of tokens, they can be traded in for the back-up reinforcers. The token system has a number of advantages over other forms of material reinforcement. The first of these is that tokens allow the teacher to reinforce the child immediately after the desired response has occurred without as much distraction as would occur if the back-up reinforcer itself were to be presented. Also, tokens permit the teacher to require more performance to be executed by the child before the back-up incentive is given. This makes the token system more economical and more nearly approaches the manner in which the child will be rewarded in later life.

Social and Verbal Incentives

A good token program always pairs the presentation of the token with social or verbal incentives. Here the child receives some form of attention or praise from an adult or peer contingent upon the desired behavior. This type of reinforcer is more economical than the material reinforcers and is one which occurs naturally in everyday life. There is occasionally a problem with social reinforcement, however, as some children will not respond for this type of stimulation. In these cases, the child must be given the material reinforcers along with such social stimulation in order that an association may be learned and the social stimuli can take on the rewarding value of the material incentives. Some examples of social or verbal incentives are saying things such as, "That was very good!" or "You did that very well!" or even being close to the child and playing with him.

Meddock, Parsons, and Hill (1973), for instance, demonstrated the incentive value of the presence and verbal praise of adults in a study using a simple motor task of dropping marbles into a box. The study measured the rate at which 4- and 5-year-olds dropped marbles into a small hole in a box. An adult was either present in the room or not present in the room, and the adult responded to the marble dropping with praise or no praise. The major findings were that the rate of dropping the marbles increased both when the adult was presented and when the adult praised the marble dropping. Furthermore, these effects were additive, showing that adult presence increases the rate at which a child will work at a repetitive task and that the rate is further increased if the adult verbally praises the work. This can be a valuable tool for a teacher in tasks requiring repetitive drill. Too often the adults in our society come to expect children to perform without encouragement. The child must be taught that such work is valued by those who are important to him.

Activity Incentives

Very often, within the context of a school program, using the incentive of allowing children to work for activities is helpful. The pupils may be allowed to exchange their tokens for the right to participate in various activities that are specially planned or occur normally in the daily school routine. Free play out of doors or in a special playroom, a trip to the zoo, tumbling on mats, staging a play, playing games, or running errands for the teacher are but a few possible activity incentives that the teacher has at her disposal.

Osborne (1969) used the activity of free time away from schoolwork to improve the attending behavior in a classroom of six deaf children. The children were out of their seats a great deal and distracted others in the class as a result. The children were offered free-time away from schoolwork at a specific time during the morning sessions contingent upon their remaining seated during their work periods. Results showed that at the end of the 66 days of the study, practically no out-of-seat behavior occurred during work time as compared to a rate of more than one out-of-seat occurrence per 15-min session before the contingencies were in effect. Also, a postcheck 6 weeks later showed that the procedures were still effective.

SELECTING INCENTIVES FOR CHILDREN

One problem often encountered in establishing an incentives program is to determine what to use as the incentives. There have been three general approaches for selecting incentives. One approach is to offer objects selected on the basis of what the adult conducting the program believes will be effective. There is an inherent problem in this approach in that these objects are likely to have a different incentive value for each child in the group and may not be of value at all to a few. In a second approach, a single object that has been arbitrarily selected is offered to all of the children. The single incentive will probably have a different value to each child and, therefore, will have a different effect on learning. The third procedure for selecting an incentive is to allow each child to select his or her own incentives from a large variety of objects or activities. This makes the incentives for each child more nearly equal in value but requires more planning and slightly more time during the administration of the program.

Dmitruk (1973) conducted a study in which he investigated the effectiveness of the first two types of procedures for selecting incentives. In particular, his study examined the incentive preferences of children as a function of age and sex. He also looked at the correspondence between the actual preferences of the children and college students' estimates of these preferences. The results of this study indicate that both of the previously discussed techniques for selection of incentives items may be of questionable merit. There was very little correspondence between what the college students estimated and the actual preferences of the children. Additionally, it was found that children of different sex and age groups tended to select very divergent preferred incentives. This suggests that the use of arbitrarily selected incentives could produce programs in which some children learn very well while others suffer.

The preschool teacher wishing to use an incentives system will have to make a choice among the various means of selecting incentives. The teacher must weigh the advantages and disadvantages inherent in each of the systems. In the case of arbitrarily selected incentives, a decision must be made as to whether or not the loss of some incentive effect is more important than the sacrifice of simplicity associated with individually determined incentives. This decision must be based upon the purpose of the program and the nature of the preschool children with whom it will be applied.

In the selection of the type of incentives to use, it is important to remember the Premack principle cited earlier in this chapter. The person wishing to use positive reinforcement need only look at what the child does most often to find a wealth of possible incentives. This may require close analysis of what goes on in the classroom and on the grounds. Incentives such as being permitted to sit in a particular location in the room are easily overlooked and can be effective and economical. Once a list of possible incentives has been compiled, considerations of practicality can be used to limit the range. Those left can then be tested through their contingent application and objective data can be kept to determine their effectiveness.

VARIABLES INFLUENCING THE EFFECTS OF INCENTIVES

Several variables have been shown to influence the effects of incentives on learning. Persons seeking to use incentives effectively in an instructional setting should have a basic knowledge of these factors.

Quality and Quantity of Incentives

The person wishing to use incentives with preschool children will have to determine the optimal level of both quantity and quality of the reinforcer for their particular population. Any reinforcer which produces a strong behavioral change can be considered of high quality. An important point to remember when considering the quantity of an incentive to use is that its quality will be inversely proportional to the amount of the incentive the child has experienced in the recent past. Most people would expect that chocolate pudding would be a useful incentive, particularly if the child had not had pudding or anything else to eat in the past few hours (deprivation). However, if the chocolate pudding is given to the child repeatedly in large amounts as a reward for performance at a task, then the child will get tired of the pudding and eventually even refuse to eat any more of it (satiation). Thus, it appears that the quantity and quality of the reinforcers are particularly important in tasks which require repeated rewarding of behavior over short periods of time.

Another important point to remember concerning the amount of incentive to offer is that if the reward is offered during the training session, time will be lost from the on-task period and, consequently, time will be lost in learning. There exists a general principle for the use of incentives as a result of this consideration. That is, always try to obtain the most performance for the least amount of reinforcer. This means that it would likely prove most effective to use a high quality incentive in a small quantity to obtain the desired behavior. The correct proportions of such an incentive can best be determined by its effects in the specific situation.

Deprivation and Satiation

Studies concerning deprivation and satiation are usually based on a theory of reinforcement that holds that an inverse relationship exists between the number of times a reinforcer has been presented previously and its subsequent reinforcing effects. There have been many attempts to determine if this principle also works with social incentives. Gewirtz (1967) reviewed the various studies concerning preschool and elementary school children in which varying amounts of social reinforcement were used to evaluate deprivation and satiation effects. He concluded that the strength of social reinforcers can be affected by depriving children of the opportunity to receive such reinforcers or by administering large amounts of social reinforcement. Gewirtz's conclusion has important implications for the preschool teacher. It demonstrates the necessity of using a large variety of social reinforcers such as praise, patting, holding, whispering, and attention. This will permit the teacher to maintain the reinforcing effects of social incentives without undermining their effects through repeating them too often over a short time period.

Delay of Reinforcement

Another factor influencing the effectiveness of the incentive is the delay of the reward after the desired behavior has been performed. Various lines of research have shown that there is a relationship between the learning of a response and its temporal relationship to the reinforcer. This has been termed the *delay of reinforcement gradient* (Hull, 1932). The basic import of this principle is that the closer the presentation of the reinforcer to the desired behavior, either in time or space, the stronger the learning will be for that behavior. Correspondingly, the more delayed the reinforcer, the weaker the learning will be.

There have been several studies examining how this delay of reinforcement gradient effect is applicable to incentives systems with children. Mischel and Metzner (1962) conducted a study to determine the parameters of children's preference for a delayed as opposed to an immediate reward. The effects of variables such as age, intelligence, and length of delay were assessed. The children could indicate whether they wanted the immediate reward or the delayed reward. The study demonstrated that a preference for delayed reward was positively related to age and intelligence. It was negatively related to the length of the delay interval. These findings indicate that the immediate reinforcement may prove to be most effective in the case of preschool children. Therefore, reinforcers such as teacher attention, tokens, and in some cases, small quantities of edibles are strongly indicated for incentive systems with preschool children. Note that when using tokens with young children, the association between the token and the back-up reinforcer must be well established.

Schedules of Reinforcement

A fourth factor in influencing the effectiveness of incentives in learning is the schedule upon which the reinforcement is based (Skinner, 1938). The incentive can be offered either on a continuous schedule or on a partial schedule, depending on the desired effects. The continuous schedule is one in which the child receives the reward immediately after each correct response. This schedule is useful for rapid learning of a behavior; however, behaviors learned in this manner extinguish easily when incentives are discontinued abruptly. The partial or intermittent schedule is useful after the initial behavior has been learned; also, it is desirable to thin the schedule to one more natural to the child's environment. Additionally, partial schedules tend to make the learned behavior more resistant to extinction, possibly because more time and responding is required for the subject to learn that the contingencies have been discontinued.

There are two general classifications for partial schedules. The interval schedule reinforces the child for the first response emitted after a fixed or variable length of time. An example of an interval schedule would be the teacher giving a child a token every 15 min following a successful response to a copying task. The interval schedule usually results in a pause after reinforcement and then an increasing amount of responding if the interval is fixed in length. It results in constant rates of responding over periods of time if the interval is varied. The ratio schedule reinforces the child after some fixed or variable ratio of responses have been performed. An instance of a ratio schedule would be the teacher's giving a child a token after successfully copying 10 items. This form of intermittent schedule results in high rates of responding, particularly if the ratio is small. Large ratios are associated with a pause in responding which typically takes place after reinforcement.

The implications of the effects of the schedules of reinforcement for the person working with preschool children are evident. In order that an incentive program be maximally effective, a high-quality reward in as small a quantity as possible should be given contingently immediately following the performance of the desired behavior. To avoid taking time from the task, the reinforcer should be of the social and/or token type, if possible. Within practical considerations, the schedule of reinforcement should be continuous until it is certain that the desired behavior has been mastered. Then the schedule should be thinned on some gradually increasing ratio schedule of reinforcement until the behavior is sustained by only infrequent reinforcement.

Race, Sex, Socioeconomic Status of Children and Experimenters

Many recent studies concerning the effects of incentives on preschool-age children have focused on the influences of the race, sex, and socioeconomic status of the child and/or the experimenter. Breyer, May, and Gable (1972) conducted a study looking at the effects of the race and sex of the experimenter and subject on the responsiveness of 5- and 6-year-old children during nonreinforcement and reinforcement conditions in a simple marble dropping task. These children were equally divided according to race and sex to form four groups. The reinforcement included comments by the adult experimenter such as, "That's very good," or "You're doing very well." The results indicated that there was significantly more responding by all subjects during the reinforcement periods. For the four groups, the rate of responding (from highest to lowest) was: white females, black females, black males, and white males. Furthermore, female experimenters elicited more responses than males, while black experimenters were more effective than whites. Interestingly, whether the experimenter was the same race as the subject or not had no significant effect on reinforced or nonreinforced responding.

In a similar group of studies done by Carringer and Wilson (1974), the effects of socioeconomic status and/or sex and race of experimenter were investigated with middle and lower class black, second grade students matched for age and intelligence. The verbal reinforcers were classified as praise or correctness. The praise reinforcers such as, "You are a good boy" were directed at the subject. The correctness reinforcers such as, "That is the right way" were directed at the task. The results indicated that middle class children of both sexes were more responsive than lower class children with both kinds of reinforcers. Additionally, it was determined that subjects performed better overall for the black experimenter. The finding that middle class black children were significantly more responsive regardless of the kind of reinforcer suggests that higher motivation of middle class subjects is the critical factor rather than intellectual ability. Contrary to Breyer *et al.*, (1972), Carringer and Wilson's (1974) results support the contention that the experimenter's race affects performance, especially with lower socioeconomic class black children.

There seems to be some confusion as to the effects of experimenter characteristics on the use of the reinforcers with preschool-age children, and further research is needed. In spite of that, social reinforcement studies provide two interesting conclusions. First, that the effectiveness of social reinforcement can be influenced by characteristics of the child and the teacher. The second major point is that social reinforcement works to a significant extent with all children. It appears, however, that it works best with middle class socioeconomic status children.

Peers as Reinforcing Agents

The teacher should be aware that the relationships between the children in a class offer an important source of reinforcement. Horowitz (1962) conducted an interesting study in which children, with an average age of 3 years, 10 months or 5 years, 1 month, were reinforced in a lever-pulling task with either a picture of the child's best friend, a neutral peer, or a blue light. The findings of this study indicated that the younger group would work longer at the lever-pulling task when reinforced by a picture of their best friend. These younger children worked less for the picture of the neutral peer or the blue light. There was no difference noted with the older age groups, and no sex differences were noted. These findings suggest the potential effectiveness of friends as social reinforcers for preschoolers. Also, the opportunity to participate the dyadic tasks with a best friend may be an effective incentive.

Social Preferences and Incentives

The effects of social reinforcement upon a preschool child's social preference for those administering the incentives were examined in a study by Redd, Morris, and Martin (1975). They studied the effects of positive and negative feedback upon the performance of color-sorting or arithmetic tasks and upon off-task behavior with 4- and 5-year-old preschool children. In a third condition, nothing was said to the children. Each of the three conditions was administered by a different adult. Following each session, the three adults reentered the room and the child selected one for an additional period of interaction. The findings showed that overall the negative adult caused a higher rate of responding and more time spent on tasks than the positive or neutral adults. The positive adult produced slightly higher rates of responding and time on tasks than the neutral adult. However, the selection for additional interactions made by the children showed that the positive adult was preferred over both the neutral and negative adults, while the neutral adult was preferred over the negative adult when only these two were available. Interestingly, the data shows that while the positive adult inspired high rates of responding in early sessions, this effect quickly dissipated. The authors suggest that these findings indicate that a good behavior modifier should not use only verbal reinforcers with preschool children or he may end up being well liked but ineffective. Instead, the verbal reinforcement should be made to appear predictive of some form of back-up incentive, like a pat on the head, a hug, or free time. In the same way, negative feedback may be immediately effective in the short run but would likely become less effective if it became apparent that there would be no back-up negative reinforcer associated with it.

This notion that the incentive agent can become a discriminative stimulus for reinforcement contingencies was demonstrated in a study with retarded children by Redd and Birnbrauer (1969). Using 10 severely retarded boys, one adult dispensed food and praise for cooperative play behavior while the second adult reinforced in a similar group setting on a noncontingent fixed interval schedule. The results indicated that when the contingent adult entered the room the children began cooperative play. The noncontingent adult did not influence behavior significantly.

These last two studies characterize the problems of generalization often experienced in incentive programs. They demonstrate the need to vary the reinforcing agents as well as the types and means of reinforcement so that the learned behavior does not become situation- and/or teacher-specific. The use of several different types of incentives and several reinforcing agents will provide assurance that the child will not latch onto inappropriate, discriminative stimuli as cues for the desired behavior. Instead, he or she will perform the behavior in a variety of situations. This could also facilitate the child's discovering the "intrinsic" rewards for appropriate behavior.

Group versus Individual Incentive Systems

A number of studies have been conducted with preschoolers to investigate the differential effects of group versus individual incentive systems. The usefulness of group incentives was demonstrated by Bushell, Wrobel, and Michaelis (1968) in a study using a token system with back-up activity-type incentives. The program was directed at increasing the study behaviors of 12 preschool children ranging in age from 3 to 6 years. The students were divided into dyadic groups where one brighter student tutored a slower student and reinforcement for both children was based on the tutee's performance. The results on this study show a rise in study behaviors to approximately 80% for the preschool children from a previous low of 42%. This study demonstrates the effectiveness of group contingencies and the potential in the use of activity-type reinforcers. Additionally, it suggests a successful strategy for teaching through the use of peer tutors in a classroom under an incentives system.

Several studies have sought to discover differences between group and individual contingencies; unfortunately, these studies have had little success. They have demonstrated that both group and individual incentive systems can be effective in modifying preschool children's behaviors but have found no differences in effectiveness (Herman & Tramontana, 1971; Brown, Reschly, & Sabers, 1974).

The effects of an individual token system versus three different types of group token systems were investigated by Drabman, Spitalnik, and Spitalnik (1974) with first-grade children. The token economies were: (1) individual reinforcement, (2) group reinforcement determined by the most disruptive child in the group, (3) group reinforcement determined by the least disruptive child in the group, and (4) group reinforcement determined by a randomly chosen member of the group. Free time was used as the back-up reinforcer. This study also found no differential effects among the various incentive systems. Fortunately, several conclusions concerning the use of the four systems were derived. The group reinforcement determined by a randomly selected member of the group system required less teacher time and was the favorite of the teacher. This system was also the second choice of the children in the class.

It was discovered that the group reinforcement determined by the most disruptive child in the group system led to important sociometric changes. Although this system was liked least by the children, it resulted in the disruptive target children being rated as more responsible on sociometric questions. The conventional individual token system was not popular with the class and was thought to be too time-consuming by the teacher. Finally, the system in which the group received the amount of free time earned by the least disruptive member of the group, while proving to be the most popular with the children, was disliked by the teacher. Not only does this study show the effectiveness of group reinforcement procedures, it demonstrates a group procedure which is considered more economical in relation to the teacher's time and appears to be well liked by the preschool children participating. The teacher wishing to employ an incentive system would do well to heed the maxim of getting the most performance for the least effort and use the group contingency system based on the randomly selected target child. This would eliminate the need to keep data on every child in the class and only require data be kept on a few children selected at random by the teacher.

Effects of Token Procedures on Teacher's Contacts

There has been some recent concern about the effects of token economies on the teacher's behavior in the classroom situation. Mandelker, Brigham, and Bushell (1970) conducted a study to determine if a system requiring a contingent delivery of tokens would have an effect on a teacher's social contacts with her students. The study used a teacher in a public school kindergarten classroom with a group of six children divided into two groups. The children were alternated between contingent and noncontingent token presentations, and it was determined that the teacher's rate of social contact was higher with the children receiving the contingent tokens than with those who received noncontingent tokens.

More recently, the question of what happens to teachers' behavior after the introduction of an incentive system has been investigated without the teachers' knowledge that they were being monitored (Drabman, 1973; Drabman & Lahey, 1974). These studies have shown that teachers who do not receive feedback on their praising behavior while administering the token program may withdraw from classroom interaction and let the system take over. This is a serious misuse of behavioral procedures. To prevent incentives systems from having the unintended effect of lowering classroom interaction, it is suggested that teachers monitor their interactions and change their behavior if the data indicate they are falling into this trap (Drabman & Tucker, 1974).

STUDIES USING INCENTIVES IN
PRESCHOOL-RELATED ACTIVITIES

It is only recently that psychologists and educators have begun experimental investigation of the use of incentives in the preschool and nursery school settings. The early studies were mainly case studies in which the goal was manipulating the teacher's use of attention and praise so as to increase some appropriate social skill while eliminating some competing inappropriate behavior. These studies included the elimination of aggressive behavior and increasing of cooperative play (Brown & Elliott, 1965; Scott, Burton, & Yarrow, 1967; Hart, Reynolds, Baer, Brawley, & Harris, 1968; Pinkston, Reese, LeBlanc, & Baer, 1973), reducing isolate behaviors and increasing social interactions (Allen, Hart, Buell, Harris, & Wolf, 1964; Gallwey, 1965; Kirby & Toler, 1970; Strain & Timm, 1974), eliminating crying responses to mild frustration or pain and increasing appropriate responding in these situations (Hart, Allen, Buell, Harris, & Wolf, 1964), decreasing hyperactive behavior and increasing attention span (Allen, Henke, Harris, Baer, & Reynolds, 1967), eliminating regressive crawling and increasing already established walking behavior (Harris, Johnston, Kelley, & Wolf, 1964), and increasing apparently deficient motor skills (Johnston, Kelley, Harris, & Wolf, 1966; Buell, Stoddard, Harris, & Baer, 1968). These studies demonstrated that the preschool teacher can employ an incentives system effectively in the normal class setting and that inappropriate behavior in preschoolers can be eliminated and more appropriate behaviors increased by offering incentives for the competing appropriate behavior.

Increasing Cooperative Peer Interactions

The most recent of the studies attempting to control aggressive behavior and increase cooperative peer interactions was conducted by Pinkston *et al.* (1973). The child was a 3.5-year-old male who made frequent but unsuccessful attempts to play with peers; these often resulted in an indiscriminate attack on his playmates. The study took place in an experimental preschool classroom. First, a 7-day base-line period was conducted in which aggression was recorded and the teacher responded to the child as she normally would, that is, giving attention to the child when aggression occurred. Next, a 9-day extinction period took place in which the teacher responded only to positive behaviors, ignoring aggression and giving attention only to the victim of an attack. For the first 32 days of the study, an additional baseline was kept on the peer interactions of the child. The teacher had been given no instructions on whether or not to attend to these interactions. Beginning with the 33rd day of the study a concurrent experiment was instituted on peer interaction.

The baseline on aggressive behavior showed that 28% of the child's interactions were aggressive. This declined to 5% in the final extinction phase. Peer interactions averaged 10% during the baseline period. The incentive program raised the level of peer interactions to 35%. A 1-day postcheck was conducted 1 month after the study; this showed that peer interactions had seemed to have actually improved (43%). It is important to note that neither of the behavior changes occurred until the teacher attention was manipulated.

Another study using contingent teacher attention to increase peer interaction while simultaneously reducing social isolation was conducted by Allen *et al.* (1964). A 4-year-old girl was very impressive to adults as a result of her knowledge of science and nature. Because of this she spent most of her time interacting with adults and was considered to be in need of much more interaction with peers. Within 6 days of using the teacher's attention contingent upon interaction with peers and ignoring her interactions directed at the teacher, a quick increase in peer interactions was obtained from her normal rate of 15% of the time to about 60% of the time. The teacher's attention was thinned in the final phase of the study to a level more natural to the regular class setting. Postchecks indicated that the changes were maintained without further special treatment of child by the teacher. There was an apparent bonus effect from the increased interaction with peers. The authors reported that the child's vocabulary came to include simple words more common to her peers, her slow pace of speaking quickened, and many game-playing behaviors became a part of her behavioral repertoire. These additional changes facilitated her subsequent easy introduction into interactions with new playmates. Similar bonus effects were noted in a study by Buell *et al.* (1968) in which social incentives were offered to a 3-year-old preschool child contingent upon her use of outdoor play equipment.

Increasing Compliance

One of the behaviors that most preschoolers are expected to learn is to comply with a teacher's instructions. There have been several studies conducted to investigate the effects of incentives systems upon the acquisition of these compliance behaviors. The results of these studies have shown that the use of reinforcing consequences for compliance is a valuable tool for teaching preschool children. Baer, Rowbury, and Baer (1973) conducted a study involving three extremely negativistic children in a preschool class of five 4–6-year-olds. The three were differentially reinforced for complying with a teacher's requests to complete specific preacademic tasks. The reinforcement was in the form of tokens that could be exchanged for free play time and snacks. This system resulted in clear and useful increases in compliance. It was also found that the incentives system produced an increase in the children's sampling of tasks and materials that they had previously avoided.

Most adults would agree that developing correspondence between what a child says and what he or she actually does is a good process for teaching self-control. Unfortunately, there are only a few studies that have tried to discover the best method for teaching this correspondence to preschool children. Risley and Hart (1968) suggested a procedure to increase correspondence in preschool children. The procedure encouraged the children to report correctly what they did by offering incentives for accurate reports of materials used in earlier play sessions. This procedure was effectively a "do–say" sequence. Israel and O'Leary (1973) theorized that a "say–do" sequence might be more effective than a do–say sequence in developing the correspondence between verbal and motor behavior. Using 16 black and white Head Start children, they conducted two studies to investigate the differential effects of the two sequences. Children in the do–say sequence first played in a play area and later were asked to report the toys with which they played. Children in the say–do sequence were asked to state with which toys they would later play. Afterwards, they were observed at play. Both the experiments showed that merely rewarding the childrens' statements that they had played with a certain toy did not effectively increase the toy's use or the childrens' accurate reporting. Correspondence was increased when incentives were made contingent upon the subjects' accurate reporting of the toys they would use in the later play situation (say–do sequence). This study indicates that the say–do sequence is the more efficient method of developing correspondence between the verbal and motor behaviors of preschool age children. Israel and O'Leary (1973) suggest that there may be an additional advantage to the use of the say–do sequence in that it could produce a more generalized correspondence. A child who has learned to correctly describe his future behavior may be well on his way to self-control.

Modifying Verbal Behavior

The potential for influencing verbal behaviors in preschool age children was demonstrated in a study by Hart and Risley (1968). Here the task was attempting to employ incentives to establish the use of descriptive adjectives in the spontaneous speech of disadvantages preschoolers. Time in school, intermittent teacher praise, and social and intellectual stimulation had proven ineffective in increasing low rates of using adjectives of size and shape. On the other hand, group teaching of color–noun and number–noun combinations with praise and edible reinforcers was effective in increasing such verbalizations. However, these methods were found to be situation specific and produced no spontaneous generations of other combinations. Because of this, access to preschool materials in free play situations was made contingent upon the use of color–noun combinations. As a result, all children increased the spontaneous use of these adjective–noun combinations. The final phase of the study made the materials no longer contingent on color naming. Fortunately, the rate of color–noun combinations dropped only slightly. It appears that access to ordinary preschool materials can be an affective incentive for long-lasting increases in verbal responding of young children.

Other studies have focused on increasing the verbal behavior of preschool children who have extremely low rates in all verbal areas. Reynolds and Risley (1968) conducted such a study with a 4-year-old black girl. After a baseline period, the teacher provided social incentives contingent upon any verbalization by the child. During this condition, the child's verbalization increased from 11% to 75%. It was noted, however, that nearly all of the talking was in the form of requests for materials. This was an indication that the effects may not have been the result of the social incentives but were the result of the contingent access to materials. The procedure was changed to investigate this alternative explanation and, unfortunately, it was confirmed. Apparently, in some cases, low levels of vocalization may not respond to social incentives alone but may require material reinforcers to affect an increase. For those cases, it appears that the easiest means of increasing the verbal behavior of a preschool child is to make environmental materials contingent on his or her talking behaviors.

In a study by Beissel (1972), social incentives were useful for increasing verbal behavior. The child was a 5-year-old black female from the Head Start program who had been classified as a nontalker by the teacher. The teacher provided the child with exclusive attention after any verbal behavior. The results showed that the percentage of intervals containing verbalizations increased from the 5% baseline rate to 53%, thus demonstrating the effect of the contingent social reinforcement.

These two studies on increasing preschoolers' talking behaviors through the use of contingent incentives illustrate several important considerations for teachers. The fact that social incentives worked for one child and not for another shows that incentives systems have the same problems as other forms of teaching systems. There will always be a need to consider the individual differences among children in the use of teaching procedures. The effectiveness of incentives systems was demonstrated in both studies; however, one required an adjustment in the program to establish what was actually reinforcing the child. The ability to determine the need to change the procedure is a strong point in the properly conducted incentive system. Through the recording of data, the person administering the program can judge its progress by comparing the effects of various conditions. He or she can quickly decide if a procedure is or is not working and take appropriate action. Additionally, adjustments to the program can be evaluated quickly since the baseline data provide a reference with which to compare them.

Teaching Preacademic Skills

Most of the studies concerning preschool children cited thus far have dealt with the effectiveness of incentive systems in establishing a normal social behavioral repertoire for the child. These studies have been generally successful in demonstrating that all of the various types of incentives are effective for most social behavior problems. There is also a growing body of evidence that incentive systems are useful in teaching preschool-age children basic preacademic skills such as letter copying and discrimination. Most of these studies have used token incentives backed up by a variety of other types of rewards. They usually begin with very basic skills and slowly build upon these, requiring more and better work to earn the incentive.

Tawney (1972) used a token system to compare the effects of two-letter discrimination training procedures. Thirty males and females ranging from 4 years to 4 years, 9 months old were selected from a summer Head Start program. The training procedure involved teaching children to discriminate critical features of letter-like forms. It was found that offering incentives for discriminating critical features significantly improved letter discrimination. Both the control and a non-critical feature group, on the other hand, showed little improvement. This study demonstrates the effectiveness of the use of a token incentive system to motivate preschool children in training of letter discrimination.

The combination of a token system and peer tutoring was investigated by Hamblin and Hamblin (1972) in relation to its effects on learning to read by preschoolers. Disadvantaged black and white inner-city preschool children, ranging from 44 to 71 months, were divided into four experimental groups: (1) adult tutoring with tokens contingent upon reading, (2) adult tutoring with tokens contingent upon attending session, (3) peer tutoring with tokens contingent upon reading, and (4) peer tutoring with tokens contingent upon attending session. It was found that on all measures (symbols learned, words learned, and books read) the groups receiving some combination of peer tutoring and/or tokens for reading did better, at all IQ levels, than the groups in which an adult tutor dispensed tokens for mere attendance. The results of the study suggest that even young disadvantaged children are effective tutors for their peers. Additionally, the data indicated that the medium- and high-IQ children who were used as tutors learned as much while tutoring as they did when tutored by adults. In a somewhat similar study, Robertson, DeReus, and Drabman (1976) found that second grade children would maintain low levels of disruptive behavior to earn tokens with which to buy a tutoring session with a college student or an older peer. Tutoring served as an ideal reinforcer while also improving the children's reading skills. This study demonstrates that teachers can use the opportunity of being tutored to reinforce appropriate classroom behavior. That is almost like "having your cake and eating it too."

Brigham, Finfrock, Breunig and Bushell (1972) coupled a programmed handwriting procedure with a token system using a school activities and snacks as back-up reinforcers. The subjects were six kindergarten children ranging in age from 5 years, 2 months to 5 years, 6 months. Tokens were presented to the children either on a contingent or noncontingent basis. The children's accuracy of handwriting consistently improved whenever tokens were delivered contingently upon correct responding. Programmed materials are particularly well suited for use in incentive systems because of their modular construction and their versatility in allowing a child to progress at his or her own pace. They also are easily scored and easily recorded, requiring less of the teacher's time.

Hopkins, Schutte, and Garton (1971) studied the effects of access to a playroom on the rate and quality of writing in first and second grade students. Access to a playroom directly followed the completion of a daily writing task. The total amount of time permitted for the children to complete their assignment and then play was progressively shortened from 50 to 35 min. There was a corresponding progressive increase in work rates. Additionally, there was a clear trend toward fewer errors under the shortened access times. In a similar study conducted by Salzberg, Wheeler, Devar, and Hopkins (1971), contingent access to play areas was shown to improve the printing skills of kindergarten children. Six children, 5 years to 5 years, 10 months old, took part in the project. Interestingly, the contingencies were applied only to half of the students in the class, who were selected at random each day. No change in the average number of correct items resulted from a "feedback only" condition in which the children were simply informed if their printing was acceptable. This study demonstrates that the contingencies in an incentive system need only be applied to a few clandestinely selected students to increase all the subjects' work while reducing the time required of the teacher. The study also demonstrates that instruction only or feedback only often do not ensure that preschoolers will do well. In these cases, other incentives must be used.

Finally, Lahey and Drabman (1974) conducted a study with two randomly assigned groups of second-grade students using tokens for a sight-word reading task. One group received tokens plus verbal feedback indicating whether or not they were correct, while the other group received only the verbal feedback. Over three acquisition sessions, 30 words previously missed by each subject were presented. Two retention tests were conducted in which all 30 words were again presented. The results showed that the token-plus-feedback group required significantly fewer trials to reach criterion (correctly reading all 10 words in the list one time through) than the feedback-only group. Additionally, and possibly more important, the token group was found to have a significantly better retention rate in the two retention sessions. The token group was able to attain the same criterion level as the feedback-only group but with better retention and in fewer trials! There was also a significant interaction between the treatment and retention interval, indicating that the importance of the token reinforcement seemed to increase with the length of the retention interval.

The usefulness of incentive systems for teaching basic reading and writing skills to preschoolers appears evident. These systems seem to be effective in increasing both rates and quality of work produced by the children. They are flexible enough to be combined with various types of training programs and often produce an increase in the effects of the programs. Incentives provide needed motivation for preschoolers to perform preacademic tasks and provide them with a more salient demonstration of their success at academic tasks. This fact is very important in the preschool years as it will likely result in the child developing a more favorable attitude toward school-related work.

Creativity

Recently, research has been directed towards discovering if incentive systems might be effective in influencing creativity in preschool age children. Goetz and Baer (1973) investigated the effects of social reinforcement on form diversity and the emergence of new forms in children's block-building behavior. The block-building of 3- to 4-year-old preschool girls was examined to find the number of different forms used in completed block constructions. Few variations in form were found during the baseline session. Social reinforcement was made contingent on the production of any form not previously constructed during the baseline session. Consequently, the number of different forms produced per session greatly increased. Next, social reinforcement was given to all second or more appearances of a form, resulting in a decrease in the variety of forms per session. The overall conclusion was that novel forms occurred at a higher rate during the period of reinforcement of first occurrence of new forms. Apparently, preschool children can be motivated to produce novel and creative responses when social incentives are offered contingent upon their occurrence.

Promoting Racial Integration

Promoting racial integration through social and tangible incentives was studied by Hauserman, Walen, and Behling (1973). The authors believed that integration should be planned so that racial interaction is associated with positive events. Monitoring the 5 black, first-grade children, in a biracial class of 25, the authors found that interaction was very low during an initial baseline period. Observations were taken during the lunch and free play periods. A 4-day prompting phase followed the baseline period. During this phase all students were paired by the teacher with "a new friend." In the lunchroom, the teacher verbally praised those students sitting with the child they had been paired with. They were also given a ticket which they could exchange for an edible treat during free play. A child could obtain a second ticket at the end of lunch if he stayed with his assigned partner. The experimental phase lasted 9 days and differed from the prompting phase only in that the children were instructed to select their own new friend as opposed to being paired by their teacher. The data taken from the free play period was used to test for generalization of the reinforced integration during the lunch periods. The average interracial interactions for the 5 children during the free play period proved to be higher than during the baseline phase. The authors suggest that in order to get practical gains from this type of program, tangible reinforcement would need to be faded out and the experimental phase would need to be longer. It appears that positive racial interaction can be brought about directly through contingent reinforcement of integration. By reinforcing racial interaction, the children may learn that their new friends have many positive attributes, making integration more likely to occur in the future.

INTRINSIC OR EXTRINSIC INCENTIVES
IN THE CLASSROOM?

There has been much controversy recently over the possibility of extrinsic incentives undermining intrinsic incentives (Deci, 1971, 1972; Greene & Lepper, 1974; Lepper, Greene, & Nisbett, 1973). This contention is based on a theory commonly referred to as the "overjustification" hypothesis. This hypothesis states that "a person's intrinsic interest in an activity may be decreased by inducing him to engage in that activity as an explicit means to some extrinsic goal [Greene & Lepper, 1974, p. 50] ."

A very recent study by Feingold and Mahoney (1975) was conducted to test the "overjustification" hypothesis. Special emphasis was given to three methodological considerations that have been found lacking in the studies upon which the overjustification hypothesis is based. First, the extrinsic reinforcement effects were to be clearly demonstrated relative to baseline measures. Second, the procedure of the study closely paralleled the actual procedures employed in many classroom token economies. Third, continual measurements were taken that allowed temporal trends and transition states of the behavioral changes to be analyzed. The subjects were five randomly selected second-grade students from a public school. They were given access to follow-the-dots picture completion books. The baseline performance was recorded for 2 weeks. A token reinforcement phase was implemented, during which subjects received points redeemable for prizes when their daily performances exceeded their individual baseline measures. Following this reward phase, two subsequent baseline phases were instituted over a 6-week period. The results show that a significant reinforcement effect had taken place. Importantly, all subjects demonstrated increases in the average performance from the first to the final baseline assessments. This means that decreases in intrinsic motivation, as defined in the overjustification studies, were not evidenced. These results strongly cast doubt on the "overjustification" hypothesis. This study indicates that the previous studies upon which the "overjustification" hypothesis is based may suffer from methodological problems that resulted in erroneous findings. In addition, Hodges (1972) points out several other important factors about external reinforcement programs. Most persons using these extrinsic reinforcers begin by applying the minimal amount necessary to obtain the desired results. They then designed ways of reducing the amount and extending the periods over which reinforcement occurs. The systems in use have well-defined schedules for changing contingencies based upon the functioning of the children. Procedures such as these, which are standard for most extrinsic reinforcement programs, appear to be lacking in the studies used to support the overjustification hypothesis. Finally, token reinforcement systems are used almost exclusively with children and where other forms of control have failed. One of the cardinal rules of behavior modification is never to use a cannon where a BB gun will do as well (Drabman & Tucker, 1974).

The implication of the research to date is clear and convincing. It appears that incentive systems are a powerful tool for motivating preschool-age children to learn a seemingly unlimited variety of social and academic behaviors. Incentives, coupled with either regular or specially designed instructional programs, offer the preschool instructor an economical, systematic, and more effective manner in which to accomplish his or her job. As long as the contingencies are applied consistently and adequate data is kept to provide feedback for the teacher, little can go wrong to thwart the effectiveness of a social reinforcement system. On the other hand, a token economy is more complicated, and teachers should consult someone with experience in the use of behavior modification before initiating one.

Incentive systems have additional advantages for preschool-age children. They establish a concrete form of feedback for the child which confirms his or her ability to succeed in school-related tasks. Also, through the constant pairing of success at academic or social endeavors and positive incentives, the child may learn to be confident; and this could result in what many people call "intrinsic motivation."

REFERENCES

Allen, K. E., Hart, B., Buell, J. S., Harris, F. R., & Wolf, M. M. Effects of social reinforcement on isolate behavior of a nursery school child. *Child Development*, 1964, *35*, 511–518.

Allen, K. E., Henke, L. B., Harris, F. R., Baer, D. M., & Reynolds, N. J. Control of hyperactivity by social reinforcement of attending behavior. *Journal of Educational Psychology*, 1967, *58*, 231–237.

Baer, A. M., Rowbury, T., & Baer, D. M. Development of instructional control over classroom activities of deviant preschool children. *Journal of Applied Behavior Analysis*, 1973, *6*, 289–298.

Baer, D. M., & Wolf, M. M. The reinforcement contingency in pre-school and remedial education. In R. D. Hess and D. M. Baer (Eds.), *Early education: Current theory, research and action*. Chicago, Illinois: Aldine Publishing Co., 1968.

Bandura, A. *Principles of behavior modification*. New York: Holt, Rinehart and Winston, 1969.

Beissel, G. F. Increasing verbalizations by a disadvantaged preschool child. *Psychological Reports*, 1972, *30*, 931–934.

Breyer, N. L., May, J. G., Jr., & Gable, R. K. Effects of race and sex of experimenter and subject on responsiveness during nonreinforcement and reinforcement conditions. *Psychological Reports*, 1972, *31*, 515–524.

Brigham, T. A., Finfrock, S. R., Breunig, M. K., & Bushell, D., Jr. The use of programmed materials in the analysis of academic contingencies. *Journal of Applied Behavior Analysis*, 1972, *5*, 177–182.

Brown, D., Reschly, D., & Sabers, D. Using group contingencies with punishment and positive reinforcement to modify aggressive behavior in a Head Start classroom. *Psychological Record*, 1974, *24*, 491–496.

Brown, P., & Elliott, R. Control of aggression in a nursery school class. *Journal of Experimental Child Psychology*, 1965, *2*, 103–107.

Buell, J., Stoddard, P., Harris, F. R., & Baer, D. M. Collateral social development accompanying reinforcement of outdoor play in a preschool child. *Journal of Applied Behavior Analysis*, 1968, *2*, 167–173.

Bushell, D. J., Wrobel, P. A., & Michaelis, M. L. Applying "group" contingencies to the classroom study behavior of preschool children. *Journal of Applied Behavior Analysis*, 1968, *1*, 55–61.

Carringer, D., & Wilson, C. S. The effects of sex, socioeconomic class, experimenter race and kind of verbal reinforcement on the performance of black children. *Journal of Negro Education*, 1974, *43*, 212–220.

Deci, E. L. Effects of externally mediated rewards on intrinsic motivation. *Journal of Personality and Social Psychology*, 1971, *18*, 105–115.

Deci, E. L. Intrinsic motivation, extrinsic reinforcement, and inequity. *Journal of Personality and Social Psychology*, 1972, *22*, 113–130.

Dmitruk, V. M. A test of the validity of two methods of selecting incentives for research with children. *Developmental Psychology*, 1973, *3*, 338–342.

Drabman, R. S. Child- versus teacher-administered token programs in a psychiatric hospital school. *Journal of Abnormal Child Psychology*, 1973, *1*, 68–87.

Drabman, R. S., & Lahe, B. B. Feedback in classroom behavior modification: Effects on the target and her classmates. *Journal of Applied Behavior Analysis*, 1974, *7*, 591–598.

Drabman, R. S., Spitalnik, R., & Spitalnik, K. Sociometric and disruptive behavior as a function of four types of token reinforcement programs. *Journal of Applied Behavior Analysis*, 1974, *7*, 93–101.

Drabman, R. S., & Tucker, R. D. Why classroom token economies fail. *Journal of School Psychology*, 1974, *12*, 178–188.

Feingold, B. D., & Mahoney, M. J. Reinforcement effects on intrinsic interest: Undermining the overjustification hypothesis. *Behavior Therapy*, 1975, *6*, 367–377.

Gallwey, M. Modification of nursery school behavior by social reinforcement. Paper presented to the Society for Research in Child Development, Minneapolis, Minnesota, 1965.

Gewirtz, J. L. Deprivation and satiation of social stimuli as determinants of their reinforcing efficacy. In J. P. Hill (Ed.), *Minnesota Symposium on Child Psychology*, Vol. 1. Minneapolis: University of Minnesota Press, 1967.

Goetz, E. M., & Baer, D. M. Social control of form diversity and the emergence of new forms in children's blockbuilding. *Journal of Applied Behavior Analysis*, 1973, *6*, 209–217.

Green, D., & Lepper, M. R. Intrinsic motivation: How to turn play into work. *Psychology Today*, September 1974, *54*, pp. 49–52.

Hamblin, J. A., & Hamblin, R. L. On teaching disadvantaged preschoolers to read: A successful experiment. *American Educational Research Journal*, 1972, *9*, 209–216.

Harris, F. R., Johnston, M. K., Kelley, C. S., & Wolf, M. M. Effects of positive reinforcement on regressed crawling of a nursey school child. *Journal of Educational Psychology*, 1964, *55*, 35–41.

Hart, B. M., Allen, K. E., Buell, J. S., Harris, F. R., & Wolf, M. M. Effects of social reinforcement on operant crying. *Journal of Experimental Child Psychology*, 1964, *1*, 145–153.

Hart, B. M., Reynolds, N. J., Baer, D. M., Brawley, E. R., & Harris, F. R. Effects of contingent and non-contingent social reinforcement on the cooperative play of a preschool child. *Journal of Applied Behavior Analysis*, 1968, *1*, 73–76.

Hart, B. M., & Risley, T. R. Establishing use of descriptive adjectives in the spontaneous speech of disadvantaged preschool children. *Journal of Applied Behavior Analysis*, 1968, *1*, 109–120.

Hartup, W. W. Friendship status and the effectiveness of peers as reinforcing agents. *Journal of Experimental Child Psychology*, 1964, *1*, 154–162.

Hauserman, N., Walen, S. R., & Behling, M. Reinforced racial integration in the first grade: A study in generalization. *Journal of Applied Behavior Analysis*, 1973, *6*, 193–200.

Herman, S. H., & Tramontana, J. Instructions and group versus individual reinforcement in modifying disruptive group behavior. *Journal of !pplied Behavior Analysis*, 1971, *4*, 113–119.

Hodges, W. L. The role of rewards and reinforcements in early education programs: I. External reinforcement in early education. *Journal of School Psychology*, 1972, *10*, 233–241.

Hopkins, B. L., Schutte, R. C., & Garton, K. L. The effects of access to a playroom on the rate and quality of printing and writing of first and second-grade students. *Journal of Applied Behavior Analysis*, 1971, *4*, 77–87.

Horowitz, F. D. Incentive value of social stimuli for preschool children. *Child Development*, 1962, *33*, 111–116.

Hull, C. L. The goal-gradient hypothesis and maze learning. *Psychological Review*, 1932, *39*, 25–43.

Hull, C. L. *Principles of behavior*. New York: Appleton-Century-Crofts, 1943.

Israel, A. C., & O'Leary, K. D. Developing correspondence between children's words and deeds. *Child Development*, 1973, *44*, 575–581.

Johnston, M. K., Kelley, C. S., Harris, F. R., & Wolf, M. M. An application of reinforcement principles to development of motor skills of a young child. *Child Development,* 1966, *37,* 379–387.

Kirby, F. D., & Toler, H. C. Jr. Modification of preschool isolate behavior: A case study. *Journal of Applied Behavior Analysis,* 1970, *4,* 309–314.

Lahey, B. B., & Drabman, R. S. Facilitation of the acquisition and retention of sight-word vocabulary through token reinforcement. *Journal of Applied Behavior Analysis,* 1974, *7,* 307–312.

Lepper, M. R., Greene, D., & Nisbett. R. E. Undermining children's intrinsic interest with extrinsic reward: A test of the "overjustification" hypothesis. *Journal of Personality and Social Psychology,* 1973, *28,* 129–137.

Mandelker, A. V., Brigham, T. A., & Bushell, D. Jr. The effects of token procedures on a teacher's social contacts with her students. *Journal of Applied Behavior Analysis,* 1970, *3,* 169–174.

Meddock, T. D., Parsons, J. A., & Hill, K. T. Effects of an adult's presence and praise on young children's performance. In F. Rebelsky and L. Dorman (Eds.), *Child Development and Behavior.* New York: A. A. Knopf, Inc., 1973.

Miller, N. E., & Dollard, J. *Social learning and imitation.* New Haven: Yale University Press, 1941.

Mischel, W., & Ebbesen, E. B. Attention in the delay of gratification. *Journal of Personality and Social Psychology,* 1970, *16,* 329–337.

Mischel, W., & Metzner, R. Preference for delayed reward as a function of age, intelligence, and length of delay interval. *Journal of Abnormal and Social Psychology,* 1962, *64,* 425–431.

Osborne, J. G. Free-time as a reinforcer in the management of classroom behavior. *Journal of Applied Behavior Analysis,* 1969, *2,* 113–118.

Pinkston, E. M., Reese, N. M., LeBlanc, J. M., & Baer, D. M. Independent control of a preschool child's aggression and peer interaction by contingent teacher attention. *Journal of Applied Behavior Analysis,* 1973, *6,* 115–124.

Premack, D. Reinforcement theory. In D. Levine (Ed.), *Nebraska Symposium on Motivation: 1965.* Lincoln: University of Nebraska Press, 1965.

Redd, W. H., & Birnbrauer, J. S. Adults as discriminative stimuli for different reinforcement contingencies with retarded children. *Journal of Experimental Child Psychology,* 1969, *7,* 440–447.

Redd, W. H., Morris, E. K., & Martin, J. A. Effects of positive and negative adult-child interactions on children's social preferences. *Journal of Experimental Child Psychology,* 1975, *19,* 153–164.

Reynolds, N. J., & Risley, T. R. The role of social and material reinforcers in increasing talking of a disadvantaged preschool child. *Journal of Applied Behavior Analysis,* 1968, *1,* 253–262.

Risley, T. R., & Hart, B. Developing correspondence between the nonverbal and verbal behavior of preschool children. *Journal of Applied Behavior Analysis,* 1968, *1,* 267–281.

Robertson, S. J., DeReus, D. M., & Drabman, R. S. Peer and college student tutoring as reinforcement in a token economy. *Journal of Applied Behavior Analysis,* 1976, *9,* 169–177.

Salzberg, B. H., Wheeler, A. J., Devar, L. T., & Hopkins, B. L. The effect of intermittent feedback and intermittent contingent access to play on printing of kindergarten children. *Journal of Applied Behavior Analysis,* 1971, *4,* 163–171.

Scott, P. M., Burton, R. V., & Yarrow, M. R. Social reinforcement under natural conditions. *Child Development,* 1967, *38,* 53–63.

Skinner, B. F. *The behavior of organisms: An experimental analysis.* New York: Appleton-Century-Crofts, 1938.

Staats, A. W., Staats, C. K., Schultz, R. E., & Wolf, M. M. The conditioning of textual responses using "extrinsic" reinforcers. *Journal of the Experimental Analysis of Behavior*, 1962, *5*, 33–40.

Strain, P. S., & Timm, M. A. An experimental analysis of social interaction between a behaviorally disordered preschool child and her classroom peers. *Journal of Applied Behavior Analysis*, 1974, *7*, 583–590.

Tawney, J. W. Training letter discrimination in four-year-old children. *Journal of Applied Behavior Analysis*, 1972, *5*, 455–465.

Part 3

ASPECTS OF
CHILD BEHAVIOR
AND COGNITION

7

Cognitive Development and Early Childhood Education: Piagetian and Neo-Piagetian Theories[1]

PAUL R. AMMON

University of California, Berkeley

Cognitive development has been an especially active area of scientific research since about 1960. Recent issues of several journals in psychology and education are replete with reports of investigations into the way children perceive, form concepts, remember, reason, and solve problems. The aim of this chapter is to glean something of value to educators of young children from the recent research on these topics. It would be impossible, however, to extract much meaning from the great mass of findings available to us now without adopting some sort of theoretical framework. Thus the discussion will focus primarily on *theories* of cognitive development—that is, on systems of concepts and principles that are intended to explain what has been observed and to predict what might be observed in the future. More specifically, two theories will be outlined and evaluated with reference to their implications for education. They are Jean Piaget's theory of cognitive development and the neo-Piagetian theory proposed by Juan Pascual-Leone. A sample of the research associated with each theory will illustrate the extent to which it seems able to account for child behavior and development. Finally, it will

[1] I am grateful for the support I have received while writing this chapter from the Institutes of Human Development and Human Learning, University of California, Berkeley, and from a Spencer Fellowship awarded by the National Academy of Education.

be argued that Pascual-Leone's approach may offer educators several advantages not found in Piaget's theory.

The present emphasis on theory is not just an expedient brought about by the plethora of available facts about cognitive development. It also reflects the view that any discussion of facts must inevitably reflect the influence of theoretical ideas anyway. Indeed, the "facts," as we know them, do not exist independent of some theory, however implicit or intuitive that theory may be. In a similar fashion, the actions of a practitioner are based not directly on facts, but on generalizations, which may or may not be consistent with the facts. A discussion of cognitive–developmental *theory* is, therefore, both more manageable and more meaningful than an attempt to survey the facts in some theoretically "neutral" fashion.

SOME CRITERIA FOR EVALUATING THEORIES OF COGNITIVE DEVELOPMENT

If we approach the topic of cognitive development from a theoretical point of view, we are immediately confronted with the question of *which* theory, or theories, to consider. We actually have several from which to choose. There is one theory, however, that stands out clearly above the rest, both in terms of the tremendous body of observations associated with it, and with regard to its impact on the current thinking of a great many psychologists and educators. That, of course, is the theory put forth by Piaget. Like Mount Everest, Piaget's theory demands our attention simply "because it is there." Nevertheless, we must try to find other, more pertinent, bases on which to assess the importance of any theory, including Piaget's. Neither its current popularity nor the sheer volume of research associated with it constitutes a sufficient, or even a necessary criterion for deciding how useful a theory might be with reference to early childhood education. What, then, are the relevant criteria to be used in evaluating cognitive theories for our present purposes?

Certainly the "truth value" of a theory is a relevant criterion. Other things being equal, one would prefer a theory that succeeds in explaining and predicting a wider range of facts. But not just any facts will do. Rather, the theory must be able to explain and predict the kinds of facts that concern educators most. One perennial issue in education is the learner's readiness for a particular kind of learning. When educators look to developmental psychology for guidance, they generally have this question foremost in mind. It does seem reasonable to assume that an account of the ways in which children think at different ages would provide the needed guidelines regarding readiness. But it is important to ask whether a given theory deals only with the kinds of cognitive skills that children acquire "normally," under "natural" circumstances, or whether it also deals with the skills that children *could* acquire, under special circumstances. Educators may often be at least as interested in the question of what a child *can* learn as in what he typically *does* learn.

Most people who work with children probably share the intuition that readiness results from some combination of *maturation* (organic growth) and *experience,* but they might have quite different ideas about the relative contributions these two factors make. Yet it is precisely this question which is most important, from an educator's point of view. The answer undoubtedly varies from one situation to another. Where the upper limit on readiness is set by maturation, one has little choice but to wait until the child "grows into" the learning task of interest. On the other hand, where experience is the major determinant of readiness, one can—at least in principle—provide the experience that is needed to bring readiness about. In order to recognize which of these possibilities is actually the case in a particular situation, one needs a theory that attempts to spell out exactly how maturation and experience interact.

The effect of experience on cognition is, of course, an important consideration not only for the child's readiness to learn, but also for the process of *learning* itself. Despite major differences in philosophical orientation, virtually all educators try to promote some sort of learning by monitoring the experiences of children in their charge. What, then, are the conditions under which learning takes place? By what processes does experience bring about cognitive change? To be educationally relevant, a theory must give satisfactory answers to these questions.

Educators frequently speak of *individual differences*—differences in learning style, temperament, and so on. These are differences that cut across the sorts of changes usually regarded as "developmental." It seems clear that such individual differences do exist and that the optimal conditions for learning will therefore vary from one individual to another. What is needed, then, is a theory that characterizes these differences in ways that can be used to predict how they will affect an individual's cognitive performance in a given situation.

Finally, theories of development differ greatly in their relative emphasis on the cognitive versus the *affective* domains. Although we can make a theoretical distinction between cognition and emotion, it is essentially impossible to consider one without the other in educational practice. The usefulness of a cognitive theory will therefore be enhanced to the extent that it specifies the role of affective factors in cognition.

It seems obvious that early childhood educators are concerned with such questions as the determinants of readiness, the conditions of learning, the nature of individual differences, and the interaction of cognition and emotion. Yet there has been a tendency—ironic in a field noted for its concern with the "whole child"—to focus on just one question or another in proposing applications of psychological theory and research. The result is a kind of patchwork eclecticism, which might be better than nothing, but is likely to be less useful in the long run than systematic application of a unified theory addressed to several of the practitioner's concerns at once. It is suggested, therefore, that a list of practical concerns should be made explicit and should serve as a set of criteria for evaluating theories of cognitive development with regard to their implications for education. The present list will perform this function in the discussion that follows.

PIAGET'S THEORY

As we have noted, Piaget's work on cognitive development is truly monumental. In addition to his formal theory, Piaget has contributed a wealth of interesting observations and a number of provocative ideas that deserve further consideration in their own right. However, attention will be concentrated here on the formal theory itself. Furthermore, because Piaget's work is nowadays quite widely known, only a very brief overview of his theory will be presented.[2]

Stages of Development

Piaget is probably best known as principal spokesman for the view that cognitive development involves a series of *qualitative* changes in a child's thinking. Young children not only know less than adults but also have distinctly different ways of understanding what they do know. The qualitative shifts in thinking are described by Piaget as a sequence of developmental stages. The major stages are known as "periods," each corresponding to a fundamentally different way of thinking. It is the child's general way of knowing, rather than his specific knowledge, that concerns Piaget most.

In the *sensorimotor period* (from birth to about 2 years), cognition consists essentially of overt responses to the immediate situation. The infant's knowledge of the world is based initially on innate reflex mechanisms relating particular sensory inputs to particular motor actions. Stimulation near the infant's mouth elicit's sucking; a touch on the hand leads to grasping; the sight of an object brings about directed looking. During the sensorimotor period, these innate structures become differentiated into a large repertoire of more refined sensorimotor "schemes": schemes for striking, lifting, pushing, pulling, and so on. The differentiated schemes are also coordinated with each other in more complex sensorimotor structures: the infant sights an object, grasps it, lifts it to his mouth, and sucks it. He can even solve problems that require him to use one object (e.g., a stick) as a means for attaining another (e.g., a toy that is out of reach). But even with these more complex structures, the infant's behavior is still highly dependent on the immediate situation (Piaget, 1954, 1963).

In contrast, the subperiod of *preoperational* thought[3] (roughly from ages 2 to 7) is characterized by the development of mental representation and, consequently, a growing separation between cognition and the immediate situation (Piaget, 1962).

---

[2] Piaget has recently presented systematic overviews of his own theory in Piaget and Inhelder (1969) and Piaget (1970a). Numerous introductions to Piaget have been written by other authors, including Baldwin (1967), Flavell (1963), Ginsburg and Opper (1969), and Rohwer, Ammon, and Cramer (1974).

[3] According to Piaget's recent terminology, the preoperational subperiod and the one that follows it comprise a "period of preparation and of organization of concrete operations [Piaget, 1973, p. 56]." By encompassing the years from 2 to 11 within a single period, Piaget draws attention to certain continuities between early and later childhood. However, for the sake of simplicity, we refer here only to the *sub*periods by name.

For example, the child can witness some bit of novel behavior on the part of another person and then deliberately imitate that behavior for the first time a day or so later. Such "deferred" imitation does not occur during the sensorimotor period because it requires a lasting mental representation of the model's behavior that can be evoked in other situations. The same sort of representational ability manifests itself in a number of other ways: The child uses play objects to represent real objects; he makes rapid progress in acquiring language and can talk about events that are remote in space and time; he begins to make drawings which (for him) represent familiar objects. The representational ability underlying these activities enables the child to discover many regularities in his environment. But in spite of all the new learning which mental representation makes possible, the preoperational child's thinking remains essentially pre-logical. It often contains contradictions that the child leaves unresolved. He might assert, for example, that the same quantity of water is both more and less than another.

The subperiod of *concrete operations* (from about 7 to 11) marks the beginning of truly logical thought. The representational schemes developed in the preceding subperiod now give rise to coordinated systems of mental actions called "operations." During this period, the child's understanding of the physical world becomes noticeably more adult-like in a number of ways. His reasoning about number, classes, and relations is also much more consistently logical than before (Inhelder & Piaget, 1964; Piaget, 1965). But the newly acquired operations of this period still have their limitations; they apply only to the child's understanding of the way things *are,* and not yet to his conception of the way things *could be.* This last constraint is finally removed in the period of *formal operations* (about 11 to 16), when logical operations are performed upon propositions about hypothetical possibilities as well as upon the actualities of experience (Inhelder & Piaget, 1958). At best, the individual's reasoning becomes purely formal and is more or less independent of particular content.

Although these periods are supposed to represent unified and qualitatively different modes of cognition, Piaget has shown, through his own observations, that there is considerable progress within each period as the child gradually masters the kind of thinking characteristic of that period. Piaget has even suggested that there are further stages and substages within each period. For example, after the initial emergence of mental representation, the preoperational subperiod can be divided into stages of "preconceptual" and "intuitive" thought (Piaget, 1950). Even smaller steps than these can be discerned with regard to specific areas of development. Nevertheless, Piaget still sees certain basic similarities within each of the major periods described above, and that is why he has not simply given us a long list of small developmental steps.

Within a given period, the child's thinking, at its best, is said to reflect a certain "whole structure" (*structure d'ensemble*). Underlying the subperiod of concrete operations, for example, is a set of interrelated "groupings"[4] of very general

[4] "Grouping" is a technical term used by Piaget for logico-mathematical structures with certain distinct properties. For an especially lucid explanation, see Baldwin (1967).

cognitive operations, such as mental addition and subtraction, which can be applied systematically to classes of objects or to relations among objects or their properties. The many instances of concrete logic found in later childhood are all attributed, by Piaget, to these underlying groupings of operations. In a similar fashion, each of the other periods is defined by its own structural core.[5] Thus development consists of a child's gradual progress through a series of global cognitive structures.

Causes of Development

What causes a child to pass through the stages of development? Piaget's position on this question has often been misunderstood as that of a "maturationist" who maintains that cognitive development results essentially from internal growth with the passage of time rather than from experience. Such misunderstandings probably stem from a variety of sources, including Piaget's statements to the effect that psychological development is "comparable to organic growth [Piaget, 1967, p.3]" or that "learning is subordinate to development [Piaget, 1964, p. 17]," along with his insistence that there are definite limits on the extent to which the child's progress can be speeded up by environmental influences. But Piaget has made it clear that, from this point of view, development can no more be reduced to maturation than to learning (e.g., Piaget, 1970a). Both are necessary but not sufficient to cause development; it is the interaction between the two that counts. Above all, Piaget stresses that this interaction takes place in the context of the child's own activity—either overt or mental—as he applies his present cognitive structures to the situations provided by his environment.

Throughout the course of development, a child's activity involves two complementary processes that Piaget calls *assimilation* and *accommodation.* Objects and events are assimilated by cognitive structures in much the same way that food is assimilated by one's digestive system. Whenever an infant attempts to close his hand around an object, it is assimilated to his sensorimotor scheme for grasping. Sometimes an object may be graspable, but not in the way the infant is going about it. If the requirements of the object are not too different from the infant's present way of grasping, then the grasping scheme will be accommodated or modified to fit the object. As a result of such accommodations, the original grasping scheme will eventually differentiate into several more specialized schemes: grasping with cupped hand, grasping with thumb and forefinger, and so on. Similar instances of assimilation and accommodation occur constantly in all stages of development and with all sorts of cognitive structures.

The frequency of assimilation by a particular structure will depend in part on environmental opportunities. Specific assimilations are further determined by affective factors, which cause the child to pursue some goals rather than others and

---

[5] It is important to note that the same cannot be said for the stages and substages within periods. Instead of having unique structural definitions, these stages seem to represent differing degrees to which a child's thinking manifests the structure that defines each period as a whole.

which energize the structures that are applied in pursuit of those goals. The extent of accommodation will depend on the demands of the material being assimilated, and perhaps also on some prerequisite degree of maturation, but most importantly it will depend on the assimilatory structure itself. That is, accommodation cannot begin to occur unless the child has the structural means for attempting an assimilation in the first place. In a sense, then, assimilation is the functional starting point for all development. Accordingly, Piaget has suggested that a developmental period begins with a preponderance of assimilation to existing structures followed by a gradual shift toward more and more accommodation to the demands of the environment, until a new set of structures emerges and the whole cycle repeats itself at a higher level (Piaget, 1967, p. 22).

According to Piaget (1967), ". . . all behavior tends toward assuring an *equilibrium* between internal and external factors or, speaking more generally, between assimilation and accommodation [p. 103, italics added]." Most important for developmental progress are those occasions on which the child's cognitive activity leads him to confront the contradictions inherent in his current way of thinking. The resulting *dis*equilibrium is regarded in Piagetian theory as a necessary precondition for advancement to a higher level of thought. The higher level is then reached through a process of *equilibration.* Experience plays a vital role in this process, but the child's readiness to profit from experience is determined primarily by his present cognitive structures or his structural "competence," a term Piaget has borrowed from the field of embryology (Piaget, 1970a). Maturational factors are undoubtedly involved to some (unknown) extent, but the main limit on the rate at which readiness is attained comes from the sheer number of steps needed for construction of the required structural competence, even under optimal environmental conditions. That is why Piaget says development cannot be rushed.

Early Childhood

From a Piagetian point of view, early childhood is essentially the subperiod of preoperational thought. The beginning of this subperiod is marked by the emergence of mental representation. Just as the infant constantly assimilates objects to his sensorimotor schemes, the 2- to 4-year-old busily engages in assimilating materials to his new representational schemes. The primacy of assimilation at this time is especially evident in the child's use of language and in his symbolic play. He calls a horse "doggie"; he pretends that pebbles are candy, using certain actions now to *represent* eating and not just to eat. Piaget calls the child's thinking at this point "preconceptual" because there is no clear differentiation between specific objects and general categories, such as dogs. Particular objects are simply assimilated to a mental "dog" scheme on different occasions.

Equipped with such representational schemes, the child develops "intuitions" about many relationships in his environment. At first these intuitions are quite global. For example, if the child is asked to make a row of white disks that is equal in number to a standard row of black ones, he makes a row that is only the same *length,* without regard to the spacing between the disks.[6] It is as if his intuition tells him that the number of items in a row is a simple function of the row's length—a rule that actually holds true in many situations. But the experimental situation is a special case and is inappropriately assimilated to this intuitive rule. Later, as the balance shifts toward more accommodation, the child's intuitions become "articulated." Given the same task with black and white disks, the child establishes a one-to-one correspondence between his own row and the standard, and thereby succeeds in producing a numerically equivalent row. But it can be shown that the child's understanding is still intuitive: if one row is spread out further, he thinks it must contain more disks than the other. In Piaget's terms, the child fails to "conserve" the numerical equivalence in his thinking.

In general, the problem with intuitive thought is that the child "centers" his thinking on just one obvious aspect of the immediate situation. Centrations of this sort result in erroneous conclusions when appearances are misleading and other aspects of the situation must be taken into account. Toward the end of the preoperational subperiod, the child begins to show some signs of *de*centering. For example, he sees that one row of disks is longer than the other, but then he recalls the earlier one-to-one correspondence. Although two aspects of the situation are now being considered, this is done by means of successive centrations, which are still not coordinated in a logical understanding of the problem (Piaget, 1950). The child's thinking about such problems is thus inconsistent and will not be completely decentered until he has attained the groupings of concrete operations.

According to Piaget, the young child's readiness to learn is constrained by the kind of intuitive thought described above. That is, he can learn simple relationships, but he cannot be expected to understand special cases that require a more complete logic to overcome misleading appearances. Eventually, however, the child comes to recognize that the special cases are problematic, either because his intuitive expectations are repeatedly disconfirmed by experience, or because he notices that these situations actually involve conflicts between his intuitive rules. The disequilibrium resulting from such conflicts sets the stage for construction of more adequate rules, for example, rules to determine numerical equivalence and the like. This disequilibrium obviously presupposes that the child has already acquired the intuitive rules which engender it. The acquisition of those intuitions and the conflicts they eventually produce are derived from the child's own activity in coping with his environment—including both the physical environment, which contains materials to be acted upon, and the social environment, which asks questions, gives directions, and provides models of behavior. Likewise, the child's activity is also required for the subsequent equilibration that leads to construction of the concrete operational groupings. It is at this time of final transition that the child is especially susceptible to environmental influences designed to promote the acquisition of operational thought—not before.

---

[6] This example is taken with slight modifications from an experiment discussed by Piaget (1973).

Alongside this picture of cognitive development in early childhood, Piaget has pointed (with far less emphasis) to certain parallels in the child's social and affective life. The widespread phenomenon of symbolic play, for example, is seen as motivated, in part, by emotions arising from the young child's attempts to deal with a world in which he has very little actual control. Because the child has the representational ability to engage in symbolic play, he can express his feelings in fantasy in ways that would be impossible in the real world. The "centered" quality of preoperational thought is also manifested in the child's social interactions, where he is often unable to adopt points of view other than his own and therefore cannot yet engage in true cooperation with others, as in the playing of games with rules. As with any other form of activity, the child's social activity reflects an underlying structure and also contributes to the developmental process of *re*structuring through equilibration.

In sum, Piaget views early childhood as the period of preparation for and transition to concrete operational thought. The preparation consists of the emergence of mental representation and the learning of intuitive rules regarding regularities in the child's environment. The time of transition begins in earnest when the child experiences the conflicts brought about by his centered way of thinking and it ends with attainment of the operational whole structure called groupings. We turn now to a brief consideration of some research related to this view of early childhood.

PIAGETIAN RESEARCH

As we have seen, Piaget's theory contains both a formal description of *what* is acquired in the course of development (cognitive structures, such as the groupings of concrete operations) and a general explanation of *how* it is acquired (the process of equilibration through assimilation and accommodation). Our main purpose here is to discuss the current research literature as it relates to these two major components of Piaget's theory. Only a small sample of studies will be cited to illustrate some conclusions that can fairly be drawn from the much larger body of research available to us now. Because Piagetian researchers have investigated the emergence of concrete operations more than any other aspect of development, that will be the focus of the present discussion as well.

Stages, Structures, and Performance

The great appeal of Piaget's theory undoubtedly derives in large measure from the hope that his developmental stages will provide a basis for predicting the kinds of cognitive tasks a given child can and cannot perform. Thus, if one believed that a particular 6-year-old was in the preoperational subperiod, for example, one might predict that he would be unable to solve any problem which, theoretically, requires concrete operations, such as the conservation of number. A research question of prime importance, then, is the extent to which Piaget's structural stages actually permit us to predict performance in this way.[7]

Piaget's notion of a concrete operational period is based on his observation that a great variety of cognitive tasks are generally performed successfully only by children of 7 or older, and that these tasks all seem to involve the same kind of logic—a logic that is represented formally by the mathematical structures Piaget has called groupings. There is a good deal of corroborating evidence that the majority of children do begin to solve many different concrete logical problems between the ages of 7 and 11, as Piaget's work has led us to expect. Children in this age range begin to conserve a variety of physical quantities, such as the number of objects in a row, the length of a piece of string, the amount of substance in a ball of clay, and so forth. They also can sort objects into hierarchically organized classes and subclasses, and they begin to give logical answers to questions about quantitative relations between classes and subclasses. They can systematically construct series of objects that are graded in terms of size and other dimensions, and they make transitive inferences such as "if A is greater than B and B is greater than C, then A is greater than C." Similar advances can be seen in other areas, including the child's thinking about space, time, and causality. Flavell (1970) has reviewed much of the evidence that was available prior to 1970 on the emergence of concrete operational thought.

To be sure, there have also been some discordant notes in this generally harmonious body of data, such as reports of number conservation in 2-year-olds (Mehler & Bever, 1967), or evidence of greatly delayed or even unattained conservation among Australian aborigines (Dasen, 1973). However, these exceptions generally involve problems of method and interpretation, which make them less exceptional than they might at first appear (for example, see Rothenberg & Courtney, 1968; Cole & Scribner, 1974). By and large, the existing data are remarkably consistent—in their broad outlines—with Piaget's own observations.

It might be said, then, that the research surrounding Piaget's theory provides approximate age norms regarding the development of concrete logic. Such norms could be useful to educators as rough guidelines for the planning of curriculum and instruction. For his own part, however, Piaget has never been especially concerned with the specific ages at which cognitive changes take place. Instead, he sees the *sequence* of development as a much more important question, and he has insisted that, above all, his periods form a fixed developmental sequence which children must go through one step at a time. Oddly enough, though, the sequentiality of Piaget's periods hardly seems to be an empirical research question at all. It can be argued that the structures that define the periods form a necessary sequence on logical grounds alone, in the sense that each more advanced structure presupposes or incorporates the ones that precede it. If so, then Piaget's position on the

---

[7] Several other authors have already addressed the same question (Wohlwill, 1963; Pinard & Laurendeau, 1969; Pascual-Leone, 1973). However, it seems desirable to discuss the issue again here, to make clear its relevance for readers with an interest in educational practice.

sequentiality of his structures is unassailable. But do these structures actually explain child thought? *Do they account for the kinds of performance that distinguish one period of development from another?* This is the most fundamental question of all. To answer it, one must examine behavior and development *within* each period, to see if one finds the regularities that are predicted from Piaget's notion of whole structures.

Taking Piaget's formal theoretical system at face value, one is led to make a very strong prediction about the onset of concrete operations: Once a child begins to manifest concrete operations in some situations, he should—at the same time—begin to manifest the same type of thinking in all other situations as well. The transition from preoperational thought need not be abrupt; the child may initially fall back on intuitive thought quite often. But this sort of inconsistency should occur across the board and to the same degree in all areas of thinking. In other words, the child's thinking over a variety of conceptual domains should exhibit the kind of developmental "synchrony" generally emphasized by Piaget. It is clear now, however, that this prediction of synchronous development is often disconfirmed. Brainerd (1975), for example, cites a body of evidence indicating that children perform certain tasks involving seriation earlier than theoretically equivalent tasks requiring classification. Interestingly, a slight delay in classification versus seriation was also noted by Inhelder and Piaget (1964), who suggested that seriation tasks sometimes permit intuitive perceptual solutions that are not possible in classification. In general, however, such time lags between different areas have not been prominent in Piaget's own work because he usually has observed a particular child's thinking in just one area at a time. Other studies, by examining each child's performance on a variety of tasks, have made the lack of expected synchronies much more obvious.

Perhaps it is too much to expect all eight groupings of concrete operations to emerge in lockstep fashion as one grand whole structure, even though Piaget has emphasized their interconnectedness and synchrony in development. One alternative, considered by Flavell and Wohlwill (1969), is to regard each grouping or domain of cognition as a separate whole structure by itself, related to but not necessarily synchronous with the others. This proposal, while weakening the unity of the concrete operational period, would at least be consistent with the kind of asynchrony mentioned above (although one would then want some explanation as to why the groupings or domains emerge in one order rather than another). Moreover, it would still lead us to expect synchronous developmental changes in performance of tasks that are supposed to involve the same grouping of operations, or which fall within the same domain.

Unfortunately, the empirical facts do not accord very well with this more limited view of whole structures either. Even within the same domain of cognition, several years may separate the ages at which "concrete operations" are manifested with respect to different content. Piaget and his associates discovered long ago that, while children generally conserve *amounts* of a substance at about age 7, they do not conserve *weight* until about age 9, or *volume* (as indicated by the displacement of water) until about 11 (Piaget & Inhelder, 1941). Essentially the same time lag in conservation has been found more recently by other researchers as well (e.g., Elkind, 1961; Uzgiris, 1964). Because this discrepancy between tasks occurs on the same developmental level, Piaget has called it a "horizontal decalage," and has suggested that it results from differences between physical properties in the extent to which they "resist" assimilation to the operations of conservation.[8] However, the factors producing this differential resistance have not been clearly explained, and there is no adequate basis for predicting other horizontal decalages that are observed. In general, then, the phenomenon of horizontal decalage raises serious questions as to the predictive utility of Piaget's concrete operational groupings, even when they are taken only one at a time.

So far we have considered evidence of sequential development where one might have expected synchrony. While this evidence casts doubt on the particular structures identified by Piaget to account for performance, it might still be compatible with the general idea that development consists of a fixed sequence of more or less global cognitive structures. That is, it might be argued that such structures do exist but have yet to be described in a fashion that would enable us to predict a child's performance from one task to another. However, there are two additional complications in the existing data which would pose problems for any theory of structural stages along Piagetian lines. First, the observed order of acquisition between two concrete operational tasks has sometimes varied from one study to another (Achenbach & Weisz, 1975). Second, the relative difficulty of two or more tasks has also been observed to vary from one *child* to another within the same study. In other words, it is not unusual to find, with two structurally related tasks, that some children pass Task A and fail Task B, while others pass B and fail A. Since individual differences of this sort seem especially important from a practical standpoint, we will discuss one example from the research literature in some detail.

Uzgiris (1964) gave children from grades one through six a set of tasks involving the conservation of amount, weight, and volume with four different kinds of material. She found strong evidence of the horizontal decalage between amount, weight, and volume *within* each type of material, but she also found that correlations of overall conservation performance *among* the various materials were not as high as one would expect. For example, the correlations between performance with plasticine balls and with metal cubes ranged from .31 in the fifth grade to .80 in the first grade, with the average correlation being about .57. It seems unlikely that this finding of only moderate correlations can be attributed entirely to unreliability of the scores in view of the great regularity with which the different forms of conservation ordered themselves for each type of material. Thus the data appear to reflect true individual differences in performance—differences in something other than the overall rate of development. Uzgiris suggests that the performance differences she observed were due to differences in past experience with the kinds of

---

[8] It has been suggested in some places (e.g. Inhelder & Piaget, 1958) that the conservation of volume actually requires formal operations, and therefore represents a *vertical* decalage relative to substance and weight conservation. However, the present argument would still apply to the decalage between substance and weight.

materials used in her experiment. As plausible as this explanation may be, there are at least two reasons why it should not be accepted uncritically. First, it begs the question of *how* experience affects performance. It is not enough to say that more experience with a particular kind of material leads to a higher level of performance with that material. For both theoretical and practical reasons, we would like to know exactly what kind of experience and how much of it will make a difference. Second, it is highly unlikely that all individual differences can be reduced to differential experience with particular content, as we will see below.

In sum, it appears that the whole-structure notion is not sufficient to account for many of the observed relationships among tasks that are supposed to involve concrete operations. Later we shall consider the possibility that Piagetian whole structures are not even *necessary* in psychological explanations of cognitive performance.

Equilibration, Learning, and Development

A particularly popular type of Piagetian research, especially among American psychologists, has been the training experiment. Numerous investigators have attempted to teach children to perform one or another of Piaget's tasks. In many instances, these attempts appear to have successfully induced operational thinking where it was initially absent and presumably would not have emerged for some time to come. In other cases, such training has failed. We may try, then, to assess Piaget's notions regarding the processes of cognitive development and learning in light of the successes and failures that have been reported in training experiments.[9]

Some of the early interest in training seems to have been based on erroneous assumptions about Piaget's theory. It was thought that if children as young as 4 or 5 could be taught to conserve, for example, then Piaget's maturational timetable would be called into question. As we have seen, however, Piaget's theory makes no commitment to specific age norms or to maturation as the prime cause of development. In fact, successful training seems quite compatible (at least up to a point) with the Piagetian view of experience as a provider of content for assimilation to existing cognitive structures and as a source of disequilibrium that leads to restructuring.

Training experiments have also aroused a more practical interest among people who would like to find methods for speeding up the rate of development through teaching. Although Piaget has acknowledged the possibility of accelerating development, he has also suggested that attempts to do so might generally do more harm than good (Piaget, 1964). It may be that Piaget's skepticism in this regard comes more from personal opinion than from his theory, but he certainly is correct in questioning the assumption that faster development is necessarily better (see Rohwer, Ammon, & Cramer, 1974, Pp. 243–245). Even where acceleration does

---

[9] For extended reviews and discussions of the literature on Piagetian training experiments, see Beilin (1971), Brainerd and Allen (1971), Glaser and Resnick (1972), Strauss (1972; 1974), and Brainerd (1973).

seem desirable, it probably is not enough just to know that certain training procedures have proven effective in previous experiments. Practical applications of research findings are much more likely to succeed if one understands *why* the experimental procedures have produced positive effects. Thus we are still faced with the problem of interpreting the training research from a theoretical point of view. In the present context, we want to see whether Piaget's theory provides a satisfactory interpretation.

Piaget's ideas about the process of equilibration are much less clear than his description of the structures that are supposed to underlie cognition, but there are two general propositions about learning and development that can be assessed in connection with the results from training experiments. These are the claims that a child (*1*) must experience disequilibrium in order to restructure or consolidate his thinking, and (*2*) must already possess the structural "competence" for specific experiences to have a progressive effect. Each of these propositions will be considered in turn.

Some investigators have set out deliberately to provoke disequilibrium in young children and thereby to induce the emergence of concrete operational thinking. In one study, Smedslund (1961) gave preoperational children aged 5 and 6 a series of modified conservation problems involving two quantities of plasticine that were initially identical in size and shape. With the child watching, one quantity (A) was then deformed to appear greater (or less) than before, while the second quantity (B) was actually increased (or decreased) by the addition or subtraction of a small piece of the plasticine. Finally, the child was asked to judge which quantity, if any, was larger. This procedure was intended to bring about a conflict between the child's tendency to respond on the basis of perceptual appearance (A > B) and his tendency to respond on the basis of his knowledge that addition causes an increase in amount (B > A). Presumably those children who resolved the conflict in favor of their addition—subtraction schemes would be more likely to see, in the standard conservation task, that two quantities remain the same despite the perceptual deformation of one, so long as nothing has been added or taken away. In fact, when Smedslund administered the standard conservation task as a posttest, he obtained results that were consistent with this prediction. About one-third of the subjects resolved the training conflicts in favor of addition—subtraction and then gave correct conservation responses on the posttest.

Because these subjects acquired conservation without ever being told whether or not their answers were correct during training, Smedslund's results have been taken to indicate the importance of disequilibrium in the process of development. However, other studies have shown that simply *telling* children when they are right and when they are wrong can also be an effective means of training conservation (Bucher & Schneider, 1973). Here, too, it is possible to interpret the results as support for the role of disequilibrium, although the conflict in this case is between the child's view of what is correct and an external indication that his view is wrong. A similar interpretation in terms of disequilibrium has been suggested for other successful training methods as well, such as exposure to a model who exhibits conservation responses, or procedures that demonstrate to the child that his intuitive predictions are disconfirmed when the materials are weighed or tested in some other fashion (see Brainerd, 1973). In fact, it is hard to imagine *any* training method which, if successful, could not be said to involve disequilibrium of some sort. Even if a child just learns a verbal rule that he then invokes in the conservation task (Beilin, 1965), one could still argue that either the initial learning or the subsequent application of the rule entailed disequilibrium, in that it conflicted with the child's former way of thinking. At this point, it seems that the existence of disequilibrium as a necessary part of cognitive change may be another nonquestion, so far as empirical research is concerned.

Of course not all attempts at training have succeeded; failures are easy to find in the literature, even in those experiments that have been identified as instances of successful training through disequilibrium. Recall, for example, that the majority of Smedslund's (1961) subjects continued to judge quantity by perceptual appearance and did not acquire conservation. Proponents of Piaget's theory may contend, however, that subjects who are left unchanged by training simply lack the structural means to resolve the disequilibrium that is involved, or even to experience the disequilibrium subjectively. This brings us to the second of our Piagetian propositions about learning and development.

If a certain structural competence is required for training to have a progressive effect, then it should be possible to predict which children can be trained successfully and which cannot. A frequent finding in training experiments is that training succeeds more often with subjects who exhibit a mixture of intuitive and operational thought before training, as opposed to subjects who seem "purely" intuitive. Sometimes the mixture of stages appears as inconsistent performance on the to-be-trained criterion task, in which case the subjects are often called "transitional" (e.g. Inhelder, Sinclair, & Bovet, 1974). Another kind of stage mixture is the cooccurrence of consistently intuitive thought on the criterion task along with evidence of concrete operations in the performance of other tasks (e.g., Langer & Strauss, 1972). In either case, it can be argued that training simply "brings out" a structure that was already present, in keeping with Piaget's views about the dependence of learning on development.

The same results have also been cited as evidence that disequilibrium is a necessary part of cognitive change (e.g., Strauss, 1972), the assumption being that children who vacillate between different ways of thinking are in a state of disequilibrium. Thus the data demonstrating greater trainability in the presence of stage mixture seem consistent with both of the Piagetian propositions about learning and development. However, these data would be consistent with just about any other theory as well, and therefore do not constitute especially strong support for Piaget (see Brainerd, 1973).

Furthermore, positive effects of training *have* been obtained with children who seem truly intuitive, by virtue of age and pretest performance. Gelman (1969) trained kindergartners to discriminate the cues involved in judgments of number versus length and then found a high level of transfer to the conservation of liquid and solid amounts, not to mention length and number. All of her subjects had been consistent nonconservers on a pretest. Strauss (1972) has suggested that Gelman's subjects may well have had certain structural prerequisites anyway—structures that would not have been present in younger children. In support of this argument, he cites a study by Christie and Smothergill (1970) in which a modified version of Gelman's training procedure failed to produce positive results with children whose average age was only 4 years, 3 months as opposed to 5.5. But even if one overlooks some potentially important changes in procedure, the Christie and Smothergill study seems rather unconvincing as counterevidence in the light of more recent evidence that 4-year-olds can be trained to perform conservation tasks (Bucher & Schneider, 1973; see also Lefebvre & Pinard, 1974).

Wherever training is successful, it can always be argued that the needed structural competence was actually present, at least in some latent form. As a general principle, this obviously must be true. But in order to prevent the argument from being entirely circular in a particular instance, it is necessary to specify—in advance—some independent criterion by which structural competence can be assessed. At this point it becomes important to ask exactly what this competence might be. In those instances where "transitional" subjects respond well to training, the putative competence seems to be the very structure that is the object of training. But the to-be-realized structure clearly cannot always be its own prerequisite because one must ultimately account for the initial emergence of a given structure. Evidently it is not enough, either, to say that intuitive thought in general provides the structural competence for acquisition of concrete operations, since some concrete operational tasks are difficult, if not impossible, to teach to some intuitive subjects. It seems, then, that in speaking of structural competence one must at least identify the specific intuitive schemes that are relevant to the criterion task, and even that still may not be sufficient (see the discussion of Pascual-Leone's "M operator" below).

In sum, Piaget's ideas regarding disequilibrium and structural competence are so general that they seem capable of explaining virtually everything *post hoc,* but incapable of generating *a priori* predictions about the effects of specific experiences on learning and development. In other words, they suffer from the same sort of limitation as Piaget's ideas about the logical structures underlying cognition.

A BRIEF EVALUATION OF PIAGET'S THEORY

There is no question that Piaget has made a tremendous contribution to our knowledge about cognitive development, by demonstrating how different the young child's thinking is from that of older children and adults, and by showing that similar developmental changes occur in many different areas of thought. Our concern here, however, is not with Piaget's data, but rather with the formal theory he has proposed to account for it. Having summarized the theory and reviewed some of the research that bears upon its basic premises, we turn now to the question of how well the theory speaks to those issues identified earlier as the particular concerns of educators.

Readiness

According to Piaget's theory, a child's readiness is determined by the stage he is in or, more precisely, by his present cognitive structure. As we have seen, however, the structures that define the major Piagetian periods do not enable one to predict a child's performance with much precision. In general, one is more likely to find thinking that seems "concrete operational" with 7-year-olds than with 5-year-olds. In general, a child who exhibits concrete operations in one task is more likely to do so in other tasks. However, there are also many instances in which a child's performance varies between intuitive and operational from one situation to another. The theory contains ways of explaining situational variation in performance *after it has been observed,* but it does not provide a general framework for identifying the sources of variation ahead of time. Consequently, it is often difficult to know what kind of thinking one can take for granted with a given child in the context of a particular learning task.

The difficulty of using Piaget's theory to determine readiness is further compounded by the fact that it really has very little to say about the trainability of thinking skills that have not already developed spontaneously. Both the theory and the rough age norms associated with it are based on observations of "spontaneous" development in "normal" environments. Thus a child's readiness to learn through special interventions may often by underestimated. Moreover, although the theory assumes that readiness results from both maturation and experience, it does not spell out exactly how each factor contributes to readiness at a particular point in development. As a result, it generally is not clear how far one can go in *promoting* readiness through experience (instead of waiting for it to emerge through maturation).

Learning

If Piaget's theory does not spell out the contribution of experience to readiness, it is because the theory does not contain an adequate explanation of learning in general. As we noted earlier, the concepts of assimilation, accommodation, and equilibration are used in Piagetian theory to characterize the processes by which cognitive structures are modified and reorganized through the individual's activity. It follows from these concepts that structural (i.e., assimilatory) competence and disequilibrium are necessary internal conditions for cognitive change to occur. But, just as these notions do not lead to predictions that can be falsified, they do not imply any specific procedures or even general strategies to promote learning.

Some followers of Piaget have emphasized the principle that experiences will be most conducive to learning and development if they are neither too easy nor too difficult for the child to assimilate (e.g., Hunt, 1961; Ginsburg & Opper, 1969).

How, though, can we know with any precision what a child will be able to assimilate and what he will not? This is the same problem we faced in trying to predict a child's performance from one situation to another. Even if we were to proceed on a trial-and-error basis, the business of recognizing the optimal "match" between a child and a set of alternative learning experiences would still be quite uncertain. If a particular experience is assimilated in the desired way immediately, is it therefore unproductive? If it is *not* assimilated immediately, is it therefore too difficult? The fact is that Piaget's theory simply does not specify the conditions under which learning will occur in a way that is practically useful.

Individual Differences

On the face of it, Piaget's theory seems to allow for individual differences of just one sort—namely, differences in the rate of progress through the stages of development, due either to heredity or to general effects of the environment. Yet we have seen evidence that there are also important individual differences in performance within the set of tasks that Piaget has used to define one of his major stages, the subperiod of concrete operations. We might add that individual differences of this sort become even more obvious in the period of formal operations.

Piaget (1972) and other theorists have argued that such differences are not imcompatible with the notion of structurally defined stages since the structures might be applied to some fields of content and not others, according to an individual's experience and interests. But without explicit accounts of learning and motivation, this way of reconciling whole structures with individual differences seems entirely gratuitous. Like the problem of learning, individual differences have suffered more from neglect that from mistreatment in the context of Piaget's theory.

Cognition and Affect

Another neglected area, and one which might account for some individual differences, is the relationship between cognition and affect. Piaget has acknowledged that interests, needs, and values are involved in all behavior, in that they energize activity and determine its goals. At the same time, he has said that all behavior involves cognitive structures too, as they determine the ways in which selected goals are approached. There is, then, a relationship of mutual dependence between cognition and affect. But Piaget has mainly been concerned with describing the cognitive structures themselves, and—to a much lesser extent—with showing the structural parallels between cognitive and affective development. He has not concerned himself with the specific functional relations between cognition and affect in the determination of behavior, and therefore he has not provided a theoretical basis for taking account of affective influences on cognition in actual practice.

In conclusion, we have seen that, with regard to each criterion of evaluation, Piaget's theory leaves much to be desired, either because it offers no specific predictions or because the predictions that can be derived from it are often disconfirmed. Of course Piaget's interest in cognitive development has been philosophical rather than practical, and his theory may therefore by quite consistent with his own goals. Nevertheless, when the theory is evaluated from a practical point of view, a number of shortcomings can be seen. Further consideration of these shortcomings with specific reference to early childhood education will be postponed until we have summarized and evaluated a second theory in the same fashion as Piaget's.

THE NEO-PIAGETIAN THEORY OF PASCUAL-LEONE

In recent years, a growing number of developmental psychologists have recognized the need to go beyond the explicit theory proposed by Piaget in order to deal with such problems as horizontal decalages and individual differences. In general, two courses of action are possible. One is to accept Piaget's basic theory as far as it goes and then add other theoretical components to make the theory a more powerful predictor of child behavior. An extension of this sort has been outlined by Flavell and Wohlwill (1969), for example. The second approach is to *revise* Piaget's theory, at least in part, before proceeding with extensions. A prime candidate for revision would appear to be Piaget's notion of "whole structures," because the use of such structures to define developmental stages and explain performance seems to create more problems than it can solve. In fact, this is the course taken by Juan Pascual-Leone in his "theory of constructive operators," to which we turn our attention now.[10]

Pascual-Leone's theory has been selected for the present discussion for several reasons. First, it is more fully worked out, both in breadth and depth, than other alternatives to Piaget that have been proposed to date, although it certainly should not be regarded as a finished product. Second, there is a small but growing body of evidence supporting its unique assumptions and suggesting that it can successfully make rather strong predictions about a child's ability to perform (or to learn) a particular cognitive task. And, third, the theory seems especially promising as a tool for educators because of the extent to which it addresses educationally important issues. Each of these points will be considered in turn in the present section and those that follow.

Schemes and Scheme Boosters

We began our summary of Piaget's theory with an overview of his developmental stages. The idea of stages, or levels of development, lives on in the theory of

[10] At present it is difficult for readers to gain access to Pascual-Leone's theory through published writings. The most systematic accounts of his approach are contained in Pascual-Leone (1969; 1973). However, the theory is also discussed in more abbreviated form in Pascual-Leone (1970; 1976a), Pascual-Leone and Smith (1969), and Case (1972a; 1974).

constructive operators too, although the levels are defined in a very different way. In order to understand these levels—and a good deal more about Pascual-Leone's theory—we must begin with the fundamental concepts of schemes and scheme boosters (Pascual-Leone, 1976a).

Recall Piaget's use of the term *scheme* for certain repeated patterns of action or thought. In general, a scheme is a psychological entity which one postulates to account for observed regularities in behavior. According to the theory of constructive operators, all cognitive functioning can be analyzed in terms of the activity of schemes. The schemes themselves vary with regard to the functions they perform. Some schemes produce mental representations of particular "facts" or states of affairs; for example, "The sky is blue right now." Other schemes transform or "operate" on such facts to produce new facts; for example, a scheme representing the rule "When the sky is blue, it does not rain" might be applied to "The sky is blue right now" to produce "It is not raining right now." (The verbal mode of representation is used as a matter of convenience here, but schemes like these are not necessarily verbal.) In addition, schemes may also vary with regard to their level of generality or abstractness. For example, there might be schemes for representing particular people and a scheme for representing the class or category of people in general.

Despite these variations in schemes, all schemes function as *units* that contain a *releasing* component and an *effecting* component. The releasing component refers to the antecedent conditions under which a scheme will be released or activated. These conditions may be either sensory inputs from the environment or prior mental events (or both). The effecting component of a scheme refers to the immediate consequences that result once the scheme has been released. The consequences can be purely mental, such as representations of particular facts, transformations of old facts into new ones, or representations of transformations. A scheme's effecting component can also involve certain observable motor acts, including speech.

At any given moment, a large subset of all the schemes in a person's repertoire is likely to be "active." In Piagetian terminology, the active schemes are attempting to assimilate various aspects of the situation. The subset of active schemes is known as the *field of activation* and changes constantly from moment to moment in response to changes in internal and external conditions. Imagine a child of 3 or 4 who is taken into a room full of toys. As soon as the child enters the room, the sight of the toys will immediately lead to the activation of several schemes in his total repertoire— schemes representing the toys and their attributes, and schemes for actions that could be performed with them. As the child begins to explore the room, his field of activation will change somewhat because he will discover additional toys that were not obvious at first and the schemes released by these "new" toys will become part of the field of activation. Other schemes will drop out of the field as they become inactive. In addition to the schemes released more or less directly by visual input, the child's field of activation may also include schemes that are released by the visually activated schemes themselves in a kind of chain reaction. Other schemes may even remain active from whatever the child was doing before he entered the room.

The field of activated schemes at any moment could cause the child to do a number of things in the room full of toys, since he might approach any of the toys he has seen and then play with each one in several different ways. The outer limit on these many possibilities is set only by the schemes the child has in his repertoire for perceiving, thinking about, and acting upon the toys. But the child obviously will not pursue all of these possibilities—at least not all at once. What, then, determines the particular toys the child will attend to and the particular activities he will engage in once he enters the room? The final arbiter in this decision, according to Pascual-Leone's theory, is the relative "weighting" of the schemes in the field of activation. Some schemes are activated more strongly, or weighted more highly, than others. Those schemes with the highest *activation weights* will be the ones that actually apply to (i.e., assimilate) the situation.

Obviously the theory must also explain what determines the activation weights of a scheme. We have already noted that schemes are activated by "input" from the environment or from the person's previous cognitive activity. Their relative weights are already determined in part by the content of this input. Some schemes are activated more strongly than others because their releasing components are more "satisfied" by the input. For example, the sight of a particular toy might activate both a "doll" scheme and a "puppet" scheme, but the doll scheme would be weighted more heavily if the input from the object were more doll-like than puppetlike, from the child's point of view. Subjectively, the child might simply perceive the object in question as a doll, but unconsciously he would, in effect, have "considered" both possibilities.

But that is not the whole story by any means. The relative weighting of schemes can also be modified. The changes are brought about by cognitive "operators" which are known as *scheme boosters,* because they have the effect of increasing the activation weights of the schemes on which they operate. Thus the total activation weight of a scheme is determined jointly by the content of the input to the scheme along with the various boosters acting upon it. We will discuss briefly three scheme boosters that seem particularly important for understanding cognitive performance, learning, and development.

As the child in our example scans the room full of toys, some of the schemes activated by the sensory input will immediately receive an increased weighting because the input to those schemes is particularly salient or striking. In other words, the child's attention tends to be drawn to some objects more than others, perhaps because of their bright colors or large size. In Pascual-Leone's theory, such salience effects are seen as one manifestation of a scheme booster called the F *operator* (Pascual-Leone, 1969, 1974, 1976b). The same booster can also change the activation weights of schemes in accordance with a principle of cognitive simplicity. Suppose, for example, that the child is asked to point to the left hand of a doll that is facing him. Although he knows left from right with reference to himself, he nonetheless points to the doll's *right* hand. It is cognitively simpler for him to do so because the doll's right hand is directly opposite his own left hand. The basic idea behind the F operator, then, is that certain forces inherent in the field of activation will naturally increase the activation weights of some schemes more than others.

The weighting of schemes can also depend on affective or emotional factors. The sight of a doll might elicit certain feelings in the child which, in turn, may then increase the activation weights of schemes associated with those feelings. Pleasant feelings might lead to a higher weighting of such actions as cuddling or talking softly to the doll; unpleasant feelings might weight the schemes for hitting or scolding the doll. Pascual-Leone has proposed an affective scheme booster, called the *A operator,* to account for the effects of emotion on performance. The A operator works through a special set of affective schemes whose effecting components increase the activation weights of other schemes (such as the motor schemes applied to the doll in our example). The affective schemes may themselves be activated by immediate input from the environment or by past experiences. In the latter case, our hypothetical child might already have certain positive or negative feelings when entering the room as a result of previous interactions with other children or adults. If so, the presence of the doll simply provides an opportunity for specific expressions of those feelings. (Note the similarity to Piaget's view of the relationship between emotion and symbolic play in early childhood.)

So far, our discussion of the child-and-toys example may give the impression that the child's behavior in the presence of the toys is quite aimless, as he responds to whatever happens to strike him from one moment to the next. It is true that the behavior of young children often seems to have a reactive quality of this sort. But, even in early childhood, one can also find many examples of more planful, goal-directed behavior—times at which a child ignores certain distractions in the immediate situation to work toward a more distant objective. For instance, a child might want to build a "house" with some blocks and then proceed to do so. When behavior is directed toward a goal in this way, it is under the control of an *executive scheme,* or—to put it another way—the child's house-building scheme is performing an executive function. What this means is that other schemes in the child's repertoire are activated because they are means to the end of building a house. These other schemes might include the ones involved in finding a block that has the right size and shape to be a "wall," picking the block up, and placing it in proper relation to other parts of the house. Thus, executive schemes can have a hand in determining the total activation weights of other schemes too, along with the input and the F and A operators.

Executives perform this function by directing attention or "mental energy" toward schemes that are particularly relevant to the goal of behavior. The mental energy mobilized by executive schemes is, therefore, another scheme booster, which Pascual-Leone has called the *M operator* (Pascual-Leone, 1969, 1970). It is this mental energy that enables a person to focus on nonsalient aspects of the situation at hand, to perform mental transformations on his representation of the situation, and to think in a directed fashion about objects and events that are remote in time and space. Without an M operator, people would always be at the mercy of immediate input, field forces, and emotions. In other words, they would never get beyond the sensorimotor period!

Indeed, the M operator is a most important scheme booster in terms of development because Pascual-Leone regards M energy as a quantity that increases steadily with age, until adulthood. The growth of M energy is reflected in the number of schemes that can be M-boosted at any given moment, that is, the number of psychological units that can be the focus of attention without assistance from input and other scheme boosters. Table 7.1 indicates the maximum number of schemes that can be M-boosted simultaneously, along with an executive scheme, at each age from early childhood through adolescence. As usual, the ages listed in Table 7.1 are intended as averages that do not preclude individual variations in rate of development. In general, however, it is expected that a child's capacity to boost schemes with the M operator will increase by one scheme every 2 years or so, beginning at about age 3.

With the introduction of these M levels, we have finally arrived at the neo-Piagetian counterpart to Piaget's periods of development, but with three important differences. First, notice that there are more M levels than periods between the ages of 3 and 16. In fact, Pascual-Leone's M levels correspond more or less to the major stages *within* Piaget's periods, which suggests that the M levels may provide a way of explaining the horizontal decalages and other changes that have been observed within the periods. Second, each neo-Piagetian "stage" is defined in terms of a *capacity* to coordinate schemes, and not in terms of a global logical structure. Cognition and behavior are determined by functional structures, called schemes, but the M levels place limits on the kinds of schemes a child can construct and on the ways he can use his schemes in performing a cognitive task. Finally, unlike the Piagetian stages, the growth of M energy is assumed to be virtually independent of specific experience, and therefore it represents mainly a contribution of maturation to development.

TABLE 7.1
Neo-Piagetian M levels in Relation to Age and Piagetian Stages[a]

Age	Piagetian stage	M level
3–4	Early preoperations	$e + 1$
5–6	Late preoperations	$e + 2$
7–8	Early concrete operations	$e + 3$
9–10	Middle concrete operations	$e + 4$
11–12	Late concrete–early formal operations	$e + 5$
13–14	Middle formal operations	$e + 6$
15–16	Late formal operations	$e + 7$

[a]Based on Case, 1974.

Aside from its role in explaining cognitive development, Pascual-Leone believes the concept of an M operator is needed to account for "truly novel" behavior, that is, behavior that cannot be attributed directly to past learning. Novel behavior occurs when one or more schemes are applied to a situation *for the first time* through the boosting effect of the M operator. In fact, many developmental tasks require exactly this sort of novel behavior, at least when they are first presented to untrained subjects. In any case, it might be said that mental energy enables people to transcend their past experience. On the other hand, the M operator can also enter into the very process of learning from experience too, as the following discussion will show.

Two Processes of Learning

According to the theory of constructive operators, cognitive development results not only from changes in a child's mental capacity, but also from changes in his repertoire of schemes. Thus we turn now to the question of how new schemes are acquired, that is, the question of learning. Piaget has noted that certain inborn, reflexive schemes are already present in the neonate, and he maintains that these initial schemes are modified by experience to become the cognitive structures that characterize each succeeding stage of development. In his view, there is both differentiation of new schemes from old ones, by simple assimilation and accommodation, and integration of new structures through "reciprocal" assimilation among old schemes. Following this lead, Pascual-Leone (1969, 1976a) has distinguished two basic processes by which new schemes are constructed: a gradual process something like conditioning, called *C learning*, and a more "insightful" and often rapid process, called *L learning*.

In C learning, which concerns the "content" of schemes, new cues are added to the releasing component of an old scheme.[11] In other words, the new scheme is differentiated from the old one by the additional cues and is activated by the old and new cues in combination. To illustrate C learning, suppose a young child initially regards many horselike animals as "horsies." In other words, the child has a "horsie" scheme which is released by a set of features that horses and many horselike animals have in common. Gradually, through repeated exposure to horses, other features that distinguish horses from their near relations (donkeys, ponies, etc.) will be added to the releasing component of the original horsie scheme to produce a new, more refined horse scheme. In order for this to happen, the original horsie scheme must be activated strongly on several occasions when other schemes representing the additional features are also activated to some extent, as would occur in the presence of a true horse. Because the child's attention is not on the new features per se, but on the horse as a whole, the learning process may take

---

[11] C learning can also involve the addition of new elements to the *effecting* component of a scheme, as well as to the releasing component, but we need not discuss both of these possibilities here.

quite some time, and the child will probably remain unaware of what the new features are. Eventually, however, there is a differentiated horse scheme, which is more strongly activated than the old horsie scheme in the presence of true horses, but not in the presence of other horselike animals.

It is conceivable that the refinement of a child's horse concept could also be accomplished, more rapidly, through the process of L learning. Suppose the child learns a rule to the effect that "horses have shorter ears and longer necks than donkeys." (Again, we use a verbal statement of the rule merely as a convenience, without implying that L learning is essentially verbal.) The learning (or discovery) of such a rule illustrates L learning because it involves the conscious integration of several constituent schemes—horse, donkey, ears, neck, long—short—into an overall structure. According to Pascual-Leone's theory, such conscious integrations are possible only when the constituent schemes simultaneously receive high activation weights on at least two occasions (two being the minimum needed to establish the regularity involved in the rule). In many cases the condition of simultaneous high weightings can only be fulfilled if some (or all) of the schemes are boosted by M. Thus a child's M level sets an upper limit on his ability to integrate schemes into more complex structures through L learning. Structures acquired by L learning have a kind of flexibility not ordinarily found in schemes that are differentiated through C learning. In our example, the "rule" structure might enable the learner not only to discriminate visually between horses and donkeys, but also to answer such questions as "How are horses different from donkeys?" or "What has longer ears, a horse or a donkey?"[12]

The two learning processes, C and L, are not mutually exclusive. In fact, a certain amount of C learning is always bound to accompany L learning, because the conditions for the latter include the conditions for the former; however, the reverse is not true. In any case, the schemes in a person's repertoire are essentially the products of past C and L learning. The subsequent application of those schemes in the performance of a cognitive task depends on their momentary activation weights as determined by the input to the psychological system along with the various scheme boosters. In addition, both learning and performance are also influenced by individual differences in "cognitive style."

Cognitive Style

A number of investigators have noted what appear to be reliable individual differences in the way people perform cognitive tasks. Because these differences seem to arise from the general approach a person takes to a variety of problems,

---

[12] It seems quite consistent with the theory of constructive operators to imagine complex structures being integrated through C learning too. This might occur if the effecting component of one scheme became incorporated in the releasing component of another. Long chains or networks of schemes could be constructed from such links, and the links could even be bidirectional. However, given the gradual nature of C learning, a limiting factor in constructions of this sort would be the sheer amount of experience required.

they have come to be known as differences in "cognitive style." A particularly well researched dimension of cognitive style is one called *field dependence–independence* (Witkin, Dyk, Faterson, Goodenough, & Karp, 1962). Field-*de*pendent people find it difficult to overcome the forces inherent in a perceptual field, as evidenced, for example, by the difficulty they have in adjusting a tilted rod to the true vertical when it is surrounded by a tilted frame. Field-*in*dependent people are better able to perform such a task because they impose another, more helpful, frame of reference on the misleading perceptual field.

Pascual-Leone (1969, 1974) has attempted to explicate field dependence–independence in terms of the theory of constructive operators. His analysis is too complex to be presented in detail here, so it must suffice to say that he believes field-independent people tend to make maximum use of their M energy to overcome misleading field effects. In contrast, field-dependent people are inclined to apply exactly those schemes that are strongly boosted by the F operator, even when it would be within their capacity to M boost other schemes that would be more appropriate for the task at hand. Individual tendencies to be field dependent or independent reside in general stylistic schemes which are somewhat akin to affective schemes in that their effecting components boost other schemes. In this case, the other schemes are executive strategies that cause the individual to approach a task in one way or another. The style schemes themselves are released by features of the task situation. Pascual-Leone has proposed a similar analysis for the related style dimension of "adaptive flexibility," and the same thing could presumably be done with other dimensions of cognitive style as well.

If the use of M energy is the key to greater field independence, and if available M energy increases with age, this suggests an explanation for the empirical fact that field independence also increases with age. But differences in field dependence–independence are not entirely developmental. Along with the developmental trend toward greater field independence, there are still important individual differences on this dimension at each M level. These differences must be taken into account when an individual's performance is predicted for a particular task. If the task presents a conflict between inappropriate F-boosted schemes and appropriate M-boosted schemes, then field-dependent subjects ought to perform as if their M capacity were lower than it actually is, whereas field-independent subjects would not have this discrepancy between functional and potential M levels. On the other hand, if the task contains no such conflict, then individual differences in field dependence–independence might not matter. Finally, there might be tasks where field dependence could even be an advantage. Which of these possibilities actually obtains in a given instance can only be determined by a detailed analysis of the task at hand.

Early Childhood

When viewed from the perspective of Pascual-Leone's theory, the early childhood years are distinguished particularly by the child's very limited capacity to engage in thinking that requires mental energy for attention to relevant information. As we have seen, this capacity is defined as the number of schemes that can be boosted simultaneously by the M operator: only one scheme at ages 3 and 4, two at ages 5 and 6, and three at ages 7 and 8. If we go on to examine the implications of these M levels, a number of similarities and differences can be seen between the Piagetian and neo-Piagetian points of view.

The fact that Pascual-Leone's theory does attribute *some* mental attentional energy to children as young as 3 seems quite consistent with Piaget's view that mental representation begins to develop significantly at the end of the sensorimotor period. After all, the M operator is postulated, first and foremost, to account for a person's ability to think about objects and events which are not salient in the immediate situation, and that seems to be the defining characteristic of representational thought according to Piaget. Furthermore, the idea that young children have only a severely limited capacity for such representation seems perfectly congruent with Piaget's emphasis on the "centered" nature of preoperational thinking. With only enough M energy to boost one or two schemes at a time, the child's thinking is bound to be centered in any case; but the problem is further compounded by the F and A operators, which—more or less by default—can often dominate the child's cognition and cause him to center on salient or compelling aspects of the situation at hand. In addition, the increments in M capacity between the ages of 3 and 8 parallel the shifts in Piaget's theory from preconceptual to intuitive to operational thought. Thus it appears that both theories have distinguished three cognitive levels in early childhood.[13]

Despite these similarities between the two approaches, there are also important differences. The most basic difference is that Pascual-Leone defines developmental levels in terms of a capacity and not in terms of cognitive structures, such as the groupings of concrete operations. For Piaget, the preoperational subperiod is characterized primarily by the *lack* of concrete operations, as the name implies. Of course, the older preoperational child does possess certain intuitive rules, which may be invoked on some occasions, e.g., "the longer the row, the greater the number of objects in it." But it is still difficult to predict behavior in early childhood from Piagetian theory because one is in a better position to say what a child will *not* do, or what he *might* do, than to say what he *will* do. It is not possible to predict behavior solely on the basis of Pascual-Leone's M levels, either. When and how an individual will *use* the M capacity he has depends on his repertoire of schemes, including affective schemes and cognitive style schemes, along with features of the particular situation under consideration. However, the theory of constructive operators does provide a basis for making behavioral predictions when all of these factors are taken into account.

---

[13] The division of the preoperational subperiod into just two developmental levels still seems far too gross to account for all the cognitive changes that can be observed from 3 to 6. Case (personal communication) has suggested recently that this period is characterized by rapid growth of a "figurative" capacity which differs from the more "operative" M capacity in that it concerns the number of *input* units a child can attend to at once. This proposal may ultimately give the theory of constructive operators greater "resolution" for analyzing early childhood, but it remains to be elaborated further.

The neo-Piagetian focus on capacity rather than structure has important implications regarding the young child's readiness to learn. Of the two learning processes, L learning would be more adversely affected by low levels of M capacity because the child would lack the mental power to boost schemes to the high level that is required for their rapid integration into a more complex structure. Consequently, there might be many things that older children can learn quickly, through L learning, that younger children can only learn through the more arduous process of C learning. Moreover, any schemes acquired in the latter way might still lack the flexibility normally found in structures acquired through L learning. Piaget has suggested similar differences in learning between younger and older children, but he has not explicated these differences in terms of two general learning processes and the development of mental capacity per se.

The question of readiness pertains not only to *how* children can learn, but also to *what* they can learn. According to Piaget's theory, readiness is determined by the presence (or absence) of a particular cognitive structure. Thus the child can only learn to perform tasks which involve a structure the child already has, or is about to acquire. In general, then, one would not expect a 4-year-old to learn how to behave like an 8-year-old in performing a conservation task, for example. (As we have seen, however, such learning has been observed in training experiments.)

On the other hand, if the ultimate constraint on learning is only the child's mental capacity, as Pascual-Leone maintains, then it should be possible, in principle, for a child to learn how to perform *any* task, so long as the task can be broken down into a set of schemes that the child can acquire and apply within the limits of his capacity. In practice, the child's readiness may be further constrained by the ingenuity of his teacher in identifying the necessary schemes and promoting their acquisition, and by the sheer amount of time needed for the learning to occur (it might even take so long that the child would outgrow his need for a long instructional sequence before the sequence was completed). But even within these practical constraints, there is reason to believe that young children can learn more than one might expect from a structural definition of readiness based on Piaget's theory.

In sum, the neo-Piagetian view of early childhood agrees with Piaget's in that autonomous mental representation is regarded as an important but limited aspect of the young child's cognition. It is consistent with both theories to maintain that the child understands his world in terms of relatively simple, intuitive rules. But according to Pascual-Leone's theory, the real hallmark of early childhood is not the set of intuitive rules per se, nor is it the absence of a more advanced cognitive structure; it is the child's limited capacity to coordinate schemes.

NEO-PIAGETIAN RESEARCH

The theory of constructive operators proposed by Pascual-Leone seems quite relevant to the concerns of educators simply by virtue of its explicit attention to such issues as maturation, learning, individual differences, and affective factors in cognition. But does the theory actually succeed in explaining and predicting child behavior? In order to be considered a viable successor to Piaget's theory, the new theory must be able to explain what the old theory could explain, and *more*. It must also account for old data that have posed problems for Piaget's theory, and it must ultimately predict new data too. In fact, Pascual-Leone and his associates have already offered several neo-Piagetian interpretations of past research findings and they have also conducted a number of new studies based directly on the theory of constructive operators. Although the amount of work in both of these areas is still small compared to that which surrounds Piaget's theory, there is enough evidence now to give some indication of the new theory's explanatory and predictive power, as illustrated by the following examples.

New Interpretations of Old Findings

Let us begin with what is probably the best-known finding in all of Piaget's research, namely that children normally do not conserve an equivalence between two quantities of substance until they are about 7. If it is established that quantity A = quantity B, and B is then visibly transformed to B', the 7-year-old understands that A = B'. According to Piaget's theory, the child's understanding of conservation is based on a cognitive structure (concrete operations) which enables him first to see that B = B'—because a change in one dimension of B compensates for a change in another, or because B' could be transformed in reverse back to B—and then to see that, if B = B' and A = B, then A = B'. From the Piagetian perspective, substance-equivalence conservation is seen as just one symptom of the concrete operational whole structure because the child begins to display the same kind of logic in a number of other tasks as well, at about the same time.

How could the same finding be explained in terms of Pascual-Leone's theory? To answer this question, one must begin with a *task analysis* of the conservation task. In general, the object of a task analysis is to set down a series of cognitive operations which, if followed step by step, would lead to successful performance of a particular task. In other words, it is like writing a computer program to solve some sort of problem. With regard to the development of substance-equivalence conservation, the purpose of the task analysis is to construct a theoretical model of the process by which successful 7-year-olds actually solve the problem. Pascual-Leone (1973; 1976b) has suggested that the task involves the following steps, when performed by untrained subjects.

1. Note the initial equivalence of A and B.
2. Bearing in mind that A = B, note that B is transformed into B' (e.g., by pouring).
3. Bearing in mind that A = B and that B → B', and remembering that a transformation like B → B' does not change quantity, conclude that B = B'.
4. Bearing in mind that A = B and B = B', conclude that A = B'.

Each of these steps has been analyzed further into the particular schemes that are required and the ways in which they are activated. From this analysis, it can be shown that the third step is the most difficult. In the first place, it requires the simultaneous activation of *four* schemes: an executive scheme for judging equalities of quantity on the basis of previous events in the task situation (versus the final appearance of the quantities); a scheme representing the initial equality A = B; a scheme representing the transformation B → B'; and a scheme representing the rule that the kind of transformation involved in B → B' (i.e., pouring) does not change the quantity of the substance. Furthermore, *all* of these schemes must be boosted by the M operator because there is nothing in the immediate situation at Step 3 to keep any of their activation weights at a high level. The initial equality A = B is no longer visible, but it must be kept "alive" mentally until Step 4, where it is needed for the final conclusion. Likewise, the transformation B → B' has already occurred, but it must be remembered long enough for the subject to conclude that B = B'. This conclusion is reached by application of a general rule that pouring per se does not change quantity, and that rule itself must also be boosted by M. Finally, the executive scheme (*e*) must be kept in charge throughout the entire task, or else the subject will lose track of what he is doing and fail to boost the other schemes that are needed.

Because step 3 requires the greatest number of schemes to be M-boosted at the same time, the *M demand* of the task as a whole is *e* + 3. This means that substance-equivalence conservation is within the capacity of a child whose M level is also *e* + 3. However, unless the child is relatively field-independent, he might still fall prey to the misleading differences in appearance between A and B', and then conclude, say, that B' is greater. Children who have not yet attained the M level of *e* + 3 (and who have not received special training) would have no choice but to follow the misleading strategy, since they would lack the M capacity to execute the correct strategy, even if they had all the individual schemes that are necessary.

The preceding task analysis constitutes a plausible explanation for the emergence of substance-equivalence conservation in 7-year-olds if one accepts the following assumptions: (*1*) that most children will have acquired all of the schemes involved in Steps 1 through 4 by about age 7, and (*2*) that most children do not attain an M level of *e* + 3 until about age 7. The first assumption seems acceptable on intuitive grounds alone, but it can also be supported by some data and by a formal analysis of the conditions under which the schemes might be acquired, including an assessment of the M levels required for their acquisition. The second assumption has been tested directly, as we will see below, and it gains additional support from the fact that other tasks first performed at age 7 seem to have the same M demand of *e* + 3, as determined by similar task analyses (Pascual-Leone, 1969). Notice that the neo-Piagetian explanation of substance-equivalence conservation makes no appeal to a global structure of concrete operations. The synchronous emergence of conservation and other "concrete operational" tasks is attributed to their common M demand, rather than their common logical structure.

So far it may appear that Pascual-Leone and Piaget simply provide alternative, but equally good, explanations of the same phenomenon. Remember, however, that some conservation tasks, though logically similar to substance-equivalence, are *not* passed by 7-year-olds—a fact that is difficult to explain in terms of Piaget's theory. If Pascual-Leone's approach can account for the horizontal decalages in conservation, then the theory of constructive operators would appear to surpass Piaget's theory in its explanatory power. As it happens, Pascual-Leone (1973) has, in fact, produced task analyses for equivalence conservation of weight and volume, which are generally passed at ages 9 and 11. According to these analyses, the respective M demands are $e + 4$ and $e + 5$. Thus the time lags that have been found in the development of conservation can be attributed to the continued growth of M energy after the initial appearance of conservation behavior. The plausibility of the task analyses for weight and volume conservation rests, again, on assumptions regarding the growth of M and the availability of required schemes in the repertoire. And, once again, there is both empirical and theoretical support for these assumptions. Indeed, Pascual-Leone has actually incorporated some leads from Piaget in his own explanation of the conservation decalages.

By means of task analysis; it is possible to model not only the performance of "naive," untrained children, but also the performance of children who have mastered a particular task earlier than usual as a result of special training. To illustrate this possibility, Pascual-Leone and Smith (1969) have suggested a neo-Piagetian explanation of the success achieved by Kohnstamm (1967) in training young children to solve Piaget's "class inclusion" problem. In a classic instance of this problem, the subject is presented with 20 wooden beads—17 brown and 3 white—and then is asked "Are there more brown beads or more wooden beads?" Children below the age of 7 or 8 almost always reply that there are more *brown* beads, even though they know perfectly well that *all* the beads are wooden. Kohnstamm, however, succeeded in training 5- and 6-year-olds to give reliably logical answers. In essence, his training procedure consisted of repeated practice on a variety of class inclusion problems, with corrective feedback and constant reminders that the test question always required a comparison between one subclass (brown beads) and the *superordinate* class (wooden beads). From a neo-Piagetian perspective, it is not reasonable to assume that the subjects trained in this way were constructing correct responses by the same operations as untrained subjects, because they still would not have had the M capacity ($e + 3$) to execute the usual strategy. But it *is* reasonable to assume that Kohnstamm's training procedure induced the acquisition of a new scheme—one which would not be acquired ordinarily, but which could produce correct responses to the task. After a lot of training, this scheme would be more strongly activated by the task situation than the old, inappropriate scheme. Moreover, its presence would reduce the M demand of the task to $e + 2$, as Pascual-Leone and Smith have shown from a modified task analysis for class inclusion.

If task analysis based on Pascual-Leone's theory can be used to explain the results of past training experiments, it should be possible to *predict* such results as well. The same kind of task analysis could even serve as a blueprint for the content of training by identifying new schemes the learner could use to perform the criterion task. As we will see below, both of these possibilities have been explored to some extent already.

New Findings

A central tenet of Pascual-Leone's theory concerns the growth of the M operator with age, according to the schedule shown in Table 7.1. Several studies have attempted to measure, more or less directly, the number of schemes that children of different ages can M-boost at the same time (Pascual-Leone, 1970; Case, 1972b; Diaz, 1974). In the study by Case, for example, children aged 6, 8, and 10 were shown a series of numbers one at a time, from left to right, such as 3, 8, 12, 6. Their task was to indicate where the last number belonged in the preceding sequence. Thus the 6 above would belong between 3 and 8. Since each number was exposed for just 1.5 sec, the children could only perform this task with consistent success by keeping in mind all of the numbers in a series. According to the theory of constructive operators, a subject should be able to do this by M-boosting a scheme to represent each number, so long as the length of the series does not exceed the subject's M level. The results of Case's experiment confirm this prediction: at age 6 ($M = e + 2$) the majority of subjects could perform perfectly with series of two numbers, but not with series of three; 8-year-olds ($e + 3$) could handle series of three, but only 10-year-olds succeeded with series of four. Diaz (1974) has found similar support for Pascual-Leone's developmental M scale with a task more suited for use with preschool children. The task requires a child to remember which body parts are colored in line drawings of a clown who "keeps changing his clothes." The number of colored parts is varied from trial to trial to determine the child's M level.

Aside from these measures of mental capacity, the theory of constructive operators has also been used to predict performance on other non-Piagetian tasks where the focus is not so much on memory per se. Pascual-Leone and Smith (1969) worked with four variations of a simple communication task. Each test item involved a pair of objects that were similar in some respects but different in others. In the "encoding" tasks, the subject had to indicate which of the two objects he was thinking of by giving the experimenter a clue. The clues were either single words referring to object properties or they were pantomime gestures concerning the object as a whole. In the "decoding" tasks, the experimenter presented the clues, either verbal or gestural, and the subject had to select the object he thought the experimenter had in mind. The M demand of each task was determined by task analysis, with the following results: encoding verbal = $e + 3$, encoding gestural = $e + 2$, and decoding verbal or gestural = $e + 1$. Data collected from children aged 5 to 9 on all four tasks were consistent with these analyses. In the encoding verbal task, for example, 5-year-olds were almost as likely to mention a property that the two objects had in common as they were to give a distinctive clue. At 7-years old, children performed only moderately well on the same task, and 9-year-olds were near perfect.

Case (1972a) used the same four tasks to assess the effects of a kindergarten program that was designed (independently) to promote the development of conceptual skills. A detailed analysis of the curriculum in this program led to the hypothesis that kindergartners who had gone through it would have acquired certain schemes that were relevant to the communication tasks. On the basis of task analyses, it was further hypothesized that the new schemes would reduce the M demands of the two encoding tasks so that specially trained kindergartners would perform the encoding verbal task as well as fourth graders who had received normal instruction, and the encoding gestural task at least as well as normally instructed second graders. When the tasks were administered to appropriate groups of subjects, the results confirmed Case's predictions.

Case (1974) used Pascual-Leone's theory to predict the effects of training in another study, with results that are, in some ways, even more striking than those we have just seen. In this experiment, the training procedure itself was based on a neo-Piagetian analysis of the criterion tasks, which were similar to the "control of variables" problems investigated by Inhelder and Piaget (1958). The apparatus for one task, called Bending Rods, consisted of a vertical baseboard from which a row of 10 different rods projected horizontally. It was explained to the subject that the phenomenon of interest was the degree to which the various rods would bend when weights were placed on them. The problem was to figure out what things caused a given rod to bend more or less. There were actually five factors which affected the degree of bending, including the length and diameter of a rod and the material from which it was made. Once these variables had been pointed out, the subject's task was to conduct experiments that would prove conclusively whether each of them affected bending or not. He was also asked to evaluate inadequate proofs that were suggested by the experimenter.

A problem like Bending Rods can be solved most readily by varying only one factor at a time while all others are held constant. Thus, if a subject wanted to test the effect of length, he would have to select two rods that differed in length but not in any other respect. According to Piaget's theory, the method of "all other things being equal" normally requires formal operations, because the subject must anticipate the alternative hypotheses that would be tenable with an uncontrolled test. In general, then, one would not expect to find this method being used until the ages of 11 or 12. Younger children would think it a sufficient "proof" that length affects bending if *any* long rod bent more than *any* short rod, as Inhelder and Piaget have shown in their own research.

With this background in mind, Case set out to teach 8-year-olds how to control variables using the method of "all other things being equal," expecting on theoretical grounds that he would succeed. His optimism was supported by the following line of analysis. First, task analyses for proof construction and proof checking indicated that the M demand in each case was $e + 3$, which is the capacity of a normal 8-year-old. Furthermore, an examination of the individual schemes involved suggested that all of them would probably be found in the repertoire of a normal 8-year-old, except for the *executive* schemes. Evidently children that age have not yet acquired executives which lead them to make sure that all other things are equal in a proof situation. Another task analysis led to the hypothesis that 8-year-olds could acquire such schemes through training. Specifically, it appeared that repeated exposure to the uncertainties of inadequate proofs would suffice to induce the construction of an adult proof concept, and that the M demand of this construction would again be $e + 3$. Both the prediction of successful training and the training procedure itself followed from this analysis.

Successful training was predicted for 8-year-olds who were field-independent and who conserved substance but not weight. The subjects were selected in this way so that their M levels would be neither higher nor lower than $e + 3$ and they would make maximum use of the M capacity they had. The training procedure was also administered to field-independent 6-year-olds and to field-dependent 8-year-olds, with the expectation that neither group would have the functional M capacity to profit from training. Three parallel groups of children served as untrained control subjects. All subjects were given a posttest that included Bending Rods and another control of variables task called Spinning Wheels, neither of which were used for training. The field-independent 8-year-olds who had received training performed at a distinctly higher level than all other groups. After four brief training sessions, they had learned to solve control of variables problems of the sort represented by Bending Rods.

Case's findings show quite clearly that children can be taught to perform a "formal operations" task long before they would do so normally. The findings do *not* show that 8-year-olds can be taught formal operations per se, in the Piagetian sense of a general ability to engage in hypothetico-deductive thinking. (In fact, the same subjects who learned how to control variables were no better than untrained subjects in performing a combinatorial task that is also supposed to require formal operations.) Nor does it follow from Case's study that 8-year-olds *should* be taught to control variables or perform any other formal operations task. Even though it appears that such learning could be relatively easy and fun for many children, the time spent on it might be devoted to other, more productive activities. The real import of Case's experiment does not lie in the particular results that were obtained, but in the fact that those results were obtained and predicted with the aid of Pascual-Leone's theory. In other words, this last sutdy and the others we have reviewed are of interest primarily because they support theoretical principles that educators may be able to use for their own purposes.

A BRIEF EVALUATION OF PASCUAL-LEONE'S THEORY

In discussing Pascual-Leone's theory and related research, we have alluded a number of times to the evaluation criteria that were applied earlier to Piaget's theory. Consequently the present section will simply summarize the points that have already been made and add a few more remarks about the current state of the theory.

The basic developmental factor in Pascual-Leone's theory is a mental capacity (the M operator) which grows with age and is essentially independent of specific experience. This explanation of development has two important implications with regard to *readiness*. First, it speaks directly to the question of what children at a given age *can* learn, and not just what they ordinarily *do* learn. Second, it makes explicit the contribution of *maturation* as a factor that sets limits on the effects of experience. The contribution of *experience* is explicated as the construction of a repertoire of schemes by the processes called L and C learning. Because the processes of *learning* are spelled out in some detail, the theory provides a basis for arranging conditions in which the construction of a particular scheme will occur. In addition, the schemes that need to be learned for performance of a given task can be determined by task analysis. *Individual differences* of a nondevelopmental sort are explained in two ways. First, individuals may respond differently in the same situation because of differences in the specific schemes they have acquired from past experience—differences which, in principle, can be predicted from the neo-Piagetian theory of learning. Second, more general differences in performance are attributed to cognitive style schemes, which act upon other schemes to introduce certain biases across a variety of situations. Finally, the role of *affect* is explained in a similar fashion, there being affective schemes in the repertoire which, when activated, selectively boost the activation weights of other schemes.

Looking back at Piaget's theory, it seems clear that Pascual-Leone's approach compares favorably on all of the evaluation criteria under consideration. However, it should also be clear that Pascual-Leone has borrowed a great deal from Piaget in developing his own theory. For one thing, the tremendous body of observations collected by Piaget provided an invaluable data bank for Pascual-Leone to work with. In addition, Piaget's theoretical discussions contain the seeds for many of Pascual-Leone's most important ideas. We have not tried to point out all the influences of Piaget's thinking on the theory of constructive operators as it stands today, but Pascual-Leone has often acknowledged his debt to Piaget in his own writings. Despite the many parallels between the two theories, however, the fact remains that one theory is concerned primarily with logical structures, like the groupings of concrete operations, while the other is concerned with functional structures, called schemes, and this difference has far-reaching consequences for each theory's ability to predict and explain child behavior.

Looking ahead, it is apparent that a lot of theoretical and empirical work has yet to be done before the full potential of Pascual-Leone's approach can be adquately assessed. Most of the work to date has had to do with age differences in performance and with individual differences on the cognitive style dimension of field dependence—independence, so that we now know more about the M and F operators than anything else. The distinction between C and L learning has many precedents in other psychological theories, but exploration of the two processes in the context of Pascual-Leone's theory has barely begun. The most undeveloped area of all is the A operator. According to the theory, affective schemes should, by definition, obey the same basic laws as other schemes, but we actually know very little about the ways in which affective schemes are acquired and how they influence behavior. As for the rest of the repertoire, an area of particular importance for further elaboration is the acquisition, structure, and function of executive schemes. Finally, the process of task analysis, without which the theory cannot be applied, needs to be explicated more fully.

With so much left to be done, it may seem foolhardy even to contemplate the educational implications of Pascual-Leone's theory at this time. Yet the theory does deal with educationally relevant issues, and the evidence of its explanatory and predictive power is really quite impressive so far. Thus, with cautious optimism, we turn now to a final comparison between Piaget and Pascual-Leone, with particular reference to early childhood education.

SOME IMPLICATIONS FOR EARLY CHILDHOOD EDUCATION

In recent years Piaget's work has been cited as the theoretical foundation for several experimental programs of early childhood education, and it has had varying degrees of influence on countles̈ others. It is not our purpose here to review these programs,[14] or to outline yet another program on the basis of Pascual-Leone's theory. Rather, we will continue to discuss, in a general way, some of the problems one encounters in trying to apply Piaget's theory, and some of the advantages that might be gained by using Pascual-Leone's approach instead. The major topics for discussion are the perennial questions of *what* to teach and *how* to teach it, or—if you will—curriculum and instruction. It should be noted that the term *teaching*, in the present context, refers to any deliberate attempt to promote learning, however direct or indirect it might be.

Curriculum

The question of what to teach young children obviously entails the question of what they are able to learn. Both of the theories we have discussed can be brought to bear on this question, but because they define readiness in different ways, they give somewhat different answers. Piaget's theory suggests a definition of readiness in terms of very general logical structures: The child is ready to learn only those things that can be assimilated to the structure which characterizes his present stage of development. Therefore children below the age of 7 generally should not be ready for learning tasks that involve the logic of concrete operations, because they

---

[14] For reviews of Piagetian influences on early childhood education, see Evans (1975) and Almy (1975).

lack the necessary logical structure. For Pascual-Leone, readiness depends ultimately on capacity rather than structure: if a task that is normally performed at older ages can be brought within the learner's present mental capacity through the acquisition of appropriate schemes, then the learner is ready to learn that task, even though he might not currently perform any other task that involves the same logical structure as the one he is about to learn. In practice, then, the set of tasks that can be learned is limited only by an educator's ability to organize those tasks in a form that fits within the learner's functional capacity. The research evidence we have reviewed seems more consistent with this view than with the Piagetian view. In general, Piaget's theory seems to underestimate what young children can learn.

Aside from the issue of what *can* be learned, the two theories offer somewhat different perspectives on what *should* be learned. Evidently accelerated learning is possible in many instances, but is it also desirable? While conceding that acceleration training can be effective, Piaget has suggested that it often results in a very limited sort of learning. Sometimes a truly operational understanding of a new task can be induced by training, but only in children who already have the relevant operations, at least in some incipient form. In other cases, however, the child will learn a specific procedure for performing a criterion task, but he will not perform the task in the same way as someone who has mastered it "spontaneously." The implication, then, is that accelerated learning generally does not have much importance.

If, like Piaget, we were concerned primarily with the development of a general way of thinking, then we might agree that the learning of "specific procedures" would not be of much interest. But from a practical standpoint, a specific procedure, though limited, may nonetheless serve an important purpose. Suppose it was deemed desirable for a particular child to engage in a learning activity that required the conservation of number when sets of objects were rearranged in different ways. And suppose the child was not yet conserving number on his own. If he could be taught to conserve number, even by using an "unnatural" procedure, this might enable him to profit from the learning activity in question, even though he might still be unable to conserve amounts of substance or perform other concrete operations tasks. In other words, the learning of a specific procedure could be highly desirable under some circumstances. It might still be argued that the short-term advantages of accelerated learning are outweighted by long-term disadvantages. One particular worry is that the child might cling to his specific procedure later on, when he is capable of a more general understanding. But from a Piagetian point of view, there is no obvious reason to expect that the early learning of a specific procedure must necessarily interfere with later learning. In fact, Piaget has written of a basic "conservatism" in cognitive development, such that the child persists in assimilating new contents to old structures until he is more or less forced to accommodate or restructure his thinking. Developmental progress is not impeded by this conservatism; rather, it depends on it.

The neo-Piagetian view of accelerated learning is quite similar to Piaget's, but it also goes further. Clearly Pascual-Leone's theory can account for the learning of both "natural" and "unnatural" procedures for performing a particular task. In the first case, training supplies the learner with schemes that are needed to perform the task in the normal way—schemes which, for some reason, the learner has not yet acquired on his own, even though his mental capacity is already equal to the M demand of the criterion task. Case (1974) illustrated this possibility when he taught 8-year-olds to solve "control of variables" problems. On the other hand, accelerated mastery of a task may also be attributed to the learning of special schemes—schemes which lead to successful performance by means of a different procedure than is normally used by older subjects. This possibility has been illustrated by the neo-Piagetian analyses of the conceptual skills program for kindergartners (Case, 1972a) and Kohnstamm's class inclusion training (Pascual-Leone & Smith, 1969). In both of these examples, the learning of special schemes reduced the M demand of the task to a level that matched the mental capacity of the learner.

Furthermore, it follows from Pascual-Leone's theory that either kind of acceleration would result in a limited sort of learning, in the sense that one would not expect a trained subject to perform like an older, untrained subject in all respects, even on tasks closely related to the criterion task. On the whole, specially trained subjects should still not be able to accomplish as much, because of their lower M levels and smaller repertoires of schemes. Within these limits, however, it should be possible to make predictions about the extent of transfer from special training— both positive and negative—by analyzing specific transfer tasks with respect to the schemes and the mental capacity they require. Thus on the basis of a neo-Piagetian analysis, it should be easier to decide when special training is desirable and when it is not. Piagetian theory does not allow one to go so far because it attributes training effects to unanalyzed "specific procedures" or to the application of a general structure whose degree of generality cannot be determined a priori with any precision.

Although we can imagine times when acceleration training might be desirable, there are also many times when it would appear to be unnecessary. After all, most children will eventually be able to perform many concrete operational tasks spontaneously, without special training. Unless there is a specific need for mastery of a particular task, it seems a waste of time to train children on that task at an early age. But how, then, should the time be spent? Are there particular learning activities or bodies of content that are especially important for young children to experience?

From a Piagetian perspective, with its emphasis on general ways of thinking, practically any activity or content will do, so long as it allows the child to use the kind of thinking that is characteristic of his present developmental stage. Thus many activities involving symbolic play, talking, or drawing could give the young child experience in representational thinking. Similarly, activities which enabled the child to construct intuitive rules about the regularities in his interactions with the environment would provide a foundation for the eventual attainment of concrete operations. Within these general guidelines, however, the particular content for such activities cannot be specified on the basis of Piaget's theory because the theory leads one to regard specific content only as food for thought, with no particular value other than its contribution to general development. Therefore the specific content would have to be determined, in one way or another, by the child's culture.

Once these educational implications of Piaget's theory are made explicit, it becomes apparent that the traditional child-centered nursery school is quite in tune with them (cf. Kohlberg, 1968). With its abundant stock of representational toys, its supply of materials for graphic and plastic arts, its books to be seen and heard, and its opportunities for fantasy or dramatic play, and for verbal interaction in general, the traditional nursery school seems an ideal environment for the development of representational thought. Because it encourages frequent and sustained interactions with materials, equipment, and other people in a safe and semistructured setting, it seems likely to facilitate the construction of intuitive rules and the beginnings of operational thought as well. For similar reasons, it is easy to see why Piaget's theory has also been mentioned frequently in connection with "open" approaches to primary education.

Interestingly, the traditional nursery school seems quite consistent with Pascual-Leone's theory too. From this point of view, however, the content of the early childhood program is significant, not simply as a medium for the development of general cognitive structures, but rather as a source of a great many specific schemes which will be added to the child's repertoire as a result of his experience in the school setting. These additions to the repertoire would include schemes for representing various objects and their properties, schemes for transforming objects or their mental representations, and schemes for representing the transformations themselves. Moreover, and most important, many of these schemes would be relevant to later learning and performance because the content of the traditional program is likely to mirror the content of the larger physical and social world in which the child lives. Thus the learning of these schemes would appear to be quite desirable.

Despite these assurances, from both theoretical perspectives, about the desirability of the learning that would generally occur in a traditional nursery school setting, one is still left with the feeling that some of the things that young children could learn are more important in the long run than others, and that it would be especially desirable to promote those important learnings in particular. Certainly, in most communities, the skills used in performing simple computations would be regarded as more important than, say, the ability to distinguish between a horse and a donkey. Piaget's theory does not offer much guidance for deciding which specific learnings would be especially valuable, due to its emphasis on general structures. But Pascual-Leone's theory does deal explicitly with specific schemes and may, therefore, be more helpful.

It seems reasonable to suggest that there are both quantitative and qualitative criteria for assessing the practical importance of a given scheme. That is, a scheme may be important because it is required for a large number of the tasks that a person must perform, or because it is required for particular tasks which are, themselves, highly valued. Basic computational schemes would appear to be important by either of these criteria. But now we come to a major obstacle. If one actually started using the above criteria to identify all of the truly important schemes, the amount of work to be done would be staggering. The quantitative criterion, especially, would require a tremendous number of task analyses, but even the number of tasks which are, themselves, singularly important might be quite large. And the project would be complicated further by the fact that there is not just *one* task analysis per task, because the same problem can be solved by different means.

Fortunately, though, it probably would not be necessary to identify all of the important schemes anyway. For one thing, many of them would not have to be *taught* at all, because they are constructed spontaneously in the course of growing up, without any deliberate intervention by parents or teachers. Most of the schemes involved in spontaneous performances of the standard Piagetian tasks would fit into this category. Yet there must also be some important schemes that cannot generally be taken for granted. Their existence is suggested by the fact that some learning tasks seem especially problematic, in that children do not master them easily when they are expected to. If these difficulties can be attributed to particular schemes that are missing from the repertoire, and if these schemes *could* have been learned previously, then it certainly would be desirable to teach them. Thus the search for particularly important schemes could be based on analysis of learning tasks which, sooner or later, present difficulties for the children who must master them. This strategy is, of course, not a new one. It can be found, for example, in programs of "compensatory" education for young children who are expected to be at a disadvantage when they enter school (e.g., Bereiter & Engelmann, 1966). But it generally has not been based on adequate analyses of the criterion tasks or their components. When coupled with Pascual-Leone's theory, the strategy of working backwards from problematic learning tasks may prove a more effective means of identifying important objectives for instruction (cf. Case, 1975).

Instruction

In theory, the question of how to teach can be answered very simply: a good teaching method is one that creates the psychological conditions needed for learning to occur. If the teacher knows, in general, what those conditions are, then he or she can find activities which seem likely to bring them about. The main theoretical question, then, is what the conditions of learning actually are. In practice, however, the matter is much more complicated. Any instructional activity may create a whole complex of psychological conditions, some of which might be conducive to learning and some of which might not. Furthermore, any activity may impinge on a number of instructional objectives at once, promoting some of them perhaps, but possibly jeopardizing others at the same time. Finally, all instructional activities are constrained by the availability of resources, both human and material. Despite all these practical complications, we must nevertheless discuss the instructional implications of cognitive—developmental theory with regard to the conditions of learning in general. A discussion at this level cannot be entirely satisfactory to the practitioner, but it is the level at which the theories under consideration have something to say, and what they say may be of some use.

According to Piaget's theory, changes in cognitive structure result from a process of equilibration. Disequilibrium is therefore regarded as a necessary condition for change to occur. As we noted earlier, however, this proposition seems too abstract to have any explanatory or predictive value, and consequently it has no discernible implications for instruction either. But Piaget has also maintained that all cognitive progress results from the child's own "activity," and this point does have some implications that can be discussed. In fact, Piaget's emphasis on activity seems to have influenced educational practice already, as evidenced by recent interest in toys and games that enable children to develop thinking skills through overt manipulation. What Piaget's theory actually implies, though, is that the really essential activity for cognitive growth (beyond the sensorimotor period) is *mental* activity, which may or may not be accompanied by overt, physical actions. Thus the main point is simply that a child will not learn from mere exposure to objects and events; rather, there must be an attempt at assimilation on the part of the child.

Fortunately, most early childhood educators seem to have a natural understanding of this point. (Unfortunately, there are many teachers of older children and adults who seem to believe that learning from passive exposure is possible.) Even when reading young children a story, a good teacher engages the mental activity of the learner by asking questions and eliciting responses in other ways. Notice that the learner's overt responses in a situation like story time are not just ends in themselves. Rather, they are means of getting the learner to attend to and "act" upon the story. They also enable the teacher to see whether these mental activities are actually taking place. Thus an emphasis on overt activity is not, itself, the essential condition for learning. In fact there may be times when overt actions actually interfere with learning, when the necessary mental activities would be more likely to occur if the learner just observed. But in order to decide whether a particular learning activity will facilitate the appropriate *mental* activity or not, it is necessary to know exactly what the appropriate mental activity is. Piaget's theory is not much help at this point, because it lacks an explicit account of learning.

With regard to Pascual-Leone, it is immediately obvious that cognitive learning requires mental activity according to his theory too. Both C and L learning have as necessary conditions the activation of schemes to a level where they apply on (assimilate) the input. In this case, however, it is possible to determine exactly which schemes must be activated, and when their activation must occur, in order for a particular learning objective to be attained. When Case (1974) set out to teach 8-year-olds a "control of variables" scheme, his task analysis suggested that in order for this complex scheme to be assembled, certain other schemes had to be activated in a particular sequence. At one point in the checking of proofs, for example, it was important for the subject to consider alternative explanations for the phenomenon being tested. In one of the training sessions, the subject was asked to check proofs that one rubber ball was inherently "bouncier" than another. If one ball was thrown to the floor harder than the other, and the subject failed to consider that this uncontrolled variable might have affected the results, then the experimenter said "How do you know it didn't bounce higher because it was thrown harder?" The experimenter's question was intended to activate the schemes involved in considering the alternate explanation. After this was done a number of times, the subject began to go through the whole sequence of reasoning on his own, without any prompting from the experimenter. Of course Case's task analysis did not tell him to use rubber balls or to ask questions, but the materials and procedures used for instruction were consistent with the task analysis.

It is important to note that, theoretically, Case's instructional procedure was appropriate for subjects who (*1*) already possessed the prerequisite schemes, (*2*) had sufficient M power (*e* + 3) to boost certain schemes when they were needed, and (*3*) were field-independent. If any of these requirements were not met, the procedure would not be expected to work. In fact, Case showed that it did not work in the absence of (*2*) and (*3*), and it seems safe to assume that it would not have worked in the absence of (*1*) either. It is conceivable that the control of variables scheme might still be taught to children who lacked one or more of these prerequisites, but each kind of deficit would require a different sort of modification in the instructional procedure. If missing schemes were the only problem, it could be remedied by a preliminary instructional sequence designed to teach them. This is the strategy mentioned earlier in our discussion of curriculum, and it is also the one that has been elaborated most fully in the "cumulative learning" theory of Gagné (1970). However, as Case (1975) has pointed out, this strategy would not be sufficient if the learner lacked the level of M energy or the field independence required to profit from the present instructional method. These two problems require different solutions.

If the learner is relatively field-dependent, he is likely to apply schemes that are strongly boosted by the F operator. And if these schemes are inappropriate, as they will be in tasks that contain misleading features, they will prevent the learner from applying the schemes that are needed to perform the task successfully. The activation weights of appropriate schemes might be increased at least temporarily by repeated reinforcement, but the tendency to apply the F-boosted scheme would still be there because it is more or less built into the learner from early childhood and is elicited automatically by the task situation. Thus a better remedy, according to Case (1975) is to teach the learner a superordinate scheme that enables him to distinguish those situations where the F-boosted scheme *is* appropriate from those where it is not. In other words, when a subject says that Ball A must be bouncier than Ball B, because Ball A obviously bounced higher in the test that was just performed, he would actually be correct if the experimenter were simply asking which ball bounced higher, instead of which ball was bouncier. Thus the child would have to learn to distinguish between these two questions by means of a special scheme like the one mentioned earlier in connection with class inclusion training (Pascual-Leone & Smith, 1969).

If the learner does not have sufficient M capacity for the instructional method at hand, then there seem to be three basic ways in which the method could be modified. First, the learning task could be broken into "chunks," so that the learner could use his limited capacity to integrate the smaller number of schemes required within each chunk. Once they were integrated, the chunks would each function as one scheme and could then be integrated with other schemes (Case, 1975). In other words, this would be a sort of stepwise process of L learning. The second strategy would be to promote L learning by providing instructional supports that would cause some of the necessary schemes to be boosted by F or A rather than M. Additional verbal prompts by the experimenter might be helpful in this regard. Finally, through sheer repetition, one could rely on the gradual process of C learning with its low M demand.

We mentioned earlier that young children probably acquire many of their schemes by C learning anyway, due to their limited M capacity. Since a lot of repetition is a necessary condition for C learning, it might appear that drilltype repetition would be a desirable instructional technique. But there are many other ways to provide repetition too, as illustrated again by the traditional setting: There are daily routines, there are the same toys and peers to play with day after day and opportunities to persist in the same activity for extended periods of time, there are standard songs with standard refrains, and on and on and on. All of this repetition could contribute to learning. Piaget (1963) showed his appreciation for repetition, too, when he spoke of "functional assimilation" and "circular reactions" in the sensorimotor period, but he seems to have neglected the role it might play in later learning as well.

The general point we have tried to make is that Pascual-Leone's theory can be used as a basis for deciding how to teach, and for adjusting the method of teaching to the experience, the developmental level, and the cognitive style of the learner. Of course, not all teaching can be as carefully planned as the instructional sequence in Case's training experiment. But teachers, educational psychologists, and other specialists working together can at least use cognitive–developmental theory in a heuristic fashion to make decisions about curriculum and instruction. Any approach to instruction, however consistent it may be with theory, must ultimately be tested in practice, in what Piaget (1970b) has called "experimental pedagogy." Such tests are much more likely to be enlightening if they are based on theory rather than trial and error. If a method works, one has a theory that explains *why* it worked. One is led, then, not to use the same *method* again (unless the same theoretically relevant conditions obtain) but rather to use the same *principles* again. If a method based on theory does *not* work, it does not necessarily mean that the theory is wrong, because there is plenty of room for "slippage" between theory and application. In fact, the theory can be used for trouble shooting, to diagnose the problem with a method. But if methods with a clear theoretical rationale are found to fail repeatedly, then the theory may need modification. In this way, early childhood education can contribute to the further development of cognitive theory.

ACKNOWLEDGMENTS

I wish to express my appreciation to Barbara Nakakihara for all her help in preparing the manuscript, and to Millie Almy, Mary Sue Ammon, Jeanne Block, Robbie Case, Harry Hom, Juan Pascual-Leone, Paul Robinson, and Deborah Tharinger for their comments on the first draft.

REFERENCES

Achenbach, T. M., & Weisz, J. R. A longitudinal study of developmental synchrony between conceptual identity, seriation, and transitivity of color, number, and length. *Child Development,* 1975, *46,* 840–848.

Almy, M. The impact of Piaget on early childhood education. Paper prepared for meetings of the Jean Piaget Society, Philadelphia, June, 1975.

Baldwin, A. L. *Theories of child development.* New York: Wiley, 1967.

Beilin, H. Learning and operational convergence in logical thought development. *Journal of Experimental Child Psychology,* 1965, *2,* 317–339.

Beilin, H. The training and acquisition of logical operations. In M. F. Rosskopf, L. P. Steffe, and S. Taback (Eds.), *Piagetian cognitive developmental research and mathematical education.* Washington, D. C.: National Council of Teachers of Mathematics, 1971.

Bereiter, C., & Engelmann, S. *Teaching disadvantaged children in the preschool.* Englewood Cliffs, New Jersey: Prentice-Hall, 1966.

Brainerd, C. J. Neo-Piagetian training experiments revisited: Is there any support for the cognitive-developmental stage hypothesis? *Cognition,* 1973, *2,* 349–370.

Brainerd, C. J. Structures-of-the-whole and elementary education. *American Educational Research Journal,* 1975, *12,* 369–378.

Brainerd, C. J., & Allen, T. W. Experimental inductions of the conservation of "first order" quantitative invariants. *Psychological Bulletin,* 1971, *75,* 128–144.

Bucher, B., & Schneider, R. E. Acquisition and generalization of conservation by preschoolers, using operant training. *Journal of Experimental Child Psychology,* 1973, *16,* 187–204.

Case, R. Learning and development: A neo-Piagetian interpretation. *Human Development,* 1972, *15,* 339–358. (a)

Case, R. Validation of a neo-Piagetian mental capacity construct. *Journal of Experimental Child Psychology,* 1972, *14,* 287–302. (b)

Case, R. Structures and strictures: Some functional limitations on the course of cognitive growth. *Cognitive Psychology,* 1974, *6,* 544–573.

Case, R. Gearing the demands of instruction to the developmental capacities of the learner. *Review of Educational Research,* 1975, *45,* 59–87.

Christie, J. F., & Smothergill, D. W. Discrimination and conservation of length. *Psychonomic Science,* 1970, *21,* 336–337.

Cole, M., & Scribner, S. *Culture and thought.* New York: Wiley, 1974.

Dasen, P. R. The influence of ecology, culture and European contact on cognitive development in Australian Aborigines. In J. W. Berry and P. R. Dasen (Eds.), *Culture and cognition: Readings in cross-cultural psychology.* London: Methuen, 1973.

Diaz, S. *Cucui: Technical manual.* Stockton, California: Multilingual Assessment Program, Stockton Unified School District, 1974.

Elkind, D. Children's discovery of the conservation of mass, weight, and volume: Piaget replication study II. *Journal of Genetic Psychology,* 1961, *98,* 219–227.

Evans, E. D. *Contemporary influences in early childhood education* (2nd Edition). New York: Holt, Rinehart & Winston, 1975.

Flavell, J. H. *The developmental psychology of Jean Piaget.* Princeton, New Jersey: Van Nostrand, 1963.

Flavell, J. H. Concept development. In P. H. Mussen (Ed.), *Carmichael's Manual of Child Psychology,* (3rd Edition), Vol. 1. New York: Wiley, 1970.

Flavell, J. H., & Wohlwill, J. F. Formal and functional aspects of cognitive development. In D. Elkind and J. H. Flavell (Eds.), *Studies in cognitive development.* New York: Oxford University Press, 1969.

Gagne, R. M. *The conditions of learning* (2nd Edition). New York: Holt, Rinehart & Winston, 1970.

Gelman, R. Conservation acquisition: A problem of learning to attend to relevant attributes. *Journal of Experimental Child Psychology,* 1969, *7,* 167–187.

Ginsburg, H., & Opper, S. *Piaget's theory of intellectual development.* Englewood Cliffs, New Jersey: Prentice-Hall, 1969.

Glaser, R., & Resnick, L. B. Instructional psychology. In P. H. Mussen and M. R. Rosenzweig (Eds.), *Annual review of psychology.* Palo Alto, California: Annual Reviews, Inc., 1972.

Hunt, J. McV. *Intelligence and experience.* New York: Ronald, 1961.

Inhelder, B., & Piaget, J. *The growth of logical thinking from childhood to adolescence.* New York: Basic Books, 1958.

Inhelder, B., & Piaget, J. *The early growth of logic in the child.* New York: Norton, 1964.

Inhelder, B., Sinclair, H., & Bovet, M. *Learning and the development of cognition.* Cambridge, Massachusetts: Harvard University Press, 1974.

Kohlberg, L. Early education: A cognitive-developmental view. *Child Development,* 1968, *39,* 1013–1062.

Kohnstamm, G. A. *Teaching children to solve a Piagetian problem of class inclusion.* Amsterdam: North Holland, 1967.

Langer, J., & Strauss, S. Appearance, reality and identity. *Cognition,* 1972, *1,* 105–128.

Lefebvre, M., & Pinard, A. Influence du niveau initial de sensibilité au conflit sur l'apprentissage de la conservation des quantités par une méthode de conflit cognitif. *Canadian Journal of Behavioural Sciences,* 1974, *61,* 398–413.

Mehler, J., & Bever, T. G. Cognitive capacity of very young children. *Science,* 1967, *158,* 141–142.

Pascual-Leone, J. Cognitive development and cognitive style: A general psychological integration. Unpublished doctoral dissertation, University of Geneva, 1969.

Pascual-Leone, J. A mathematical model for the transition rule in Piaget's developmental stages. *Acta Psychologica,* 1970, *63,* 301–345.

Pascual-Leone, J. A theory of constructive operators, a neo-Piagetian model of conservation, and the problem of horizontal décalages. Unpublished manuscript, York University, 1973.

Pascual-Leone, J. A neo-Piagetian process-structural model of Witkin's psychological differentiation. Paper prepared for the meetings of the International Association for Cross-Cultural Psychology, Kingston, Ontario, 1974.

Pascual-Leone, J. Metasubjective problems of constructive cognition. *Canadian Psychological Review,* 1976, in press. (a)

Pascual-Leone, J. On learning and development, Piagetian style: I. A reply to Lefebvre-Pinard. *Canadian Psychological Review,* 1976, in press. (b)

Pascual-Leone, J., & Smith, J. The encoding and decoding of symbols by children: A new experimental paradigm and a neo-Piagetian model. *Journal of Experimental Child Psychology,* 1969, *8,* 328–355.

Piaget, J. *The psychology of intelligence.* London: Routledge & Kegan Paul, 1950.

Piaget, J. *The construction of reality in the child.* New York: Basic Books, 1954.

Piaget, J. *Play, dreams, and imitation in childhood.* New York: Norton, 1962.

Piaget, J. *The origins of intelligence in children.* New York: Norton, 1963.

Piaget, J. Development and learning. In R. E. Ripple and V. N. Rockcastle (Eds.), *Piaget rediscovered.* Ithaca, New York: Cornell University School of Education, 1964.

Piaget, J. *The child's conception of number.* New York: Norton, 1965.

Piaget, J. *Six psychological studies.* New York: Random House, 1967.

Piaget, J. Piaget's theory. In P. H. Mussen (Ed.), *Carmichael's manual of child psychology.* (3rd Edition) *1,* New York: Wiley, 1970. (a)

Piaget, J. *Science of education and the psychology of the child.* New York: Orion, 1970. (b)

Piaget, J. Intellectual evolution from adolescence to adulthood. *Human Development,* 1972, *15,* 1–12.

Piaget, J. *The child and reality.* New York: Grossman, 1973.

Piaget, J., & Inhelder, B. *Le développement des quantités chez l'enfant.* Paris: Delachaux et Niestlé, 1941.

Piaget, J., & Inhelder, B. *The psychology of the child.* New York: Basic Books, 1969.

Pinard, A., & Laurendeau, M. "Stage" in Piaget's cognitive-developmental theory: Exegesis of a concept. In D. Elkind & J. H. Flavell (Eds.), *Studies in cognitive development.* New York: Oxford University Press, 1969.

Rohwer, W. D., Ammon, P. R., & Cramer, P. *Understanding intellectual development.* Hinsdale, Illinois: Dryden Press, 1974.

Rothenberg, B. B., & Courtney, R. Conservation of number in very young children: A replication of and a comparison with Mehler and Bever's study. *Journal of Psychology,* 1968, *70,* 205–212.

Smedslund, J. The acquisition of conservation of substance and weight in children. V. Practice in conflict situations without reinforcement. *Scandinavian Journal of Psychology,* 1961, *2,* 156–160.

Strauss, S. Inducing cognitive development and learning: A review of short-term training experiments. I: The organismic-developmental approach. *Cognition,* 1972, *1,* 329–357.

Strauss, S. A reply to Brainerd. *Cognition,* 1974, *3,* 155–185.

Uzgiris, I. C. Situational generality of conservation. *Child Development,* 1964, *35,* 831–841.

Witkin, H. A., Dyk, R. B., Faterson, H. F., Goodenough, D. R., & Karp, S. A. *Psychological differentiation.* New York: Wiley, 1962.

Wohlwill, J. F. Piaget's system as a source of empirical research. *Merrill-Palmer Quarterly,* 1963, *4,* 253–262.

8

Language, the Child, and the Teacher: A Proposed Assessment Model[1]

MARION BLANK

Rutgers Medical School

> Language permeates school life. Boys and girls in their attempts to master the school curriculum and in the process of growing up have to call upon their language resources. Moreover they are expected to increase these resources by making the language encountered in their school learning a living part of their thinking and communicating. . . . They are expected to reason, speculate, plan, consider theories, make their own generalizations and hypotheses. These are in many respects language activities, that is, language is the means by which they are carried out, the means, therefore, by which children do much of their learning [Barnes, 1969, pp. 160–162].

The above statement, selected from a report on the development of new curricula in Great Britain, typifies the increasing importance accorded to language in the teaching–learning process. But the quote does more than highlight some of the numerous functions that language is expected to serve. Contained within it is an important, albeit implicit, dichotomy about the role of language in the classroom—a dichotomy that reflects the fact that language is central to both the means and goals of education. Thus, a major goal of the school is the enhancement of the child's language, but in turn the means for this enhancement is seen to depend largely on language—that is, the language of the teacher (including the language of the curriculum that he or she employs). This dual role of language is so well accepted that it is an almost unquestioned part of the educational scene. Neverthe-

[1] The writing of this chapter was supported by the Grant Foundations and U.S.P.H.S. Grant #MH 21051.

less, it represents a cleavage that has significantly affected the way in which the language of the school has been studied. Specifically, some investigators are drawn to language as a means of education; for them, there is a strong inclination to focus on the language of the teacher. Others are drawn to language as a goal of education; for them, the inclination is to focus on the language of the child.

This distinction in interests becomes evident as soon as one begins to examine the research carried out in this area (see Criper & Davies, 1974, for a comprehensive review). For the most part, the language of the child has been investigated by psychologists, linguists, and sociologists who have concentrated on such questions as: How is language used by the child? How are language skills acquired? How are these skills in accord, or in conflict, with the language demands of the school? On the other hand, the language of the teacher has been investigated much more by educators who have concentrated on such questions as: What are the demands that teachers place on the children?, What percentage of time does the teacher control the interchange? and What are the differences in the strategies used by effective as contrasted to ineffective teachers?

Since the phenomena under study are so broad and complex, one can easily recognize the interests and pressures that have led investigators to study, in relative isolation, the language of the two major classroom participants. But the isolation has been costly, for it has resulted in our being left without the knowledge to cope with what is perhaps the major educational problem confronting us at this time— namely, the high rate of failure among children in our schools. It has become increasingly common to attribute such failure to a lack of effective communication between the teacher and the child (see Boggs, 1972; Dumont, 1972; Labov, 1969; Rosen, 1969; and Silberman, 1970). This view is reflected in the following statement by Hymes (1972): "In many communities not only is it normal for the language of the classroom and the language of the home to be different; they may be mutually unintelligible [p. xxiii]."

The hypothesis of a communication breakdown has become increasingly popular in recent years. Because of the division between the language of the teacher and the language of the child, however, we have almost no techniques to determine whether this hypothesis is valid. For example, with most currently available techniques, it is possible to assess teachers on such parameters as the number of open-ended questions they ask or the amount of didactic information that they offer. Similarly, it is possible to assess children on such parameters as the number of correct grammatical sentences that they utter or the type of dialect they employ. However if we are to determine if there is a breakdown in communication, statements such as those outlined above are not sufficient. Rather, the information or questions put forth by the teacher must be assessed as to whether or not they were received and understood by the child; analogously, statements made by the child must be assessed as to how appropriately they were responded to by the teacher.

Because we currently lack the systems needed to answer these sorts of questions, we have almost no solid information on the factors that underlie effective teacher—

child interaction. But due to the prevalence of strong theoretical biases in education, we have not felt the absence of this information as strongly as we might. These biases have permitted us to believe that we know the components of teacher–child communication when in fact such information has not been determined. The biases are widespread and often compelling. For example, one common assumption is that effective teaching depends upon the teacher asking a broad range of stimulating, open-ended questions. Such questions are thought to capture the child's interest and thereby lead him to higher levels of thinking. This sounds most reasonable—and I, like others have been strongly guided by this notion. However, when I began actually working with children, I found the idea severely wanting. The work to which I am referring was concerned with fostering cognitive development in preschool-age children whose performance suggested they were likely to fail in school (Blank, 1973; Blank, Koltuv, & Wood, 1972; Blank & Solomon, 1969). When I and my colleagues attempted to pose apparently stimulating questions, we did not find the children's reactions to be those of excitement and interest; instead, their responses involved confusion, anxiety, and withdrawal. Upon reflection, their reactions were understandable. These children were in the teaching program because of their cognitive difficulties. The asking of seemingly stimulating questions, therefore, demanded precisely the skills in which they were most deficient. Accordingly, with their weaknesses exposed in this way, they responded—as any of us would—by trying to withdraw to safer territory.

There were numerous other examples in which we found the assumptions of "good teaching" in sharp conflict with the facts of classroom life. For instance, a well-accepted tradition in preschool education urges teachers not to impose on the child, but rather to follow the child's lead. When we tried to adhere to this course in our work with poorly functioning children, however, we found that the children led us into a series of scattered, fleeting, unproductive exchanges about whatever was salient to them at the moment. We had unwittingly participated in a new Pygmalion effect—we had not changed the children to become more thoughtful and reflective; instead, they had changed us to become as distractible and hyperactive as themselves.

Many readers, particularly those committed to certain schools of training, might find themselves disagreeing with these observations and interpretations. At this point, however, the statements cannot truly be challenged because there are no data available to confirm or refute them. In turn, the absence of such data is a direct consequence of the absence of systems to assess communication in the classroom; in particular, systems that will allow us to differentiate between effective and ineffective teacher–pupil interaction.

The present chapter represents an initial effort to grapple with this problem. It offers a model for the exploration of the language interactions that occur between teachers and young children. The model includes a coding system for evaluating the language functioning of both participants and for identifying the strengths and weaknesses of each. The material does not offer answers as to how most teachers and young children interact with each other in actual settings. Indeed, the current coding system has been devised for the purpose of obtaining such information. Once obtained, it is hoped that we will then be able to use the information to determine the factors that underlie effective and ineffective interchange so that ultimately we will be able to foster the former and reduce the latter.

The system of analysis that will be used is one that evolved from a tutorial program I developed for young children whose performance suggested that they were liable to fail in school (see Blank, 1973, for a description of the program). In that setting, a sustained dialogue took place between the teacher and the child for a period of about 15 min each day. This situation offered a unique opportunity to monitor a broad range of the behaviors displayed by both the teacher and the child, and it thereby provided an optimal setting for examining, in detail, the quality of exchanges that occur between teachers and children.

Even though the scales are geared to focus on teacher—child exchange, for purposes of exposition, the scales for each of these participants are initially presented separately. Thus, the first scale that is outlined deals with the child's linguistic performance. The next set of scales deals with the language of the teacher. The integration of the scales is then illustrated (1) by applying them to two actual teaching lessons and (2) by offering a number of assessment measures that are designed to reflect the effectiveness of the teacher—child exchange. The assessment measures may cause some difficulty in that they require the reader to hold in mind simultaneously the behavior of both the teacher and the child. Hopefully, the problem will be eased by the fact that the area under study is restricted to a relatively limited age, that is, the preschooler in interaction with his teacher, and to a relatively limited domai   that is, the language that is used in teaching situations directed towards fostering ognitive development.

ASSESSING THE LANGUAGE PERFORMANCE
OF THE CHILD

Choosing a Path through the Labyrinth of Language

As soon as we begin to examine the child's verbal ability, we confront the many complexities that have led investigators to term this sphere of functioning "the labyrinth of language [Black, 1968]." Even when the child is still at the preschool age, his language ability is comprised of hundreds of varied and complex skills—skills that permit him to learn new vocabulary, produce and understand a remarkable range of different types of sentences, and use language to express a wide variety of his thoughts and interests (see Halliday, 1973). The presence of this enormous repertoire is, in part, responsible for the debate on language that has dominated the educational scene. The debate to which I am referring is best known as "the difference—deficit controversy." The key issues in this controversy are captured in the following statement from a Scottish report on spoken language[2] in the primary school:

> We start from the fact that much of the work on language in education has begun from the standpoint of educational failure. Language has been seen as a cause of failure but at the same time as open to remedial action. There are two contrasted viewpoints on why language can cause failure in school. One argument runs that some children are lacking in the essential words and structures necessary for them to think and argue: therefore they must be given the words and structures and drilled in them until they can use them freely. The counter argument is that these children already have the structures and most of the words and are just as capable of thinking and arguing amongst their peers as anyone else. Where they differ is in the use of the language which teachers and others believe to be suitable for school. According to this argument, their use of language and their attitudes are not inferior, just different, and society needs to recognize these differences. The teacher's job is therefore to make children use their existing language structures and words appropriately in different contexts [Criper & Davies, 1974, p. 1].

In essence then, two major groups exist—one which believes that children who fail are deficient in language skills, the other which believes that the children who fail have all the necessary language skills, but that these skills are in a different form, which the school deems inferior. As indicated above, however, this controversy exists partly because of the enormous range of behaviors subsumed under language. Thus, each time that the deficit proponents point out a skill that the children are thought to lack, the difference proponents offer data to indicate that the children possess the same skill in a different form, or that they possess a different skill of comparable complexity and usefulness.[3]

As long as the debate is permitted to encompass the entire realm of language skills possessed by the child, the issues are bound to remain undecided. It is as if a man wanted to plant a garden and chose, as his universe for consideration, the entire range of plants available in the world. Having failed to set any constraints on the material that he will consider, he will find himself having to evaluate an overwhelming amount of information that has little order or meaning. His detailed search then will have led only to confusion, rather than to clarity. The situation changes dramatically, however, if at the start of his search the man in question had set up constraints whereby he would limit his study to plants that would be suitable given the conditions that apply to his territory—that is, the climate, the type of soil,

---

[2] The term "spoken language" is used in this context and throughout the chapter as a contrast to the term "written language." Therefore, it does not represent simply the language produced by the child; rather, it encompasses the skills of both production and comprehension available to the child in the oral language sphere.

[3] The "deficit–difference" controversy has been so extensively discussed and reported in so many different quarters that it is not necessary to review the specifics of the issues at length in this chapter. For readers who are interested in pursuing the controversy in a detailed manner, useful references are Angel, 1972; Baratz and Baratz, 1970; Bereiter and Engelmann, 1966; Bernstein, 1969; Blank, 1970; Cazden, John, and Hymes, 1972; Deutsch, 1975; Houston, 1970; Labov, 1969; Lawton, 1968; Spolsky, 1972; Tough, 1973; and Williams, 1970.

the amount of sun, and so forth. Analogously, if we are to move in our understanding of the language in the classroom, we must resist the temptation to allow any and all of the child's linguistic skills to enter the realm of investigation. Instead, we must confine our search to those aspects of language that are most likely to be essential to mastering the formal learning situation that is the essence of classroom life. This approach naturally entails hazards, since there is little solid information as to what type of language is needed for success in formal schooling. Nevertheless, I believe that educated guesses as to what conditions apply to the classroom are still preferable to the alternative of allowing all language skills to be seen as of potentially equal merit. Accordingly, the analysis of the child's language to be presented below will be focused on those aspects of the child's language that I believe are essential to mastery of the demands of the classroom.

The Child's Role in the Classroom

In effecting the approach outlined above, the first problem naturally revolves around establishing meaningful limits on the types of language that will be considered. To this end, the work of Bellack and his colleagues (Bellack, Kliebard, Hyman, & Smith, 1966) is particularly useful. A guiding theme of their investigations is that "linguistic activities assume different forms and structures according to the functions they come to serve in different contexts" and "that verbal activities in various contexts follow certain rules or conventions appropriate to the activities under way." They then go on to liken these rules to a game, for, as in a game, "players have to learn the rules, the purpose of the rules, and how the various parts of the game are related. Only by learning these rules can they play the game successfully [p. 3]."

With the situation defined in this way, the problem becomes one of defining the rules that govern the classroom game. Based upon their research, Bellack *et al.* conclude that the rules of the classroom game involve "one person called a teacher and one or more persons called pupils. The object of the game is to carry on a discourse about subject matter, and the ostensible payoff of the game is measured in terms of the amount of learning displayed by the pupils after a given period of play [p. 237]." Of central importance to this view of the classroom is the notion that each player (i.e., the teacher or the child) has different rules to follow. The teacher's role is to foster learning by offering tasks that lead the child to acquire information or skills that he did not previously possess; the child's task, on the other hand, is to master the imposed tasks. Clearly, these roles are interdependent in that the teacher is successful only if he or she offers the child tasks that are within his interest and within his ability to cope. Nevertheless, this view of the classroom does permit us to limit our study of the language of the child. Specifically, the child's behavior that is most relevant in this context is his ability to meet the tasks imposed by the teacher.

Some readers may object to interpreting the child's behavior in a way that focuses solely on his ability to meet imposed demands and that thereby omits any assessment of his cognitive–linguistic skills in other areas (e.g., in his peer relationships in the school setting). But, as the discussion above indicated, a major source for the educational concern about the child's language is his poor performance in school. In large measure, such poor performance is synonomous with the child's failure to meet the demands set by the teacher and the curricula. To the extent that he fails to meet these demands, he is not fulfilling the role that is expected of him as a student and to that extent his behavior is inadequate in the situation. Therefore, unless schools abandon all efforts at teaching (i.e., transmitting information and skills to the child that he previously did not have, as occurs in the teaching of reading), an essential aspect of the child's behavior that must be assessed is his ability to meet the demands of the teacher. (Interestingly, the school is not the only situation that is marked by the adult imposing problems on the child. Examination of many of the reported interchanges between parents and young children indicate that the adults' verbalizations commonly take the form of questions that they clearly expect the children to answer [Ervin-Tripp, 1970; Gleason, 1973; Snow, 1972]. Indeed, in one study, it was found that questions were the most frequent types of utterances in adult speech with young children [Savić, 1975]. It therefore seems that imposed demands—offered in the form of questions—represent a technique by which mature speakers unconsciously attempt to engage and even teach the more immature members of their community.)

Evaluating the Child's Behavior: A Proposed Scale

Having selected the child's ability to meet imposed demands as the area upon which to concentrate, we are still left with many problems. As all who work with children are well aware, there is a seemingly endless variety to the responses they can give in any situation. For example, a situation as simple as holding up a square and asking the child to give you its name ("What is this called?") may lead to such varied answers as "box," "yellow," or "I got one of those at home." The situation, of course, becomes even more complex when one considers the endless range of more complex questions that in turn lead to an even greater variety of answers. If this variety is not to stymie our efforts to analyze the child's behavior, we must be able to offer a coding system that reduces the seemingly infinite variety of answers to a definable system with a reasonably small number of categories.

The Adequacy of Response scale presented in Table 8.1 has been constructed to meet these goals. It allows one to code, on a 9-point scale, a young child's response to any cognitive demand. In order to illustrate its use, a sample problem is presented along with the coding for each type of response. As the reader will note, the coding of the responses proceeds in general from fully adequate responses to responses that are increasingly less adequate. The progression, however, is not exact (e.g., a request for help need not necessarily be a poorer response than is an "ambiguous" answer).

The application of this scale will be illustrated in the next section of the chapter. From the schematic form in which it is presented, however, it may seem that the

TABLE 8.1
Adequacy of Child's Response

Sample Task: Child is shown a toy balance scale containing weights on each side. The adult holds up a small weight and asks, "What will happen to the scale if I put another one here?"

Coding of response	Rule for coding	Example of response
1. Fully adequate	Child offers a valid answer which fully meets the demands of the task:	(pointing) *That side will go down.*
2. Adequate	a. Child gives valid answer but it is vague or poorly formulated:	(points) *down*
	b. Answer is correct technically, but it does not describe the focal result:	*There'll be another thing in the cup.*
	c. Answer includes detracting irrelevant information:	*It will go down 'cos it's white.*
3. Ambiguous	The response is formulated so that it is not possible to determine if answer is adequate or inadequate:	*It'll move.*
4. Requests information	Child requests additional information or help:	*What did you say?*
5. Inadequate–invalid	Child's response shows an understanding of the question, but the answer is incorrect:	*It will go up.*
6. Inadequate–association to material	Child's response is focused on the material, but it indicates no understanding of the question:	*It's red.*
7. Inadequate–irrelevant	a. Child's response shows no understanding of the question nor any analysis of the material:	*I got one of those at home.*
	b. Child imitates all or part of teacher's words or actions:	*It will happen.*
	c. Child denies the problem stated:	*You won't put it on.*
8. Inadequate–*Don't know.*[a]	Child states he cannot answer the problem:	*I don't know what'll happen.*
9. Inadequate–no response[a]	Child offers no verbal response to problem:	shrugs

[a]These two types of failures to respond are separated because, clinically, they seem to be different behaviors. The verbalization of "I don't know" ... that the child wishes to continue the exchange, whereas the nonverbal response is more indicative of a withdrawal from the dialogue.

scale, like much of the developmental work on language, focuses only on the child and not on the linguistic interaction between the teacher and child. The isolation is illusory, however, for no response could be judged as adequate or inadequate with reference to the child alone; instead, the judgment of the child's behavior must be made relative to the demand imposed by the teacher. For instance, the specific examples in Table 8.1 are coded into their respective categories only in relation to the specific problem illustrated. Were the same answers given even to a slightly different question, (e.g., "What will happen to the scale if I take one out?") their coding would have been altogether different. These qualifications suggest that the ratings must be made relative to the imposed demands. Of even greater importance, however, is that these qualifications imply that it is impossible to make sense out of the child's behavior unless we have a full understanding of the demands of the teacher to which the child is responding. In other words, we must be able to code the teacher's behavior in comparable detail to the coding just outlined for the child. It is this issue that will now be considered.

ASSESSMENT OF THE TEACHER'S LANGUAGE

The Goals of Assessment

As was pointed out at the start of the chapter, investigators interested in the means or processes of education have focused on the language of the teacher.[4] The literature in this latter area is extensive and growing rapidly (see Amidon & Hough, 1967; Bellack et al., 1966; Bennett & Jordan, 1975; Coulthard, 1974; Flanders, 1970; Simon & Boyer, 1968; and Taba, Levine, & Elzey, 1964, for samples of the research being conducted.) Because the research is so broad, as one would expect, it is characterized by a multiplicity of goals. However, the major effort seems to be toward describing what has been termed "the interaction processes in the class-room," answering such questions as: What percentage of the time does the teacher initiate the exchange? What are the children's reactions to these initiations? How does the teacher convey feedback to the children regarding the quality of the responses they have offered?

Given that these questions clearly involve not simply the teacher, but the

[4] At times, investigators interested in the language of the child, and, in particular, in changing that language have also focused on the language of the teacher. In general, though, their studies have involved limited assessments of teacher behavior. For example, many intervention programs designed to effect changes in the child have not in fact yielded the hoped-for gains. This "failure" has led to a focus on the teacher since it was felt that a likely cause for the negative results might be the teacher's failure to have correctly implemented the designated program. (See Bissell, 1971; Dopyera, 1969; Lay, 1972; and Rosenshine & Furst, 1973, for illustrations of this approach.) Following this line of reasoning, the analysis is directed towards the degree to which there is or is not correspondence between the stated program and the teacher's behavior. Rarely is there any analysis of the success or failure of the actual interactions that occur between teachers and children.

interaction between the teacher and child, the reader may wonder if investigators have not already identified the difficulties in communication that occur between teachers and children who function poorly in school. For a number of reasons, such information is not available. First and foremost is the fact that most studies of the classroom are focused on characterizing *general* features that hold across most teacher–pupil interactions. Rarely is any differentiation made among the interactions of teachers with different types of pupils; in particular, there is almost no research on the interaction between teachers and those children who fail versus the interaction between teachers and those children who succeed. The need to have techniques that differentiate between groups is essential if we are to begin to identify at what points, and in what way, the teacher–pupil exchange breaks down. Second, most of the work in this area has been directed towards analyzing the teacher's behavior in situations where there is a formal curriculum to impart (e.g., social studies, match, etc.). Consequently, the situations almost always involve teachers in interaction with older, school-age children; relatively little effort has been directed towards assessing the interchange in the preschool situations—even though this is the age range where the teacher is deemed to play a vital role in affecting the child's learning. As a result, there are relatively few techniques and findings available to guide the analysis in this area.

Despite these limitations, many of the ideas that have guided the development of the various classroom coding systems to seem applicable in initiating an assessment of the teacher of the preschool-age child. For example:

1. The behavior of the teacher (like the behavior of the child) can be reduced to a finite number of categories that will reveal the patterns that the teacher employs in dealing with students. (This point is central to the belief of many investigators that differential use of these patterns is the key feature that distinguishes effective from ineffective teachers—see Flanders, 1970.)

2. The particular categories used in any analysis may vary according to the aspect of classroom interaction selected for study (e.g., the same categories may not be applicable to different behaviors, such as classroom management routines used for discipline versus the formal instruction used for teaching specific subject matter). In other words, one cannot simply develop *a system* for assessing classroom interaction. Instead, different categories must be developed, depending upon one's educational priorities.

3. Teacher behavior should not be considered by itself, but rather as part of a teacher–pupil relationship. Therefore, any behavior on the part of the teacher should not be coded as an isolated act; instead it must be evaluated on such criteria as its relevance to what the child has just said or done. In other words, if it is to be adequate, any coding system for classroom interaction must capture the reciprocal nature of the teacher–child exchange.

With these principles providing a framework for analysis, it becomes possible to develop a system for coding the teacher's behavior with preschool-age children. Given the framework of the classroom game outlined above, main areas of teacher behavior that ought to be assessed concern the types of cognitive—linguistic demands that the teacher places on the child. The delineation of these demands provides us with a first step in identifying which of the demands typically presented by teachers actually foster the desired learning and which precipitate difficulties for the children. The section that follows presents the details of this coding system.

A Cognitive—Linguistic Code

One of the obstacles to progress in this area is that there are almost no guidelines for determining the range and type of appropriate questions and demands that one can present to a preschooler.[5] Rough, intuition-based guidelines do exist. For example, it is commonly accepted that one would not ask a 4-year-old a question demanding the logic of Piaget's formal operational stage. But these guidelines, based largely on our knowledge of developmental stages, are so broad as to be of limited value when faced with trying to define a broad range of meaningful but different questions suitable for a particular child at a particular age (e.g., What are the types of problems that one can put to a 1-year-old as opposed to those that can be asked of a 7-year-old?) Therefore, in setting out to assess the teacher's behavior with the preschool child, the first goal was to develop a coding system that would define the range and quality of the cognitive—linguistic demands made by the teacher.

In an effort to approach this problem, a classification was made of the large range of the questions that adults (both parents and teachers) ask of young children in the course of their everyday exchanges. The focus of this analysis was not on the content of the questions (e.g., whether they dealt with information about animals, clothing, or furniture) but on the type of cognitive process required for an adequate response (e.g., did the question demand *labeling, memory, prediction*?). Adults rarely think explicitly about this problem. For example, a parent will not be aware that in asking a question such as "What did you do today in school?" he or she has placed a memory demand on the child. The adult is usually focused on the content sought by the question and not on the type of cognitive demand that the question imposes. But while adults are not explicitly conscious of the types of demands they make, they are remarkably adept in this sphere on an intuitive basis. For example, in an attempt to foster communication, parents will automatically simplify not only the content, but also the structure of their language when talking with young children (Blank & Allen, 1976; Newport, Gleitman, & Gleitman, 1975; Snow, 1972). The existence of this behavior means that the problem is not to devise *de nuovo* a set of questions that would be meaningful for a young child; rather, the problem is to give explicit definition to the broad range of demands and questions that adults commonly ask when in interaction with the preschooler.

[5] The difficulties in defining the cognitive demands employed by the teacher are by no means restricted to the preschool age, although they may be somewhat more extreme for this age period. Interested readers are referred to Bloom (1956) for a careful analysis of the problems and techniques in creating a reasonable taxonomy of demands in the educational setting.

TABLE 8.2
Coding of Cognitive–Linguistic Demands

1. Imitation
   a. Action
      Example–Teacher says, *Do what I do,* and proceeds to tap a table.
   b. Language
      Example–Teacher says, *Say what I say. The flower is nice.*
2. Following simple commands
   Example–Teacher says, *Put the book over here.*
3. Identifying objects
   a. By sight
      Example–Teacher holds up a cup and asks, *What is this?*
   b. By touch
      Example–Child feels an object hidden in a bag (e.g. a spoon) and is asked,
      What is this called?
   c. By sound
      Example–A bell is rung and child is asked to select which of four objects made
      the noise.
4. Scanning a complex array
   a. By matching
      Example–Teacher holds up a crayon; than displays a card with many objects on
      it and says, *Find one like this.*
   b. By verbal cues
      Example–Teacher points to a table covered with many objects and says, *Find me
      something here that I can use to draw with.*
5. Completing a sentence
   Example–Teacher says, *You finish this sentence. Children like to eat_____.*
6. Memory (for objects, or labels)
   a. Immediate
      Example–Teacher holds up an apple, hides it and says, *Tell me what you just saw.*
   b. Short-term (within the lesson)
      Example–At the beginning of the lesson, the teacher reads a story about a bird. At the
      end of the lesson, the teacher says, *Can you remember who was in the story?*
   c. Long-term (referring to events prior to lesson)
      Example–*What toy did you play with when you came in here last time?*
7. Description of an event
   a. Present
      Example–A picture is shown of children playing ball. The teacher asks, *What is
      happening in this picture?*
   b. Past
      Example–*What did you do at the zoo when you visited there?*
   c. Future
      Example–A picture of a boy riding a bike is shown as part of a story. The teacher says,
      He finished riding his bicycle. What do you think he'll do next?
8. Concepts
   a. Concepts of actions (verbs)
      Example–Teacher points to a paper and says, Turn *this* over.
   b. Attribute concepts
      Example–Teacher holds out several objects and says, *Find me the one that is* rough.
   c. Relational concepts
      Example–Teacher points to two boxes and says, *Which is* bigger?
   d. Part–whole relationships
      Example–Teacher points to the screw in a scissors and asks, *What is* this part for?
   e. Spatial concepts
      Example–Teacher gives the child a pencil and says, *Put this* next to *the box.*

TABLE 8.2
Continued

  f. Multiple concepts
   Example–Teacher shows several objects and says, *Find the* big, red *block.*
  g. Concepts of exclusion
   Example–Child has drawn a circle, teacher says, *Now draw me something that is not a circle.*
  h. Temporal concepts
   Example–Child has heard a story. Teacher says, *Who came into the room first, the dog or the man?*
  i. Auditory concepts
   Example–*Tell me a word that* rhymes *with man.*
  j. Concepts of difference
   Example–Teacher shows two nonidentical pencils and asks, *How are these* different?
  k. Concepts of similarity
   Example–Teacher shows a truck and a bus and asks, *How are these the* same?
  l. Definitions
   Example–Teacher says, *Tell me what* shoes *are.*
 9. Dialogue skills–role taking
  Example–Teacher in telling a story says, *The man's car was broken and he took it to the garage. What do you think the man in the garage said when he brought in the car?*
10. Following a set of commands
  Example–Teacher says, *Put the ball on the chair, taken the pencil off the book, and then turn the book over.*
11. Formulating a generalization
  Example–Teacher shows a sequence depicting a boy getting ready to go to bed. Teacher asks, *What is happening in this story?*
12. Prediction
  Example–Teacher shows a balance scale andd asks, *What will happen to the scale if I put this (weight) in?*
13. Identifying causes
  a. Event observed
   Example–Child has seen a truck knock down a tree. Teacher asks, *What made the tree fall down?*
  b. Event not observed
   Example–Child sees a crumpled paper and a smooth paper. Teacher asks, *What could have happened to make the paper look like this?*
14. Offering explanations
  a. For barrier to action
   Example–Child tries to reach a toy on the top of a cabinet and is unsuccessful. Teacher says, *Why can't you reach the toy?*
  b. For proposed (predicted) action or observation
   Example–The teacher reads a story about a boy looking for a pair of scissors because he needed to make a piece of cardboard smaller. Teacher then asks, *Why did he want a pair of scissors?*
  c. For construction of objects
   Example–After child has recognized that a boot is made of rubber, teacher says, *Why is it made of rubber instead of something else, like paper?*
  d. For an inference
   Example–Child has noted that a child (in a picture) looks sad. Teacher asks, *How could you tell she is sad?*
  e. For prediction about hypothetical changes
   Example–Teacher shows a sponge and asks first, *Would this still be a sponge if it were green instead of yellow?* Then, *Why?*

In addition to the problem of definition, there is a subsidiary problem—namely, the problem of question difficulty. For example, those familiar with young children will "intuitively" know that a "what" question (such as "What is this?") is generally easier than a "why" question (such as "Why do we use bricks in making houses?")—easier in the sense that a child of 2 years could readily answer the former question, while it might not be until 5 years that a child could answer the latter problem. The problem of question difficulty is particularly crucial in the classroom setting, for it is the teacher's role to pose problems that are matched or appropriate to the level of attainment that characterizes the child's functioning at any particular time. Unfortunately, adequate information on the issue of task difficulty within the preschool-age range is extremely sparse. However, based on a test currently being developed in our unit, it was possible to obtain estimates of the relative ease or difficulty of a large range of cognitive demands that one poses to young children (see Blank, 1975).

These two issues (i.e., type and ease of question) are reflected in Table 8.2, where the range of linguistic–cognitive demands made of the preschooler are listed in roughly increasing order of difficulty (based on research currently being conducted in our laboratory, it has been found that the order of difficulty is by no means exact). The list follows a pattern in which the initial set of items (i.e., types 1–5) are coped with successfully by most 3-year-olds; the intermediate set (i.e., types 6–9) are handled by 4-year-olds; while it is not until 5 years that most children can deal with the later set of items (i.e., types 10–14).

The list as shown is far from complete in that many additional types of demands could be added. Nevertheless, it does cover a wide range of the linguistic–cognitive based demands that can be asked of young children. The labels attached to the different demands are not meant to represent clearly defined, independent skills · For example, even a relatively simple item such as identifying an object (Type 3) requires a host of different skills (e.g., *visual recognition* of the object; *memory for the label* associated with the object, *auditory recognition* of the words "What is this?"). Thus, the category names are not meant to be precise; instead, they are meant to serve as useful mnemonics for what appear to be essentially different demands on the child.

Coding a Teaching Exchange

Rather than elaborating further on the qualifications in the coding, it seems most useful at this point to discuss the ways in which the coding might be utilized. Considered on its own, the scale can be used to answer a number of issues that are frequently raised about teaching practice, for example: How varied is the teacher's repertoire? Does he or she limit the range of demands to a very few types (e.g., repeatedly asking for *identification of objects* or repeatedly demanding *memory*)? Does he or she cover the range of processes appropriate to a young child? Those sorts of questions are valuable, but they focus solely on the teacher and therefore do not necessarily help us understand the patterns of interaction that occur between teacher and child in response to the imposition of these demands.

Insight into the interaction can be attained, however, if one evaluates the Cognitive Demand scale in conjunction with the Adequacy of Response scale outlined earlier. In essence, the two scales in combination reflect the two sides of the teaching–learning exchange, thereby permitting assessment of the effectiveness with which each participant in the exchange is coping with his respective task. For example, the child's performance can be assessed in the following way: the demands he meets adequately offer a picture of his cognitive–linguistic strengths in the formal learning situation; the demands he does not meet adequately offer a picture of his weaknesses in that situation. Conversely, the combination of the scales offers a diagnostic picture of the appropriateness of the teacher's behavior. For example, if a large percentage of the teacher's demands lead to inadequate responses, then the teaching may be deemed inappropriate since it is causing the child to be inundated with failure. The "lesson" then would have served no purpose other than to reinforce the child's sense of inadequacy in the school setting. On the other hand, if the teaching is such that the child offers adequate responses to all the demands posed, then it is likely that the lesson may be too easy since it is touching only upon skills that the child has already fully mastered before he entered the lesson.

This line of analysis suggests that a first step in adequate teaching is the imposition of demands that lead to a "reasonable balance" of success and failure on the part of the child. Since there has been little research in this area, it is impossible to state what the appropriate ratio of success and failure ought to be. But the raising of this issue indicates one of the primary ways in which the scales offered here may be used in studies of teacher–child interaction. Specifically, it is important to determine the degree of success and failure that children need if their interest and self-confidence are to be maintained while they are simultaneously challenged by relatively complex demands that move them to achieve higher levels of understanding.

Some Sample Dialogues

Questions about the desirable balance between success and failure cover complex and controversial areas that might simply lead to endless unproductive debate. For example, many might argue vehemently with the need to elicit any degree of failure from the child. In an effort to prevent heated controversy, it seems best to remove the ideas from the realm of theoretical speculation alone and show how they may be used in coding actual teacher–child exchanges. To this end, the material that follows is drawn from two lessons with a 4-year-old child whose test performance was indicative of likely school failure. The first lesson was carried out by a teacher trained in a tutorial program outlined briefly at the start of the chapter (see also Blank, 1973). The second lesson with the same child is conducted by a traditionally trained nursery school teacher. Both teachers were asked to carry out a lesson that they felt would be appropriate and meaningful to a child of this age.

Because of space limitations, the sections of the lessons that are presented are far shorter than those that would be needed for a truly adequate assessment of any teacher–child exchange. However, the full dialogues (from which these sections are drawn) are available elsewhere and therefore the total exchanges can be examined by interested readers (see Blank & Solomon, 1969). Each interchange in the dialogue is accompanied by the coding that the particular behavior would receive according to the scales outlined above (i.e., the teacher's comment is coced according to the type of cognitive demand that it represents; the child's response is coded according to the adequacy with which it meets the teacher's demand).

In the first lesson, the teacher and the child had been discussing a blackboard, means of erasing writing on the blackboard, and so on. At this point in the exchange, the teacher says:

Teacher	Child
1. *Now, I'd like you to draw something for me on the blackboard.* (Type 2)	2. *What color?* (Request information)
3. *What color would you like to use?* (Type 8b)	4. *Green* (and selects green crayon). (Fully adequate)
5. a. *Green is fine.* b. *Draw some green lines for me.* (Type 2)	6. *I'll make some big ones* (and proceeds to draw). (Fully adequate)
7. a. *Okay, we can work with big ones.* b. *Oh. Those are very big ones.* c. *What will happen if you wipe the sponge on those lines?* (Type 10)	8. *I don't know.* (Inadequate. *Don't know.*)
9. a. *Think about it, Julie.* b. *If you put this sponge over your lines and wipe them, what will happen?* (Type 10)	10. (Moves sponge over drawing) (Inadequate association)
11. *What's happening to the lines, Julie?* (Type 7a)	12. (With surprise) *They're not there anymore!* (Fully adequate)
13. (Holds sponge down to prevent child from lifting it) *If I lift up the sponge, what color is going to be on the sponge?* (Type 10)	14. *White.* (Inadequate association)
15. *Why white?* (Type 14a)	16. *Green.* (Ambiguous)
17. a. *Tell me why you said green.* b. *Why do you think it will be green?* (Type 14a)	18. *Cause I wipe it off.* (Adequate)
19. *What did you wipe off?* (Type 6b)	20. *The green color.* (Fully adequate)

21. a. *Let's see if you're right.*
    b. (lifts sponge) *Green!*
    c. *You're right.*
    d. *Very good.*

The section that follows is, as stated above, with a different teacher but the same child. At the start of the lesson, Julie had looked at some flowers that were in the room, reading for planting outdoors in the school garden. The teacher responded by asking:

Teacher	Child
1. *Have you seen the flowers?* (Type 6a)	2. *I saw a beautiful flower outside.* (Ambiguous)
3. a. *A beautiful flower?* b. *What color was it?* (Type 6c)	4. *I don't know. It's a beautiful flower.* (Inadequate–*don't know*)
5. *Did you put it in the ground?* (Type 6c*)[6]	6. *I picked it up.* (Ambiguous)
7. a. *You picked it up.* b. *What kind was it?* (Type 6c)	8. *I don't know.* (Inadequate–*don't know*)
9. a. *Was it little and yellow?* b. *Maybe it was a dandelion?* (Type 6c*)[6]	10. (Nods). (Ambiguous)
11. *Why don't you draw a picture of the flower and then we can see what color it is?* (Type 8b)	12. *I'd like to do any color flower.* (Inadequate–association)
13. *I'd love to have a drawing of it.*	

Even a rapid reading of the exchanges indicates that there are marked differences between the lessons. Yet the coding of each individual response does not capture these differences. Therefore, one may well be puzzled as to what has been achieved by the intricate coding process. The coding of individual responses cannot, or is it meant to, yield a picture of the teacher–child interaction. It is only a first step in the process. The coding becomes helpful only if it used to evaluate the total set of interchanges. Table 8.3 presents one such evaluation; it showes the total range of demands that were made by the teacher and the child's response to each of these demands in both lessons.

---

[6] The asterisk refers to questions that are not open-ended in that they demand only a "Yes–No" type of response.

TABLE 8.3
Assessment of Teacher–Child Interaction

Adequacy of child's response	Type of cognitive demand by teacher[a]							
	2 Commands	6a Memory	6b Memory	6c Memory	7 Description	8 Concepts	10 Prediction	14 Rationale
Fully adequate	(5, 6)		(19, 20)		(11, 12)	(3, 4)		
Adequate								(17, 18)
Ambiguous		(1, 2)		(5, 6) / (9, 10)				(15, 16)
Requests help	(1, 2)							
Inadequate: Invalid								
Inadequate: Association						(11, 12)	(9, 10) / (13, 14)	
Inadequate: Irrelevant								
Inadequate: *Don't know*				(3, 4) / (7, 8)			(7, 8)	
Inadequate: No Response								

[a]For reasons of space, the full range of possible cognitive demands is not shown. Instead, the categories here are limited to those demands that were made in the reported exchanges. The numbers above the diagonal refer to the coding of Lesson 1; the numbers below the diagonal refer to the coding of Lesson 2. In each case, the numbers refer to the particular exchange in the dialogue as recorded above.

There are a number of ways in which this type of data can be assessed. Two of the key ratios are:

		Lesson 1	*Lesson 2*
1.	$\dfrac{\text{Number of adequate responses}}{\text{Number of demands}}$	$5/10 = 50\%$	$0/6 = 0\%$
2.	$\dfrac{\text{Number of adequate responses to demands}^7}{\text{Number of different types of demands}}$	$5/5 = 100\%$	$0/3 = 0\%$

The first ratio indicates that in the first lesson the child offered adequate responses to 50% of the demands, while in the second lesson no response adequately met the demand posed. The second ratio indicates that the first lesson also offered the child not only a broader range of cognitive demands, but a range with which she coped more successfully than she did in the second lesson. Thus, the first lesson offered her a greater success experience in terms of both number of demands and variety of demands. In addition, in the second lesson, the teacher repeatedly concentrated on a type of demand—that is, memory—that the child could not handle effectively. As a result, the teacher in that lesson essentially reinforced an area of weakness that was preventing the child from coping well in the academic setting. If this lesson is characteristic of some of the exchanges between teachers and those children who are likely to fail, it becomes clear as to how the academic setting, even the very early academic setting, can be frustrating to many children. However, the optimum ranges necessary to avoid this frustration—or, conversely, necessary to enhance learning—remain to be determined. This could be one of the major areas in which the scales could be applied. That is, observation of a large number of teachers might enable us to determine the ranges that lead to optimum interaction between the teachers and the children.

The Value and Treatment of Failure

Although the first lesson offered a much greater degree of success to the child, it is clear from the number of inadequate responses that the lesson was not one of total success. However as indicated earlier, there are valid reasons for not wanting any lesson to be one of total success, for that degree of success would mean that the lesson did not challenge the child to move beyond the point where he or she was prior to any teaching. In addition, as long as they are not of overwhelming proportions, inadequate responses can be extremely valuable in that they can serve as indicators of the areas in which the child needs help. In other words, any type of demand that the child fails can be viewed as representing an idea that needs strengthening.

But diagnosis is not sufficient. It is useful only if the teacher is able to cope with the child's failure and ultimately help him to overcome his errors. In other words, effective teaching hinges not simply on the type of cognitive demand that is

---

[7] This figure represents the number of different types of demands that received at least one adequate response; there need not be consistently adequate responses to every demand within a category.

imposed, it also hinges on the teacher's ability to manage the inadequate responses triggered by some of the cognitive demands. In turn, the management of these responses depends upon the teacher's use of simplification techniques that restructure and reduce the problem so that the child will be able to meet the demand that was originally failed or avoided. In many ways, the concept of simplification shares many of the basic ideas of task analysis, wherein a task is systematically reduced to its less complex subcomponents. The child must then master these subcomponents before having to grapple with the more complex task (see Gagné, 1965). However, in the main, task analysis has not been concerned with analyzing the subcomponents of normal conversational exchange, such as those that a teacher might use with a child. For example, a preschooler may systematically fail "Why?" questions because he does not yet understand the concept of "why?" Task analysis offers almost no guidelines as to how this type of verbal concept may be reduced to simpler subcomponents. By contrast, the simplification techniques listed below are designed precisely to deal with this issue; they represent the range of practices whereby a teacher can reduce the typical language demands of a preschool setting when the child offers evidence (in the form of inadequate responses) that he cannot, or is not, coping with the demand posed.

Table 8.4 lists the simplification techniques that are applicable for use with the preschool-age child. A number of different rules govern the successful application of these techniques, and these are described elsewhere (Blank, 1973). One need not delve into the rules, however, to determine success or lack of success, for the child's response offers an unparalleled criterion. Specifically, if the techniques lead the child to recognize and apply the more appropriate response, then the techniques are judged to be successful; if they have failed to do so, then they are judged unsuccessful.

These ideas concerning the use of simplification are illustrated in Table 8.5, where the excerpts from the two lessons presented earlier are coded for the type of simplifications used by each of the two teachers. Again, as with the analysis of the cognitive demands, the focus is not on any particular exchange but on the pattern that characterizes the teacher's behavior within a full lesson or across lessons. This aspect of the teacher's behavior can be analyzed on a number of parameters. These include the following ratios that were calculated for the lessons above.

1. The first measure is a sign of the frequency with which simplification techniques were used relative to the number of times they could have been used. This is calculated by

	Lesson 1	*Lesson 2*
Number of times simplifications used	5/6 = 83%	3/6 = 50%
Number of other than fully adequate responses		

TABLE 8.4
"Simplification" Techniques for Management of Nonadequate Responses

1. Delay
   Sample problem: Teacher—*Pick up the_____. Child starts grabbing objects.
   Teacher—*Wait a minute. Listen to what I want you to pick up.*
2. Focus for attention
   Sample problem: Teacher—*Go to the sink and get me the pot.* Child goes to the sink and
   reaches for the first thing he sees, which is a glass. Teacher—*Do you remember what I
   asked you to bring?*
3. Repeats demand
   Sample problem: Teacher—*Put your coat on the chair next to the table. No, not on the
   table, put it on the chair that's next to the table.*
4. Synonymous rephrasing
   Sample problem: Teacher—*Lift the box off the floor.* Child does nothing. Teacher—*I mean
   I want you to pick it up with your hands.*
5. Partially completes task
   Sample problem: Teacher—*What is a pail for?* Child says nothing. Teacher—*It can carry
   w_____.*
6. Dissects or restructures task to highlight specific components
   Sample problem: Teacher—*Why do you think we couldn't get this sponge into the (small)
   cup and we could fit the marble?* Child—*Because it's a sponge.* Teacher—*Okay, I'll cut
   this sponge into two. Now it's still a sponge. Why does it go into the cup now?*
7. Offers relevant comparison
   Sample problem: Teacher—*Where did the ball go?* Child says nothing. Teacher—*Well, let's
   see—did it go under the table or did it go under the chair?*
8. Didactic presentation of information
   Sample problem: Teacher—*Could you go over there and get me the strainer?* Child goes to
   table and looks bewildered. Teacher—*Do you know what a strainer is?* Child shakes head.
   Teacher—*Look, this one is a strainer.*
9. Makes child clarify response
   Sample problem: Teacher (while pouring milk into some pudding) asks—*What's happening?*
   Child says, *Milk.* Teacher—*Yes, there's milk, but what is happening to the milk?*
10. Repeats demonstration for clarification
    Sample problem: Teacher—*Where did I put the key to get the door to open?* Child shrugs.
    Teacher—*Well, watch again. I'm going to do it over—and then you can show me.*
11. Relating unknown to the known
    Sample problem: Teacher—*Now the spaghetti is hard. How do you think it will feel after it
    is cooked?* Child says, *I don't know.* Teacher—*Well, do you remember when we cooked the
    potatoes? How did they feel?*
12. Directed action to recognize salient characteristics
    Sample problem: Teacher—*How is the ice different from the water?* Child says, *I don't
    know.* Teacher says, *Well, let's see. Turn over the cup of water and turn over the tray
    of ice.*
13. Focus on relevant features
    Sample problem: Teacher—*Why did you pull your hand away from the stove?* Child says
    nothing. Teacher—*Well, how did the stove feel?*

TABLE 8.5
Application of Simplification Techniques to Dialogues

Child's previous response	Repeat	Rephrases	Dissects	Clarify	Features	No simplification used
Adequate					18+ /	
Ambiguous			10– /	16+ /		
Requests inform.	2+ /				2– /	/ 6
Invalid						
Association				10+ /		14 /
						/ 12
Irrelevant						
I don't know	8– /					
No response					/ 8–	/ 4

*For reasons of space, the full range of possible simplifications is not shown. Instead, the categories here are limited to only those simplifications used in the reported exchanges. Numbers in upper left of diagonal reflect the exchanges where the error was made in Lesson 1; in the lower right where it was made in Lesson 2.
+child's response to simplification is adequate
−child's response to simplification is inadequate

2. The second measure reflects the success that the simplification measures achieved. This is reflected in:

	Lesson 1	Lesson 2
Number of times simplification led to adequate responses / Number of times simplification used	4/5 = 80%	0/3 = 0%

3. The third measure reflects the flexibility with which the teacher employs the range of simplification techniques. This is reflected by:

	Lesson 1	Lesson 2
Number of different simplification techniques used / Number of times simplification used	4/8 = .80	2/3 = .67

These ratios reflect some of the key differences between the teaching styles in the two lessons, and they serve to highlight the exact areas with which the teacher is experiencing difficulty. For example, the analysis of the second lesson indicates that the teacher's problem was not so much in a failure to use simplifications or in a failure to use a variety of simplificiations (ratios 1 and 2). Instead, her major difficulty lay in experiencing a lack of success with the techniques. Further analysis suggests that part of the difficulty lay in the fact that the attempted simplification could not possibly lead the child to answer the original problem. For example, when the child could not, or did not, offer the color of the flower (exchanges 3 and 4), the teacher attempted a simplification that had nothing to do with colors. Instead, she asked if the child put the flower in the ground. Even if one were certain that the child could answer this latter question, it would in no way help the child to answer the original question concerning color. As these comments suggest, effective use of simplification demands complex skills on the part of the teacher. It is not possible within the scope of the present chapter to discuss the training of teachers in this area. The points above were raised solely in an effort to point out ways in which one might begin to analyze the teacher's behavior in this important, but often neglected, sphere of interaction.

The Supportive Role of Language

Both scales of teacher language thus far presented are concerned with the purely cognitive aspects of the situation; that is, with the type of demands he or she puts to the child and the techniques he or she has available to help the child over difficulty. Even in the most formal of lessons, however, no interchange is stripped down to these limited uses of language. Many other types of language are present to support the teaching (e.g., as in the comments of Lesson 1 where the teacher said, "Green is fine," and "Okay, we can work with the big ones"). Frequently, the comments to which I am referring fall into groupings that the teacher interaction literature categorizes as "praise," "acceptance of ideas," and "offers rationale for the presentation of material."

In general, the supportive language used by the teacher is a sign of his or her sensitivity to the situation confronting the child (e.g., the teacher offers an explanation because he or she realizes that the child might not understand the reason for a particular material being brought out). This sensitivity is essential if the teacher is to attain one of the most widely accepted goals of teaching—namely, elicitation of the child's active cooperation and involvement in the learning process. "Support" language is central to the goal, for it serves to signal to the child how his responses are being evaluated and how accepting the teacher is of his views. Because of its importance, almost every system for coding teacher behavior makes some provision for scoring this type of behavior. For example, Flanders' widely used system employs categories such as "accepts feelings," "praises or encourages," "accepts or uses ideas of." Again, because so little of the work in this area is designed to deal with the teacher in interaction with the young child, and in particular the poorly functioning young child, it was necessary to devise a set of

TABLE 8.6
Categories for Coding Teacher's "Support" Language

"Positive" behavior A	"Negative" behavior B
1. Accepts child's comment, idea or suggestion (*Okay, let's try it*) 2. Acknowledges child's comment or behavior (e.g., *Oh, you're making a train*) 3. Praises adequate response by child (e.g., *That's very good*) 4. Structures and/or explains presentation of material (*We're going to the zoo tomorrow, so I thought that today we would read a story about animals*)	1. Rejects child's suggestion (*No, I'm afraid that wouldn't work*) 2. Ignores child's comment or request 3. Criticizes child (*If only you would listen*) 4. Praises an inadequate response given by the child (Child picks up a circle when he was asked to select a square; teacher says *That's very good*)

categories that would highlight the "support" language most likely to be used with this age group.

It is apparent that the range of teacher behavior in this area can be extremely broad, and the list outlined below in Table 8.6 is by no means a complete representation of the comments that the teacher may display. However, they are designed to cover a large percentage of the teacher's "support" language when interacting with the preschool-age child. It will be noted that the behaviors are grouped into A and B categories. In general, the methods listed under A tend to be what would be deemed positive or appropriate responses and those under B to be what would be considered negative or inappropriate responses. This distinction is made since it is deemed of importance in helping to identify the key factors responsible for effective versus ineffective exchanges (e.g., traditionally negative comments are thought to inhibit the communication between teachers and children).

Far more important than the positive or negative aspect of the behavior, however, is the relevance or appropriateness of the behavior in the context. For example, it may well be that the teacher uses positive ("desirable") support language when the child is performing well (i.e., offering adequate responses), but that he or she finds it difficult to respond to the child in a positive or supportive way when the child offers inadequate responses. In an effort to tap this factor, in the current coding system the teacher's support language is evaluated with reference to the child's functioning. This is done by grouping the teacher's responses separately according to whether

1. the child's immediately preceding response was adequate,
2. the previous response was not adequate,
3. the previous response was ambiguous,
4. the previous response was a request for help or information,

TABLE 8.7
Teacher's Supportive Comments

Child's previous response	Positive				Negative			
	Accepts	Acknow.	Praises (adequate)	Structures	Rejects	Ignores	Criticize	Praises (inadequate)
Adequate	5a / 7a	7b / 21c	21d	21a 21b				
Inadequate				9a				
Ambiguous	3a / 7a							13
Requests info.								
No prior response required								

The numbers and letters refer to the exchanges in the dialogue; those in the upper left are from Lesson 1 and those in the lower right from Lesson 2.

5. the situation was such that no previous response was required (e.g., the teacher is introducing a new idea and has not yet made any demands on the child).

In order to illustrate these ideas, Table 8.7 presents the coding of the support comments used by the two teachers in Lessons 1 and 2. Again, as with the two previous scales, any specific response is not of concern. Instead, the teacher's overall behavior is assessed through a number of ratios that tap the appropriateness of the teacher's response according to the child's preceding response. For example, the first measure assesses the teacher's support comments when the child's response is adequate. This is reflected in the ratio:

$$\frac{\text{Number of appropriate comments when child's response is adequate}}{\text{Number of all comments when child's response is adequate.}}$$

Four comparable ratios are computed according to whether the child's preceding respones were: (1) inadequate, (2) ambiguous, (3) requests for help or information, or (4) not required. Unfortunately, the samples of dialogues presented from Lessons 1 and 2 are too sparse to permit one to gain a picture of the teachers' behavior in this sphere (although Table 8.7 is sufficient to illustrate the way in which the coding would be done). Analysis of the full lessons (available in Blank & Solomon, 1969) indicates that both teachers were highly supportive—with the qualification that the teacher in the first lesson used praise when the child offered adequate responses, while the teacher in the second lesson commonly used praise in response to ambiguous and inadequate answers. This latter course of behavior may be questionable, since it may cause the child to become confused regarding the most appropriate response to the problem stated. However, this judgment, as well as almost all judgments in this area, can only be tentative since there are almost no guidelines so to what are optimum or desirable patterns to follow. The absence of information in this sphere is particularly unfortunate since it is probably here that the oft-discussed issue of cultural differences between the teacher and child becomes of prime importance, raising such questions as: How do children of different ethnic groups respond to praise and to criticism? What sorts of feedback do they expect from the adult? How are they accustomed to initiating an exchange about a particular issue? "Difference" proponents have often raised the possibility that cultural differences may interfere with teacher—child exchange, but they have offered almost no systematic techniques for assessing this aspect of the interaction. In the few cases where there is an analysis of the teaching situation, generally the material remains solely on an anecdotal level (e.g., reporting an exchange between a teacher and a child). (See Gumperz & Hernandez-Chavez, 1972, and Mischler, 1972, for articles illustrating this approach.) Systematic evaluation of the support comments used by the teacher may offer a useful entry into this important but little studied area.

A SUMMARY STATEMENT

As noted earlier in the chapter, the coding system outlined here is geared to the demands and goals of a specialized teaching program for preschool-age children who are likely to fail in school. The coding system will almost certainly have to be modified for use with other programs and for research with different goals. Nevertheless, it is hoped that the ideas and techniques it employs can be adapted by other investigators interested in the area of teacher–child communication. In particular, the major themes that guided its development are:

1. Language is an extraordinary complex behavior that involves a host of different skills and functions. If we are to be able to analyze it in a meaningful way, we must impose a structure that will permit us to limit our attention to those aspects of language that seem most relevant to particular situations. In the case of the classroom, it was suggested that the roles assigned to the teacher and to the child could provide one such structure. As the formal learning situation is presently constituted, it is the teacher's role to impose tasks, problems, and material that will enhance the child's learning, and it is the child's role to cope with these imposed demands.

2. Utilizing this framework, sets of scales were developed to capture the behaviors used by the teacher and the child in meeting their respective roles. A 9-point scale titled Adequacy of Response was developed to represent the patterns of response that a child might offer in response to any linguistic–cognitive problem placed before him. Analogously, a set of three scales was developed to represent the quality and appropriateness of the demands that the teacher places on the child. One scale assessed the type of demand that the teacher made; a second assessed the way in which the teacher simplified problems for the child when he was in difficulty; a third assessed the type of language used by the teacher in presenting material to the child or in offering feedback to the child about the quality of his responses.

3. These scales are designed to be used in coding actual dialogues that take place between the teacher and child. Each interchange between the two participants can be coded on one or more of these scales (e.g., a problem put forth by the teacher can be coded both as a particular type of cognitive demand and as a type of simplification that he or she is using to ease a problem that the child has failed). The quality of the communication between the teacher and child, however, is never judged on the basis of any single exchange that has taken place. Instead, the effectiveness of the teacher–child communication is based on a total range of interachanges that have taken place. This is done through a series of ratios that are designed to evaluate how effectively the two participants responded relative to each other. For example, one such ratio assesses the times the child could adequately meet the problems imposed by the teacher. It thereby reveals the extent of the child's success or failure in that lesson. Another ratio assesses the percentage of

times the teacher uses simplification techniques when the child is in some form of difficulty. It thereby shows the sensitivity of the teacher in trying to help the child overcome his failures. In combination, the total range of ratios gives a comprehensive picture of the strengths and weaknesses of both the teacher and child.

4. Because of the detail needed in the coding of the interchanges, the scales cannot be used, nor are they intended to be used, on an "everyday" basis. Rather, they are intended for use in those situations where on wishes to analyze, on a systematic basis, the patterns of functioning that characterize particular teachers and particular children. It is hoped that this type of analysis will allow us to begin to identify the precise factors underlying effective communication. Much of current educational theory is based on the premise that these factors are already known. The high failure rate in schools, however, suggests that either we have not correctly identified the factors that permit effective teaching—learning exchange or else we have not effectively trained teachers to implement these principles in their actual work with children. In either case, if we are to begin to move on the problem of school failure, we must begin to identify exactly where the difficulties lie. It is hoped that the assessment model presented here can allow us to make some progress on this vital issue.

REFERENCES

Amidon, E. J., & Hough, J. B. (Eds.), *Interaction analysis: Theory, research and application.* Reading, Massachusetts: Addison-Wesley, 1967.

Angel, F. Social class or culture? A fundamental issue in the education of culturally different students. In B. Spolsky (Ed.), *The language education of minority children.* Rowley, Massachusetts: Newbury House, 1972.

Baratz, S. S., & Baratz, J. C. Early childhood intervention: The social science base of institutional racism. *Harvard Educational Review,* 1970, *40,* 29–50.

Barnes, D. Language in the secondary classroom. In D. Barnes, J. Britton, and H. Rosen (Eds.), *Language, the learner and the school.* Harmondsworth, England: Penguin, 1969.

Bellack, A. A., Kliebard, H. M., Hyman, R. T., & Smith, F. L. Jr. *The language of the classroom.* New York: Teachers College, 1966.

Bennett, S. N., & Jordan, J. A typology of teaching styles in primary schools. *British Journal of Educational Psychology,* 1975, *45,* 20–28.

Bereiter, C., & Engelmann, S. *Teaching disadvantaged children in the preschool.* Englewood Cliffs, New Jersey: Prentice—Hall, 1966.

Bernstein, B. A critique of the concept of compensatory education. In D. Rubenstein and C. Stoneman (Eds.), *Education for democracy.* Harmondsworth: Penguin, 1969.

Bissell, J. S. Implementation of planned variation in Head Start. Washington, D.C.: U.S. Department of Health, Education and Welfare, Office of Child Development, 1971.

Black, M. *The labyrinth of language.* New York: Praeger, 1968.

Blank, M. Some philosophical influences underlying preschool intervention for disadvantaged children. In F. Williams (Eds.), *Language and poverty: Perspectives on a theme.* Chicago: Markham, 1970.

Blank, M. *Teaching learning in the preschool: A dialogue approach.* Columbus, Ohio: Charles E. Merrill, 1973.

Blank, M. Mastering the intangible through language. In D. Aaronson and R. W. Rieber (Eds.), *Developmental psycholinguistics and communication disorders.* Annals New York Academy Sciences. New York, 1975, *263,* 44–58.

Blank, M., & Allen, D. A. Understanding "why": Its significance in early intelligence. In M. Lewis (Ed.), *Origins of intelligence.* New York: Plenum, 1976.

Blank, M., Koltuv, M., & Wood, M. Individual teaching for disadvantaged children: A comparison of two methods. *Journal of Special Education,* 1972, *6,* 207–219.

Blank, M., & Solomon, F. How shall the disadvantaged child be taught? *Child Development,* 1969, *40,* 47–61.

Bloom, B. S. (Ed.). Taxonomy of educational objectives: Handbook I. *Cognitive domain.* New York: David McKay, 1956.

Boggs, S. T. The meaning of questions and narratives to Hawaiian children. In C. B. Cazden, V. P. John & D. Hymes (Eds.), *Functions of language in the classroom.* New York: Teachers College Press, 1972.

Cazden, C. B., John, V. P., & Hymes, D. (Eds.). *Functions of language in the classroom.* New York: Teachers College Press, 1972.

Coulthard, M. Approaches to the analysis of classroom interaction. *Educational Review,* 1974, *26,* 229–240.

Criper, C., & Davies, A. Research on spoken language in the primary school. A report to the Scottish Education Department, Department of Linguistics, University of Edinburgh, September 1974.

Deutsch, M. The role of social class in language development and cognition. American *Journal of Orthopsychiatry,* 1965, *1,* 78–88.

Dopyera, J. E. Assessing the micro-environments of individual preschool children. Final report, OEO Head Start, Research Division, OEO 4120, 1969.

Dumont, R. V. Jr. Learning English and how to be silent: Studies in Sioux and Cherokee classrooms. In C. B. Cazden, V. P. John & D. Hymes (Eds.) *Functions of language in the classroom.* New York: Teachers College Press, 1972.

Ervin-Tripp, S. Discourse agreement: How children answer questions. In J. R. Hayes (Ed.), *Cognition and the development of language.* New York, Wiley, 1970.

Flanders, N. A. *Analyzing teacher behavior.* New York: Adison Wesley, 1970.

Gagné, R. R. *The conditions of learning.* New York: Holt, Rinehart & Winston, 1965.

Gleason, J. B. Code switching in children's language. In T. E. Moore (Ed.), *Cognitive development and the acquisition of language.* New York: Academic Press, 1973.

Gumperz, J. J., & Hernandez-Chavez, E. Bilingualism, bidialectalism and classroom interaction. In C. B. Cazden, V. P. John, and J. D. Hymes, (Eds.), *Functions of language in the classroom.* New York: Teachers College Press, 1972.

Halliday, M. *Explorations in the functions of language.* London: Edward Arnold, 1973.

Houston, S. H. A re-examination of some assumptions about the language of the disadvantaged child. *Child Development,* 1970, *41,* 947–963.

Hymes, D. Introduction. In C. B. Cazden, V. P. John, and D. Hymes (Eds.), *Functions of language in the classroom.* New York: Teachers College Press, 1972.

Labov, W. The logic of non-standard English. In J. S. Alatis (Ed.), *Linguistics and the teaching of standard English.* Monograph Series of Language and Linguistics, No. 22. Washington, D.C.: Georgetown University Press, 1969.

Lawton, D. *Social class, language, and education.* London: Routledge & Kegan Paul, 1968.

Lay, M. Z. *The responsive care model: A program manual and report of implementation.* Syracuse, New York: Syracuse University Early Childhood Education Center, 1972.

Mishler, E. G. Implications of teachers strategies for language and cognition: Observations in first-grade classroom. In C. B. Cazden, V. P. John, and D. Hymes (Eds.), *Functions of language in the classroom.* New York: Teachers College Press, 1972.

Newport, E. L., Gleitman, L. R., & Gleitman, H. Contributions to the theory of innate ideas from learning: A study of mother's speech and child language acquisition. Paper presented at the Society for Research in Child Development, Denver, Colorado, 1975.

Rosen, H. Towards a language policy across the curriculum. In D. Barnes (Ed.), *Language, the learner and the school.* Harmondsworth, England: Penguin, 1969.

Rosenshine, B., & Furst, N. The use of direct observation to study learning. In R. Travers (Ed.), *Second handbook of research on teaching.* Chicago: Rand McNally, 1973.

Savić, S. Aspects of adult-child communication: The problem of question acquisition. *Journal of Child Language,* 1975, *2,* 251–260.

Silberman, C. E. *Crisis in the classroom: The remaking of American education.* New York: Random House, 1970.

Simon, A., & Boyer, E. (Eds.), *Mirrors for behavior: An anthology of classroom observation instruments.* Classroom Interaction Newsletter, 1968, 3.

Snow, E. E. Mothers' speech to children learning language. *Child Development,* 1972, *43,* 549–565.

Spolsky, B. (Ed.). *The language education of minority children.* Rowley, Massachusetts: Newbury House, 1972.

Taba, H., Levine, S., & Elzey, F. Thinking in elementary school children. Cooperative Research Project No. 1574., U.S. Office of Education, 1964.

Tough, J. The language of young children: The implications for the education of the young disadvantaged child. In M. Chazan (Ed.), *Education in the early years.* Swansea: University College of Swansea, Wales, 1973.

Williams, F. (Ed.). *Language and poverty: Perspectives on a theme.* Chicago: Markham, 1970.

9

Prosocial Behavior

JAMES H. BRYAN

Northwestern University

INTRODUCTION

Increasingly, psychologists have been addressing their efforts toward the study of the development and elicitation of helping behavior. Indeed, since 1970, one book (Macualay & Berkowitz, 1970), two *Psychological Bulletin* review articles (Bryan & London, 1970; Krebs, 1970), an entire journal issue (Wispe, 1972), not to mention literally hundreds of journal articles, have been devoted to theories and data regarding helping activities of adults and children alike. This interest appears to have been stimulated by several factors. Wispe (1972) suggests that student activism, humanistic psychology, and the peace movement have played a prominent catalytic role. The apparently increasing brutality of citizens toward each other has also been expressed as a stimulant to such studies (Bryan, 1972). There is no question that practical concerns to produce a "better society," one in which the principle of the Good Samaritan is given not only verbal but behavioral allegiances, has played an important role in stimulating and maintaining empirical efforts in the study of helping activity. "Can the educational institutions, the parent, and the mass media, better teach behavioral allegiances to the value of concern for others and thereby reduce social and economic inequalities, the distress of victims, and the brutality of the citizenry towards themselves and others? Many investigators feel that the answers must be in the affirmative and have begun their efforts to determine what might be done to affect such changes [Bryan, 1975, p. 128]."

The present chapter will present an overview of these theoretical and research efforts, but before so doing, several characteristics of this area of investigation should be made explicit. Most of the investigations of the development of helping behavior have been made within a laboratory rather than a naturalistic setting. Additionally, such studies are based upon children who are attending primary school classes. There are relatively few studies concerned with the helping activities of preschool-age children. The applicability of many of the findings to such young children can therefore be argued.

The experiments so far conducted have, by and large, shown certain theoretical and methodological similarities such that certain influences on helping are well known, and other potential sources thoroughly neglected. By and large, most work on helping has been theoretically guided by the work of Bandura (1969), whose focus has been on the role of observation upon the learning and performance of children and adults. The emphasis in studies of helping is upon the impact of the child's observing others giving, the effects of such giving upon the benefactors, and the characteristics of the giver. The role of exemplars, or models, has been that which has drawn the most attention. Methodologically, most studies expose a child to a giving model, and then attempt to assess that child's helping behavior on the basis of whether the child will also give a valued object to an unfortunate other. Insofar as most investigators are interested in altruistic, or self-sacrificing responses under conditions of minimum external coercions, the majority of the studies are concerned with the child's private rather than public aiding.

Insofar as educators are likely to serve as important models to children in their charge, the study of model effects are particularly important for them to understand. Insofar as such studies by design exclude many important influences likely to be found in the classroom, such studies will not capture the many complexities affecting helping behavior within that setting. Like the story of the gambler in a small town who was willing to gamble on a rigged roulette wheel since it was the only good game in town, the current chapter will necessarily review modeling studies since they provide almost the only data in town.

Finally, there is some question as to the degree to which any one particular measure of helping, such as donating a commodity to the needy, correlates with other measures of helping, such as rescuing a victim in distress. Can on predict, from knowledge that the child will contribute money to the needy, whether or not a child will be nurturant toward a friend? As pointed out elsewhere (Bryan, 1975), studies conducted within the laboratory context have generally failed to find that measures of helping are positively associated with one another (Mussen, Rutherford, Harris, & Keasey, 1970; Staub, 1969; Staub & Sherk, 1970; Weissbrod, 1974). Several studies, however, did find such a correlation. Elliot and Vasta (1970) reported a correlation between children's donations of money and of candy to a stranger, and Midlarsky and Bryan (1972) found that children's donations within a laboratory setting were predictive of their generosity towards needy children within a classroom setting sometime later. Moreover, observational studies conducted within the classroom have produced evidence that helping behaviors are correlated, although far from perfectly. Friedrich and Stein (1973) found that nurturant and cooperative behaviors were highly correlated in their sample of preschool boys, and moderately correlated in their sample of preschool-age girls. Baumrind (1971) found that such behaviors as bullying, helping, and sympathy and nurturance towards peers were correlated in such a fashion as to suggest reliable differences among children in their consideration for others. Rutherford and Mussen (1968) found that boys who were generous in their donations of candy to two friends were also more likely to be rated by their teachers as generous than children who gave little to their friends.

The remainder of this chapter will review research relevant to the elicitation and development of children's helping behavior. Initially, a discussion of the role of exemplars will be presented with subsequent sections devoted to the impact of affects, competition, and individual differences in children's helping activities.

EXEMPLARS

There is little question that children who observe helping others are likely to be more helpful than those who do not. Whether the observer is attending a preschool or is an adult shopper, exemplars affect their generosity (cf. Bryan & Test, 1967; Hartup & Coates, 1967). Children's imitation of a generous model has been demonstrated with regard to rescue acts (Staub, 1971a) and to the donation of a wide variety of prized objects (Schwartz & Bryan, 1971a, b; Bryan & Walbek, 1970a, b; Harris, 1971; Liebert & Poulos, 1971; Midlarsky & Bryan, 1972; Rosenhan & White, 1967; Rushton, 1975; White, 1972). Moreover, there is evidence that the impact of the generous model may show enduring effects, a surprising finding for a laboratory-produced behavior. Midlarsky and Bryan (1972), Rushton (1975), and White (1972) found that children who viewed a generous model within the laboratory were not only more likely to donate within that context immediately after viewing the model but also were more likely to aid others in a test given days later. Increasingly, recognition is now given to the importance of the nature of the behaviors that the child sees about him.

Explanations of Modeling Effects

There are several explanations that have been advanced to account for the impact of the generous model upon the observing child. One hypothesis is that children learn a *norm* which dictates that one should help a dependent other, the Social Responsibility Norm (Berkowitz & Daniels, 1964; Krebs, 1970), and that the generous model reminds the child, through his actions, of this norm. Once reminded, the child is thought to conform to the norm. There is evidence that children, by the time they are in the primary grades, do learn such a norm. If asked, they respond that it is good to give; they will evaluate others on the basis of the others' willingness to aid needy strangers and will urge others to be generous even in the fact of hearing a model exhort selfishness (Bryan & Walbek, 1970a; Bryan, Redfield, & Mader, 1971; Schwartz & Bryan, 1971a). The question does remain, however, as to whether children will *act* more generously *because* of such reminders. The data are such as to reject this hypothesis. Experiments have been conducted in which some children are reminded of this norm through verbal exhortations, and their generosity is compared with that of children who are not verbally reminded of the norm. Statements such as "It is good to give," or "One should give," have not been found to increase children's donation actions (Bryan & Walbek, 1970a; Liebert & Poulos, 1971; Walbek, 1969). There is some evidence that such moral exhortations may affect giving at some later date for reasons not yet fully understood (Rushton, 1975). What is clear, however, is that simple moral exhortations containing "shoulds" and "oughts" in and of themselves do not immediately increment children's generosity. Moreover, to assume that the effects of the model's generous actions are attributable to norm reminders would require the assumption that the model's actions are better norm reminders than verbal explications of such norms, a very tenuous assumption.

A second explanation of the impact of the exemplar upon the observing child is that the model's behavior defines the proprieties of the situation to the child. The term *demand characteristics,* when applied to imitative altruism, reduces to the idea that children will do what they think is required of them within an experimental setting and will weigh heavily both the model's actions and the consequences of such actions in inferring the requirements. Presumably, the actions can either be demonstrated or verbally described, both being important in affecting the child's expectancies of the proprieties surrounding the situation. The verbal inputs, unlike the moral exhortations previously noted, describe the model's past or future behaviors to the child. While the model's motoric actions influence the child's willingness to donate, the impact of their verbal descriptions show complex relationships with the age and sex of the observing child. The results, while not entirely consistent, suggest that verbal descriptions of past or future behavior by the exemplar are likely to be effective with girls between the ages of 7 to 11, and for boys over the age of 11, but only if the children have had explicit instructions that such donation behavior from them is allowable (Grusec, 1972; Grusec & Skubiski, 1970).

The overall greater effects of the model's behavior compared to his verbal influence attempts on children's aiding might be attributable to several sources. Grusec and Driscoll have suggested that the child's observation of a generous model elicits a comparison process between the child and the model by the observing child. It is hypothesized that the child compares himself with the model and if the model actually donates the child's feelings of self-worth will be attenuated unless he does likewise. A second possibility is that the model's actions better demonstrate the acceptability of giving than the model's verbal statements. It is one thing to be informed that giving will be done or has been done with apparently no untoward consequences, and quite another to view such actions and to note the absence of negative consequences. Whatever mediates the modeling effect, noteworthy is the increasing evidence that the impact of an altruistic model shows durability in time and generalizability across space.

It now seems clear that a model's actions speak louder than his moral exhortations, that generous behavior is more readily elicited from children when they see generous-acting others than when they are simply provided a "lip-service" morality. The preschool teacher should be sensitive to her actions as well as her words. At this point, it should be noted that all models are not equal—certain characteristics of the model may facilitate imitative helping. These characteristics include the warmth, affective expression, power, and moral consistency of the model.

Warmth of the Model

The nurturance or warmth of the model has been demonstrated to be of significance in imitative behavior in general and has had a long history of central importance in theories of identification (Bandura, 1969; Mowrer, 1950). Generally, it is hypothesized that the warmth enhances the child's identification with the socialization agent. Experimental analogues of this process typically involve an interaction of a child with a model in which, for a very brief time, the model acts friendly, supportive, and interested in the child. While it is clear that such a brief interaction hardly approximates the duration and nature of the relationship between a child and a loving teacher or parent, it is also clear that the relationship between such a parent or teacher is not simply one of loving. Other interactions between child and teacher occur in the real world, such as interactions involving discipline, assignments of responsibilities, periods of high affect arousal, indifference, or despair. Thus, while the experimental studies of the impact of model warmth on children's helping behavior are necessarily artificial, they also allow investigators to isolate the particular or special effects of warmth, unconfounded by other factors, on children's imitative helping.

Studies concerning the impact of model warmth have yielded relatively consistent, albeit complex, results. Apparently, the effect of model warmth depends upon just what kind of helping behavior is being assessed. Model warmth has been found either to have no effect upon children's willingness to imitate a model who donates to needy others, or to retard such imitation (Grusec, 1971; Grusec & Skubiski, 1970; Rosenhan & White, 1967; Weissbrod, 1973). By contrast, the warmth of the model has been shown to increase the child's willingness to rescue a peer in distress (Staub, 1971a; Weissbrod, 1973).

For example, in a most thorough and careful study, Yarrow, Scott, and Waxler (1973) studied the rescue behavior or nursery school children. Unlike the usual study, these investigators presented either warm or cold models to the child within a naturalistic setting for an extended period of time (6 weeks). Additionally, care was taken to document the fact that the teacher actually acted either warmly or coldly. Finally, while specific attempts were made to train the child to be helpful, the measure of rescue activity was unrelated to the training tasks. As expected, children were more likely to aid an infant after having had a warm rather than a cold relationship with an authority who had modeled helpful actions.

The differential effect of model warmth upon children's donation and rescue activity may be resolved by the following hypothesis, one that assumes that the model's warmth liberates the child to maximize his own gain. It is reasonable to assume that most children do not wish to contribute money to needy others, and indeed most studies find that many children simply refuse to do so. When the model is warm, the child's fear of model or experimenter disapproval for not donating might be reduced. On the other hand, in a situation where a peer is in distress, it is likely that the child will experience distress through empathic processes (cf., Aronfreed, 1968; Yarrow & Waxler, 1975). One means of reducing such distress is to aid the victim, thus terminating the aversive stimulation. To terminate distress, the child must sometimes initiate novel actions, actions that may well be associated with negative consequences from others. The warm model or experimenter may serve to reduce the child's concerns about such negative consequences, thus freeing him to pursue his self-interest by means of aiding another.

Other studies of model warmth involving behaviors that children might consider aversive suggest such a liberating dynamic (Bandura, Grusec, & Menlove, 1968; Parke, 1967). That is, the greater the warmth of the model, the less likely are children to imitate a behavior that is aversive to them. As pointed out elsewhere (Bryan, 1975), it is important to note that within the naturalistic setting warm models are also likely to be helpful ones. If such is the case, then the warm model is also likely to be a frequent exemplar of helping behavior to the observing child.

Model Expressiveness

Some attention has been drawn to the role of model affects in evoking imitative helping or imitative donation behavior. The question revolves around the issue of whether or not the model's affective expressions, *when contingent* with his behaviors, will affect children's imitations of that model. Aronfreed (1968) has suggested that if an observing child experiences a change in affect that is increasingly positive, and if this change is associated in time with his helping act, the affect will become attached to the act and the child's disposition to aid others will increase. It can also be argued that if the child observes someone who helps another and who expresses strong positive affect in association with the helping act, then the child will connect his own vicariously experienced positive affect with donation behavior. Midlarsky and Bryan (1972) predicted that a model who demonstrated positive affect immediately following either a donation or a selfish act would elicit more imitation than a model who exhibited the same affect displays *not* contingent upon keeping or giving. As expected, the children who were exposed to a selfish model who expressed happiness about keeping his gains gave the least, while those children who viewed a model who expressed happiness about giving gave the most. Bryan (1971) found that children donated more, and more precisely imitated the actions of the model when the model had previously expressed positive affect immediately after donating than when the model had expressed the same affect somewhat delayed in time from the donation act. The results of these studies suggest that self-expressed affect by the model during the time of aiding behavior may significantly affect the observing child. Models who are trying it and *at the same time* liking it are likely to be more influential upon the observing child than those who are simply trying it.

Power of the Model

The power of the model has been demonstrated to be an important determinant of imitation (Bandura, 1969). It is certainly reasonable to assume that parents and teachers are generally powerful people in the world of their charges. A model's power to determine the distribution of a valuable prize has been found to affect children's imitation of a generous model. The generous model who has such power is more likely to be imitated than a generous exemplar who does not (Grusec, 1971). Hartup and Coates (1967) found that nursery school children responded differently to models who dispensed various reinforcements within the classroom than to those who did not. How these young children responded was based upon their own experiences with reinforcements in the classroom. Children who received a relatively great number of reinforcements from their peers were likely to imitate the model who dispensed reinforcements; those who received few reinforcements matched the behavior of the model who gave few reinforcements in the classroom. For nursery school children, it would appear that the powerful model, powerful in the sense of distributing social or material rewards, does increase imitative helping, at least for children who have had a history of being a recipient of peer rewards.

Studies that have manipulated power by other methods, however, have not been successful in demonstrating the impact of model power upon imitative helping. Bryan and Walbek (1970b) and Marshall (1972) had one group of children view the experimenter in the role of the model and another group view a model who was not an experimenter. Presumably, the experimenter-model would appear more powerful insofar as he had control over the laboratory. The results of neither study demonstrated an effect of power. Walbek (1969) manipulated the power of the model by telling some children that the model was to be their teacher during the following academic year, while other children were told that the model was simply a college student. No differences between the models were found in their ability to evoke anonymous donations from the children.

Hypocrisy

During the course of everyday social intercourse, it is likely that children are often confronted with individuals who preach various virtues and then subsequently violate them behaviorally. It would seem likely that preaching morality is generally less costly than practicing it and that, if such is the case, incidents of moral inconsistency will be ubiquitous in the child's world. In effect, it is likely that children are often confronted by the hypocritical behaviors of their parents, peers, and teachers.

Surprisingly little theorizing has been offered regarding the possible impact of hypocrisy upon the development of the young child. It appears to be generally agreed upon by the public that hypocrisy is not only bad but that individuals who demonstrate it are likely to have a deleterious effect upon the observing child (Rosenhan, Frederick, & Burrowes, 1968). Studies of hypocrisy effects have generally presented to the child a model, sometimes an adult, sometimes a peer, who exhorts the child to be either generous or selfish to other children, and who then acts either selfishly or generously himself. Thus, some models preach charity and practice it; others preach selfishness and practice it; others preach charity while practicing selfishness; others preach selfishness but practice charity. Little evidence has been forthcoming to indicate that hypocrisy with respect to helping has widespread effects. That is, the child exposed to the hypocritical model is not less likely to anonymously donate to needy others or more likely to commit antisocial behaviors such as stealing or less apt to like the hypocritical models than children exposed to other model types (Bryan & Walbek, 1970a, b; Bryan, *et al.,* 1971; Midlarsky & Bryan, 1972; Ruston, 1975; Schwartz & Bryan, 1971a; Walbek, 1969).

This does not mean to say that children are entirely unaffected by moral inconsistency. Several recently completed studies have demonstrated that the interactions of the model and the child may be importantly affected by a model's hypocrisy. Midlarsky, Bryan, and Brickman (1973) found in two separate experiments with children from the second through fifth grades that when a model exhorted charity but failed to be charitable, his social approval following the child's donation acts served not to increase, but to inhibit, the child's subsequent donations. In a recently completed study, Bryan, Slater, & Bertelson (unwritten study) found that while social approval from an inconsistent model did not inhibit donations, the child was more likely to be judged, by independent and blind raters, as being less happy and less interpersonally involved with the model than children interacting with a consistent model. Apparently, social approval from one who is inconsistent in his preachings and actions or inconsistent in his behavior from the implicit "demands" he makes of the child will become aversive to the recipient.

Children's Views of the Helping Model

Relatively little attention has been paid to children's perceptions of helping models, and what information is available is concerned with the children's evaluations of such models. Typically, the child views a model who either is or is not generous and one that preaches either generosity or selfishness. The child is then asked to rate the model as to his niceness, goodness, or such. The charitable model in either actions or preachings is consistently evaluated more favorably than the selfish one, however that selfishness is communicated (Bryan & Walbek, 1970a, b; Rushton, 1975; Schwartz & Bryan, 1971a). Moreover, these verbal ratings are correlated with a behavioral measure of attraction, that is, whether the child will choose a balloon with the model's name on it (Schwartz & Bryan, 1971a).

Brickman and Bryan (1975) have pointed out that the simple act of helping another may take several forms. That is, children might help a needy other by sacrificing some of their own goods or by donating property belonging to others. Specifically, these investigators were interested in children's judgments of peers who distributed resources from one party to another. They found that fifth grade females did view a Robin Hood action more favorably if the resulting distribution of goods created equality than if it served to accentuate an initial inequality of resources among a fictitious group. Likewise, self-sacrifice was viewed more favorably if equality of the resulting distributions was achieved than if it was not. In effect then, charitable actions, be they a result of self-sacrifice or the product of a theft, are viewed more favorably when the result is an equality rather than an inequality of resource distributions among group members.

Conclusions

The evidence is abundant that children will imitate the helping activities of models whether those models are alive and present or televised and absent. The list of responses shown to be affected by observing models is almost endless and it is not surprising that helping actions can also be added to this list. Additionally, while studies of imitative helping by preschool-age youngsters have not been extensive, the evidence is abundant that children of this age are affected by observing the behaviors of others (Bandura, 1969).

It is also clear that some types of models affect imitative helping more than do others, although it is not certain whether all of the model characteristics so far implicated in imitative altruism would apply to the preschooler as well as to older children. On the face of it, however, it would appear likely that the findings so far presented are not age-specific.

One important characteristic of a model is that of his power over the resource distributions available to the child. The teacher, as well as the parent, may be a particularly powerful model to the child, even the nursery-school-age child. They are powerful in that they dictate the distributions of rewards and punishments to the child. Many teachers are probably reluctant to recognize, much less employ, sanctions and power over the child. Yet there is reason to believe that demanding that the child conform to fair standards and a willingness to employ sanctions that control the child's behavior facilitate the development of an individual who will show kindness to others (Baumrind, 1971; Staub, 1973). At the very least, it is likely that the child is sensitive to the power of the teacher to control his destiny for a short period of time and that if the teacher shows benevolence, the child is also likely to show kindness.

It would appear from the experimental studies that the warmth of the model may have differential effects upon children's aiding. Rescue activities appear to be facilitated, while donation activities are inhibited, by the model's warmth. A hypothesis concerning the impact of the model's warmth suggests that such warmth is likely to facilitate those forms of helping activity in situations where the proprieties of the situation are vague. Certainly, children are constrained by a variety of considerations from executing any action within a novel situation, one consideration being the fear of reprimand. When the proprieties of the situation are vague, yet the child is motivated to aid another, then the warm model may well reduce the child's fear of punishment and consequently liberate the child to aid another and, indirectly, himself. Extending this hypothesis, it would seem that the warm socializing agent would generally produce an expectation by the child of a benevolent world, thus providing him with more courage to pursue his own aims, be they devilish or benevolent.

Finally, it is inevitable that most socialization agents demonstrate, time and again, their own moral inconsistency to the child. Perhaps they enact behaviors that violate their preachings, perhaps they enforce double standards of morality, likely they do both. One outcropping of adult hypocrisy is likely to be the production of hypocritical children (Bryan, 1969). Moreover, it is likely that inconsistency will serve to attenuate the socialization agent's power to influence the child by means of social approval, at least within the domain of actions relevant to the moral issue at stake. Parents and teachers alike would benefit from careful consideration of their own moral consistencies. Attention must be paid to not only words but deeds.

It should also be noted that simple moral exhortations concerning charitable actions have not been found to be particularly effective in producing anonymous helping activities by children in the primary school years. At this point it is certainly unclear as to whether such exhortations would be similarly ineffective for the preschool-age child. Several considerations, however, suggest that children should be exposed to such exhortations. First, knowing the proprieties concerning sharing and giving may not be a sufficient basis for eliciting donations, but may well be a necessary one. Without learning the Social Responsibility Norm, it is possible that donation behaviors will be greatly reduced. Secondly, it should also be noted that children of the primary school age appear to judge each other on the basis of verbal exhortations as well as behavioral enactments. In fact, interpersonal attraction can be enhanced by a verbalized morality without behavioral conformities, that is, by a lip-service morality. To be deprived of such a lip-service morality is to be deprived, perhaps, of some favorable interpersonal judgments and actions. It is also becoming clear, however, that lip-service morality is not enough, that children also need to be taught the behavioral commitments associated with verbal statements. Preaching helping is not enough. There is a need to demonstrate how such preaching carries obligations for specified actions and how these actions may be accomplished. For the preschool teacher, one method of instruction is that of modeling—not only to present a verbal description of the shoulds and oughts of the situation but also to enact helping responses that the child, with his limited repertoire of motor acts, might accomplish.

A question must be raised as to the power of the model to produce lasting effects upon the child. It would be naive to assume that a brief exposure of the child to a helping model would produce a prosocial child. The fact that helping models can have some lasting effects has been demonstrated in several investigations (Midlarsky & Bryan, 1972; Rushton, 1975; White, 1972), but also shown is the fact that when children are exposed to a model who imposes different standards upon himself and on the child, the child will adopt those standards that maximize his personal gain (Rosenhan *et al.,* 1968). Moreover, if a model implies either through words or deeds that a standard may be violated, children will violate such a standard or rule in order to maximize their gains (Stein & Bryan, 1972). If children are exposed to multiple models who vary their own standards for rewarding themselves, children will adopt the most lenient standards for self-reward (Bandura *et al.,* 1968). If the milieu in which the child moves about reflects self-indulgence, the impact of a particular helpful model will be short-lived. For helping models to be effective, repeated exposures from a variety of models within a variety of settings are likely necessary.

AFFECTS AND HELPING

In a society such as ours where there are many and often contradictory norms and values (Darley & Latané, 1970), it is probable that moods and affects will play an important role in affecting behavior. Moods do play an important role in affecting adult helping (Bryan, 1975). If such is true of the adult, it is likely to be more true of the child, an individual who has had little opportunity and perhaps capacity to arrange various values and norms into a hierarchy of moral priorities.

Methods

There have been a variety of methods used to induce moods in children and the results of studies in this area ppear to be dependent upon the method employed. Feelings of happiness, security, or comfort might be induced by means of observing the moods of others in the environment. Results from studies employing variations in the model's moods have previously been discussed. A second method of inducing moods is to contrive a situation wherein the child has either a success or a failure experience on some task: presumably, successful children would feel happy, those who have failed, sad (Staub, 1968). More recently, moods have been manipulated by having the child recall some past event which either produced considerable sadness or happiness for him (Moore, Underwood, & Rosenhan, 1973). Finally, there have been attempts to associate children's moods and actions through conditioning procedures (Aronfreed & Paskal, 1968; Midlarsky & Bryan, 1967).

Positive Affects

As previously indicated, the warm model may decrease the child's willingness to make self-sacrifices. On the other hand, Moore *et al.* (1973) found that children who were asked to recall happy events were much more likely to donate a prized object to needy others than children asked to recall a saddening event. The authors suggest that "people who are experiencing positive affect tend to be kind to themselves and to others in a variety of ways. They tend to reward themselves and others, to attend to their own assets more than their liabilities [p. 102]." But why should these two methods of inducing affect, the warm model and the recall method, produce such different results? A possibility is that the two methods appear to take place in very different psychological settings. In studies of model warmth, there is an emphasis upon children's having fun. They are presented with a warm model, they play games and win prizes. In the recall method, the experimenter is serious, games are not available, prizes are not won, but rather money is earned for helping the experimenter with a serious task. In effect, the situations vary in their implications for the permissibility of self-indulgence. In the warm model condition, self-indulgence seems to be much more encouraged than in conditions employing the recall methods. The facilitating effects of a child's positive affect upon his donations to the needy then might pivot upon the emphasis within the situation of self-gratifying activities.

Empathy, or the child's ability to experience the feelings of distress and joys of others, has often been suggested as important in the development of a concerned child (Aronfreed, 1968; Berger, 1962; Hoffman, 1973; Yarrow & Waxler, 1975). Aronfreed has proposed that altruistic helping is based upon the conditioning of empathetically experienced states of joy with the act of giving. (Essentially, if the child experiences pleasure produced by the recipient's positive response to the giver, that affective state will become conditioned to the act of giving.) Such affect may then serve either as an incentive or a reinforcement for the child's helping actions. Aronfreed and Paskal (1968) and Midlarsky and Bryan (1967) tested these ideas using primary-school-age girls. In these studies, when the experimenter paired her verbal expressions of joy with hugging of the child, the latter presumably inducing positive affect in the child, the girl was more likely to sacrifice a prize to gain the experimenter's joyous responses. Hugs or statements alone were not sufficient to elicit such sacrifice. Moreover, Midlarsky and Bryan found that for those subjects given the conditioning procedure, such altruistic acts generalized to donations made anonymously to needy children. Apparently, positive mood states can be directly conditioned to generous actions and can thereby increment children's helping of others.

Negative Affects

Children's negative affects do not appear to depress their donations, at least when such states are produced through experiences of failure. However, Moore *et al.* (1973) did find that children who were asked to recall sad events in their past were less likely to donate than children not given such instructions. Isen, Rosenhan, and Horn (1973) have suggested that negative affect states might produce donations if by donating the child could repair his self-image. These investigators have provided evidence that such is the case, at least when testing children over preschool age. There is some question about just how concerned a preschooler might be about repairing his image in the eyes of adults, but apparently slightly older children do manifest such concern.

One negative affect state that has received considerable attention in research on adult helping is that of guilt. There is some evidence (as well as controversy about the evidence) that adults who are presumably made to feel guilty within an experiment are more likely to aid others than adults not so compromised (Carlsmith & Gross, 1969; Freedman, Wallington, & Bless, 1967; Wallace & Sadalla, 1966). Very little work has been conducted upon the role of guilt, however, defined, upon children's helping behavior. Neither Silverman (1967), who had children cheat on a task, nor Test (1969), who had then inadvertently break a valuable toy of a peer, found that such experiences incremented children's willingness to donate prize objects. It is doubtful that children's "guilt" over their moral transgressions increase helping behaviors.

COGNITIVE PROCESSES

While the early research in children's helping was addressed primarily to the role of models, recently attention has been drawn to the cognitive processes involved in helping. Such processes are thought to be important because of the relatively consistent finding that children's helping behavior is positively associated with the age of the child (Barnett & Bryan, 1974; Handlon & Gross, 1959; Harris, 1971; Midlarsky & Bryan, 1967; Rushton, 1975; Rushton & Weiner, 1975; Skarin, 1975; Ugurel-Simin, 1952; Walbek, 1969; Wright, 1942). Since the child is presumed to be learning norms and experiencing changes in his cognitive capabilities during this period, as well as becoming apparently more helpful, concern for the correlations of cognitive processes with aiding behavior has been evidenced. Thus children's concerns about deservedness, their egocentrism and role-taking skills, and the nature of their moral judgments in affecting helping have become topics of study.

Social Comparison and Deservedness

That children's sharing behaviors are affected by their comparisons of their own gains to those of others, *even absent others,* has been shown in a series of studies by Masters. Masters (1971) found that the donations of 4- and 5-year-olds to an absent partner was significantly affected by whether the child had received rewards equal to, greater than, or less than, a peer partner. Those children who had received an equal number of rewards to the partner were likely to be the most generous; those who received less than their partner the least generous. Interestingly, when children believed that rewards had been given to "all the other children in the nursery school," children showed little generosity. This was true whether the child's donations were to be given to an absent partner or to an absent friend. Thus the young child does apparently view his rewards within a larger context of the rewards given to a "generalized other," and if the generalized other is relatively affluent, the child will be more reluctant to make donations.

It would also appear that at least some kinds of children are reluctant to give away what they have earned through merit. Long and Learner (1974) have hypothesized that children who believe that the world is just and that one gets what one ultimately deserves would be more reluctant to give up deserved gains, but more willing to donate undeserved gains, than children without such a belief. They suggested that one index of a belief in a just world is the child's willingness to delay personal gratification, since such delays imply a faith that merit will ultimately be rewarded. These investigators found, when testing fourth and fifth grade children, that children who could delay gratification were more likely to give away undeserved rewards than children who were less inclined to show such delays. On the other hand, children who could delay gratification were less likely than those who could not to donate deserved rewards.

The notion that children compare their rewards with those obtained by others and evaluate such rewards on the basis of deservedness provides some explanation of the depressing effects of competition upon helping actions. In a correlational study, Rutherford and Mussen (1968) found that nursery school boys who were judged to be highly competitive in a game also demonstrated less sharing behavior with their friends than did boys who were judged not to be as competitive. Confirmation of this finding was provided by Rushton and Weiner (in press). Barnett and Bryan (1974) tested second and fifth grade boys in a situation in which some children won, others tied, others lost, and still others did not participate in a competitive encounter. Second grade boys were not affected by the competitive situation, but fifth graders were. Competition in all but the winning condition depressed donations relative to the noncompetitive situation. Children who had won the competition were as generous as those who had not competed. This was generally to be expected because children who had won were likely to be happier or feel more competent than children who had either tied or lost in the contest. It is clear that the competitive encounter is likely to depress children's donations, except those from a winner. Perhaps children who have competed feel that they deserve the rewards and, given the absence of positive affect, will be less likely to distribute them to needy others.

Role Taking and Moral Judgment

As previously mentioned, empathy has often been suggested as important in the development of a concerned child. Presumably, children who are more able to assume the role of others are more likely to experience empathy with a victim (Rosenhan, 1969). Rubin and Schneider (1973) found that children who were able to take the perspective of others were also more likely to donate candy to poor children and to help a peer on a task than children less able to assume another's perspectives. Elmer and Rushton (1974), however, failed to find a relationship between role-taking ability and generosity among children 7 to 13 years of age. Likewise, Yarrow and Waxler (1975) were unable to demonstrate that the capacity of children between the ages 3 and 7 to assume the roles of others was significantly correlated with prosocial interventions. Rushton and Wiener (in press) also failed to find that generosity to either a friend or to a charity was correlated with assessments of various cognitive skills (including several measures of role taking). It would seem surprising if egocentrism and role-taking abilities were unrelated to prosocial activity by children, but as yet there is more theory than evidence suggesting such a linkage.

There is some evidence that the maturity of the child's moral judgment is associated with helping behavior. Rubin and Schneider (1973) found that children with more mature moral judgments were also more likely to donate candies and help another child on a clerical task than were children with less mature judgments. Likewise, Elmer and Rushton (1974) found that the level of the child's moral judgment was associated with the child's willingness to donate prizes to a charity for poor children.

Conclusions

While maturity of moral judgments appears to be associated with helping behavior, several points need to be made. First, very young children, while they may have the ability to experience empathy (Hoffman, 1973; Yarrow & Waxler, 1975), are not likely to be frequent helpers (Hartup & Keller, 1960; Hoffman, 1970; Rosenhan & White, 1967). The relatively low incidence of helping by the preschool-age child is not surprising; their moral judgments are likely to be primitive, resting on a principle that whatever is pleasing must be good and whatever is aversive must be bad (Kohlberg, 1964). Their role-taking abilities are no doubt limited and their practice of implementing solutions to the accurately perceived difficulties of others infrequent. This does not mean to imply that helping by the preschool children cannot be elicited, rather that such helping is not frequently revealed. Secondly, concern for the impact of cognitive development upon helping behavior was, in part, generated from the frequent laboratory-based finding that age and helping were positively associated. In more complex settings, however, such positive associations are not necessarily found. For example, Severy and Davis (1971) demonstrated that within a classroom setting advanced cognitive development may be negatively associated with helping. These researchers found that mentally retarded children between the ages of 8 and 10 years old were more likely to aid another on a task then either younger retardates or older normals. Moreover, retarded children were more likely to offer psychological comfort than were intellectually normal children. Severy and Davis suggest that in spite of the normal child's greater capacities to recognize and to render aid, it is likely that such aid is inhibited by their learning of competing values and behaviors. They hypothesize that the child's learning of values stressing achievement and independence increases the child's competitiveness. This competitiveness inhibits helping. In light of the findings that competitiveness increases with age (Bryan, 1975) and that competitiveness is negatively associated with helping, Severy and Davis's hypothesis is reasonable. If the aim of the preschool teacher is to increase children's consideration towards others, it would behoove the teacher to be especially sensitive to the matter of competitiveness. In effect, each teacher should ask whether or not the price of competition-producing activities is worth the product obtained.

INDIVIDUAL DIFFERENCES

It has long been noted by investigators that children differ greatly in their helping behavior even though exposed to the same laboratory treatments. Already discussed have been such individual differences as competitiveness, maturity of moral judgments, cognitive development, and role-taking abilities. Other social and personality characteristics have also been studied and will now be reviewed.

Sex

A question frequently posed is whether or not there are sex differences in helping activities. Often sex differences are not found (Grusec, 1971; Harris, 1970, 1971; Masters, 1971) or are found to be complexly determined by variations in experimental procedures (Grusec & Skubiski, 1970; Rosenhan & White, 1967). If sex differences are found, they are in the direction of demonstrating that girls are more helpful than boys (Midlarsky & Bryan, 1967; Moore et al., 1973; Rosenhan, 1969a; Skarin, 1975; Staub, 1973; White, 1972). Moreover, the experimentally elicited generosity of girls is more likely to be stable over time than that demonstrated by boys (White, 1972). Several hypotheses, not necessarily mutually exclusive, have been advanced to account for such sex differences in helping. One hypothesis is that females are socialized to be "other-oriented" while males are trained to achieve and compete (e.g., Skarin, 1975). Another speculation is that the greater generosity of girls compared to that of boys stems from their more frequently experiencing nurturant, and probably helpful, interactions with adults (Bryan, 1975). Yarrow et al. (1973) found that nursery-school-age boys who frequently sought help from an adult within the school setting were more likely to elicit rejecting or negative responses than were girls who sought help. Thus boys may be more frequently exposed to a nonhelping model or to a model who reluctantly helps. No doubt further work will show any simple statements concerning sex differences in helping to be erroneous. Varieties of helping are variously appropriate to female and male sex roles and thus the relationship of helping to sex of helper is likely to be complexly determined.

Economic Status

Rarely investigated is the relationship between children's helping and the family's socioeconomic status. At least for those forms of helping that require donations, it would seem that children with more would give more. Apparently, this intuition has not yet been found to be true. Studies by Bryan (1971), De Palma (1974), and Rosenhan (1969a) have failed to find a relationship between social class and aiding. Perhaps the categorization of social class within these studies has not been refined enough. For example, Berkowitz and Friedman (1967) found in their study of adolescents that children from middle class families whose occupations were service oriented rather than entrepreneurial were more likely to render aid to another who had not previously aided them. Similar distinctions within the middle class grouping might be necessary before reliable social class correlates of children's aiding behavior will be determined.

Personality and Helping

There have been two approaches to the study of helping and personality. One approach examines whether particular personality characteristics might be related to helping others. That is, does the child with a high need for social approval, a high degree of trust, or a desire to be socially desirable also demonstrate a high frequency of helping others? A second approach has been to study individual consistency in helping behavior. That is, if the child is likely to be helpful in one situation, will he be helpful in other ways as well? Is the child who offers sympathy also one who is likely to give aid to a peer on a task, donate money to a charity, or rescue a peer in distress?

In trying to isolate particular individual traits that might be associated with helping behavior, investigators have appeared to rely considerably on their intuitions rather than on some well-defined theory concerning personality and helping. Already mentioned is the fact that children with relatively mature moral judgments are more likely to be generous than children with a less developed sense of moral judgment. Results implicating other personality characteristics are generally based upon but one or two studies and do not reflect findings that can be considered, at this time, highly reliable.

Perhaps because of psychology's interest in reinforcements, one popular idea concerning children's helping behavior is that children give in order to obtain social approval from others. There have been two techniques for attempting to assess this hypothesis. The first is to index the frequency with which children bother to tell others that they had in fact donated to others; the second is to assess the children's need for social approval, with the assumption that children with a high need for social approval will donate more than children with a lower need. Bryan and Prentky (1973) found that less than half of the children who donated money to the March of Dimes mentioned that fact when leaving tape-recorded messages for persons of their choice. Weissbrod (1973) found that only 3 of her 72 subjects mentioned to her that they had donated money to the March of Dimes. Using a questionnaire designed to assess need for social approval, Staub and Sherk (1970) found that children high on this need were less likely to donate than those low on the need, although noteworthy was the fact that such children were also less likely to claim their rewards in the first place. Bryan and Walbek, in an unpublished study

(1968), found that children with high need for social approval were more likely to donate than those lower on the need, but the differences were slight. It is probably true that one motive for donation is the desire for social approval, but such desires will affect helping differently in different situations. One hypothesis is that when the situation is so structured that there is little question concerning the appropriateness and acceptability of helping, the child with high need for social approval will help. However, in those situations that require novel responses, the proprieties of which are in doubt, the high-need child may be less likely to help than his low-need counterpart.

Emotional expressiveness, willingness to seek aid, and aggressiveness have been linked to children's aiding activities. Lenrow (1965) found that nursery school children who were expressive of their own distress in their everyday activities were also more likely than those who were not to aid a puppet in distress. Hartup and Keller (1960) found that children between 3 and 5 years of age who were nurturant towards their peers were also those who frequently sought out aid. Yarrow and Waxler (1975) have found that among 3- to 7-year-old children, the frequency of their being victims of aggression was related positively to their sharing with and comforting peers. The authors suggest that frequency of being a target of misfortune may, among children who are relatively secure, increase sensitivity to the feeling states of others and thereby increase aiding behaviors. Finally, Yarrow and Waxler found that young children who were moderately aggressive, which they interpreted as assertive, were more likely to render aid than those who showed high aggression or hostility or those who showed little aggression. Likewise, Friedrich and Stein (1973) found that cooperative behavior by girls and cooperative and nurturant behavior by boys of nursery school age were positively related to interpersonal aggression during the school day.

There are a number of explanations that may account for these relationships of need for social approval, aggressiveness, and emotional expressiveness to helping. Perhaps children who are relatively free from interpersonal inhibitions, allowing them to be assertive, can be somewhat indifferent to social approval, can show their distress and actively seek relief from it, and are more capable of initiating novel actions to aid another. Freedom can produce courage. Perhaps children who are free to express themselves are those most frequently exposed to helpful models. Finally, perhaps children who show such expressiveness, who seek help, and who show assertiveness, are those children who experience a greater intensity of affective arousal. Such children then may have greater motivation to render aid to the distressed or needy other. Perhaps all three hypotheses are correct, for they are not mutually exclusive.

Consistency in Helping

Is there consistency in aiding behaviors? At least four studies conducted *in vivo* would suggest that there is a moderate relationship among various forms of helping by young children. Yarrow and Waxler (1975) found that sharing and comforting were correlated positively with each other but neither was associated with helping as measured by the child's willingness to help an adult who had spilled some materials. Friedrich and Stein (1973) found in their study of preschool children that nurturant and cooperative behaviors by boys were correlated. Dlugokinski and Firestone (1973) found in their study of fifth to eighth grade children that children's kindness, as indexed by both self-reports and peer ratings, and the amount children donated to UNICEF were slightly correlated. Baumrind (1971) rated preschool children on such dimensions as sympathy and nurturance, helping, selfishness, thoughtlessness, and insulting behavior. All of these behaviors were found to correlate in such a fashion as to suggest that children can be reliably differentiated on the general dimension of consideration for others. It does appear to be the case that children who are kind in one manner are likely to be kind in some other manners, though certainly not invariably. No doubt situational factors and transitory mood states play a role in affecting some forms of helping and thus high correlations of helping behavior across time and space are hardly to be expected.

Conclusions

There is relatively little information concerning the personality and social characteristics associated with the development of helping persons. One relatively consistent finding, however, is that children who are assertive are also more likely to comfort and help others. It is likely that the young child, faced as he is with learning the rules of life, is somewhat timid in initiating novel actions. Children who feel free to express themselves, who are not precoccupied with evaluations from others, may well have the courage to take a risk of interacting with others in situations relatively novel to them. The early emphasis by socialization agents upon children's rule following, obedience, and conformity may well attenuate children's willingness to aid and comfort others. Clearly a balance between training obedience and self-expression by children is among the preschool teacher's most necessary and difficulty tasks. Too much or too little obedience training may well produce a conformity that is not in the best interest of either the public or the person. Finally, it is probably true that it is an ill wind that blows no good, and preschool teachers might find it wise to refrain from too quickly evaluating children on the basis of their conformity. In the long run, the somewhat disruptive child may also be the child who first renders aid to others.

SOCIALIZATION PRACTICES

The following discussion will review parental socialization practices that seem to facilitate children's helping behavior.

Most efforts devoted to understanding the role of parental socialization practices have been addressed to the role of parental discipline. Baumrind (1971), in her study of the parents of nursery school children, found that parents who specified "aims and methods of discipline, promoted their own code of behavior, could not be coerced by the child and set standards of excellence for the child [p. 62]" were the most likely to produce friendly and cooperative children. Hoffman and Saltz-stein's (1967) study of parental discipline techniques has been quite influential in affecting thinking concerning helping and discipline. These investigators classified discipline procedures as either power assertive, love withdrawal, or induction. Parents who employ power assertion frequently use physical punishment and material deprivation; those who used induction techniques emphasize the negative consequences of transgression upon the lives of others, while those employing love withdrawal imply their anger, hurt, or disapproval, but do not explain the negative effects of transgressions upon others. These researchers found that when either the father or mother primarily employed induction techniques, the female offspring were most likely to show consideration of others than when parents primarily employed other forms of discipline. Boys' consideration of others was enhanced by power assertive discipline. Mussen et al., (1970) report that boys who were rated by their peers as being altruistic appeared to have mothers who were "directive, authoritative and not highly permissive [p. 83]." For altruistic girls, however, Mussen et al. found a different pattern of maternal behavior. The altruistic girl was likely to have a permissive and considerate mother. Before leaving this topic, noteworthy is Staub's (1971b) failure to find within a laboratory setting that the use of induction statements concerning the positive consequence of helping another in an emergency subsequently affected the helping behavior of either kindergarten boys or girls. However, it should be noted that when testing fifth and sixth grade children, Staub (1973) found that children exposed to induction statements along with training in actually aiding another were more likely to subsequently write letters to hospitalized children than were the children exposed simply to induction statements or to the training sessions. The combination of training and induction action was particularly effective in altering the girls' rather than the boys' behaviors. Midlarsky and Bryan (1972) used exhortations to give in which were embedded statements as to the positive consequences of such giving for the recipients. Donations from girls in a primary school were incremented by such exhortations. While the evidence is still somewhat weak, there is a suggestion that induction techniques, particularly when used with primary-school-age girls, are likely to increase that child's consideration of others.

Another familial circumstance that may facilitate children's helping actions is responsibility assignment. Essentially, it is believed that if children are assigned the personal responsibility for tending to the needs of others, they will become more sensitive to and more appropriately responsive to another in distress. Staub (1970) found that when kindergarten and first grade children were "in charge" during the experimenter's absence, they were more likely to intervene to help a distressed peer in another room than if no such simple instructions were given. The responsibility hypothesis, however, has been more often investigated through correlational than through experimental procedures. Specifically, it is assumed that if a child has a younger sibling, then that child will have more frequently been assigned caretaking activities and thus be more responsive to another's need states. While Midlarsky and Bryan (1972) failed to find any correlation between donations and number of siblings, Rosenhan (1969a) found that among children 9 and 10 years of age, those with younger siblings donated more than those with no siblings. Staub (1970) found that while sharing and donations were not related to family size, young children with siblings were more likely to be helpful than those without siblings. Staub (1971b) later found, however, that family size was uncorrelated with boys' helping and negatively correlated with girls' rescuing another in distress. The evidence is far from clear that family size has some predictable correlation with aiding behavior, but at least one experiment (Staub, 1970) has demonstrated the importance of responsibility assignment to eliciting young children's aiding responses in an emergency situation.

While suggestions have been made that prosocial behavior could be increased if parents and teachers paid greater attention to the teaching of "do's" than "don'ts," only one study has examined parental value orientations and young children's helping activities. Olejnik and McKinney (1973) divided parents of 4-year-olds into those who administered rewards and punishments on the basis of a prescriptive value system, that is a system which emphasizes the "do's," and those whose value system is proscriptive, the emphasis being upon what not to do. Whether parents use rewards or punishments was not found to be critical to whether the child would be generous in his donations to poor children, but parents with prescriptive values had children who were more generous than those who had proscriptive values.

IMPLICATIONS

This chapter has reviewed those studies concerned with the development of prosocial behavior, studies primarily conducted within a laboratory and governed by a stranger to the child, producing perhaps some short-term changes in behavior. The studies do give us some leads as to the procedures that may be effective in developing a child who is concerned about and willing to aid others in need.

There is little question that an altruistic model will affect aiding behavior even in children as young as those attending a preschool. The model, in his demonstrations, communicates both the acceptability and the specific mechanisms associated with helping. The model is thus an important source of information from which the young child learns. Moreover, if the model is happy about his helping, "sincere" if you will, perhaps then the child can also learn the joys as well as the mechanisms of aiding others.

It is important to realize that in the everyday social intercourse of the teacher and parent, both may model not only aiding behavior, but selfishness and hypocrisy as well. Such modeling is probably inevitable since behavioral enactments of stated values are often inappropriate within a particular social situation or individual condition. Sometimes generosity is not called for, sometimes intervention is not helping but intrusive and therefore resented. Given that displays of hypocrisy and selfishness are often based upon sound judgments concerning immediate situational constraints and long-term individual needs, such incidences of negative modeling provide the adult an opportunity to communicate such distinctions to those about him. Certainly children observe violations of norms and values and they probably could benefit from knowing the distinctions that justify such moral transgressions. The adult must be sensitive to the effects of his behaviors as well as his verbalizations upon the child. These behaviors simply cannot be neglected by the conscientious child trainer.

There are, of course, many ways employed in attempting to produce a helping child. Certainly values and rules of conduct must be taught. In this writer's opinion, moral exhortations are not likely to have much effect upon children's self-sacrificing behaviors. This does not mean to say that exhortations are not important in their own right, for they do spell out values and norms that the child must know. It is also clear that children at an early age may learn the norm that one should help others (Bryan & Walbek, 1970a; Shure, 1968). But faith that a child who learns such norms and values will show behavioral conformity to them is unwarranted. This "lip-service morality" is important for the child to acquire insofar as it is likely to affect his relationships with peers and adults alike, but certainly more desirable is the condition where the verbalized morality corresponds to the behavioral enactments of the child. Care then must be taken not only to teach values, but to see that the child learns that value statements carry an implication of appropriate behavior. This author had the occasion to interview fourth, fifth, and sixth grade children after having exposed them to a peer who had preached charity but had practiced selfishness. When this inconsistency was pointed out to them within the interview, the modal response on their part was, essentially, "So what, it is at least better to say that than not to say anything!" To many children, the preaching of values do not carry implications for behavior. The problem then is that of training the child to translate a norm or value into appropriate motoric actions. Both Baumrind (1971) and Staub (1973) have indicated that firm enforcement policies that include employment of negative reinforcements along with explications of just and fair standards are likely to be helpful in developing a prosocial child. Presumably such practices reflect the parent's willingness to insist upon the child's conformity to verbalized standards of conduct. Attention needs to be paid to the training of children to connect their verbalizations to their behavior, and parental control is necessary for such training. A greater emphasis in socialization upon the "do's" than the "don'ts" is needed.

Recently, there have been studies by Staub (1973) pointing to additional ways in which prosocial behavior may be increased. Children who have had a responsibility towards others assigned to them may assume more responsibility towards their peers. Moreover, children who have been given the responsibility to train others in prosocial activities and the reasons for them seem themselves to be markedly affected by their teaching. The teacher of prosocial behaviors might learn more from the lesson than the student.

It should be noted, however, that there are certain values and training experiences that probably attenuate helping behavior by children. Most important in this respect are circumstances that increase the child's competitiveness. Where achievement is accomplished at the expense of another, where rewards are given on individual rather than group merit, or where the individual is ranked within rather than being a part of a group, cooperation and helping among children is likely to be reduced (Bryan, 1975).

It is almost a cliché to indicate that contingent rewards to the helper for helping others are likely to have an important impact in developing a child who is concerned for others. Children are likely to do that which gets them what they want, and given that they know and want the incentive, they will even help others for it. Moreover, children learn from observing the rewards given to others. A reward to a youngster for helping may well increase not only his helping actions but the aiding activities of those children who observed the rewarding sequence. The opportunity to elicit in helping actions by providing material and social approval appear to be plentiful within the classroom. Young children seem particularly eager to help the classroom teacher, and opportunities for children helping can and should be frequently provided so that children can be trained in helping.

The evidence is reasonably strong that the secure and happy child, one who perceives himself in a nonthreatening environment, will be the one who has the courage to initiate novel helping actions such as is often required in an emergency situation. Some forms of aiding require of the child nonconforming behaviors, and apparently the child who feels safe will respond to the needy in situations that require unorthodox behavior. On the other hand, courage or security allows one to defy the orthodox as well. Such children appear to be less likely to render aid when aid is assessed by means of donations. Perhaps these children feel coerced and are more courageous in resisting such pressures and exerting their rights to refuse such aid, or perhaps they have a better sense of their needs than the child more concerned with social approval. Whatever the case, it would appear that a nurturant environment and a secure child may stimulate some forms of aiding and inhibit others.

Finally, a repeat of a caveat is warranted. As written elsewhere, "A helpful person may well be intrusive (e.g., invade our privacy), moralistic (e.g., prevent us from 'doing our thing'), or simply conforming to the status quo of proprieties [Bronfenbrenner, 1970]." "That is, a helpful person with all his 'good' intentions may well violate a variety of personal freedoms that we cherish. Whatever the nature of the costs, it is naive to assume that there will be none. Perhaps the price will be worth paying. At least it should be known [Bryan, 1972, Pp. 101–102]."

REFERENCES

Aronfreed, J. *Conduct and conscience: The socialization of internalized control over behavior.* New York: Academic Press, 1968.

Aronfreed, J., & Paskal, V. Altruism, empathy and the conditioning of positive affect. In J. Aronfreed, *Conduct and conscience*. New York: Academic Press, 1968.

Bandura, A. *Principles of behavior modification*. New York: Holt, Rinehart and Winston, 1969.

Bandura, A., Grusec, J. E., & Menlove, F. L. Some social determinants on self-monitoring reinforcement systems. *Journal of Personality and Social Psychology*, 1968, *8*, 99–108.

Baumrind, D. Current patterns of parental authority. *Developmental Psychology Monograph*, 1971, *4*, 1–103.

Barnett, M. A., & Bryan, J. H. Effects of competition with outcome feedback upon children's helping behaviors. *Developmental Psychology*, 1974, *10*, 838–842.

Berger, S. M. Conditioning through vicarious instigation. *Psychological Review*, 1962, *69*, 450–466.

Berkowitz, L., & Daniels, L. Affecting the salience of the social responsibility norm: Effects of past help on the response to dependency relationships. *Journal of Abnormal and Social Psychology*, 1964, *68*, 275–281.

Berkowitz, L., & Friedman, P. Some social class differences in helping behavior. *Journal of Personality and Social Psychology*, 1967, *5*, 217–225.

Brickman, P., & Bryan, J. H. Evaluation of theft, charity, and disinterested transfers that increase or decrease equity. *Journal of Personality and Social Psychology*, 1975, *31*, 156–161.

Bronfenbrenner, U. *Two worlds of childhood: U.S. and U.S.S.R.* New York: Russel Sage Foundation, 1970.

Bryan, J. H. How adults teach hypocrisy. *Psychology Today*, 1969, *3*.

Bryan, J. H. Model affect and children's imitative behavior. *Child Development*, 1971, *42*, 2061–2065.

Bryan, J. H. Why children help: A review. *Journal of Social Issues*, 1972, *28*, 87–104.

Bryan, J. H. Children's cooperation and helping behaviors. In M. Hetherington (Ed.), *Review of child developmental research*. Vol. 5. Chicago: University of Chicago Press, 1975.

Bryan, J. H., & London, P. Altruistic behavior by children. *Psychological Bulletin*, 1970, *73*, 200–211.

Bryan, J. H., & Prentky, R. Public responses to children's altruism. Unpublished manuscript, Northwestern University, 1973.

Bryan, J. H., Redfield, J., and Mader, S. Words and deeds about altruism and the subsequent reinforcement power of the model. *Child Development*, 1971, *42*, 1501–1508.

Bryan, J. H., Slater, J. E., & Bertelson, K. Unwritten study. Evanston, Illinois: Northwestern University, 1975.

Bryan, J. H., & Test, M. Models and helping: Naturalistic studies in aiding behavior. *Journal of Personality and Social Psychology*, 1967, *6*, 400–407.

Bryan, J. H., & Walbek, N. Preaching and practicing generosity: Children's actions and reactions. *Child Development*, 1970, *41*, 329–535. (a)

Bryan, J. H., & Walbek, N. The impact of words and deeds concerning altruism upon children. *Child Development*, 1970, *41*, 747–757. (b)

Bryan, J. H., & Walbek, N. Unwritten study. Evanston, Illinois: Northwestern University, 1968.

Carlsmith, J. M., & Gross, A. E. Some effects of guild on compliance. *Journal of Personality and Social Psychology*, 1969, *11*, 232–239.

Crandall, B. D., Crandall, V. J., & Patkovsky, W. A children's social desirability questionnaire. *Journal of Consulting Psychology*, 1965, *29*, 27–36.

Darley, J. M., & Latané, B. Norms and normative behavior: Field studies of social interdependence. In J. Macaulay and L. Berkowitz (Eds.), *Altruism and helping behavior*. New York: Academic Press, 1970.

De Palma, D. J., Effects of social class, moral orientation, and severity of punishment on boy's moral responses to transgression and generosity. *Developmental Psychology*, 1974, *10*, 890–900.

Dlugokinski, E., & Firestone, I. J. Congruence among four methods of measuring other-centeredness. *Child Development*, 1973, *44*, 304–308.

Elliott, R., & Vasta, R. The modeling of sharing: Effects associated with vicarious reinforcement, symbolization, age and generalization. *Journal of Experimental Child Psychology*, 1970, *10*, 8–15.

Elmer, N. P., & Rushton, J. P. Cognitive-developmental factors in children's generosity. *British Journal of Social and Clinical Psychology*, 1974, *13*, 277–281.

Freedman, J. L., Wallington, A., & Bless, E. Compliance without pressure: The effect of guilt. *Journal of Personality and Social Psychology*, 1967, *7*, 117–124.

Friedrich, L. K., & Stein, A. H. Aggression and prosocial television programs and the natural behavior of preschool children. *Monographs of the Society for Research in Child Development*, 1973, *38*, 1–64.

Grusec, J. E. Power and the internalization of self-denial. *Child Development*, 1971, *42*, 93–105.

Grusec, J. E. Demand characteristics of the modeling experiment: altruism as a function of age, and aggression. *Journal of Personality and Social Psychology*, 1972, *22*, 139–148.

Grusec, J. E., & Skubiski, L. Model nurturance, demand characteristics of the modeling experiment and altruism. *Journal of Personality and Social Psychology*, 1970, *14*, 352–359.

Handlon, B. J., & Gross, P. The development of sharing behavior. *Journal of Abnormal and Social Psychology*, 1959, *59*, 425–428.

Harris, M. B. Reciprocity and generosity: Some determinants of sharing behavior. *Child Development*, 1970, *41*, 313–328.

Harris, M. B. Models, norms and sharing. *Psychological Reports*, 1971, *29*, 147–153.

Hartup, W. W., & Coates, B. Imitation of a peer as a function of reinforcement from the peer group and the rewardingness of the model. *Child Development*, 1967, *38*, 1003–1016.

Hartup, W. W., & Keller, E. D. Nurturance in preschool children and its relation to dependency. *Child Development*, 1960, *31*, 681–689.

Hoffman, M. L. Moral development. In P. H. Mussen (Ed.), Vol. 2, *Carmichael's manual of child psychology*. New York: John Wiley, 1970.

Hoffman, M. L. A theoretical perspective: The development of altruistic motives. Paper delivered at the Conference on Contemporary Issues in Moral Development, 1973.

Hoffman, M. L., & Saltzstein, H. D. Parent discipline and the child's moral development. *Journal of Personality and Social Psychology*, 1967, *5*, 45–57.

Isen, A. M., Rosenhan, D. L., & Horn, N. Effects of success and failure on children's generosity. *Journal of Personality and Social Psychology*, 1973, *27*, 239–247.

Kohlberg, L. Development of moral character and moral ideology. In M. L. Hoffman and L. W. Hoffman (Eds.), *Review of child development research*, Vol. 1. New York: Russell Sage Foundation, 1964.

Krebs, D. Altruism—An examination of the concept and a review of the literature. *Psychological Bulletin*, 1970, *73*, 258–302.

Lenrow, P. B. Studies in sympathy. In S. S. Tomkins and C. E. Izard (Eds.), *Affect, cognition, and personality: Empirical studies*. New York: Springer, 1965, Pp. 269–294.

Liebert, R. M., & Poulos, R. W. Eliciting the "Norm of Giving": Effects of modeling and the presence of a witness on children's sharing behavior. Paper presented at the meeting of the American Psychological Association, Washington, D.C., 1971.

Long, G. T., & Lerner, M. J. Deserving, the "Personal Contract," and altruistic behavior by children. *Journal of Personality and Social Psychology*, 1974, *29*, 551–556.

Macaulay, J., & Berkowitz, L. (Eds.), *Altruism and helping behavior*. New York: Academic Press, 1970.

Marshall, H. M. The effect of vicarious punishment on sharing behavior in children. *Dissertation Abstracts International*, 1972, *32*, 6539.

Masters, J. C. Effects of social comparison upon children's self-reinforcement and altruism toward competitors and friends. *Developmental Psychology*, 1971, *5*, 64–72.

Midlarsky, E., & Bryan, J. H. Training charity in children. *Journal of Personality and Social Psychology*, 1967, *5*, 408–415.

Midlarsky, E., & Bryan, J. H. Affect expressions and children's imitative altruism. *Journal of Experimental Research in Personality*, 1972, *6*, 195–203.

Midlarsky, E., Bryan, J. H., & Brickman, P. Aversive approval: Interactive effects of modeling and reinforcement on altruistic behavior. *Child Development*, 1973, *44*, 321–328.

Moore, B. S., Underwood, B., & Rosenhan, D. L. Affect and altruism. *Developmental Psychology*, 1973, *8*, 99–104.

Mowrer, O. H. *Learning theory and personality dynamics*. New York: Ronal Press Co., 1950.

Mussen, P., Rutherford, E., Harris, S., & Keasey, C. B. Honesty and altruism among preadolescents. *Developmental Psychology*, 1970, *3*, 169–194.

Olejnik, A. B., & McKinney, J. P. Parental value orientation and generosity in children. *Developmental Psychology*, 1973, *8*, 311.

Parke, R. D. Nurturance, nurturance withdrawl, and resistance to deviation. *Child Development*, 1967, *35*, 1101–1110.

Rosehan, D. L. Studies in altruistic behavior: Developmental and naturalistic variables associated with charitability. Paper presented at the meeting of the Society for Research in Child Development, Santa Monica, California, 1969. (a)

Rosenhan, D. L. The kindnesses of children. *Young Children*, 1969, *25*, 30–44. (b)

Rosenhan, D., Frederick, F., & Burrowes, A. Preaching and practicing: Effects of channel discrepancy on norm internalization. *Child Development*, 1968, *39*, 291–301.

Rosenhan, D. L., & White, G. M. Observation and rehearsal as determinants of prosocial behavior. *Journal of Personality and Social Psychology*, 1967, *5*, 424–431.

Rubin, K. H., & Schneider, F. W. The relationship between moral judgment, egocentrism, and altruistic behavior. *Child Development*, 1973, *44*, 661–665.

Rushton, J. P. Generosity in children: Immediate and long term effects of modeling, preaching, and moral judgments. *Journal of Personality and Social Psychology*, 1975, *31*, 755–765.

Rushton, J. P., & Wiener, J. Altruism and cognitive development in children. *British Journal of Social and Clinical Psychology*, in press.

Rutherford, E., & Mussen, P. Generosity in nursery school boys. *Child Development*, 1968, *39*, 755–765.

Schure, M. B. Fairness, generosity, and selfishness: The naive psychology of children and young adults. *Child Development*, 1968, *39*, 875–886.

Schwartz, T., & Bryan, J. H. Imitation and judgments of children with language deficits. *Exceptional Children*, 1971, 157–158. (a)

Schwartz, T., & Bryan, J. H. Imitative altruism by deaf children. *Journal of Speech and Hearing Research*, 1971, *14*, 453–461. (b)

Severy, L. J., & Davis, K. E. Helping behavior among normal and retarded children. *Child Development*, 1971, *42*, 1017–1031.

Silverman, I. W. Incidence of guilt reactions in children. *Journal of Personality and Social Psychology*, 1967, *7*, 338–340.

Skarin, K. Altruism and rivalry: An analysis of age and sex differences. Paper presented at the meeting of the Society for Research in Child Development, 1975.

Staub, E. The effects of success and failure in children's sharing behavior. Paper presented at the meetings of the Eastern Psychological Association, 1968.

Staub, E. Determinants of children's attempts to help another child in distress. Paper presented at the meeting of the American Psychological Association, Washington, D.C., September, 1969.

Staub, E. A child in distress: The effects of focusing responsibility on children on their attempts to help. *Developmental Psychology*, 1970, *2*, 152–154.

Staub, E. A child in distress: The influence of nurturance and modeling on children's attempts to help. *Developmental Psychology*, 1971, *5*, 124–132. (a)

Staub, E. The use of role playing and induction in children's learning of helping and sharing behavior. *Child Development*, 1971, *42*, 805–816. (b)

Staub, E. To rear a prosocial child: Reasoning, learning by doing, and learning to teach others. Paper presented at the Conference on Contemporary Issues in Moral Development, 1973.

Staub, E., & Sherk, L. Need for approval, children's sharing behavior, and reciprocity in sharing. *Child Development*, 1970, *41*, 243–252.

Stein, G. M., & Bryan, J. H. The effect of a television model upon rule adoption behavior of children. *Child Development*, 1972, *43*, 268–273.

Test, M. A. Children's responses to harm doing: A behavioral study. Unpublished dissertation, Northwestern University, 1969.

Ugurel-Semin, R. Moral behavior and moral judgment of children. *Journal of Abnormal and Social Psychology*, 1952, *47*, 463–474.

Walbek, N. H. Charitable cognitions and actions: A study of the concurrent elicitations of children's altruistic thoughts and deeds. Unpublished master's thesis. Northwestern University, 1969.

Wallace, J., & Sadalla, E. Behavioral consequence of transgression: I. The effects of social recognition. *Journal of Experimental Research in Personality*, 1966, *1*, 187–194.

Weissbrod, C. S. The effect of adult warmth on reflective and impulsive children's donation and rescue behavior. Unpublished doctoral dissertation, Northwestern University, 1973.

White, G. M. Immediate and deferred effects of model observation and guided and unguided rehearsal on donating and stealing. *Journal of Personality and Social Psychology*, 1972, *21*, 139–148.

Wispe, L. G. Positive forms of social behavior: An overview. Journal of Social Issues, 1972, *28*(3), 1–19.

Wright, B. A. Altruism in children and the perceived conduct of others. *Journal of Abnormal and Social Psychology*, 1942, *37*, 218–233.

Yarrow, M. R., Scott, P. M., & Waxler, C. Z. Learning concern for others. *Developmental Psychology*, 1973, *8*, 240–261.

Yarrow, M. R., & Waxler, C. Z. The emergence and functions of prosocial behaviors in young children. Paper presented at the meeting of the *Society for Research in Child Development*, 1975.

10

Behavior Disorders in Preschool Children

THOMAS M. ACHENBACH

National Institute of Mental Health

Preschoolers are among the most fascinating people in the world. Their bountiful energy, the marvelous ways in which they contort language, the creative power of their fantasy, their tender empathy, their clever misinterpretations of the physical and social worlds, their ability to see the humor of their own distortions, and their fantastic rates of learning and development admirably equip them to captivate and delight adults. Preschoolers can also be among the most puzzling and exasperating people in the world. The negativism of the 2-year-old, shameless recalcitrance over toileting, perpetual motion, obsessional insistence on doing grown-up things, language barriers of both comprehension and production, demands for attention, incessant spilling and messing, deliberate and inadvertent destruction, irrational fears and rituals, aggression and temper tantrums—these, too, preschoolers offer in abundance.

So much is happening so quickly during the years from 2 to 5 that it would be surprising indeed if no friction arose between the child and the constraints of adult mores, cautions, aspirations, and convenience imposed upon him. Further friction is bound to arise from the disparity between the goals the preschooler can envision for himself and his abilities to adapt his goals to the realities of the world and his own capabilities. Accordingly, an understanding of behavior disorders manifested during this period requires coordination of multiple perspectives on development. While these perspectives emphasize different causes for behavior disorders, the perspectives are in many ways mutually complementary. An overview of these perspectives will provide the context within which we will consider behavior disorders.

PERSPECTIVES ON DEVELOPMENT

The Organic Perspective

The most conspicuous aspect of development during the preschool years is, of course, the physical maturation of the child. From a clumsy toddler tentatively feeling his way about the world, the child—when all goes well—becomes a highly mobile and precisely coordinated organism firmly in command of an amazing variety of skills, from speech to bowel control to roller-skating to drawing and coloring. However, there are many ways in which the course of physical development can contribute to behavior problems.

To begin with, nutrition is critical in determining the child's rate of growth, the adequacy with which his sensorimotor equipment functions, and his general state of responsiveness to his environment. Nutritional influences include not only the child's current food intake, but his nutritional history dating back to conception and his mother's nutritional history dating back to her own childhood. The child's prenatal nutritional history is important because many organic deficits occurring prior to birth cannot be overcome later. In particular, most nerve cells of the brain develop prior to birth and new nerve cells cannot be formed at later periods. The child's mother's nutritional history is important because it affects the quality of the intrauterine environment she provides and her vulnerability to illness during pregnancy. Disorders of pregnancy and delivery increase the risk of brain damage which, in turn, increases the risks of mental retardation, learning problems, and behavior disorders.

Slow organic maturation during the preschool period, whether it is due to specific organic abnormalities, poor nutrition, or normal variation in constitutional characteristics, can result in behavior disorders. The child who is not physically able to use language, to control his sphincter muscles, or to manipulate objects effectively by about the age of 3 will receive a biased exposure to many of the typical socializing experiences. Whether he responds by withdrawing, aggressing, or manifesting other behavior problems, it is important to recognize that slow maturation per se may not be the direct cause of his behavior problems. On the contrary, the slow maturation may contribute to behavior problems merely because it creates a gap between a child's capabilities and those of his peers. It is the psychological consequences of this gap—including the ridicule, pity, overprotection, annoyance, frustration, failure, and inferiority feelings it elicits—that are the primary causes of the behavior problems.

Specific organic handicaps in children who are developing at the normal rate can likewise be responsible for behavior problems. Even minor vision or hearing problems can shut a child off from subtle environmental cues that are important in social relationships. When unrecognized, handicaps of this sort often create the impression that a child is being deliberately unresponsive or defiant. This may create a vicious circle whereby a child's failure to respond to normal levels of input elicits angry (and less subtle) cues from adults, which, in turn, cause the child to respond, thereby reinforcing the adult's harsh approach to the child and establishing a negatively toned communication system between child and adult.

Unrecognized seizure disorders can also be a source of what may be perceived merely as inattentiveness or orneriness. A child who is observed to have momentary "absences" during which he stares blankly or his eyelids flutter may be suffering from petit mal epileptic seizures. Not only may the seizures block off environmental cues, but the organic defect causing the seizures may interfere with sensorimotor functioning and may be a manifestation of a progressive disease.

The Psychodynamic Perspective

The preschool years provide some of the most compelling illustrations of the psychodynamic principles proposed by Sigmund Freud and elaborated upon by later analysts such as Anna Freud and Erik Erikson. Because these principles have been derived largely from clinical observations on child and adult patients rather than from formal research studies, they are still subject to considerable debate.

Freud hypothesized that from about 18 months to 3 years the anal region becomes the focus of *libidinal* (sexual) energy and children become preoccupied with anal pleasures. This period, which Freud called the *anal stage*, is usually, though not always, stressful for parents and children alike. Despite most children's desire to be grown up and their occasional spontaneous interest in using toilets, a collision is almost inevitable between adult strictures on toileting and children's accustomed pleasure in relieving themselves when and where they please. The force and outcome of these collisions vary as much as do children and their parents, but the rarity of a smooth and quick transition to adult toilet behavior means that exasperation is in store for most families. However, unlike the typical scenario in Freud's Vienna, in which the child was prematurely beaten into submission—only to risk long-term fixation on toileting—current problems seem to stem more from parents' ambivalence about establishing clearcut expectations that their child use the toilet (Spock, 1968). While empirical studies fail to support Freud's hypothesis that extremes of toilet training produce "anal" personalities (Beloff, 1957; Hetherington & Brackbill, 1963), there is no doubt that toilet training can become the focus of serious conflicts between a child and the adult world and that failure to achieve adequate continence by about the age of 3.5 years is a cause for concern.

In his "psychosocial" reformulation of the psychoanalytic view, Erik Erikson (1963) substitutes the broader concept of an *anal–urethral–muscular* stage for the anal stage. According to Erikson, the significance of this period stems not so much from the focusing of libidinal energy in the anal region, as Freud believed, but from the interaction between social demands upon the child and the child's own conflicts over control of his impulses. Toilet training is aimed at regulating two conflicting modes of bodily activity, retention and elimination. These modes of activity have parallels in many types of social interaction in which the indiscriminate release of impulses must be replaced by self-control, without the child's becoming so fearful of his impulses that he cannot express them even when appropriate. Erikson formulates the child's concerns of this period in terms of a conflict between feelings of *autonomy*, on the one hand, and *shame and doubt* on the other. If toileting and other elementary skills, such as speaking, eating, and dressing, are successfully mastered, the child develops a sense of autonomy and pride in his ability to do things for himself. However, if the child fails to master these tasks, he is left with a sense of shame about himself and doubt about the value of what he can do.

The reasons for failure to master the tasks of this period are diverse. They include excessively stringent demands by adults, the failure of adults to be flexible and supportive in helping the child to gradually meet higher standards, and handicaps on the part of the child that may result from slow organic maturation, from specific debilities, or from failure to develop healthy emotional relationships during earlier stages of development. The reasons for failure also include failure on the part of adults to unambiguously and unambivalently convey to the child that he is expected to meet more advanced standards and that they will be firm in their insistence that he learn to do things for himself.

Whatever the reason for a particular child's failure to master toileting and other elementary skills, such failure can begin to interfere with his accomplishment of further developmental tasks. He is likely to become subject to other children's ridicule and to adults' pity or annoyance. Even in a child who is otherwise quite normal, the absence of an important elementary skill may become a source of other difficulties if it interferes with his mastery of succeeding stages.

The other important stage hypothesized by Freud to occur during the preschool years is the *phallic stage,* which spans approximately the ages 3 to 5. During the phallic stage, libido becomes centered in the penis of the boy and clitoris of the girl. Motivated by sexual curiosity and heightened genital sensitivity, the child—without necessarily understanding the mechanics of sex—seeks an intimate and exclusive relationship with the opposite-sex parent. This, in turn, generates rivalry with the same-sex parent and elicits real or fantasied threats of retaliation from him. The oedipal conflict between desires for the opposite-sex parent and a combination of love and fear of the same-sex parent was theorized to be resolved through *identification* with the same-sex parent—that is, the child introjects the mores of the same-sex parent as a guiding part of his own personality and attempts to be like the same-sex parent. In identifying with the same-sex parent, the child unconsciously accomplishes two ends—he reduces his fear of the same-sex parent and he vicariously shares in the special relationship his same-sex parent maintains with his opposite-sex parent. The introjected mores of the same-sex parent form the basis for the conscience or *superego,* while the image of the same-sex parent to which the child seeks to conform constitutes the *ego ideal.*

Although there is little formal research on the subject, everyday observations show that most preschoolers have intense sexual curiosity and desires, and that many express the wish to marry their opposite-sex parent. Their attempts to compete with and exclude their same-sex parent can also cause significant friction. Furthermore, if something should happen to the same-sex parent during this period, a child may experience intense guilt because his wishes to be rid of the parent have been fulfilled.

However, there is far more going on during this period than the oedipal formulation would suggest. In recognition of the broader psychosocial nature of this stage, Erikson (1963) calls it the *locomotor and infantile genital stage*. Not only is the child motivated by sexual feelings and curiosity, but he also seems "turned on" to thrusting himself into other people's lives in other ways as well. Erikson describes the child's dominant mode of action during this period as *intrusive*, the intrusiveness being expressed "in ambulatory exuberance, in aggressive mentality, and in sexual fantasies and activities [p. 88]." Although Erikson describes both sexes as being "on the make," he believes that sex roles typically become differentiated during this period: In the boy, intrusiveness remains overt and direct, whereas in the girl it shifts to "making" more by teasing or provoking or by making herself attractive and endearing.

In Erikson's view, the basic conflict of this period is between a sense of *initiative* and feelings of *guilt*. If the child's aggressive initiatives result in real or fantasied damage, he may develop a sense of guilt over his goals and powers. Besides the guilt that can arise from harm to or loss of the same-sex parent, excessive guilt can also arise on the one hand from overreactions by adults to the normal aggressiveness of this period, and on the other hand from the failure of adults to set limits that will prevent the child from going so far that he does real damage.

The Cognitive Perspective

A third important perspective concerns the development of thought processes. According to our most comprehensive theory of cognitive development, that of Piaget, the child between the ages of about 2 and 5 has acquired the capacity for thinking in terms of symbols but has not yet acquired the coherent system of logical operations that becomes manifest between the ages of about 5 and 7. The ability to create mental representations—to picture the world to oneself by means of thought—sets the preschooler off dramatically from the child in the preceding "sensorimotor" period, during which behavior is geared exclusively to physically present stimuli and the physical actions that can be performed on them. Mental representation enables the child to re-present to himself previous experiences at will, to mentally transform the world through pretense, to recognize language as a system for symbolic communication, to engage in mental trial-and-error problem solving, and to envision and pursue distant goals.

The acquisition of mental representation brings the child a giant step closer to the world of adult thought, but, during the long period required to subjugate this powerful capacity to the constraints of logic, the child can occasionally be overwhelmed by his own mental creations. This is when monsters, witches, wild animals under the bed, dreams, and things that go bump in the night can become as real as anything else that can be conjured up in the mind's eye. While the older child can master an occasional frightening dream or fantasy by means of logical "reality testing," the preoperational child as yet possesses neither the system of logical operations nor the faith in logic that will later enable him to resolve contradictions between fantasy and logic in favor of logic. Thus, even when fantasy images are playfully created by the child or by a friendly adult, they may get out of hand merely because the child does not clearly distinguish between the reality of the external world and his own very compelling mental imagery.

On the other hand, the child's capacity for mental transformation enables him to gain control of many frightening fantasies through processes like those that engender the fantasies in the first place. A 2-year-old boy who was afraid of monsters under the bed, for example, stopped complaining of monsters after he began taking a large toy frog to bed. He had not previously liked the frog and still did not cuddle with it. In fact, whenever his parents handed it to him in bed, he pushed it aside, facing it toward his feet. Finally, upon being asked why he kept turning the frog away from him, he expalined: "Dat fwoggie ugly—it keep da monsters fwom comin' up da wall by me bed!" The belief that the ugly frog would keep the monsters cowering beneath the bed was perfectly consistent with the system of thought that had created the monsters in the first place.

Fantasy companions are another aid to mastering emotional stresses, as the child can control such companions in ways he cannot control the real people in his life. However, fantasy companions are also likely to serve a more cognitive function in the development of the mental dialogue that is first manifest in young children's overt talking to themselves but that becomes progressively more covert with age.

Occasional preoccupation with fantasy and fantasy companions is a normal, healthy, and often delightful aspect of emotional and intellectual development. Preschoolers who do not engage in fantasy may be failing to use a very important part of their adaptive capacities (Singer, 1973). On the other hand, if fantasy life becomes so intense that a child is shut off from interactions with others or from the acquisition of age-appropriate skills, it may interfere with the development of more logical and reality-oriented modes of adaptation. It is therefore important that the preschooler be given accurate information and feedback about reality, including other people's reactions to him, so that, even if he does not fully assimilate it all at once, he can gradually adjust his mental world to it. While attempting to interfere with children's fantasies by too stringent an insistence on reality may undermine the adaptive value of fantasy, the other extreme of attempting to protect the fantasies by failing to provide honest information can deprive the child of contact with the reality to which he must ultimately adapt.

The Behavioral Perspective

The emphasis in the perspectives discussed so far has been upon aspects of development that are inferred from behavior. The behavior provides observational data, but inferences about underlying physical functioning, motives, fantasies, and cognitive organizations are made in order to facilitate understanding of behavior. A further perspective from which to view development is that which originated with the "behaviorists." John B. Watson (1913) was responsible for the term *behaviorism* as a label for the view that the subject matter of psychology should be restricted to overt behavior and the physical stimuli that elicit it. His definition of psychology in terms of stimuli and responses and his explanation of behavioral change in terms of conditioning became hallmarks of American experimental psychology.

Although Watson and a few others applied behaviorist principles to the treatment of children's behavior problems during the 1920s and 1930s, it was only during the 1960s that behaviorist principles were applied on a large scale to the modification of problem behavior. The methods most relevant to preschoolers have included *operant conditioning, systematic desensitization,* and *modeling. Operant conditioning,* also known as "instrumental" conditioning, refers to the process whereby the consequences that follow a response affect the probability or intensity with which that response will be made again in similar circumstances. The response is referred to as an "operant" (or "instrumental" response) because it operates upon the environment to bring about an effect. Thus, an operant that produces a reward is likely to be repeated, whereas one followed by nonreward or punishment is likely to be extinguished.

Since a particular consequence may not have the same rewarding or punishing effects on everybody, operant conditioners attempt to identify the precise environmental contingencies that affect specific responses by specific individuals. In doing so, they divide the consequences of behavior into three classes: positive reinforcement, negative reinforcement, and punishment. A *positive reinforcement* is an event that increases the future probability or intensity of the preceding response. *Negative reinforcement* is like the other side of the same coin in that it refers to the strengthening of a response through *termination* of an aversive condition. *Punishment,* of course, refers to events that decrease the probability or strength of the responses preceding them.

As Skinner (1971) has argued, operant conditioning is not confined to deliberately contrived situations like the Skinner box, but is occurring in everybody's life all the time. Parents, teachers, and other socializing agents are especially intent on manipulating rewards and punishments in order to control the behavior of young children. However, these attempts at control are rarely carried out systematically enough to enable the socializing agents to determine whether or not they in fact have the desired effects. As a result, many of the reinforcement and punishment contingencies encountered by young children either fail to promote adaptive behavior or actually promote maladaptive behavior. Operant conditioners have been especially adept at pointing out the ways in which certain types of undesirable behaviors are inadvertently reinforced by adults. For example, excessively dependent behavior in a preschooler may earn extra attention from a sympathetic teacher (e.g., Allen, Hart, Buell, Harris, & Wolf, 1964). Likewise, scolding intended as punishment may inadvertently reinforce destructive behavior by a child who is ignored except when he is being scolded. Furthermore, in families where there is a great deal of teasing and other mutually aversive stimulation, a child's aggressive responses may be reinforced because they temporarily stop the noxious behavior of others (Patterson & Cobb, 1971). Even in a normal nursery school environment, aggression is frequently reinforced by the compliance of its victims (Patterson, Littman, & Bricker, 1967).

The first step in determining what may be supporting a troublesome behavior is to observe carefully the conditions under which it occurs and the immediate consequences of its occurrence. A behavior that repeatedly has the same consequences is probably being reinforced by those consequences. A variety of strategies can be employed to ascertain whether the hypothesized relationship between a particular behavior and environmental contingencies indeed holds. One strategy is to manipulate environmental consequences in order to see whether behavior changes accordingly. For example, does the excessively dependent child spend more time with other children if the teacher attends to him only when he is with other children? Do children whose aggressive behavior is not reduced by adult interference become less aggressive when adults start praising them for cooperative behavior and ignoring their aggressive behavior, as was found by Brown and Elliott (1965)?

Another strategy for identifying the relationships between a particular behavior and environmental contingencies is to reduce aversive conditions that may elicit the unwanted behavior. For example, teaching family members to increase their positive behavior toward one another may reduce aversive stimulation that invites aggressive responses which, in turn, are reinforced because they momentarily terminate the aversive stimulation (Patterson & Reid, 1970).

By the time a behavior is troublesome enough to become the focus of an operant analysis, it is often quite entrenched and may be bringing the child a variety of not easily changed environmental consequences, such as hostility or ridicule from peers. In such cases, more powerful combinations of intervention are often needed. These may include simultaneous manipulation of a variety of contingencies so that new adaptive behavior is reinforced while attempts are being made to extinguish maladaptive behavior. Thus, the child whose destructiveness is reinforced by scolding may need not only positive attention when he is not destructive and withdrawal of attention when he is destructive, but placement in a room by himself whenever he is destructive so that he is deprived of all attention, as well as of the opportunity to continue being destructive. The excessively aggressive child may need not only withdrawal of the aversive stimulation against which aggression was directed, but reinforcement for specific new ways of getting along with people.

The second major method of behavior modification, *systematic desensitization,* is based upon *respondent conditioning* (also known as "Pavlovian" or "classical" conditioning). This type of conditioning occurs when a neutral stimulus is repeatedly paired with a stimulus that already produces a response until the previously neutral stimulus alone acquires the power to elicit the response. Thus, in Pavlov's original studies, dogs learned to salivate to the sound of a bell that had been repeatedly paired with presentation of meat. It is believed that respondent conditioning accounts for the acquisition of many irrational fears and anxieties. This occurs when harmless stimuli become associated with a frightening event, the result being that the harmless stimuli subsequently elicit fear. For example, a child who is frightened by the sudden bark of a dog may generalize his fear to all cues of "dogness," no matter how harmless a particular dog might be.

Systematic desensitization is a method for overcoming irrational fear responses by replacing them with other responses. Joseph Wolpe's (1958) claims for the success of systematic desensitization with adult neurotics were an important factor in the rapid growth of behavior modification in the 1960s. Wolpe's method entails training the patient to completely relax his body. Once relaxation responses have been learned, the patient is asked, often with the aid of hypnosis, to imagine situations that provoke mild anxiety. When he experiences anxiety, the patient is trained to invoke relaxation responses incompatible with the feeling of anxiety. By invoking relaxation responses to stimuli progressively higher in the patient's "hierarchy" of anxieties, the patient is ultimately supposed to overcome his irrational fears, that is, to become *desensitized* to previously feared stimuli.

Wolpe's technique for training relaxation responses and pairing them with imagined stimuli cannot be used effectively in its pure form with very young children. However, the basic principles of identifying a graded hierarchy of anxiety-provoking stimuli and of exposing a child to progressively more extreme stimuli in the hierarchy while encouraging nonanxious responses can be employed. For example, if a child is afraid of dogs, desensitization can start with encouragment to look at pictures of dogs in books while an adult points out how nice they are (e.g., Obler & Terwilliger, 1970). Later, the child can be gradually exposed on successive occasions to a small friendly dog at progressively closer range until he can be encouraged to pet the dog. Thereafter, he can be encouraged to interact with an increasing variety of dogs.

The third type of behavior modification, *modeling,* entails providing models who perform the desired behavior. Although children appear to have a natural, probably innate, propensity to imitate, Albert Bandura (1972), the foremost exponent of modeling theory, maintains that modeling involves far broader effects than imitation. In addition to direct response mimicry, modeling includes learning to generalize observed behavior to new situations in a manner consistent with the model's behavior even though the model was never observed in these situations. The effectiveness of modeling in reducing young children's fears has been demonstrated by Bandura, Grusec, and Menlove (1967). They showed that, among nursery school children who feared dogs, those who observed another child successively approach, pet, feed, and interact with a dog over four occasions were later less afraid of dogs than children who had merely been exposed to the dog without the model. Other applications of modeling are reviewed in Zimmerman's chapter in the present volume.

Although behavioral methods may have a powerful influence, the usefulness of the behavioral approach to children's problems must be assessed within a developmental context. The negativistic behavior of many 2-year-olds, for example, may be in some sense a response to environmental contingencies, but what makes these environmental contingencies more reinforcing, aversive, or anxiety provoking for 2-year-olds than for younger or older children? And how does one decide whether certain annoying behaviors of the 2-year-old are maladaptive enough to warrant systematic behavioral intervention or whether they represent normal stages of development, or are simply not significant enough to risk tampering with?

Several guidelines are relevant. One is a knowledge of the typical sequence of development as it occurs in our culture and as it is outlined in the preceding sections on the organic, psychodynamic, and cognitive developmental perspectives. Many behaviors that would be quite abnormal in older children are not at all abnormal in preschoolers and should not, therefore, be considered targets for intensive intervention. This does not mean that behavioral principles should not be employed to encourage more mature ways of coping, but that tolerance for a broad range of behavior is important and that major changes in behavior should be sought only when the behavior is very persistent, clearly detrimental to further develop- ment, and/or responsible for making the child unhappy.

When behavioral methods are to be used, it is often best to discuss the problem behavior with the child and to outline the plan for helping him. This should be done in such a way as to stress the rewards the child can earn through changing his behavior rather than to threaten him with punishments if he fails to change. Behavioral approaches can be especially effective if they are geared to the child's developmental level so as to take advantage of his motivation to master new tasks. For example, a *token reinforcement system* whereby a child earns gold stars or other token rewards that he later exchanges for a more tangible reward can be especially appealing to 4- and 5-year-olds. It is important, however, that the adult only introduce a system that he is himself willing and able to maintain. Incon- sistency in providing the agreed upon response contingencies is a surefire way to sabotage a system and to make new attempts at behavior change far more difficult.

The Sociological Perspective

Much of the current interest in early childhood education stems from two major changes in American social policy. One has been the advent of federal support for preschool education for disadvantaged children, primarily in the form of Project Head Start. The second has been the exponential growth of day care, first for the disadvantaged as a product of the War on Poverty, and now increasingly in demand by parents of all social strata. Whereas preschool education had previously been restricted almost exclusively to middle class nursery schools, the goals of providing an educational head start for poor children and day care for children whose parents want more than babysitting have brought a variety of sociological complications to early childhood education.

Some of these complications, such as language differences among socioeconomic and ethnic groups, have received considerable attention. The work of Labov (1970) and Baratz (1969), for example, has made it clear that children's language development is not defective merely because they speak something other than white standard American English. Whereas lack of experience with a teacher's language may create barriers which, in turn, lead to behavior problems, failure to master the teacher's language should not be regarded as an abnormality unless the child also fails to learn the language spoken at home. Where there is a significant difference between preschoolers' language and that of their teachers, an educational strategy must be adopted to overcome the barriers. This may involve systematic teaching of the teachers' language to the children, learning of the children's language by the teachers, or, preferably, some of each.

Besides obvious differences in language and social customs, a variety of more subtle sociological factors should be considered in assessing behavior problems. One is that preschool education for the poor is typically expected to deliver measurable benefits in terms of academic test scores. Although it has been implicitly assumed that traditional nursery schools provide an academic head start, this has never really been demonstrated even for middle class children, much less for disadvantaged children. The failure of many disadvantaged children to make rapid academic progress in preschool settings may, therefore, not reflect any particular disabilities on their part. Instead it may reflect the ineffectiveness of present approaches to preschool education. Many of these approaches now differ markedly from the traditional nursery school, but the history of preschool education for the disadvantaged has been far too short to produce definitive conclusions about how much to expect of any particular child in any preschool program.

A second factor is that much of the socializing structure of the nursery school is predicated upon the type of experience brought by middle class children. Middle-class nursery school children generally come from homes having a small number of children and a high degree of adult-imposed structure. Consequently, middle class nursery schools tend to be oriented toward providing peer group experience, with large blocks of free time during which children are expected to play together in the sandbox, dress-up corner, and so on. Most disadvantaged children, by contrast, come from environments in which there are many children and relatively little adult-imposed structure. They thus have much peer group experience but little experience in structured activities. For them, the peer interaction provided by free play periods may be superfluous, while their lack of experience in structured activities may make it difficult for them to conform to the norms of decorum expected during free play periods. Rather than regarding failure to make good use of free play as reflecting a behavior problem on the part of a disadvantaged child, it might often be better to substitute adult-structured activities for free play.

A facet of experience common to many disadvantaged children and to middle class children placed in day care is that they receive relatively little adult attention at home. The large number of children per home and high proportion of families in which there is only one parent or where both parents work prevent many disadvantaged children from having much one-to-one contact with adults. The increasing proportion of middle class families in which there is only one parent or in which both parents work, coupled with the rarity of live-in relatives in middle class homes, means that more and more middle class children also lack the abundance of one-to-one experience with adults that middle class nursery school children have typically brought with them.

Deprivation of one-to-one adult attention may result in excessive clinging, demands for attention, showing off, and "outer-directedness"—reliance on cues from adults rather than on one's own ideas. Excessive need for attention by children receiving little at home can put the teacher in a double bind situation in that indiscriminately providing attention can risk reinforcement of dependency or attention-getting behavior. On the other hand, if a child in fact receives insufficient adult encouragement and guidance in mastering skills, he may remain excessively impulsive and outerdirected. The careful provision of one-to-one adult attention and praise for the accomplishment of tasks may therefore be an important facet of the education of preschoolers who otherwise receive little adult attention.

TYPES OF BEHAVIOR DISORDERS

Official Diagnostic Categories

One of the most troublesome questions in the study of early childhood psychopathology is how to categorize disorders in a useful way. The dominant system for classification is maintained by the American Psychiatric Association (1968) and is employed for official record keeping in most treatment settings. The system follows a quasi-medical model according to which behavior disorders are conceptualized as if they were diseases. Traditionally, the three major categories of psychopathology have been *neurotic disorders, personality disorders,* and *psychotic disorders,* but problems arise in applying these categories to disorders of early childhood.

Neurotic disorders are defined by the presence of chronic anxiety, generally assumed to be caused by unconscious conflicts that have become so intense that behavioral symptoms are created to help in controlling the conflicts. According to the psychoanalytic theory of neurosis, true neurotic conflicts cannot occur until the superego has developed to the point where its prohibitions create unconscious conflicts over the expression of sexual and aggressive impulses. Consequently, neurotic disorders theoretically do not emerge before the age of about 5 or 6.

Whether or not caused by unconscious conflicts between the superego and instinctual impulses, neurotic disorders are in fact rarely seen in early childhood. Anxiety in young children generally has a specific focus in fantasy or the external world, although other troublesome behavior designed to avoid a feared situation may complicate the picture. For example, "neurotic" symptoms such as obsessions, compulsions, and bodily complaints having no physical cause can appear in response to specific anxiety-provoking situations.

Personality disorders are ingrained patterns of behavior that, unlike neurotic disorders, are not characterized by anxiety. Even though the behavior of a person diagnosed as having a personality disorder may seem abnormal and may cause problems for people around him, the person himself is not usually very concerned about it. A particularly troublesome type of personality disorder, the antisocial personality (previously known as the "sociopathic" personality), is marked by repeated irresponsible, destructive, and often criminal behavior, unaccompanied by feelings of guilt or genuine remorse. Other personality disorders include the obsessive–compulsive personality—characterized by an excessive concern with conformity and conscience; the hysterical personality—characterized by excitability, emotional instability, and dramatic attention-getting behavior; and the passive–aggressive personality—characterized by expression of aggression through pouting, intentional forgetting, and stubbornness.

While some preschoolers may show behaviors resembling those of personality disorders, the diagnosis of personality disorder is not really appropriate because personality is still very malleable, and guilt, remorse, and concern for the effects of one's behavior on others do not normally appear until late into the preschool period anyway. However, if a pattern of behavior resembling a personality disorder continues over the entire preschool period—during which most children undergo numerous changes of behavior pattern, then there is certainly cause for intervention to help the child develop new patterns of adaptation.

Psychotic disorders comprise the third and most severe category of disorders. According to the American Psychiatric Association's (1968) *Diagnostic and Statistical Manual of Mental Disorders,* "Patients are described as psychotic when their mental functioning is sufficiently impaired to interfere grossly with their capacity to meet the ordinary demands of life. The impairment may result from a serious distortion in their capacity to recognize reality [p. 23]." Adults diagnosed psychotic usually show clear evidence of distortions in their interpretations of reality. However, there is considerable question as to whether this concept of psychosis is applicable to young children since it is difficult to establish an appropriate baseline for "reality" with which a young child's thinking can be compared for evidence of psychotic distortion. The preoperational stage of cognitive development is normally characterized by a great deal of distortion and a lack of capacity for critical logical assessment of one's own thinking. Furthermore, the great intraindividual and interindividual variation in the development of symbolic, communicative, social, and logical abilities makes it difficult to determine whether apparent defects in mental functioning involve abnormal distortions of reality or just lack of development.

Leaving aside the question of whether distortion of reality is an appropriate criterion for childhood psychosis, disorders severe enough to be labeled psychotic are extremely rare in children. Estimates of prevalence range up to only about 6 in 10,000 children (Werry, 1972). Of the children diagnosed psychotic, most are considered to have either early infantile autism or childhood schizophrenia, although the classification system of the American Psychiatric Association lumps all childhood psychotic disorders into the category of childhood schizophrenia. While these terms are often applied indiscriminately and interchangeably to severely disturbed children, the diagnosis of early infantile autism is properly restricted to children who from very early infancy show a lack of social involvement with others and who are greatly upset by alterations in their environments and routines. Failure to look people in the eye, lack of cuddliness, and general lack of attention to people are hallmarks of autism. Furthermore, few autistic children develop normal speech. Those who acquire speech at all during the preschool period typically engage in repetitive echoing ("echolalia") of other people's words, TV commercials, and mechanical sounds. Their usage of personal pronouns is often reversed in that they refer to themselves as "you" and they call other people "I." Autistic children are distinguished from retarded children by their peculiar refractoriness to social stimulation and occasionally by evidence of specialized abilities. Exceptionally good memory, precocious interest in maps and mechanical gadgets, and average or better sensorimotor skills have been reported for autistic children.

In contrast to those diagnosed as being autistic, children diagnosed schizophrenic do not show such extreme lack of relatedness from early infancy onward. Instead, they may appear relatively normal until they begin to withdraw from others and show signs of distorted thinking in middle or later childhood. When a child as young as preschool age is called schizophrenic, it is usually for lack of a better term for an extremely disturbed child who is not clearly autistic, even though he may fail to show clear signs of distortion of "reality."

From the 1940s through the 1960s, there was a widespread tendency to blame childhood psychosis on parental behavior, especially that of the mother. Rank (1949) and Despert (1947), for example, maintained that psychosis is caused by mothers who are narcissistic, overintellectual, and incapable of mature emotional relationships. Bettelheim (1967) maintained that childhood schizophrenia (or "autism," which he used interchangeably with "schizophrenia") is caused by mothers who "wish that [their] child should not exist [p. 125]." However, research has yielded little support for the view that psychoses of early childhood are caused by parental behavior (e.g., Block, Patterson, Block, & Jackson, 1958; DeMyer, Pontius, Norton, Barton, Allen, & Steele, 1972; Klebanoff, 1959; Pittfield & Oppenheim, 1964; Schopler & Loftin, 1969; Zuckerman, Oltean, & Monashkin, 1958). There is growing evidence that at least some children diagnosed as psychotic suffer from brain damage (Gittelman & Birch, 1967; Goldfarb, 1974; Gubbay, Lobascher, & Kingerlee, 1970; Menolascino, 1965; Pollack, Gittelman, Miller, Berman, & Bakwin, 1970; Rutter & Bartak, 1971; Weber, 1970; White, 1974), but the specific causes of most childhood psychoses remain a mystery. Early infantile autism is particularly controversial, with hypotheses about biochemical abnormalities currently being among the most heavily researched.

Despite the emphasis on possible organic causation, the most successful treatment methods for psychotic children so far have been behavioral, although success is generally measured in terms of teaching very elementary skills (e.g., Hamblin, Buckholdt, Ferritor, Kazloff, & Blackwell, 1971). The moderate success of behavioral methods in no way argues against possible organic causation, as such methods merely demonstrate that psychotic children are capable of being taught new behavior. No treatment has yet been demonstrated to transform psychotic children into essentially normal children (cf. Achenbach, 1974, for a more complete review). In addition to the major categories of psychopathology, the official classification system contains a few categories for problems specific to children. The category of *adjustment reaction of childhood* refers to disturbances that are assumed to be temporary reactions to stress. The symptoms displayed may include fears, bed-wetting, insomnia, eating problems, aggression, temper tantrums, obsessions, compulsions, or almost any other problem behavior that might also characterize other categories of nonpsychotic psychopathology. Because the diagnosis of adjustment reaction covers so many possibilities, and because the other nonpsychotic categories have limited applicability to children, the vast majority of children seen for psychiatric treatment are diagnosed as having adjustment reactions (Rosen, Bahn, & Kramer, 1964; Achenbach, 1966). As a result, the diagnosis of adjustment reaction conveys little information about differences among children.

The most recent edition of the American Psychiatric Association's (1968) classification system has added several other categories of childhood disorders, of which two may have some applicability to preschool-age children. These are *hyperkinetic reaction,* "characterized by overactivity, restlessness, distractibility, and short attention span"; and *withdrawing reaction*, "characterized by seclusiveness, detachment, sensitivity, shyness, timidity, and general inability to form close interpersonal relationships [p. 50]." Little information is yet available on how frequently these categories are being employed.

Empirical Clustering Approaches

The introduction of categories such as hyperkinetic reaction and withdrawing reaction—defined by specific behavior problems rather than by more theoretical concepts like neurosis, personality disorder, psychosis, or adjustment reaction—reflects an increasing emphasis on empirical description of children's problem behavior in preference to inferring underlying "disease" entities. This emphasis has resulted both from the lack of any widely accepted theoretical frame of reference for children's disorders and from recognition of the inappropriateness of applying the categories derived from adult pathology to children's disorders.

As yet, most attempts to derive empirical categories for child psychopathology have concentrated on children above the age of 5, although a few have been directed at identifying clusters of behavior problems in preschoolers. In a study by Kohn and Rosman (1972), for example, lists of 58 behavior problems and 90 social competence items were constructed. The list of behavior problems included such items as "fails to play with other children" and "child treats other children with deliberate cruelty; bullies other children or hits or picks on them." The social competence items included "child gets interested in what he's doing" and "child cooperates with rules and regulations." Kohn and Rosman attempted to identify clusters of behavior by factor analyzing symptom checklists and social competence checklists filled out on day-care center children by their teachers.

While factor analysis is designed to empirically identify statistical groupings or dimensions of items that occur together, each of the various types of factor analysis requires decisions by the user as to the number of dimensions to extract. On the basis of previous findings with older children, Kohn and Rosman chose to extract just two dimensions for both the symptom checklist and the social competence checklist. One social competence dimension was defined by items indicative of high degrees of interest, curiosity, and assertiveness, whereas the other dimension was defined by items indicative of cooperation with the rules and routines of the classroom. By contrast, one dimension derived from the symptom checklist was indicative of lack of involvement with tasks and people, whereas the second dimension was defined by aggressive and disruptive behavior. The social competence and symptom dimensions actually represented opposite sides of the same coins, as indicated by the finding that children's scores on the first social competence factor correlated −.75 with their scores on the first symptom factor, while their scores on the second social competence and symptom factors correlated −.79. There were thus two basic dimensions of behavior, one of which was given the label "Interest–Participation versus Apathy–Withdrawal" and the other "Cooperation–Compliance versus Anger–Defiance."

The stability of children's standing on these two dimensions was assessed by having different teachers fill out the checklists at 6-, 12-, and 18-month intervals. Despite the changes in teachers and classroom environments, the children's initial scores on both dimensions were significantly correlated with their scores at each of the succeeding intervals. In another study, Kohn and Rosman (1973b) found significant correlations between scores on their two dimensions obtained during the preschool period and scores obtained on two similar dimensions by combining first grade teachers' ratings from two other behavior checklists, the Peterson Problem Checklist (Peterson, 1961) and the Schaefer Classroom Behavior Inventory (Schaefer & Aaronson, 1966). Continuing stability in these dimensions following first grade is indicated by Schaefer's (1975) findings of significant year-to-year correlations in scores on his behavior inventory throughout elementary school. Scores on the Kohn-Rosman preschool factors have also been found to correlate with independent assessments of emotional disturbance (Kohn & Rosman, 1973a) and to predict subsequent elementary school achievement test scores, with children receiving high scores for Apathy–Withdrawal and Anger–Defiance doing poorly in school achievement (Kohn & Rosman, 1974).

An empirical clustering approach can be valuable insofar as it provides objective means for summarizing children's behavioral problems and competencies and for conducting research on relations between the behaviors thus identified and other characteristics, such as long-term emotional and school adjustment. However, considerably more work is necessary to provide norms that can guide judgments about whether a particular child's behavior pattern is deviant enough to warrant special intervention and to optimally match techniques of intervention to a child's particular problems.

Furthermore, the fact that Kohn and Rosman obtained only two dimensions of behavior does not mean that these two provide the most effective means for identifying problems and helping children. At the opposite extreme, Baker and Dreger (1973), using a different factor-analytic approach, identified 22 factors in behavior problem checklists filled out by the parents of 4- to 6-year-olds. However, many of the Baker–Dreger factors consisted of either a very small number of items or of items that redundantly referred to the same behavior, and many can be viewed as subtypes of the two very general groupings obtained by Kohn and Rosman. Application of a more flexible factor-analytic approach has in fact revealed a hierarchical relationship between two general groupings like those found by Kohn and Rosman and more specific clusters like those found by Baker and Dreger (Achenbach, 1966). However, the real test of any empirical groupings of symptoms will be in the degree to which they reliably distinguish among children whose problems are ultimately found to have different causes and/or different prognoses under various conditions of intervention and nonintervention.

Specific Behavior Problems

Since there is as yet no well accepted system for grouping young children's behavior disorders with respect to causes and appropriate treatments, it may be helpful to deal with some of the most common individual behavior problems one by one. Nevertheless, it should be noted that determination of the cause, seriousness, and most appropriate treatment for each specific problem requires consideration of such contextual factors as the child's developmental level, cultural background, general pattern of coping, environmental stresses, and other behavioral problems and strengths.

Surveys of behavior problems in "normal" children (i.e., children not referred for clinical services) show a high frequency of many types of problem behavior. Table 10.1 portrays the percentage of children in a longitudinal study reported by their mothers to have various behavior problems at the ages of 3 and 5 years (Macfarlane, Allen, & Honzik, 1954). Table 10.2 portrays the percentage of 5-year-olds reported by their teachers to have various problems observable in school (Werry & Quay, 1971).

In addition to the generally high frequency of problems, sex differences are also evident, especially in Table 10.2, which shows that teachers reported many problems significantly more often for boys than for girls. This corresponds to the experience of most mental health agencies, where referrals of boys typically outnumber referrals of girls by three or four to one. While the biggest sex differences tend to involve failure to conform to the school culture (e.g., attention-seeking, disruptiveness, short attention span, fighting, disobedience, hyperactivity, and distractibility), boys are also more frequently reported to show problems such as "crying over minor hurts and annoyances" and "incoherent speech." The differences in Table 10.1 are smaller and do not so consistently favor girls. Whether this is because the types of problems observable at home tend to be more evenly distributed between the sexes, because the school environment elicits more problem behaviors from boys, or because teachers tend to evaluate boys' behavior more

TABLE 10.1
Percentage of Children Reported By Mothers to Have Various Problems
at Ages 3 and 5 Years

Problem	Boys	Girls
1. Attention demanding		
3 years	20	26
5 years	10	15
2. Bed wetting		
3 years	18	31
5 years	8	10
3. Specific fears		
3 years	43	67*
5 years	46	36
4. Jealousy		
3 years	29	29
5 years	36	38
5. Temper tantrums		
3 years	69	63
5 years	59	38*
6. Excessive activity		
3 years	37	33
5 years	46	35
7. Speech problems		
3 years	24	18
5 years	18	8
8. Lying		
3 years	14	12
5 years	49	42
9. Stealing		
3 years	12	18
5 years	10	4

Data from Macfarlane *et al.*, 1954.
*Difference between sexes is significant at $p < .05$.

negatively is not clear. For the two problems tabulated from both the mothers' and teachers' reports—excessive activity and speech problems—mothers as well as teachers reported both problems more frequently for boys than for girls. Because the first of these problems, hyperactivity, is currently receiving more publicity than perhaps any other single behavior problem of early childhood, it will lead our discussion of specific behavior problems.

Hyperactivity

Whether due to cultural cycles that affect the attention paid to particular behavior problems at various times or due to an actual increase in its occurrence, hyperactivity has gained prominence in the popular media as well as in educational and mental health circles. Its prominence may be due in part to the reactions it elicits from adults. If a child truly manifests the behavior of the "hyperkinetic

TABLE 10.2
Percentage of 5-Year-Olds Reported By Teachers to Have Various Problems

Problem	Boys	Girls
1. Oddness, bizarre behavior	22	9*
2. Attention seeking, showing off	39	25*
3. Self-conscious, easily embarrassed	49	47
4. Disruptive, tendency to annoy others	52	21*
5. Feelings of inferiority	35	29
6. Short attention span	55	30*
7. Crying over minor annoyances and hurts	28	19
8. Preoccupation, "in a world of his own"	22	16
9. Shyness, bashfulness	43	48
10. Social withdrawal, preference for solitary activities	25	25
11. Incoherent speech	16	6
12. Fighting	45	9*
13. Anxiety, chronic general fearfulness	23	21
14. Excessive daydreaming	17	11
15. Disobedience, difficulty in disciplinary control	35	11*
16. Hyperactivity, "always on the go"	39	19*
17. Distractibility	58	32*

Data from Werry & Quay, 1971.
*Difference between sexes is significant at $p < .05$.

reaction" described in the classification system of the American Psychiatric Association (1968), he is extremely annoying to adults around him. Furthermore, use of drugs for hyperactivity—in particular, dextroamphetamine (Dexedrine) and methylphenidate (Ritalin)—has elicited violent controversy over whether children are being "drugged into insensibility" merely because they annoy adults and whether psychoactive medication increases the risk of subsequent drug abuse.

The controversy over hyperactivity and its treatment is fed by ignorance about causes, how to identify children in whom hyperactivity is indeed the primary problem, and how to match hyperactive children to the most appropriate treatments. The problems that arise in determining whether a child is really hyperactive in the first place are illustrated by a study in which, of 100 children referred to a clinic for hyperactivity, only 13 were judged hyperactive by all three staff members who evaluated them. Fifty-eight of the children were not judged to be overly active by *any* staff members (Kenny, Clemmens,Hudson, Lentz, Cicci, & Nair, 1971). It is thus likely that the term hyperactivity is currently used far too broadly to label annoying behavior of which high activity is at most an insignificant aspect.

Problems of diagnosis are further compounded by the tendency to attribute hyperactivity to organic dysfunction, whether or not there is evidence of such dysfunction. The tendency to assume that hyperactivity results from brain damage may be due in part to early work by Strauss which showed that brain-damaged retarded children were more active than nonbrain-damaged children (Strauss & Lehtinen, 1947). From these findings, the conclusion was drawn that hyperactivity is typically a sign of brain damage. The apparently beneficial effects of amphetamines and methylphenidate on hyperactivity (cf. National Institute of Mental Health, 1973) has also been used to support the conclusion that hyperactivity is caused by organic dysfunction (e.g., Wender, 1971), although the means by which these drugs reduce hyperactivity is unknown. Since these drugs have stimulant effects on adults, their calming effects on hyperactive children are in fact regarded as paradoxical.

Neither the fact that some brain-damaged children are hyperactive nor that drugs reduce hyperactivity in some children necessarily indicates that hyperactivity is typically a result of organic dysfunction. That hyperactivity may not be generally indicative of brain damage was demonstrated by Shaffer, McNamara, and Pincus (1974). They measured the activity levels of four groups of boys in a series of standardized situations. The groups consisted of brain-damaged boys reported to have conduct problems, brain-damaged boys without conduct problems, boys with no evidence of brain damage but reported to have conduct problems, and boys having neither brain damage nor conduct problems. It was found that brain-damaged boys as a group were not more active than nonbrain-damaged boys, but that the two groups of boys with conduct problems were more active than the other two groups. It was concluded that hyperactivity could not be regarded as typically indicating organic damage, but that it is better regarded as a psychologically based behavior problem that may or may not accompany organic damage.

In another study, children known to have suffered early brain damage were compared during the preschool period with children having no evidence for brain damage (Ernhart, Graham, Eichman, Marshall, & Thurston, 1963). Although the brain-damaged children were found to be more infantile, negativistic, and compulsive, they were also rated as being more *inactive* and no more aggressive than the undamaged children.

Whatever the initial cause of hyperactivity, it may prevent a child from learning social and other skills at the appropriate age, leaving him without means for constructive adaptation when, as typically occurs, his activity level declines during late childhood (Menkes, Rowe, & Menkes, 1967). Thus, even though hyperactive children may "outgrow" their hyperactivity, some sort of intervention may be desirable if a child's behavior is causing him to be excluded from normal socialization and learning experiences. Despite the apparent efficacy of amphetamines and methylphenidate with some children, these drugs have the undesirable side effects of depressing appetite and causing insomnia, and they must in most cases be periodically discontinued to prevent weight loss and interference with growth. Other approaches, usable either in conjunction with or instead of medication, include making the child's environment less stimulating and more tolerant, and using operant conditioning methods to reinforce attending and task-relevant behavior (Allen, Henke, Harris, Baer, & Reynolds, 1967; Christensen, 1975; Doubros & Daniels, 1966; Patterson, Jones, Whittier, & Wright, 1965). The supposed benefits of removing certain food additives from the diets of hyperactive children have not to date received solid research support, although it is certainly possible that food additives and other potential allergens play a role in at least some cases of hyperactivity.

Aggressive and Coercive Behavior

In its current overly broad usage, the term *hyperactivity* is often extended to children who are regarded as troublesome not so much because their activity levels are abnormally high, but because their overt aggression, demandingness, and tantrums contribute to an impression of uncontrollable activity. Patterson and Cobb (1971) have analyzed these behaviors in terms of what they call a "coercion trait." Screaming, kicking, and flailing are natural responses of infants to the discomfort of hunger, cold, and pain. They are highly adaptive responses because they induce adults to relieve the discomfort. During the normal course of socialization, however, children are taught less obnoxious means for reducing their discomfort and infantile behaviors are punished or become less effective than more socially advanced behaviors. Yet, if models and reinforcement are not provided for more socialized behavior and/or if infantile aggressive behaviors continue to be reinforced, then these behaviors may remain high in the hierarchy of a child's responses to aversive conditions. Excessive aggression, demandingness, and tantrums in preschoolers may thus be best regarded not so much as intrinsically abnormal behavior, but as behavior that has not yet been replaced through the learning of more socialized behavior.

As was mentioned earlier, mild to moderately aggressive behavior may be reinforced (Patterson *et al.,* 1967) as well as reduced (Brown & Elliott, 1965) by reinforcement contingencies in the preschool setting. However, when a child's aggression reaches serious proportions and persists across various situations, it is likely that basic problems exist in his home environment. By observing the families of aggressive boys, Patterson, Cobb, and Ray (1973) have identified three parental patterns that seem especially common. One type of parent is inattentive to the sequence of coercive behaviors that culminate in major aggression such as hitting. When such aggression occurs, the parent reacts with yelling or nagging, behaviors which are unlikely to reduce aggression unless they are frequently followed by intense punishment. Since these parents do not punish aggression consistently or early enough in sequences of coercive behavior to deter major aggression, their yelling and nagging has little effect. These parents also fail to attend to and reinforce their children's prosocial behavior. Regarding the child as being generally bad, they see no reason for reinforcing prosocial behavior the child is "supposed to" show anyway. They therefore fail to train their child in prosocial adaptive responses to aversive situations.

In a second type of pattern identified by Patterson *et al.,* the parents do pay attention to their children's behavior and may reinforce prosocial behavior. However, for various reasons, they fail to apply effective contingencies to coercive behavior. For example, a working mother who feels she is depriving her child of mothering may feel guilty about stopping his coercive behavior. Some fathers, on the other hand, actively enjoy the masculinity implied by the aggressive behavior of their sons. Parents of children who have been seriously ill or who have been diagnosed as brain-damaged or retarded may also be overly timid about stopping coercive behavior.

In the third type of pattern, one parent (usually the father) assumes the role of a despot who is excessively harsh with the child, while the other parent attempts to compensate for the harshness by being excessively warm and permissive. As a result, aggressive behavior is likely to occur mainly in the absence of the punitive parent, especially outside the home.

Since inappropriate parenting is usually the source of severe aggressive problems in young children, alteration of parent behavior is an important element of treatment. One approach has been to train parents in techniques like those taught by Bernal, Duryee, Pruett, and Burns (1968) to the mother of a boy manifesting the "brat syndrome" of aggressive and demanding behavior. Interactions between the boy, Jeff, and his mother were recorded on audiotape at home and on videotape at the clinic. Using the videotapes and a cue light that could be flashed to the mother while she was with Jeff in an experimental room, the first step was to train the mother to reduce her indiscriminate, meek, soft, monotone responses and to ignore Jeff's abusive behavior. If ignoring did not stop a particularly abusive behavior, she was to express anger and order Jeff to stop. If he still did not stop, she was to spank him, having already provided clear cues of anger that were expected to become conditioned punishment stimuli after being followed several times by spanking. The mother was also to identify Jeff's acceptable behaviors and praise him warmly when they occurred.

Observation showed that the mother ignored only 11% of Jeff's abusive behavior during a pretreatment session but that this jump to 100% after training. Jeff obeyed 100% of his mother's commands after training, compared to none before training, and the percentage of time his mother was affectionate went from zero to 20%. Other investigators have also reported success in training parents to change reinforcement contingencies in order to reduce aggressive behavior (e.g., Patterson & Brodsky, 1966; Zeilberger, Sampen, & Sloane, 1968).

Unfortunately, follow-ups have shown that the improvements are often short-lived because parents return to their initial patterns, thereby reinstituting the contingencies that originally supported their children's aggression (Patterson *et al.* 1973). In an attempt to produce more permanent changes, Patterson *et al.* tried out a multifaceted 3–4-month program for training parents of aggressive boys. Observers in the home recorded data on parent and child behavior prior to, during, and for a 12-month follow-up period after the parent training program. The parents received training in observation and recording of behavior and in social learning concepts. They were supervised in implementing behavior change programs with their children, their adherence to the programs was monitored through daily phone contacts, and they received additional assistance from home visitors when necessary.

Of the 13 families participating in the program, only 7 remained available for the full 12-month follow-up period. It was found that coercive behavior specifically targeted for modification decreased and remained low throughout the follow-up period for the seven aggressive boys in these families. However, parents apparently did not learn to generalize their behavior management techniques to behaviors not specifically targeted for modification, as nontargeted coercive behaviors were about as high at follow-up as they were in the initial baseline periods before the parents were trained. Furthermore, the attrition of six families suggests that the potential power of behavior modification techniques does not by itself provide adequate leverage for reducing aggressive behavior problems in children: The family of one boy terminated treatment and had him placed in a foster home; the parents of two other boys separated; the mother of another was absent from the home for an extended period (reason unexplained by the authors); and two families moved away. The realities of family disruption may thus limit even the most effective of presently available techniques for controlling aggression.

Phobias

One of the clearest differences between the psychodynamic and behavioral orientations is in their explanations for phobias. As outlined earlier, the behavioral view is that phobias result chiefly from classical conditioning whereby a neutral stimulus becomes feared because it has been associated with a frightening experience. The psychodynamic formulation, by contrast, portrays phobias as one of a large class of symptoms that result from unconscious conflicts. According to this view, the behavioral symptom is created by the ego to help keep anxiety-arousing impulses disguised and in check. A dog phobia in a 4-year-old boy, for example, might be interpreted as reflecting displacement of the unconscious fear of castration by the father on to fear of a biting dog. Since fear of castration is a response to the child's own oedipal desires toward his mother, attributing his fear to a plausible external stimulus like a dog enables the child to accept the fear while preventing its real source from becoming conscious.

The choice of a particular phobic object is hypothesized to be determined by its ability to symbolically substitute for the real fear without being so transparent as to reveal the real fear. Thus, a biting dog may effectively serve as a symbolic substitute for a castration fear because, since dogs really do bite, the essence of what is feared—bodily mutilation—is plausibly associated with the phobic object. Of all the possible objects that could represent this type of threat, the particular choice may be further determined by the fact that the child for some reason associated dogs with his father, for example, because of a slight physical resemblance, gruffness, and so on. Furthermore, if the fear of the father is successfully displaced onto dogs, the feeling of fear can be controlled by avoiding dogs. The psychodynamic model implies that, unless the unconscious conflict is relieved, simply treating the phobic symptom will either be unsuccessful or will result in the substitution of a new symptom to help in controlling the unconscious conflict.

As mentioned earlier, modeling and "real life" desensitization can help to overcome mild animal phobias in young children (Bandura *et al.*, 1967). More severe phobias may, however, require more intensive treatment. Accordingly, Miller, Barrett, Hampe, and Noble (1972) carried out a comparison of the effects of psychodynamically oriented psychotherapy, systematic desensitization, and no treatment with children having severe phobias of various types. One group of phobic children received 24 sessions of psychodynamic psychotherapy, a second group received 24 desensitization sessions, and a control group received no treatment but was assessed and reassessed at the same intervals as the treated children. For children aged 6 to 10, the two kinds of treatments were found to produce equal improvements and both were significantly more effective than no treatment. A 2-year follow-up confirmed that the improvements were maintained (Hampe, Noble, Miller, & Barrett, 1973). However, for children aged 11 to 15, neither treatment produced much improvement and there were no significant differences among the three groups. It thus appears that younger children's phobias may be less complex and more easily removable by both the psychodynamic and behavioral approaches than are phobias occurring at later ages.

In addition to phobic responses to particular objects, school phobias are fairly common during childhood. There is probably no child who has not at some time felt a twinge of fear about going to school. Such feelings are to be expected upon initial entry into school and when changes of school are made. However, they are also common after periods of illness, vacations, and other absences, and can reach such serious proportions that children vomit and develop other physical symptoms, even though they may express the wish to attend school. While the term "school phobia" is rarely applied to children before the age of mandatory schooling, reluctance to separate from parents in order to attend nursery and day-care programs is a common occurrence. When this occurs in preschoolers, it is typically interpreted as separation anxiety rather than school phobia. However, psychodynamic and behavioral theorists generally agree that school phobias of later years also reflect separation anxiety rather than truly representing fear of school per se. There is, in addition, general agreement that the longer the return to school is delayed, the more difficult it becomes.

Kennedy's (1965) findings with behavioral treatment of school phobias are, like the Miller *et al.* (1972) findings, instructive with respect to differences between phobias in younger and older children. Kennedy distinguished between school phobias regarded as neurotic crises ("Type 1") and school phobias that represent a more chronic pattern ("Type 2"). Type 1 school phobias, most frequent in elementary-school-age children, are characterized by acute onsets, frequently on Monday, following an illness the previous Thursday or Friday. Children with the Type 1 phobia often express a concern about death and about their mother's health. The parents of such children are usually well adjusted, communicate well with each other, and easily achieve an understanding of the child's problem, although the father may be competitive with the mother in household management. By contrast, Type 2 school phobias, most frequent in children above the elementary school grades, have incipient onsets and tend to occur in children whose parents are disturbed, difficult to work with, and communicate poorly with one another, and whose fathers are uninterested in the household and children.

Kennedy's procedure for treating school phobias was to have the father take the child to school—by force, if necessary—without procrastination or prolonged discussion with the child. The school principal or attendance officer insured that the child stayed in the classroom, while the mother remained in the hallway if necessary. The child was praised for whatever length of time he was able to remain in school. The stay in school was lengthened the next day, with a goal of complete removal of the symptom by the third day. A therapist also met with the child to encourage him with illustrations of the advantages of going on in the face of fear and to stress that the fear could be quickly overcome.

Kennedy reports that all 50 children with Type 1 school phobias treated in this way overcame their phobias and remained symptom-free for follow-up periods ranging from 2 to 8 years. However, this procedure did not work for children with Type 2 school phobias. This suggests that phobic behavior in most young children from normal families, including that involving separation anxiety, may typically be less complicated than in older children and is likely to be effectively handled by firmly encouraging the child to face the feared situation and not permitting continuation of avoidance behavior.

Enuresis

Bed-wetting that persists beyond the age of about 4 without organic cause is another behavioral problem that receives different interpretations from behavioral and psychodynamic theorists. Behavioral theorists see it as resulting from failure of appropriate conditioning, although they acknowledge that emotional and physiological factors may make it especially difficult for some children to learn to stop wetting. Psychodynamic theorists, on the other hand, see bedwetting as a symptom of unconscious conflict, especially over the expression of masculinity by boys whose mothers are aggressively masculine and whose fathers have doubts about their own masculinity. Both parents are hypothesized to resent the emergence of masculinity in their son and to emasculate him by being overprotective. The symptom of enuresis helps the child to reduce the anxiety thus created by marking him as emasculated and in need of protection (cf. Achenbach & Lewis, 1971).

Since the 1930s, devices have been available to wake enuretics when they begin to wet the bed (Mowrer & Mowrer, 1938). These devices consist of a bed pad electrically wired to activate an alarm when the pad becomes wet. Theoretically, the stimulus of bladder distention, after having been followed by the alarm on a number of occasions, becomes a stimulus for awakening. The enuretic should, therefore, learn to wake up and go to the toilet rather than wet the bed. Lovibond (1964), however, has pointed out that many children treated with the device learn to sleep through the night without wetting or getting up. He maintains that, rather than being conditioned to wake up in response to bladder tension, they simply learn to avoid urinating in bed because it has been followed by the aversive alarm.

Whatever the exact reason, the alarm procedure has been found to yield significantly better results than other treatments, including having a parent wake the child (Baker, 1969), psychotherapy (DeLeon & Mandell, 1966; Werry & Cohrssen, 1965), and various medications (Forrester, Stein, & Susser, 1964; Young, 1965). Follow-ups ranging from 6 months to 4 years have shown that most of the conditioned enuretics remained dry and did not develop other significant symptoms (Baker, 1969; DeLeon & Sacks, 1972; Young, 1965).

Novick (1966), however, found the effects of the conditioning treatment to differ with two types of enuretic boys, those who had never had extended dry periods ("persistent enuretics") and those who had begun wetting after having been dry for an average of 2 years ("acquired enuretics"). Although almost 90% of both groups reached a cure criterion of 14 consecutive dry nights after conditioning, the acquired group wet more frequently and showed significantly more new symptoms than the persistent group during a 10-month follow-up. Thus, faulty conditioning may indeed be the basic problem for persistent enuretics, while emotional problems may be important in cases of acquired enuresis.

That a significant proportion of older enuretics may be acquired enuretics is indicated by the rates of enuresis reported by Macfarlane et al., (1954) in their longitudinal study cited in Table 10.1. As shown in Table 10.1, 8% of the boys and 10% of the girls were reported to be enuretic at age 5. Thereafter, the rates increased, reaching 17% for boys at age 7 and 14% for girls at age 8. Even at the age of 14, 11% of the boys were enuretic, although no girls were. As with other types of behavior problems, enuresis may be relatively uncomplicated and easily treated in early childhood, but may take on a different significance later in childhood. This may be because the determinants of the problem change and/or the problem itself begins to create secondary problems, such as ridicule by others and low self-esteem.

Speech Problems

Two aspects of speech are of special concern during the preschool period. One is the course of language development from the onset of initial comprehension and production of words through the mastery of progressively more complex units of language. The first word typically appears at approximately 12 months of age. Although there is considerable individual variability, lack of any speech by the age of 2 is cause for concern. Two-word sequences generally appear between about 15 and 28 months, with the outer limit of the normal range being in the neighborhood of 3 years (Mysak, 1972). Failure to reach these milestones may indicate defective hearing, mental retardation, severe environmental deprivation, an organic deficit specific to speech, or emotional disturbance.

If the child's comprehension of language is far more advanced than his usage, this is likely to rule out deafness and retardation, and possibly environmental deprivation as well. Of course, both the child's speech production and comprehension should be assessed in terms of the language he hears at home, rather than in terms of linguistic usage to which he may not have been exposed. If comprehension is far ahead of speech production, and if there is no evidence of emotional disturbance, the possibility of a specific inability to speak, either a complete inability (*expressive aphasia*) or a partial inability (*expressive dysphasia*) must be considered. Expressive aphasia or dysphasia is likely to be due to organic damage in the speech centers of the brain. Although congenital damage having no effects other than to prevent speech is rare, Lenneberg (1962) has provided a detailed case history and film of a boy who, by the age of 8, could not speak at all but could understand language well. Organic damage can also interfere with comprehension of speech (*receptive* aphasia or dysphasia), but interference with understanding of langauge will interfere with acquisition as well. It is thus unlikely that speech production could be more advanced than speech comprehension during the preschool period unless organic damage to the receptive apparatus occurred after speech was already well established.

Where both speech production and comprehension appear to be far below normal for a child's age, evidence for symbolic functioning other than speech may be helpful in distinguishing general mental retardation from hearing impairment, organic deficits specific to speech, and emotional disturbance. The child's capacity to manipulate symbols is evident in pretend play, imitation of complex behavior he has seen on previous occasions, communication through gestures, and recognition of pictures as standing for objects. If a nonspeaking preschooler's behavior in these areas is similar in level to that of his agemates, his speech problems are unlikely to be the result of general mental retardation. Occasionally, children show *elective mutism* in that, despite knowing how, they refuse to speak in certain settings such as the preschool. When unaccompanied by evidence for significant emotional disturbance, elective mutism may be treatable through manipulation of reinforcements, for example, by making attention or other reward contingent on a series of successive approximations to speech (e.g., Bangs & Freidinger, 1949).

In addition to general language development, the second aspect of concern is mastery of the mechanics of speech. A child may comprehend language well and his utterances may be of a complexity appropriate for his age, but problems of articulation may prevent him from being understood. Articulation problems comprise approximately 80% of speech problems found in schoolchildren (Mysak, 1972). Such problems can be particularly frustrating for a child who knows what he wants to say but cannot make himself understood. Among the most common articulation problems are simple delays in the ability to make certain sounds, many of which cannot typically be made until surprisingly late ages. Templin (1957), for example, reports the following ages for achievement of consonant sounds by 75% of children: *m, n, ng, p, f, h, w*–3 years; *y*–3.5 years; *b, d, k, g, r*–4 years; *s, sh, ch*–4.5 years; *t, l, v, th*–6 years; *th*(voiced), *z, zh, j*–7 years. Since difficulties with all these sounds are common during the preschool period, and most are outgrown, it is unlikely that such difficulties should be singled out for special treatment beyond reassurance and encouragement of the child who may be upset by them.

Stuttering during the preschool period is also common and frequently outgrown. Many speech specialists maintain that excessive adult attention to it will make it worse (Mysak, 1972). However, Martin, Kuhl, and Haroldson (1972) have reported a successful behavioral treatment of stuttering in 3- and 4-year-old boys. Each boy spent weekly sessions with a talking puppet mounted in a specially designed puppet stage. The first few sessions were used to familiarize the boys with the situation and to determine how frequently they stuttered when talking to the puppet. Thereafter, the puppet became silent and the stage went dark for 10 sec each time the boy stuttered. Both boys' stuttering disappeared almost completely and remained at negligible levels, as revealed in tape recordings taken in the home and interviews over follow-up periods of approximately a year.

PROGNOSIS FOR CHILDHOOD DISORDERS

Although the lack of standardized and objective methods for classifying psychopathology in children makes it difficult to conduct research on the long-term outcomes of various problems, there is some evidence that certain types of early behavior problems are predictive of later difficulties. In a study of the relations between reports on middle class nursery school children and problems throughout the children's later school careers, Westman, Rice, and Bermann (1967) found a composite nursery school "adjustment score" to be a good predictor of later school adjustment and use of mental health services. The adjustment score was based on a combination of reports of interpersonal criteria (behavior with peers and teachers), of individual behavioral criteria (creativity, immaturity, eccentricity), and family criteria (family structure, pathological family relations). The family criteria contributed most to the prediction of later adjustment and use of mental health services. Family relations scores, followed closely by peer relations in nursery school, were the best predictors of later peer relations. However, behavioral eccentricity (e.g., withdrawal, sneakiness, phobias, hyperactivity) in nursery school was the best predictor of later behavioral problems of a similar nature.

Follow-ups of older children into adulthood have shown that, except for psychotic children, those manifesting severe antisocial behavior from the age of about 7 onward generally have the poorest outcomes (cf. Kohlberg, LaCrosse, & Ricks, 1972; Robins, 1972). Whereas most children manifesting excessive shyness, withdrawal, and neurotic behaviors are found to be reasonably well adjusted and self-sufficient as adults, many of those who are rebellious, delinquent, and very poor achievers in school are later found to manifest personality disorders and criminal behavior. Since prognosis is a function not only of a disorder itself, but of the conditions impinging on the individual, the most appropriate conclusion is probably that our present-day educational and mental health systems do not successfully treat antisocial behavior.

OBTAINING PROFESSIONAL ASSISTANCE

The normal stresses of the young child's life—adjustment to preschool, the birth of a sibling, illnesses and deaths in the family, moves, toilet training, family conflicts—coupled with his immature means for coping with stress are bound to produce behavior problems in every child from time to time. Early childhood educators are often in a position to identify behavior problems and to determine whether they are transitory or limited to particular situations, or whether they are persistent across time and setting. If problems are unresponsive to manipulation of contingencies in the preschool setting, then it may be desirable to obtain further information from the parents about the child's behavior outside the preschool. If parents share similar concerns about the child's behavior, it may be possible to work out mutually agreeable changes in the way the child is handled at home and in the preschool.

If it is not possible to bring about improvements in the child's behavior, other avenues may need to be explored. Unfortunately, mental health services for very young children are extremely meager, especially for families who cannot afford private treatment. Pediatricians are usually among the first to whom parents turn for advice on the behavior of young children, but the lack of readily available techniques for screening and diagnosing behavior problems in the course of pediatric contacts, as well as communication barriers between pediatricians and mental health professionals, leave many pediatricians to rely on reassurance that "he'll grow out of it" as an approach to problems not having clear organic causes.

Child guidance clinics tend to concentrate on children above the age of 4, but they may be helpful in making referrals to services in a community that might be appropriate for preschoolers. Congress has recently enacted legislation (Public Law 94-63, 1975) specifically requiring community mental health centers to offer children's services, but, since significant funding has not yet been allocated for these services and for training people to render them, they are a long way off at best.

A number of states have recently enacted legislation requiring that all school systems provide education by the age of 4 to children who have any problem that may significantly interfere with their learning. Intended to include physically, mentally, emotionally, environmentally, and behaviorally handicapped children, these services may constitute one of the best potential sources of help because they are intended to identify the optimal educational approach for each child without his having first to fail several years of school before being selected for special education. It is to be hoped that enough public school districts will eventually provide high quality preschool services so that early identification of problems can be routinely followed by appropriate tailoring of educational and treatment services to each child's long-term developmental needs.

One other factor that needs to be considered is the recent enactment of tough child neglect and abuse laws by many states. Contrary to the previous tendency to put parental rights above the rights and welfare of children, these laws are intended to protect children by punishing abusive parents and removing their children from them when necessary. The laws not only provide criminal penalties for child abuse, but make it a crime to fail to report child abuse. Unfortunately, the high-minded intentions of these laws have not been accompanied by funds to care for neglected and abused children. As a result, professionals who know of child abuse may have to choose whether to disobey the law or to see parents justly arrested, but their children either left with them under conditions of still greater risk or removed from them only to be passed from one receiving center or foster home to another. While the laws against abuse may at least provide deterrent leverage in some cases, it is to be hoped that ways can be found to provide more effective protection for children.

REFERENCES

Achenbach, T. M. The classification of children's psychiatric symptoms: A factor-analytic study. *Psychological Monographs*, 1966, *80*, Whole No. 615.
Achenbach, T. M. *Developmental psychopathology*. New York: Ronald Press, 1974.
Achenbach, T. M., & Lewis, M. A proposed model for clinical research and its application to encopresis and enuresis. *Journal of the American Academy of Child Psychiatry*, 1971, *10*, 535–554.
Allen, K. E., Hart, B., Buell, J. S., Harris, F. R., & Wolf, M. M. Effects of social reinforcement on isolate behavior of a nursery school child. *Child Development*, 1964, *35*, 511–518.
Allen, K. E., Henke, L. B., Harris, F. R., Baer, D. M., & Reynolds, N. J. Control of hyperactivity by social reinforcement of attending behavior. *Journal of Educational Psychology*, 1967, *50*, 231–237.
American Psychiatric Association. *Diagnostic and statistical manual of mental disorders* (2nd edition). Washington, D. C.: American Psychiatric Association, 1968.
Baker, B. L. Symptom treatment and symptom substitution in enuresis. *Journal of Abnormal Psychology*, 1969, *74*, 42–49.
Baker, R. P., & Dreger, R. M. The preschool behavioral classification project: An initial report. *Journal of Abnormal Child Psychology*, 1973, *1*, 88–120.
Bandura, A. Modeling theory: Some traditions, trends, and disputes. In R. D. Parke (Ed.), *Recent trends in social learning theory*. New York: Academic Press, 1972.
Bandura, A., Grusec, J. E., & Menlove, F. L. Vicarious extinction of avoidance behavior. *Journal of Personality and Social Psychology*, 1967, *5*, 16–23.
Bangs, J. L., & Freidinger, A. Diagnosis and treatment of a case of hysterical aphasia in a thirteen-year-old girl. *Journal of Speech and Hearing Disorders*, 1949, *14*, 312–317.
Baratz, J. C. A bi-dilectal task for determining language proficiency in economically disadvantaged Negro children. *Child Development*, 1969, *40*, 889–901.
Beloff, H. The structure and origin of the anal character. *Genetic Psychology Monographs*, 1957, *55*, 141–172.
Bernal, M. E., Duryee, J. S., Pruett, H. L., & Burns, B. J. Behavior modification and the brat syndrome. *Journal of Consulting and Clinical Psychology*, 1968, *32*, 447–456.
Bettelheim, B. *The empty fortress*. New York: Free Press, 1967.
Block, J., Patterson, V., Block, J., & Jackson, D. D. A study of the parents of schizophrenic and neurotic children. *Psychiatry*, 1958, *21*, 387–397.
Brown, P., & Elliott, R. Control of aggression in a nursery school class. *Journal of Experimental Child Psychology*, 1965, *2*, 103–107.
Christensen, D. E. Interaction effects between stimulant therapy and classroom behavior modification programs. Paper presented at American Psychological Association, Chicago, September, 1975.
DeLeon, G., & Mandell, W. A comparison of conditioning and psychotherapy in the treatment of functional enuresis. *Journal of Clinical Psychology*, 1966, *22*, 226–330.
DeLeon, G., & Sacks, S. Conditioning functional enuresis. *Journal of Consulting and Clinical Psychology*, 1972, *39*, 299–300.

DeMyer, M. K., Pontius, W., Norton, J. A., Barton, S., Allen, J., & Steele, R. Parental practices and innate activity in normal, autistic, and brain-damaged infants. *Journal of Autism and Childhood Schizophrenia*, 1972, *2* 49–66.

Despert, L. Psychotherapy in childhood schizophrenia. *American Journal of Psychiatry*, 1947, *104*, 36–43.

Doubros, S. G., & Daniels, G. J. An experimental approach to the reduction of overactive behavior. *Behaviour Research and Therapy*, 1966, *4*, 251–258.

Ernhart, C. B., Graham, F. K., Eichman, P. L., Marshall, J. M., & Thurston, D. Brain injury in the preschool child: Some developmental considerations. II. Comparison of brain injured and normal children. *Psychological Monographs*, 1963, *77*, Whole No. 573, Pp. 17–33.

Erikson, E. H. *Childhood in society* (2nd edition). New York: Norton, 1963.

Forrester, R. M., Stein, Z., & Susser, M. W. A trial of conditioning therapy in nocturnal enuresis. *Developmental Medicine and Child Neurology*, 1964, *6*, 158–166.

Gittelman, M., & Birch, H. G. Childhood schizophrenia: Intellect, neurologic status, perinatal risk, prognosis, and family pathology. *Archives of General Psychiatry*, 1967, *17*, 16–25.

Goldfarb, W. *Growth and change of schizophrenic children*. New York: Halstead Press, 1974.

Gubbay, S. S., Lobascher, M., & Kingerlee, P. A neurological appraisal of autistic children: Results of a Western Australian survey. *Developmental Medicine and Child Neurology*, 1970, *12*, 422–429.

Hamblin, R. L., Buckholdt, D., Ferritor, D., Kozloff, M., & Blackwell, L. *The humanization processes: A social behavioral analysis of children's problems*. New York: Wiley-Interscience, 1971.

Hampe, E., Noble, H., Miller, L. C., & Barrett, C. L. Phobic children one and two years post-treatment. *Journal of Abnormal Psychology*, 1973, *82*, 446–453.

Hetherington, E. M., & Brackbill, Y. Etiology and covariation of obstinacy, orderliness, and parsimony in young children. *Child Development*, 1963, *34*, 919–943.

Kennedy, W. A. School phobia: Rapid treatment of fifty cases. *Journal of Abnormal Psychology*, 1965, *70*, 285–289.

Kenny, T. J., Clemmens, R. L., Hudson, B. W., Lentz, G. A., Cicci, R., & Nair, P. Characteristics of children referred because of hyperactivity. *Journal of Pediatrics*, 1971, *79*, 618–622.

Klebanoff, L. B. Parental attitudes of mothers of schizophrenic brain-injured and retarded, and normal children. *American Journal of Orthopsychiatry*, 1959, *29*, 445–454.

Kohlberg, L., LaCrosse, J., & Ricks, D. The predictability of adult mental health from childhood behavior. In B. B. Wolman (Ed.), *Manual of child psychopathology*. New York: McGraw-Hill, 1972. Pp. 1217–1284.

Kohn, M., & Rosman, B. L. A social competence scale and symptom checklist for the preschool child: Factor dimensions, their cross-instrument generality, and longitudinal persistence. *Developmental Psychology*, 1972, *6*, 430–444.

Kohn, M., & Rosman, B. L. A two factor model of emotional disturbance in the young child: Validity and screening efficiency. *Journal of Child Psychology and Psychiatry*, 1973, *14*, 31–56. (a)

Kohn, M., & Rosman, B. L. Cross-situational and longitudinal stability of social-emotional functioning in young children. *Child Development*, 1973, *44*, 721–727. (b)

Kohn, M., & Rosman, B. L. Social-emotional, cognitive, and demographic determinants of poor school achievement: Implications for a strategy of intervention. *Journal of Educational Psychology*, 1974, *66*, 267–276.

Labov, W. The logic of nonstandard English. In F. Williams (Ed.), *Language and poverty*. Chicago: Markham, 1970.

Lenneberg, E. H. Understanding language without the ability to speak: A case report. *Journal of Abnormal and Social Psychology*, 1962, *65*, 419–425.

Lovibond, S. H. *Conditioning and enuresis*. Oxford: Pergamon, 1964.

Macfarlane, J. W., Allen, L., & Honzik, M. P. *A developmental study of the behavior problems of normal children between twenty-one months and fourteen years*. Berkeley: University of California Press, 1954.

Martin, R. R., Kuhl, P., & Haroldson, S. An experimental treatment with two preschool stuttering children. *Journal of Speech and Hearing Research,* 1972, *5,* 743–752.

Menkes, M., Rowe, J. S., & Menkes, J. H. A twenty-five-year follow-up study on the hyperkinetic child with minimal brain dysfunction. *Pediatrics,* 1967, *39,* 393–399.

Menolascino, F. Psychoses of childhood: Experiences of a mental retardation pilot project. *American Journal of Mental Deficiency,* 1965, *70,* 83–92.

Miller, L. C., Barrett, C. L., Hampe, E., & Noble, H. Comparison of reciprocal inhibition, psychotherapy, and waiting list control for phobic children. *Journal of Abnormal Psychology,* 1972, *79,* 269–279.

Mowrer, O. H., & Mowrer, W. M. Enuresis: A method for its study and treatment. *American Journal of Orthopsychiatry,* 1938, *8,* 436–459.

Mysak, E. D. Child speech pathology. In B. B. Wolman (Ed.), *Manual of Child Psychopathology.* New York: McGraw-Hill, 1972, Pp. 624–652.

National Institute of Mental Health. *Psychopharmacology bulletin: Special issue on pharmacotherapy of children.* Washington, D. C.: U.S. Government Printing Office, 1973, DHEW Publication No. (HSM) 73-9002.

Novick, J. Symptomatic treatment of acquired and persistent enuresis. *Journal of Abnormal Psychology,* 1966, *71,* 363–368.

Obler, M., & Terwilliger, R. F. Pilot study on the effectiveness of systematic desensitization with neurologically impaired children with phobic disorders. *Journal of Consulting and Clinical Psychology,* 1970, *34,* 314–318.

Patterson, G. R., & Brodsky, G. A behavior modification programme for a child with multiple problem behaviors. *Journal of Child Psychology and Psychiatry,* 1966, *7,* 277–295.

Patterson, G. R., & Cobb, J. A. A dyadic analysis of "aggressive" behaviors. In J. P. Hill (Ed.), *Minnesota symposia on child psychology, Vol. 5.* Minneapolis: University of Minnesota Press, 1971.Pp. 71–129.

Patterson, G. R., Cobb, J. A., & Ray, R. S. A social engineering technology for retraining the families of aggressive boys. In H. E. Adams, and I. P. Unikel, (Eds.), *Issues and trends in behavior therapy.* Springfield, Illinois: Charles C. Thomas, 1973.

Patterson, G. R., Jones, R., Whittier, J., & Wright, M. A. A behavior modification technique for the hyperactive child. *Behavior Research and Therapy,* 1965, *2,* 217–226.

Patterson, G. R., Littman, R. A., & Bricker, W. Assertive behavior in children: A step toward a theory of aggression. *Monographs of the SRCD,* 1967, *32,* No. 5 (Serial No. 113).

Patterson, G. R., & Reid, J. B. Reciprocity and coercion: Two facets of social systems. In C. Neuringer & J. L. Michael (Eds.), *Behavior modification in clinical psychology.* New York: Appleton-Century-Crofts, 1970, Pp. 133–177.

Peterson, D. R. Behavior problems of middle childhood. *Journal of Consulting Psychology,* 1961, *25,* 205–209.

Pittfield, M., & Oppenheim, A. Child-rearing attitudes of mothers of psychotic children. *Journal of Child Psychology and Psychiatry,* 1964, *5,* 51–57.

Pollack, M., Gittelman, M., Miller, R., Berman, P., & Bakwin, R. A developmental, pediatric, neurological, psychological, and psychiatric comparison of psychotic children and their sibs. *American Journal of Orthopsychiatry,* 1970, *40,* 329–330.

Public Law 94-63. 94th Congress. An Act to Amend the Public Health Service Act. July 29, 1975.

Rank, B. Adaptation of the psychoanalytic technique for the treatment of young children with atypical development. *American Journal of Orthopsychiatry,* 1949, *19,* 130–139.

Robins, L. N. Follow-up studies of behavior disorders in children. In H. C. Quay and J. S. Werry (Eds.), *Psychopathological disorders of childhood.* New York: Wiley, 1972. Pp. 414–450.

Rosen, B. M., Bahn, A. K., & Kramer, M. Demographic and diagnostic characteristics of psychiatric clinic patients in the U.S.A., 1961. *American Journal of Orthopsychiatry,* 1964, *34,* 455–468.

Rutter, M., & Bartak, L. Causes of infantile autism: Some considerations from recent research. *Journal of Autism and Childhood Schizophrenia,* 1971, *1,* 20–32.

Schaefer, E. S. Major replicated dimensions of adjustment and achievement: Cross-cultural, cross-sectional, and longitudinal research. Paper presented at American Educational Research Association Meetings, Washington, D. C., April 3, 1975.

Schaefer, E. S., & Aaronson, M. R. Classroom behavior inventory: Preschool to primary. Bethesda, Maryland: National Institute of Mental Health, 1966 (Mimeo).

Schopler, E., & Loftin, J. Thinking disorders in parents of young psychotic children. *Journal of Abnormal Psychology,* 1969, *74,* 281–287.

Shaffer, D., McNamara, N., & Pincus, J. H. Controlled observations on patterns of activity, attention, and impulsivity in brain-damaged and psychiatrically disturbed boys. *Psychological Medicine,* 1974, *4,* 4–18.

Singer, J. L. *The child's world of make believe: Experimental studies of imaginative play.* New York: Academic Press, 1973.

Skinner, B. F. *Beyond freedom and dignity.* New York: Knopf, 1971.

Spock, B. *Baby and child care* (2nd edition). New York: Pocket Books, 1968.

Strauss, A. A., & Lehtinen, L. E. *Psychopathology and education of the brain-injured child.* New York: Grune & Stratton, 1947.

Templin, M. C. Certain language skills in children. *Institute of Child Welfare Monograph Series,* 1957, No. 26.

Watson, J. B. Psychology as the behaviorist views it. *Psychological Review,* 1913, *20,* 150–177.

Weber, D. *Der frühkindliche Autismus unter dem Aspekt der Entwicklung.* Bern: Verlag Hans Huber, 1970.

Wender, Paul. *Minimal brain dysfunction in children.* New York: Wiley, 1971.

Werry, J. S. Childhood psychosis. In H. C. Quay and J. S. Werry (Eds.), *Psychopathological disorders of childhood.* New York: Wiley, 1972, 173–233.

Werry, J. S., & Cohrssen, J. Enuresis: An etiologic and therapeutic study. *Journal of Pediatrics,* 1965, *67,* 423–431.

Werry, J. S., & Quay, H. C. The prevalence of behavior symptoms in younger elementary school children. *American Journal of Orthopsychiatry,* 1971, *41,* 136–143.

Westman, J. C., Rice, D. L., & Bermann, E. Nursery school behavior and later school adjustment. *American Journal of Orthopsychiatry,* 1967, *37,* 725–731.

White, L. Organic factors and psychophysiology in childhood schizophrenia. *Psychological Bulletin,* 1974, *81,* 238–255.

Wolpe, J. *Psychotherapy by reciprocal inhibition.* Stanford, California: Stanford University Press, 1958.

Young, G. C. Conditioning treatment of enuresis. *Developmental Medicine and Child Neurology,* 1965, *7,* 557–562.

Zeilberger, J., Sampen, S. E., & Sloane, M. N. Modification of a child's problem behavior in the home with the mother as therapist. *Journal of Applied Behavior Analysis,* 1968, *1,* 47–53.

Zuckerman, M., Oltean, M., & Monashkin, I. The parental attitudes of mothers of schizophrenics. *Journal of Consulting Psychology,* 1958, *22,* 307–310.

11

Individual Differences: A Perspective for Understanding Intellectual Development

IRVING E. SIGEL*

Educational Testing Service

DAVID M. BRODZINSKY*

Douglas College, Rutgers University

INTRODUCTION

The purpose of this chapter is to present a rationale for the study of individual differences in young children. We begin with differentiating a nomothetic (general) from an idiographic (individual) research strategy and proceed to discuss the major factors accounting for individual variations in cognitive behavior. Following this, we focus on a particular class of behaviors that have been found to contribute to variability in intellectual performance. This class of behaviors is referred to as *cognitive styles*. We conclude with a discussion of the educational implications of the individual difference perspective in the course of demonstrating the practical utility of the cognitive style concept. Hopefully, educators as well as researchers will find this presentation useful as a guide to understanding the *how* and perhaps the *why* of cognitive performance.

*The order of the authors' names does not represent a senior–junior author relationship. Each author contributed equally to the present chapter.

Normative Research versus Individual Differences

Two fundamental research strategies have been used by developmental psychologists: the *nomothetic* and the *idiographic*. The nomothetic approach focuses on the search for general laws of development applicable to populations or large aggregates of individuals. While researchers using this approach recognize the existence of within-group variability, they deemphasize it in favor of generic principles of development. On the other hand, the goal of the idiographic approach (the term *ipsative* has also been used) is to discover laws of individual development. Here the emphasis is on examining individual variability within populations rather than generalizations across populations.

Behavioral researchers generally have adopted a nomothetic approach to the study of human development. This emphasis apparently reflects the assumption that the goal of science is primarily to discover general principles, and only secondarily to deal with isolated and/or atypical cases. Thus, most current developmental studies are designed to identify population characteristics, or similarities and differences between populations, rather than to identify and explain the variability manifested by individuals in the course of development. As such, these studies yield global generalizations about the behavior of the population or populations under study, but very little information about the determinants of an individual's behavior. For example, consider the large corpus of research that has accumulated since 1960 with respect to children's development of logical thought. To date, most of this research has been concerned with describing and evaluating the universal stage sequence proposed by Jean Piaget. The result of this multitudinous effort has been a series of generalizations about the course of intellectual development from infancy to adolescence that by and large are remarkably reliable across most Western populations. Yet, within all these generalizations there are exceptions. Not all individuals fit the expected pattern. Children develop at different rates; some lag behind their peers, while others are more advanced. Furthermore, some children never attain certain levels of development, as in the case of retarded children (Inhelder, 1968), or children who are not exposed to formal education (Bruner, Olver, & Greenfield, 1966). In addition, once having reached the final level of development, some individuals display an apparent regression in thought, although typically this is found only in cases of psychopathology or during the aging process (Bearison, 1974; Papalia & Bielby, 1974).

Most cognitive–developmental psychologists, however, have not been interested in, or have ignored, within-population variability. The reasons for the lack of interest are twofold. First, most researchers are committed to the position that the primary goal of science is to discover basic principles of development. Second, once having accepted this position, they implicitly assumed that within-group variability is largely due to sampling and measurement errors. The emphasis on sampling error, however, is not a sufficient explanation for the response variability observed within large aggregates of individuals. Not only does it limit one's understanding of the behavior of the population under study, but it also ignores the importance of individual differences.

This emphasis on generalizations of population characteristics tends to subordinate interest in sources of variability within populations, resulting in relatively more accurate predictions for groups than for individuals within groups. An individual difference emphasis, however, seeks understanding of intragroup variability as a psycho-bio-social phenomenon, not as a function of measurement or sampling errors.

Thus, the psychologist should have two goals: (*1*) the identification of generalizations that characterize a population and (*2*) the identification of individual differences within that population. The former allows for prediction of group behavior; whereas the latter extends our understanding of the individual.

SOURCES OF INDIVIDUAL DIFFERENCES

Let us begin by examining the sources that promote unformity among individuals. Humans are first and foremost biological organisms and as such are structured in a way which has been programmed through an evolutionary and genetic history. Since mankind shares the same evolutionary history, a considerable degree of organismic uniformity exists. For example, humans have certain biological limitations that define what they can eat, how they can live, how they can reproduce, and in general, what they can do to maximize their chances of survival as a species. Further, humans are vulnerable to disease and destruction from an array of sources: biological, social, psychological, economic, and political. It is the individual's basic helplessness, therefore, in conjunction with his or her biological limitations, that demand a group existence.

The sociocultural group is another vehicle that promotes uniformity among humans. In all cultures, individuals are socialized to adopt a particular language, kinship system, knowledge base, value system, and so on. The emphasis is on conformity to the larger group rather than on individuality.

Thus, we see that both the biological nature of humans and the sociocultural context in which they live contribute to organismic uniformity. Yet, when we reflect on the similarities among individuals, we are struck by their diversity. The same general factors, while creating human uniformity, also create diversity. This contradiction, however, is more apparent than real. The evolutionary history of the human species has endowed it with a variety of genetic mechanisms which promote individual uniqueness (see Scarr-Salapatek, 1975 for a review of the genetic sources of individual and group differences in intelligence). At the same time, considerable differences exist both between and within cultures, which, in turn, influence the individual's socialization experiences. Each person does have a unique developmental history since socializing agents (parents, teachers, peers) treat each one differently. Thus, the individual is programmed from conception, and socialized from birth, to be like all humans in some ways (organismic uniformity), and unlike most humans in other ways (organismic variability).

Biological Sources of Individual Differences

Recent biobehavioral research relevant to intellectual development has emphasized the role of genetic composition, nutritional status, and developmental anomalies. We shall limit our discussion to the genetic issues.[1]

Historically, the role of genetics in the development of intelligence can be traced to the time of Galton and other British investigators influenced by Darwinian thought. Over the years, the question of interest has been the degree to which familial genetic composition influences the broad spectrum of intellectual functioning, ranging from rote learning to the acquisition of verbal skills to more complex problem-solving strategies and logical reasoning.

At the turn of the century, there seemed to be little doubt among scientists that intellgence was primarily determined by heredity. As such, individual differences in intellectual performance were attributed to differences in the quality of genes (see Kamin, 1974, for an excellent review of this early conception of intelligence and the social and political implications that resulted from it). Further, it was believed that intelligence developed gradually, and that by 14–16 years of age it reached a plateau.

The fixed nature of intelligence remained a controversial issue among psychologists for many years. Only recently has it been shown that intelligence is not fixed but influenced by a host of sociocultural experiences, personality characteristics, and measurement methods (Hunt, 1961; Sigel, 1963). Further, it has also been found that certain aspects of intelligence do not reach a plateau during middle adolescence but continue to increase in complexity well into the adult years (Bayley & Oden, 1955; Owens, 1953).

With these conclusions, the issue of heredity, environment, and intelligence remained quiescent until the publication of a controversial paper by Arthur Jensen (1969) in the *Harvard Educational Review*. In that paper, Jensen argued that intelligence, as measured by the Stanford-Binet test, in particular, was largely inheritable, with 80% of the variance in the distribution of IQ scores attributed to heredity and only 20% to environment. In addition, two levels of intelligence were identified: Level I, the ability to learn by rote and deal with the world in a concrete manner, and Level II, the ability to think, reason, and deal with the world in an abstract, logical way. Jensen contended that blacks on the whole were equal to whites on problems tapping Level I ability, but that they were clearly inferior to whites on Level II problems. Further, he attributed these differences to the influence of genetics. Needless to say, Jensen's report aroused considerable criticism (Elkind, 1969; Hunt, 1969; Kagan, 1969). Some critics questioned the validity of the model which Jensen used to separate heredity and environment, while others attacked him for generalizing from the finding that IQ was heritable *within* a

[1] Nutritional studies tend to show impact in IQ scores only under extreme deprivation (Read, 1972). Biological anomalies such as birth defects are beyond the scope of this article (see Gallagher, 1975).

population to the position that the differences *between* populations were also genetic (Lowentin, 1976; Scarr-Salapatek, 1971, 1975).

One reason why Jensen's paper was so controversial was because of the educational and social implications which followed from his conclusions. The title of his paper reflects this controversy, namely "How much can we boost IQ and scholastic achievement?" The answer Jensen presents was "not much." Jensen was questioning directly the feasibility and the usefulness of such intervention programs as Head Start, which attempted to provide lower class preschool children with an enriched environment to overcome the intellectual deficits typically shown by these individuals in later life. Presumably Jensen's reasoning was as follows: If intelligence is largely determined by heredity, then it is immutable, and consequently it is essentially futile to attempt to eliminate IQ and scholastic differences between groups of individuals via large scale "enrichment" programs.

There are at least three vulnerable points to his argument. First, it is questionable just how much of what we call intelligence is genetically determined. Certainly, geneticists have not as yet defined specific genes that are responsible for one's intelligence. Secondly, even if intelligence has a large genetic component, this does not exclude the environment from playing an important role in its phenotypic expression. Thus, different environmental situations may facilitate or inhibit the development and expression of intellectual competencies (see the following section). Finally, as Lowentin (1976) points out, even if intelligence is genetically determined, this does not mean it is immutable. He states:

> The plasticity of a morphological or physiological or behavioral trait is not made greater or less by the fact that genes influence it. If "inherited" meant "unchangeable," then human clinical genetics would be a largely fruitless enterprise, limited only to counseling parents about risks of having defective children. But this is not the case. Inherited disorders can be treated and corrected as easily (or with as much trouble) as those arising from birth traumas, accidents, or environmental insults. To cure a disorder, we need to know what the metabolic or anatomical lesion is, not whether it is a result of being homozygous for a gene [p. 8].

Presumably few theorists would doubt that heredity plays some role in the child's intellectual development or in the differences manifested among children's performance on IQ tests. The critical question, however, is *how* heredity and environment interact to determine children's ability to function adequately in their world. Of further importance are the educational implications of the heritability issue. Given that individuals differ in intelligence and that one source of this variation is heredity, an important question arises regarding particular kinds of inputs that educators employ to help each of the children learn effective and satisfying ways to adapt to their world. The answer to the question is complicated by the fact that we do not yet know how to identify the individual's intellectual genetic potential let alone how to create the match between this potential and the educational environment (Lowentin, 1976). We shall have more to say about this issue in our concluding section in implications.

Sociocultural Sources of Individual Differences

To this point we have focused only on the genetic side of the heredity—environment issue. Let us now turn to a discussion of the role of environment as a source of variation in intelligence.

The first thing to note is that the environment should not be construed as a unitary phenomenon. On the contrary, the concept of environment as used by psychologists refers to a host of experiences that the individual encounters in the course of development. In the past, however, attention has been focused on very broad conceptualizations of environment, primarily through such index variables as culture, socioeconomic status, and ethnicity. Each of these variables is associated with a complex array of experiences, which in turn, are related to specific levels of performance on various intellectual and personality tests. Thus, knowing the cultural or socioeconomic status of a child provides the investigator with some predictive power with respect to the child's performance on different types of tests.

There is a danger, however, in stereotyping children on the basis of cultural or class variables. To do so is to equate each child with all other children within a particular group or population. This gets us back to the denigration of individual differences as discussed earlier. More recently, however, developmental psychologists have attempted to delineate specific factors transcending cultural or class lines that are related to individual differences in intellectual and personality functioning. The work of one of the present authors is an example. Sigel (Sigel & Cocking, 1977) has attempted to examine specific aspects of the environment that promote the development of representational competence in young children; that is, "the ability to deal competently and equivalently with representational material [Sigel, 1970, p. 103]." According to Sigel, the source of this ability lies in the structuring of the physical and interpersonal world of the child. Parents who structure the young child's world so as to allow for predictability, and/or who encourage the child to relate the present to past and future events, essentially are stimulating him/her to deal with the world in terms of *anticipated* happenings, which in turn take the form of evoked representational images. Further, Sigel suggests that these parental behaviors (termed *distancing* behaviors) facilitate the development of the ability to deal appropriately with both internal (e.g., mental images) and external (e.g., drawings, photographs, scale models) representations of the world. Although Sigel has discussed this hypothesis in the context of social class differences in young children's symbolization ability, recent work by Donovan (1975) suggests that distancing behaviors transcend socioeconomic class boundaries. Working with preschool children from middle income families, Donovan found that individual differences in representational thinking were related to parental distancing strategies.

While Sigel has tended to emphasize parental strategies that influence cognitive development directly, other investigators have studied aspects of the parent—child relationship that have a more indirect bearing on individual differences in cognitive growth. Parent—child studies have shown that linguistic environments, teaching styles, and discipline procedures vary between and within social class groups (Baumrind, 1971; Bishop & Chase, 1971; Hess & Shipman, 1967). Differences in these types of parent–child interactions also have a differential impact on the intellectual and/or personality development of the child. For example, Hess and Shipman (1967) reported that maternal teaching style was even more important than mother's IQ or social class in predicting the child's performance on simple problem-solving tasks. Further, Baumrind (1971) reported that children of authoritative parents (i.e., parents who are warm and loving, but impose rational restrictions on their children) are more achievement oriented than children of other parent groups. Thus, while parental socialization practices contribute to developmental regularities, it must be kept in mind that these very same factors contribute to individual variations.

Individual differences in intellectual performance also are affected by the child's test-taking behavior and the relevance of the test to the child's sociocultural background. In the first place, children vary in mood and ease when taking tests. Data indicate that test taking itself engenders anxiety, which in turn may hinder performance (Sarason, Davidson, Lighthall, Waite, & Ruebush, 1960). Even children as young as 2.5 years when in a testing situation have been known to ask the examiner "Is this right?" "Am I doing good?" (Sigel, Secrist, & Forman, 1973).

Another set of factors influencing performance is the relevance of testing and test items to one's experiential background. Cross-cultural studies have shown that the concept of testing is itself culture-bound (Cole & Schribner, 1974). Thus, performance differences among individuals at times may reflect differences in understanding the meaning of the testing situation, and/or the appropriateness of the items for the individuals involved.

In summary, the constellation of sociocultural variables, from the broad cultural domain to the particulars of the testing situation itself, contributes to individual differences in intellectual performance. These factors, however, tell but part of the story. To complete the picture, one must consider the individual's experiential background in concert with his/her genetic programming. It is this interaction of factors that determines the uniqueness of the individual's performance pattern.

COGNITIVE STYLE AS AN INDIVIDUAL DIFFERENCE VARIABLE: DEFINITION OF CONSTRUCT

Up to now we have discussed rather general characteristics of the child and his environment that contribute to individual differences in intellectual development. Now we shall turn to a more specific form of individual difference that has been a topic of recent interest, namely, *cognitive style*.

Cognitive style is conceptualized as a dispositional variable that mediates the way the individual processes information. Further, it is assumed that this disposition represents a stable, self-consistent, hence stylistic, mode of adaptation. As such, it is thought of as an interface between cognition and personality.

Historically, research in this area has focused on the functioning of adults (Gardner, Holtzman, Klein, Linton, & Spence, 1958; Klein, 1958; Witkin, Dyk, Faterson, Goodenough, & Karp, 1962). In the past decade, however, attention has been directed toward children. This interest comes from at least two perspectives. For some investigators, the objective is in tracking the origins and developmental course of cognitive styles per se. This research strategy has as its objective the identification of the continuities and discontinuities in development, with the aim of delineating the necessary conditions for such development (Kagan & Moss, 1962). Other investigators, however, are concerned with studying cognitive styles as a means of understanding the ongoing dynamic relationship between cognition and personality. This can be characterized as a "here and now" interest, an attitude that is important in planning and working with children (Kogan, 1976). Results from either research strategy can be of value to educators by contributing an understanding of the child's current level of functioning, by providing information on how to program learning environments to "match" different cognitive styles, and in some cases by providing information that may lead to the modification of certain styles of performance.

The cognitive style concept is used by many investigators, and differences in definition do exist (Kagan & Kogan, 1970: Kagan, Moss, & Sigel, 1963; Kagan, Rosman, Day, Albert, & Phillips, 1964; Kogan, 1973; Sigel, Jarman, & Hanesian, 1967; Sigel & McBane, 1967; Witkin *et al.*, 1962. In spite of the differences, however, the common features are encompassed in the following definition:

> [cognitive styles are] individual variations in *modes* of perceiving, remembering, and thinking, or as distinctive ways of apprehending, storing, transforming, and utilizing information. It may be noted that *abilities* also involve the foregoing properties, but a difference in emphasis should be noted: Abilities concern level of skill—the more or less of performance—whereas cognitive styles give greater weight to the *manner* and *form* of cognition [Kogan, 1971, p. 244].

The critical aspect of the definition is the distinction between *abilities* and *manner* and *form* of cognitive performance. Ability is the usual way performance level is defined. Here one is concerned with the individual's *capacity* to perform, and therefore the emphasis is product oriented. For example, in evaluating performance on an IQ test, the examiner is interested only in the correctness of the individual's answers. The basic assumption is that differences in performance can be attributed to different levels of intellectual ability.

In contrast, emphasis on the *manner* and *form* of cognition suggests that individuals develop *ways of performing* on cognitive tasks. Here one is concerned with the process employed in arriving at the product of performance.

Let us be more specific. Some individuals are characteristically quick and cursory in the manner in which they approach a problem; others are slow and methodical. Each is comparable in ability, but differs in the way he/she approaches the problem. However, it is likely that in many situations the performance of the quick, cursory individual may contain more errors or be less complete than that of the individual with the slow, methodical approach. If one were to focus only on the product of performance, one might interpret the difference between these individuals as a function of differential cognitive capacity, whereas in reality it is a difference in style.

For example, in a recent series of studies by one of the authors (Brodzinsky, 1976; Brodzinsky, Feuer, & Owens, 1975), part of which dealt with children's detection of linguistic ambiguities, it was found that children who employed a cautious and methodical approach to the task spontaneously comprehended the double meaning of ambiguous sentences and joke punch lines more than children who responded in a quick and cursory way. However, when prompted by the examiner to reflect on the possibility of alternative solutions, the difference between these groups in comprehension of linguistic ambiguities was eliminated. Thus, the performance difference on the spontaneous comprehension measure for the two groups of children should be regarded as reflecting their general *style of responding* rather than their *cognitive ability.*

Although the general definition of cognitive style presented earlier defines it as a way or manner of responding, investigators have approached the construct differently. Cognitive style research among preschool and school-age children involves three approaches: First is the approach that emphasizes accuracy of performance as manifested on perceptual tasks requiring the individual to identify a figure embedded in a larger context. This type of research is epitomized by the work of Witkin *et al.* (1962) and Coates (1972). A second type refers to work on categorization, where the aim is to determine different modes individuals use in classifying materials. This perspective is expressed in the work of Sigel *et al.* (1967), Kagan *et al.* (1963), Gardner *et al.* (1959), and Denny (1974), among others. A third approach is the work on reflection–impulsivity, where the emphasis is on the relation between an individual's response tempo and accuracy of performance. This work was originated and developed by Kagan and his colleagues (Kagan *et al.*, 1964).

We shall discuss each of these briefly for they collectively comprise the bulk of the work on children's cognitive styles. The educational implications of the various styles of performance will be dealt with in a later section.

Field Dependence–Independence

Definition and Measures of Concept

With no doubt, the group of researchers which have been the most prolific in investigation of cognitive style have been Witkin and his colleagues (Witkin *et al.*, 1962). The basic concept of style that they have focused on is *field dependence–independence,* alternatively called global–analytic functioning, field diffuseness–articulation, and psychological differentiation. Regardless of the label used, this style refers to the degree to which the individual is dependent on and distracted by the context in which an event occurs.

Three specific tests have been developed by the Witkin group to measure the individual's ability to overcome embedding contexts in perception. First is the

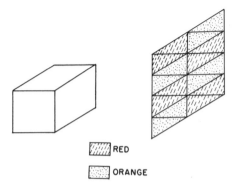

RED
ORANGE

Figure 11.1. Sample of simple and complex figures used in the embedded figures test.

Embedded Figures Test (EFT), which requires the subject to locate a simple geometric figure embedded within a more complex one (see Figure 11.1[2]). A second measure is the Rod-and-Frame Test (RFT), where the subject is seated in a darkened room facing a luminous rod within an luminous frame (both the rod and frame are tilted, either in the same or opposite directions). The subject is required to adjust the rod to true vertical while the frame remains tilted. Finally, a third procedure is the Body Adjustment Test (BAT), where the subject is seated in a tilted chair within a tilted room and the goal is to adjust the chair, and have his/her body aligned to a true vertical. Individuals who are more successful at locating embedded figures and who are better able to adjust the luminous rod and their chair to true vertical are said to be *field independent*; in contrast, individuals who have difficulty disembedding geometric figures from surrounding contexts and whose adjustments of the rod and the chair deviate more from true vertical are said to be *field dependent*. It should be noted that in the great majority of studies in this area the measures of field dependence–independence have been the EFT and RFT (the BAT poses obvious logistical problems because of the size of the apparatus).

In addition to these tests, other investigators have devised measures of this cognitive style that are more appropriate for use with children. Karp and Konstadt (1963) and Goodenough and Eagle (1963) developed versions of the Embedded Figures Test that could be used with children as young as 5 years of age (CEFT and CHEF, respectively). Both of these tests substitute meaningful complex figures for the abstract geometric designs of the EFT. As with the EFT, however, the child's task is to locate a simple figure embedded within a more complex one. Further, two forms of the EFT have been developed for use with children from 3 to 5 years of age—the Preschool Embedded Figures Test (PEFT) devised by Coates (1972), and

---

[2] Figure 11.1 is from the EFT used with older children, adolescents, and adults, but makes the same task demands as the young children's EFT.

the Early Childhood Embedded Figures Test (EC-EFT) devised by Banta (1970). Although both tests are quite similar and are basically simplified versions of the CEFT and CHEF, the PEFT is regarded as being psychometrically superior to the EC-EFT (Kogan, 1976). Finally, the development of a portable Rod and Frame Test (Oltman, 1968) has improved the ease with which this test is given, thus making it more adaptable for young children.

The research on field dependence–independence is voluminous, both for children and adults. As such, we cannot hope to cover adequately all the findings within this chapter. Therefore, we shall focus our attention primarily on the performance of young children, in keeping with the orientation taken for the other cognitive styles discussed later. The reader is referred to Goodenough (1976), Kagan and Kogan (1970), and Witkin et al. (1962) for more in-depth analyses of this style.

Developmental Trends

Two different issues have concerned the Witkin group with respect to developmental trends of field dependence–independence. The first concerns the individual's *absolute* level of performance over time. The second concerns the *relative* position of the individual with respect to his or her peer group over time.

The first issue the Witkin group has focused on concerns the question of whether individuals become more or less field independent with increasing age. Here the data are very clear. Regardless of the specific measures used, there is a progressive increase in field independence beginning during the preschool years and extending at least into later adolescence and possibly into young adulthood. For example, Coates (1972) observed improved performance across the age span of 3 to 5 years on the PEFT for both sexes. A similar finding also was reported by Dermen and Meissner (1972). Furthermore, Vaught, Pittman, and Roodin (1975) using a cross-sectional design with children from 4 to 13 years found a significant linear increase in performance on the portable RFT, while Witkin, Goodenough, and Karp (1967) using both cross-sectional (for the EFT, RFT and BAT) and longitudinal (RFT only) designs found progressive improvement in performance from 8 to 17 years.

The second issue is concerned with the following question: Will a young child who is said to be field independent in comparison to his or her peer group still be classified the same way 6 months later? 1 year later? 5 years later? 10 years later? Unfortunately, few long-term stability studies of this type are available for young children. What we do know, however, suggests moderate stability of performance for preschool children over time periods ranging from 5 months (Coates, 1972) to 1 year (Block & Block, 1973). Further, results of two longitudinal studies with older children and adolescents provide an affirmative answer to the above question. Working with a group of individuals from 8- to 13-years old and a second group from 10 to 24-years old, Witkin et al. (1967) reported coefficients of stability ranging from .48 to .92. Thus, at least from middle childhood to young adulthood, the long-term relative stability of field dependence–independence is quite good.

To summarize, as individuals get older their relative position on the field dependence–independence continuum remains reasonably stable, although they become progressively more field independent in an absolute sense.

Sex Differences

A considerable number of studies have reported sex differences in field dependence–independence for preschool (see Coates, 1974), school-age, and adult subjects (see Kagan and Kogan, 1970). The pattern of sex differences is different, however, depending upon the developmental level of the individuals involved. For example, the bulk of the data suggests that when sex differences appear for older school-age children and adults, they usually indicate greater field independence for males than females (Kagan and Kogan, 1970). In contrast, the evidence bearing on sex differences for preschool children indicates just the opposite; that is, young girls are more field independent than boys (Coates, 1974). While this latter finding may simply reflect greater developmental maturity for preschool girls than boys (see also the section on reflection–impulsivity). Coates (1974) has argued that the sex difference can be explained in terms of a more moderate position on the passivity–activity dimension for young girls, which in turn is conducive to more successful performance on the various style measures. On the other hand, preschool boys manifest excessive activity, which interferes with their disembedding performance. As children get older, however, girls become more passive and boys more moderate in activity, and as a result a reversal in the pattern of sex differences is observed; that is, boys now become more field independent than girls.

Whether Coates' position is valid is yet to be determined. In any case, a clear discontinuity in the manifestation of field dependence–independence is observable between the sexes from the preschool period to the late school years. Nevertheless, it must be remembered that with increasing age boys and girls become more field independent in an *absolute* sense. Furthermore, as we shall see, sex differences also emerge at various ages with respect to the relation between this cognitive style and other intellectual, personality, and social behaviors.

Relationship to IQ

One of the most controversial issues surrounding field dependence–independence is its relationship to intellectual ability. Witkin *et al.* (1962) maintain that this cognitive style is independent of general intelligence and verbal–conceptual processes in particular. Yet, Zigler (1963a, 1963b) contends that a link between field dependence–independence and general intelligence exists mediating most of the findings vis-à-vis other cognitive and socioemotional variables.

What evidence is there to suggest a relationship between this style and intelligence? At present, the data reveal equivocal results. At the preschool level, Coates (1972, 1975) and Coates and Bromberg (1973) found that the PEFT was related to various subtests of the WPPSI which tap perceptual–analytic functioning (Block Design and Geometric Design) but was unrelated to subtests tapping verbal–conceptual ability (Information, Vocabulary, Similarities, Comprehension, Sentences).

In contrast, significant correlations between subjects' PEFT scores and verbally oriented intelligence tests, such as the Preschool Inventory (Cooperative Tests and Services, 1970) and the Peabody Picture Vocabulary Test (PPVT) have been found (Derman & Meissner, 1972; Durrett & Henman, 1972). To complicate matters, however, Block and Block (1973) failed to find a relationship between the PEFT and various verbal intelligence measures; namely, the PPVT for 3-year-olds, and the WPPSI Vocabulary for 4-year-olds. Finally, the data for older children are just as confusing, with some investigators reporting that field dependence—independence is related to perceptual analytic functioning but unrelated to verbal comprehension (Goodenough & Karp, 1961), and other investigators noting significant correlations between this style and verbal processes (Crandall & Sinkeldam, 1964).

It is clear that this issue is far from resolved. Yet, given the few significant findings relating field dependence—independence to verbal processes, future investigators would be advised to control for this aspect of intelligence statistically (a procedure that has been seldom used in previous research).

Relationship to Other Cognitive Tasks

Relatively few studies have examined the cognitive correlates of field dependence—independence at the preschool period. The data that do exist, however, indicate that this style is related to performance on other cognitive tasks, particularly when those tasks emphasize perceptual analytic functioning, for example, Raven Progressive Matrices, (Block and Block, 1973). In addition, in an unpublished study by Coates (cited by Kogan, 1976) it was found that 4- and 5-year-old girls' human figure drawings, representing their articulation-of-body-concept (ABC), correlated significantly with PEFT scores (this was not the case for boys). In fact, for older children and young adults the ABC index is sometimes used as an additional measure of this style dimension (Faterson & Witkin, 1970).

To be sure, field dependence—independence is not always related to young children's problem-solving behavior. Keogh, Wellis, and Weiss (1972) found no relationship between 4-year-old children's RFT scores and performance on tasks measuring design copying, puzzle completion, and task persistence in a non-imitative situation. In addition, no relationship was observed between the RFT and ABC or between the EC-EFT and ABC for either sex.

To summarize, field dependence—independence accounts for some of the variability in problem-solving behavior for preschool children, although as Kogan (1976) points out, this relationship may be developed earlier in girls than in boys. At this point, however, it is unclear just which areas of problem solving are most likely influenced by this cognitive style.

Relationship to Personality and Social Behavior

A considerable body of research now exists relating field dependence—independence to a variety of personality and socioemotional behaviors, though most of this research is with older children and adults. With regard to the preschool period, the findings in this area are generally based on teacher rating data. Coates (1972) found that while autonomous achievement striving behavior were positively correlated with PEFT scores for both 4-year-old boys and girls, only the correlations for girls remained significant when verbal ability was partialled out. In contrast, in an unpublished replication of this study by Coates and Laird (cited by Kogan, 1976), the achievement striving–field independence relationship remained significant for both girls and boys even with verbal ability controlled. Kogan points out, however, that the correlation coefficients were substantially higher for girls than for boys.

The work of Block and Block (1973) also measured teacher ratings of achievement striving in preschool children. The findings of this study, however, provide only weak support at best for the hypothesized achievement striving–field independence relationship, since only some of the items related to achievement striving differentiated field-independent from field-dependent boys, while for girls no such relationship appeared. The only consistent results obtained were that 3- and 4-year-old field-independent boys were rated as more fluent, competent, attentive, and creative.

With respect to social behavior, Witkin has recently suggested that field-dependent individuals may be more socially oriented while field-independent individuals may be more task oriented (Witkin, 1973). These speculations have received considerable support with older children and adults. For example, Konstadt and Forman (1965) found that school-age field-dependent children were more "outer-directed" (i.e., more influenced by the examiner's facial and social cues) than field-independent children in an experimental problem-solving task. Similar findings also are available for preschool children. Keogh et al. (1972) found that field-dependent 4-year-olds more often glanced toward the examiner in the course of a simple problem-solving task.

Thus, it is clear that some of the relationships between field dependence–independence and personality and social functioning extend down to the preschool period. The discrepancies between various studies, however, point to the fact that these relationships probably are not very strong for young children and may be dependent upon the age and sex of the subjects and the measures used.

Origin of Field Dependence–Independence

There is a growing body of research that suggests that the antecedents of this cognitive style reside in the nature of the parent–child relationship. Although most of the research reported is with older children, it is included here because findings are equally relevant for preschool children. However, it must be kept in mind that the field-independence style is still evolving during the preschool period and hence the final determination of an individual's style is made later.

Dyk and Witkin (1965) and Witkin (1969) report that socialization practices that encourage separation from parental control lead toward greater field independence. For example, those mothers of 10-year-old boys who lack self-assurance in dealing with their children, who limit curiosity and stress conformity, who regard their children as delicate, and who because of their own fears and anxieties limit their children's activities are less likely to foster a field-independent cognitive style.

Further, it appears that paternal absence also is related to field dependence. Thus, the role of parental practices seems clearly to be a significant factor influencing this style.

Summary

What can be said about the diverse array of research findings in this area? First, there is no doubt that in the absolute sense boys and girls become increasingly field independent with age. Second, the pattern of sex differences is discontinuous between the preschool and the older school-age child. Third, field dependence–independence style has been found to account for variability in performance on intellectual and problem-solving tasks, and in interpersonal behavior. Finally, the origins of this style appear to reside in the nature of the interactions between parents and their children.

At issue is whether field dependence–independence among preschool children is functionally equivalent with this same style at older age periods. The only way this issue can be resolved is through a longitudinal study beginning with the preschool child and extending into the school-age years.

Categorization Styles

Definition and Measures of Concept

Categorization styles refer to the differences in approach individuals use to organize arrays of stimuli. Since every object, picture, or event has many attributes and since individuals are relatively free to select any particular attribute as the basis of organization of an array, respondents have options to create groupings that reflect their preferences. For example, given an array of items which include an apple, an orange, and a banana, some individuals, when asked to group the items any way they wished, would select these aforementioned items and give as their reason "They are things to eat," while other individuals selecting the same items would give a different reason, to wit, "They are fruits," or "These items belong together because they all have curved surfaces." Each of these responses is reasonable and appropriate, but each is based on a different criterion. Such arrangements of items reveal more about the respondents than just their competence in categorization. What is revealed is the individual's particular organizational preference. The question, however, is whether or not there is any psychological significance to these variations in criteria, where some arrangements are by function (things to eat), or by a class concept (fruits) or by a descriptive criterion (curved surfaces). The major objective in this section is to identify the psychosocial correlates of styles of categorization.

The existence of such a phenomenon as styles of categorization is based on observations of ways adults and children group items. To be sure, organization of items in an array involves ability to create groups by perceiving relationships among items. At the same time, however, the very fact that every item in an array is polydimensional provides the individual with the option to express preferences for particular bases for organization. It was observations of preferential behavior in free-sort situations that provided empirical support for the style construct in categorization (Kagan *et al.,* 1963; Sigel, 1953).

Among the more popular procedures employed to assess styles of categorization in preschool children is the Conceptual Styles Test (CST) developed by Kagan *et al.* (1963). The CST is made up of a set of placards containing three drawings of familiar items, for example, a ruler, a pencil, and a pad of paper, and the child is asked to select any two of the three that go together or belong together in any way. After the selection, the child is asked to state the reason for the choice. A threefold classification system was developed to code the responses: *descriptive–analytic* (selection of a manifest detail as the common element) *relational–contextual* (linking items on some theme or function) and *categorical–inferential* (inclusion of objects in a common class).

While the CST is a major test of categorization styles, it is by no means the only one. Sigel found that CST too difficult for preschool children, and constructed another task (SCST) which used a match-to-standard procedure. The child is asked to select from an array of pictures one which "goes with or is like [the standard] in any way" (see Figure 11.2). The child is then asked to give a reason for the selection. The SCST also uses the threefold classification system (Sigel *et al.,* 1967).

In assessing cognitive styles among preschool children with lower socioeconomic backgrounds, Sigel and his associates discovered that these children had difficulty responding to this task (SCST). However, when the items to be grouped were three-dimensional objects, virtually no difficulty in grouping was found (Sigel, Anderson, & Shapiro, 1966).

In view of this finding, a sorting task of three-dimensional objects was constructed that allows testing different socioeconomic and age groups and can be scored with the threefold system used with the picture tasks. The 12-item Object Sorting Task (OCT) was constructed and it comprised familiar life-size items (see Figure 11.3). A match to standard procedure was employed with the child being instructed to select from an array of objects as many items as "belong or are like" the standard. The scoring system, while applicable for middle class groups, had to be modified for lower class children. The descriptive part–whole category was extended to include color and form as descriptors (Sigel & McBane, 1967).

Development Trends

Relatively few studies have been done investigating age changes in style of categorization during the preschool period. To be sure, a body of literature exists describing categorization competence among preschoolers (Denny, 1974; Denny & Acito, 1974; Inhelder & Piaget, 1964; Ricciuti, 1965; Sigel & McBane, 1967; Sigel, 1975). However, categorization competence must not be confused with styles of categorization. In the studies referred to, the intent was to determine if children had the ability to categorize arrays of items into groups and could transfer this

Figure 11.2. Sample item: SCST.

knowledge to other situations. Children as young as 2.5 can learn to group and to manifest this competence in a number of settings (Denny & Acito, 1974). However, such experiments tended to test for ability to categorize geometric forms with a limited number of physical attributes, for example, color, form, size, and so on. Our interest in this discussion is in the style of categorization, which is a preference for particular modes of classification. To be able to manifest a style, a child has to have alternatives available. Thus when faced with a sorting task the child will respond in a way that is the preferred mode. If the child has only one strategy available because of inexperience or immaturity, it is not a style. Thus with the very young children, styles can only be identified when alternatives are available.

Sigel *et al.* (1967) using the SCST found no significant differences in categorization styles between 4- and 5-year-old boys and girls. The average number of responses for each style in descending order was descriptive part–whole, relational–contextual and categorical–inferential. Interestingly enough, the use of the analytic type of response was observed with a higher frequency than expected. Of course, it is not clear whether or not this strategy when used by younger children has the same psychological significance as when used by older individuals. This is a problem that has not been addressed empirically.

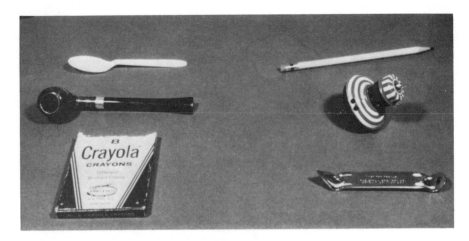

Figure 11.3. Object array: OCT.

The lack of age differences between 4 and 5 years was surprising. Actually there was a numerical increase in the use of descriptive part–whole and categorical–inferential responses, but the differences were not statistically significant. Age differences were found when older children were studied. Sigel (1965) found that older children (6–7 years old) increased steadily in the use of descriptive part–whole and categorical–inferential responses, but relational–contextual groupings showed no such increase. He also found that there was moderate consistency in the use of descriptive and categorical modes over a 3-year period. Unfortunately few other developmental studies were done with either the CST or the SCST.

Attention shifted to the OCT as interest in evaluating cognitive development among low-SES children began. Three sets of investigators worked with this task, each of whom contributed differentially to our understanding of categorization behavior.

Lindstrom and Shipman (1972) found that children ranging in age from 3 to 6, while able to label the items and create groupings, had difficulty in producing rationales that could be scored within the threefold classification system. Consequently, they used only a grouping score that measured only the ability to form groups. They found that the older children created more groupings than the younger ones. This score, however, seems to reflect ability rather than style, since it loaded on the intelligence factor in Lindstrom and Shipman's factor analysis.

On the other hand, Block and Block (1973), working with younger 3- and 4-year-olds, found that most of them were able to give reasons for their grouping. They produced mostly descriptive responses (about 66% of the 3-year-olds and 75% of the 4-year-olds). The remaining responses were relational—contextual and categorical, with the former the more prevalent of the two.

Sigel and McBane's (1967) results tend to support the Block and Block study. Working with both middle and lower socioeconomic groups, they reported that most children could provide reasons for their groupings. The younger the children, the more likely they were to produce descriptive color—form responses, with relational—contextual responses of thematic type also prevalent. Rarely were analytic-type descriptives used (structured descriptive responses). Further, middle class children increased in use with age of categorical inferential responses whereas lower socioeconomic groups showed minimal use this response style.

In summary, styles of categorization as differentiated from ability to categorize, are found among preschool children. Children from lower socioeconomic groups have greater difficulty in expressing either ability *or* preference when pictures are employed as compared to when three-dimensional objects are used. Middle class children reveal no such difficulty, producing similar developmental trends with objects or pictures, namely an increase in structured (analytic) descriptions and categorical—inferential responses. However, lower class children tend to show high frequencies of color—form descriptive and relational—contextual groupings. As they get older they continue to use these two types of styles, but increase in absolute number. There are also some indications, although slight, of increases in categorical—inferential responses.

Relationship to Personality and Social Behavior

If indeed cognitive styles are personality-type variables interfacing with cognition, then there should be some differential relationship between style and personal—social characteristics. Two studies have approached this problem with preschool children, Sigel *et al.* (1967), and Block and Block (1973).

In the study using the SCST reported earlier, Sigel and his associates obtained personal social ratings from the children's nursery school teachers. Although no significant differences were found between boys and girls in the frequency of use of the style categories, different patterns of correlations between styles of categorization and personal–social characteristics were obtained.

Boys who more often employed descriptive part–whole responses were generally rated by the teachers as more controlled emotionally, slow in responding, and high in achievement. Girls, on the other hand, were rated as not cautious, inattentive and tending to daydream. Boys inclined to use relational–contextual responses were rated by teachers as low on emotional control. No such relationships were found with girls. The relationships between categorical–inferential responses and personal–social characteristics were not significant.

What is of interest is the fact that while descriptive and relational–contextual responses tended to relate to ratings in the affective domain for boys and girls differently, categorical–inferential usage tended to relate positively to efficiency in learning for both boys and girls.

The findings reported with these children (5-year-olds) for the descriptive and relational–contextual styles are comparable to the findings reported by Kagan and Moss for older subjects (Kagan & Moss, 1962). The congruence between these results and those found for older subjects suggest that styles of categorization are beginning to be established in the personality matrix at the preschool level.

Block and Block (1973), while using different-aged samples, 3- and 4-year-olds, also found personal–social correlates with styles of categorization. However, their findings indicate that there is no consistency between what is found at age 3 for boys and girls and at age 4. Boys, for example, using descriptive styles at age 3 are rated as reflective, attentive, reasonable, creative, and thoughtful, traits resembling those reported by Sigel *et al.* (1967) for 5-year-olds. But by 4 years the correlations change, and now the boys are fidgety, indecisive and vacillating. The results for the relational–contextual are the converse.

Girls also show more dramatic changes between ages 3 and 4 for each of the two styles. Positive social characteristics typify the 3-year-old girls using descriptive responses, but by 4 there is a reversal, with negativistic social behaviors appearing. No clear-cut pattern exists between relational–contextual and personal–social characteristics.

Block and Block found that for 3-year-old boys, categorical–inferential responses had no personality correlates, but by 4, boys using such responses were judged high in intellectual strength, but as antisocial, for example, aggressive, distrustful. Girls showed a different pattern. At 3, girls using this approach were rated as undercontrolled and antisocial, but at 4 evidence showed a complete reverse; now prosocial and emotionally controlled behaviors emerge.

It is difficult to integrate the results of Sigel *et al.* (1967) and Block and Block (1973) since different samples and methods were used. But they each indicate that personal–social characteristics do relate to styles of categorization. While in some cases the relationships are similar, for example, descriptiveness with 3- and 5-year-old boys, there are certainly differences. Nevertheless, what these studies do indicate is that styles of categorization are not totally indicative of cognitive competence; rather, when competence to classify is evident, variability in criteria selected for grouping emerges as a function of personal—social characteristics. The styles of categorization do reflect a coalescence of cognitive and personal—social factors. It will require further study to identify further functional significance of these dimensions.

At this time, explanations of the significance of the various styles tend to be speculative. Kogan (1976) argues that observed styles of categorization among boys is more diagnostic of relevant personal—social adaptation than it is for girls, particularly at ages 3—4. For 3-year-old boys, use of relational—contextual responses reflect immaturity, whereas descriptive styles are indicative of maturity. It should be noted, however, that this result does not hold for 4-year-olds. At this age the categorical response seems to be indicative of a new mode of adjusting. "The self-assertiveness, aggressiveness and dominance of these children may well represent a testing of one's emerging intellectual powers . . . such testing of one's social environment may well have disruptive effects [Kogan, 1976]." Thus, the explanation of antisocial behavior for boys.

Kogan argues that the significance of the styles is different for girls. Since girls readily use descriptive—analytic types of responses, he suggests these are not of particular diagnostic significance. In fact, relational—contextual styles do not appear to play a significant diagnostic role either, a finding consistent with Sigel *et al.* (1967), for 5-year-old girls. According to Kogan, it is the categorical—inferential style that is more significant as an indicator of developmental maturity for girls.

Origins of Styles of Categorization

The major study explaining the influences of home backgrounds on styles of categorization was reported by Hess and Shipman (1967). Working with 163 black mothers from four social class groups, college-educated professionals, high school—educated blue collar workers, elementary school—educated semiskilled workers and welfare cases, Hess and Shipman administered a free-sorting task using diversified human figures with the parents (Kagan *et al.* 1963) and Sigel's revised SCST with the children.

The social status of the mothers influenced performance, with the performance of higher-status mothers relating positively to descriptive—analytic and categorical—inferential sorts and negatively to relational—contextual. For the children, the absolute incidence of descriptive—analytic, relational—contextual and categorical—inferential responses declined with decreasing status, with the relational—contextual style the most preferred among the lowest socioeconomic group. These results are consistent with the findings of Sigel *et al.* (1966).

Hess and Shipman offer a linguistic-type explanation for these results. They agree with Bernstein (1961) that there is a close link between social class and linguistic codes, with middle class mothers using a more elaborated system, while lower class mothers are more restricted. While the linguistic interpretation contributes to our understanding of the class differences, it does not explain the relationship between particular styles and linguistic codes within class. Sigel's distancing theory tries to extend the interpretation. He holds that the more likely parents are to encourage children to plan, organize and anticipate, the more likely the children will be to use analytic and categorical styles. Lower social status mothers do less of such planning and organization than their middle class counterparts (Sigel, 1970).

Modification of Categorization Styles

Studies dealing with modification of categorization skills have been done, but these tended to focus on the ability to classify rather than the styles employed in such classification (see Denny & Acito, 1974 as an exemplar). Sigel and Olmsted (1970), however, working with preschool children from lower socioeconomic backgrounds undertook a classification training program with the explicit aim of modifying bases of grouping. They used three types of training conditions: three-dimensional objects, pictures, and role playing. Small training groups of four to five children were set up for 20 min a day for 20 school days. The results, as assessed on the OCT and its pictorial counterpart (photographs of these objects presented in an identical format as the OCT), showed increases in variety of grouping only for the object- and picture-training groups. Further, these increases were found only with the OCT, but continued difficulty was observed for all children in expressing styles of categorization with pictures. In addition, the children did increase in the use of appropriate verbal explanations for their groupings, particularly with the OCT. After 8 months, it was found that children in the experimental groups did maintain gains from training but were no longer significantly different from the control group children. Sigel and Olmsted argued that had the school situation continued to foster categorization training, the children in the experimental group might have continued to gain. At least what this study does demonstrate is that children's styles of categorization are modifiable.

Summary

Styles of categorization do in fact exist among preschool children. Age changes are found between 3 and 5 with some indication of continuity from ages 4 onward. The developmental trends are as follows: Descriptive−analytic and categorical−inferential responses increase steadily with age and relational−contextual responses decrease. Further, these styles are correlated with personal−social characteristics, suggesting that styles are preferential and adaptive in nature. However, patterns of trends and correlates were found to vary between boys and girls.

Reflection−Impulsivity

Definition and Measures of Concept

A third area in which individual differences have been studied is the relation between response tempo and performance on problem-solving tasks. Kagan and his colleagues (Kagan, et al., 1963), while investigating styles of categorization, noted that some children typically responded quickly, while others took their time before offering a response. Furthermore, these response rates were associated with particular styles of categorization; namely descriptive–analytic strategies (e.g., "The apple and pear go together because they both have stems and are round.") more often resulted in longer response latencies than relational–contextual strategies (e.g., "The cowboy and horse go together because the cowboy rides the horse.")

Results of this type led Kagan to argue that the critical stylistic feature was the tempo variable; that is, the response rate. Of importance, however, was not rate per se, but what the response time signified. It was postulated that the reason for the variability in tempo was the processes involved in coming to a decision. Kagan suggested that children who were slow responders (*reflectives*) were scanning the stimulus array, checking the validity of their hypotheses, and in general, being careful and cautious in coming to a decision, particularly in situations involving response uncertainty. In contrast, children who were fast responders (*impulsives*) were less complete in scanning the stimulus, more global in the way they scanned it, and in general, less careful in their decision making.

In pursuing this research on reflection–impulsivity (R–I), however, Kagan and his colleagues discovered that some children responded quickly and accurately, while others responded quickly but with error. Consequently a new index was developed that took both accuracy and speed of response into account. This new index was adopted in conjunction with the development of the Matching Familiar Figures Test (MFF), which has become the primary instrument for measuring this cognitive style. The MFF is a match-to-standard task consisting of a standard figure and six variants, only one of which matches the standard (see Figure 11.4). The child's task is to choose the variant that exactly matches the standard figure. The test consists of 2 practice and 12 test items. Mean latency to first response and total errors across the test items are the dependent variables. On the basis of median splits for the latency and error data, children are categorized into the different cognitive style groups. Children who score above the median on response time but below the median on errors are labeled *reflective,* while children who score below the median on response time, but above the median on errors are labeled *impulsive.* In addition, two other groups of children have been identified, but seldom studied; namely, those children who score below the median on both measures (*fast–accurate*), and those children who score above the median on both measures (*slow–inaccurate*). Most research with school-age children has shown a moderately negative correlation between MFF latency and errors, with a median r of about −.56 (Messer, 1976).

In addition to the MFF, which has been used primarily with school-age children, other versions of the test have been developed for use with preschoolers. These include the Early Childhood Matching Familiar Figures Test (EC-MFF) which contains only three variants (Banta, 1970), a simplified MFF containing four variants (Lewis, Rausch, Goldberg, & Dodd, 1968), and the Kansas Reflection–Impulsivity Scale for Preschoolers (KRISP) which contains from four to six variants (Wright, 1973). Only the latter preschool test has been used with any regularity by researchers.

Figure 11.4. Sample item: matching familiar figures test.[3]

The literature on reflection–impulsivity has been increasing at a tremendous rate since Kagan's seminal work in this area. The sheer volume of material published in recent years precludes an exhaustive review. Therefore, we shall limit our discussion to an overview of the major findings, with particular emphasis on the performance of preschool children. The reader is referred to Messer (1976) and Kogan (1976) for more detailed reviews.

Before summarizing the empirical findings, however, it is important to note that the very definition and meaning of reflection–impulsivity recently has been challenged (Block, Block, & Harrington, 1974). These authors criticized the use of the double median split criterion for operationalizing the construct, particularly since most investigators have concentrated on only the reflective and impulsive cells (see Figure 11.5 for a hypothetical example of the four quadrants that result from the double mean split procedure). Furthermore, Block and his colleagues argued that most of the significant results vis-à-vis other cognitive and personality variables

---

[3] Figure 11.4 is from the MFF used with elementary school children but represents the same format used with preschool children.

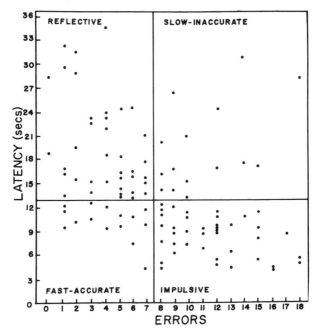

Figure 11.5. Median split of MFF responses of a hypothetical population.

could be attributed to MFF error rather than to latency scores, thus undermining the notion that *response tempo* was the critical stylistic variable. Since it is impossible to pursue this controversy in any depth within the scope of this chapter, let us simply say that while Block and his associates make many valid points, particularly in their objection to the overemphasis on the reflective and impulsive quadrants, we believe that they are unduly pessimistic in their condemnation of the validity of this cognitive style. For a more thorough analysis of this controversy, however, the reader is referred to Kagan and Messer (1975), Block, Block, and Harrington (1975), Ault, Mitchell, and Hartmann (1976), and Egelund and Weinberg (1976).

Developmental Trends

Putting aside the above issue, the first thing to note is that children typically become more reflective with age; that is, MFF response time increases and errors decrease as children get older (at least through the early school-age years). Furthermore, the correlation between MFF response time and error scores also increases with age. However, Messer (1976) notes that for preschool children the latency–error correlation is most often quite low, and therefore the reflection–impulsivity dimension may have little theoretical or practical meaning at this age level. In fact, Messer concludes that only after entrance into school does the child's delay of response become functionally connected with fewer errors. In contrast, Kogan (1976) suggests that it is unrealistic to treat preschool children as a unitary group.

While conceding that the latency and error scores are functionally unrelated for many preschoolers, he points out that this is not the case for a considerable number of young children. Kogan states that for these latter children the reflection—impulsivity dimension is just as relevant as for older school-age children.

While the bulk of the data show no consistent sex differences for R—I during the school-age years (Messer, 1976), there is some evidence to suggest different rates of development for preschool girls and boys. When sex differences appear for young children, they usually indicate greater reflectivity as well as an earlier linking of response tempo and accuracy for girls than for boys (Kogan, 1976).

Relationship to IQ

As with other cognitive styles, it is often suggested that significant findings relating MFF scores to problem-solving performance is attributable to a general ability factor. In reviewing the data on the relation between R—I and intelligence, however, Messer (1976) concludes that this cognitive style is not highly related to IQ, at least when IQ falls within the normal range. When a significant relationship between these two constructs is observed, it usually can be explained in one of two ways: (1) the IQ tests used were basically nonverbal and structured in such a way as to maximize response uncertainty, thus tapping into the very dimension measured by R—I, and/or (2) the subjects were preschool children. With respect to the latter finding, it seems that R—I is more closely tied to a general ability factor during the early preschool years, only to become increasingly (although not completely) separate from it as the child develops (Kogan, 1976).

Relationship to Other Cognitive Tasks

Given that reflection—impulsivity both has theoretical meaning and is functionally separate from intelligence, what can one say about children who employ a reflective rather than an impulsive response strategy? This question focuses on the issue of construct validation. To date, few investigators have explored cognitive functioning in young reflective and impulsive children. The little data that do exist, however, seem to favor the reflective child. For example, Siegel, Kirasic, and Kilburg (1973) found that reflective preschoolers' recognition memory was generally better than that of impulsive preschoolers. Fugua, Bartsch, and Phye (1975) also observed that young reflective children were more creative than their impulsive counterparts. In addition, as children mature and enter into the elementary-school-age years, the relationship between reflectivity and successful academic and problem-solving performance broadens to include prose reading (Kagan, 1965), serial recall (Kagan, 1966), inductive (Kagan, Pearson, & Welch, 1966) and analogical reasoning (Achenbach, 1969), diagnostic problem solving (Neimark, 1975), spatial perspective-taking (Brodzinsky & Feuer, 1976), formal operational thought (Neimark, 1975), and humor comprehension (Brodzinsky, 1975, 1976), to name just a few areas.

Further, these performance differences are often attributed to the way reflective and impulsive children scan and process information inherent within the stimuli presented to them. In fact, research on scanning strategies offers some support for this position in showing that both preschool (McCluskey & Wright, 1973; Wright, 1971) and school-age reflective children (summarized by Messer, 1976) are more complete and systematic in their scanning behavior than their impulsive counterparts.

Relationship to Personality and Social Behavior

Research on R–I has also been extended to personality (e.g., anxiety, achievement motivation, locus of control, humor responsiveness) and self-regulatory behavior (e.g., motor inhibition, delay of gratification, risk taking, aggression), for both preschool- and school-age children. The results, however, are much more equivocal in these areas. Rather than attempt to summarize a rather confusing body of research, it is sufficient to state that this cognitive style dimension does show some relation to personality traits and social behavior, but the findings are dependent upon the measures used, the age and sex of the subjects, and the specific traits and behaviors studied. In order to give the reader an idea of the relationships that have been found to exist during the preschool period, however, Table 11.1 summarizes the findings from Block et al. (1974) that are based upon teachers' Q-sort ratings of young children's personality and social functioning. In examining the descriptions it should be mentioned that several of the traits associated with the different response styles (e.g., impulsives as humorless and cautious) conflicts with data reported for

TABLE 11.1
Personality and Social Characteristics Related to Four Response Styles on the Matching Familiar Figures Test[a]

Slow–accurate (reflective)	Fast–accurate	Slow–inaccurate	Fast–inaccurate (impulsive)
Reasonable	Intelligent	Aggressive	Anxious
Calm	Cheerful	Competitive	Sensitive
Reflective	Self-confident	Difficulty in delay	Structure seeking
Circulatory	Competitive	Egocentric	Tense
Gets alone well with others	Rational	Quick, uninhibited	Humorless
Constraint	Resourceful	Does not try to master cognitive problems	Self-doubting
Docile	Vigorous in approach		Cautious
Confident	Independent Confident		Querulous Unpopular

[a]From Block et al., 1974. The authors state, "the reader should understand that the interpretive descriptions are intended comparatively; they should not be construed as representing the absolute qualities of the children in the various quadrants [p. 14]."

older children. This raises the question of the stability of the relationship between R–I and personality and social behavior. It may be that certain response styles are associated with particular traits only during certain developmental periods. Unfortunately, the type of longitudinal data needed to answer this question are not available.

Origin of R–I

A question that we have yet to discuss concerns the underlying dynamics of R–I. Why do some children adopt a slow and cautious tempo while other children respond quickly and in a cursory manner? In the past, Kagan has offered several possible etiological mechanisms, including constitutional factors, different standards of performance, and fear of failure. Only the latter explanation, however, has received serious consideration. According to this hypothesis, anxiety over error is a major antecedent of a reflective disposition. While there is some evidence to support this position (Brodzinsky & Rightmyer, 1976; Messer, 1970; Ward, 1968), it is by no means conclusive. Indeed, Block *et al.* (1974) found that impulsive preschool children were the *highest* in anxious self-concern. As Kagan and Messer (1975) point out, however, reflective children may be anxious about making errors on tasks they believe they can solve, whereas impulsive children are anxious over total incompetence.

In addition to these speculations, Buss and Plomin (1975) have put forward a temperament theory of impulsivity. According to these authors, impulsivity, which includes the behavioral components of inhibitory control, persistence, and decision time, represents a genetically based personality trait that is manifested soon after birth. To date, the only direct test of this theory, using the MFF as the measure of impulsivity, has yielded some support for this position. Working with preschool twins, Plomin and Willerman (1975) found that the heritability coefficient for MFF latency was between .42 and .48, although the comparable heritability estimate for MFF errors was considerably lower (between .19 and .24). The authors suggest that the findings indicate a genetic component for R–I. However, estimates of the heritability of impulsivity using measures other than the MFF (e.g., self and observational ratings) have produced mixed results (see Buss & Plomin, 1975 for a review). While some researchers have found reasonably high heritability coefficients for inhibitory control, the results are not consistent across studies or gender (the evidence favors a genetic component only for boys). Moreover, the data provide a weak case for a genetic factor for decision time and persistence. Thus, little can be said at the present time about the inheritance of R–I, or, for that matter, about the underlying role of sociocultural factors. Clearly, this area is in need of considerably more research before any unequivocal statements can be made concerning the determinants of this style.

Modification Studies

One final point needs to be considered. Given that impulsive children are less successful than reflective children on academic and problem-solving tasks, it is understandable that researchers should seek to determine whether the R–I style is modifiable. Generally, this has been approached by examining whether impulsive children can be trained to adopt a more reflective strategy. In summarizing the data, Messer (1976) notes that while children may be influenced by a number of environmental manipulations, including forced delay of response, direct reinforcement for specific strategies, and exposure to reflective peers and teachers, the most successful modification technique is one in which the individual is trained in specific scanning strategies directly (e.g., Meichenbaum & Goodman, 1971).

Summary

In sum, what can be said about R–I? First, there is little doubt that this dimension functions as a cognitive style, relatively independent of general intellectual ability, *but* also contributing to individual differences in intelligence test performance (Sigel, 1963). Second, reflectivity increases with age. Third, children who are reflective are usually more successful in academic and cognitive tasks that contain response uncertainty and ambiguity. Finally, R–I is modifiable when specific scanning strategies are directly trained.

To be sure, many issues still remain to be resolved. Among these are the origins of R–I, its personality and social correlates, and whether or not R–I reflects a global trait or a task-specific disposition.

EDUCATIONAL IMPLICATIONS

The purpose of this chapter was to impart a point of view, namely, to emphasize the significance of individual differences in approaching our understanding of child growth and development. The variability among children is obvious, but the understanding of the origins of such are complex. As we have indicated, our science of psychology has tended to minimize the import of individual differences in search for generalization. The educator, however, is faced with a unique problem. It is important to have a conception of general characteristics of the children with whom one is working, for that provides the framework and the guideposts by which to determine teaching strategies, materials, classroom organization and the myriad of activities teachers engage in. Without such general knowledge the teacher would be at a loss as to how to proceed. At the same time, the teacher must be and usually is aware that children vary in many ways, for reasons we have already enumerated.

The challenge to the teacher is to be able to keep two critical points in mind simultaneously; one, that children share many characteristics, and two, that there is considerable within-group variability. The coordination of these two perspectives at one and the same time is the teachers' challenge. To be sure, the two points of view are not always simultaneous in significance. There are times when planning an event that the teacher must ignore individual differences, but there are also times when the teacher can and should ignore general characteristics and attend to the individual's needs, for example, tutoring, helping a 4-year-old separate from his mother, and so on.

The cognitive styles construct is of particular relevance to educators. Cognitive styles describe how an individual comes to a task, how his or her environment is organized, and how he or she processes information. It is not intelligence as we commonly know it, nor is it purely personality. It is the combination of these working together to effectuate a response. Every task that a child engages in allows some type of stylistic response. If it is a classificatory task, one commonly employed in the classroom, the style of categorization is involved; if it is a map-reading task where the child has to disengage elements in the array, the field dependence–independence dimensions come into play; and if the task requires careful analysis and reflection, the reflective–impulsive style is involved. The degree to which all of these are related is yet to be identified among young children. It would be useful if we knew the interrelationships of the styles for each child. At this stage of knowledge we know that there is not a perfect set of relationships among them (Kogan, 1976). Thus, by having available information for each child, the educator would be in a position to know what resources the child has available in solving problems or coming to grips with any task, be it cognitive or social.

We have pointed out the developmental sequence for each of the styles discussed. What remains at issue is whether these styles have the same meaning at the preschool level as they do for older children. Since the question of continuity remains to be resolved, the educator may be well to focus on the here and now. Knowing how the child approaches a task and knowing that children have different modes of coming to terms with tasks will contribute to the sensitivity of the educator working with children.

Implied in this comment is the critical question we have avoided to this point, namely, Are some stylistic responses better than others? Is it better to be field independent than field dependent? Is it better to be reflective or impulsive? Which of the styles of categorization is better, descriptive or relational, for example? In our previous discussion, there are implied and explicit comments to the effect some styles are better than others. Are these value judgments, or are they not? Let us consider these a moment, not in isolation but in terms of the contexts in which they appear. It will be recalled that usually the particular cognitive style is correlated with some other variable, for example, reflectivity and problem solving. The reflective child does better than the impulsive, therefore it is better to be reflective. This is true for each of the areas discussed. But what is not discussed is whether this finding generalizes to all situations? Is it always better to be reflective or is impulsivity sometimes better? It will depend, then, on the task in question. At times it may be better to be quick and take a chance and possibly make an error than to be careful and correct. Sometime it may be better to be relational instead of analytic. In other words the question can not really be answered in the abstract, but will depend on the context in which the style is being expressed.

We have tried, although briefly, to discuss a complex issue, individual differences and cognitive style. There are many individual differences we might have selected.

From our point of view, cognitive styles form a central issue in human adaptation and human development. It is, in our estimation, one of the underlying constructs that with further study may shed important light on how children adapt, how they learn and what they learn.

At this point, the incompleteness of the data should not preclude careful observation by teachers so as to develop their own criteria for determination of individual differences in styles of approaching tasks, in learning, and in engaging with others. The more the teacher is tuned in to these individual differences in interaction with tasks and with people, the greater the opportunity the teacher has to plan more sensitively and carefully for each child. Hopefully this chapter has sensitized the scientist and the educator to some of the issues in this area and has contributed food for thought and rationales for careful observation.

REFERENCES

Achenbach, T. M. Cue learning, associative responding, and school performance in children. *Developmental Psychology*, 1969, *1*, 717–725.

Ault, R. L., Mitchell, C., & Hartmann, D. P. Some methodological problems in reflection-impulsivity research. *Child Development*, 1976, *47*, 227–231.

Banta, T. J. Tests for the evaluation of early childhood education: The Cincinnati Autonomy Test Battery (CATB). In J. Hellmuth (Ed.), *Cognitive studies* Vol. 1. New York: Brunner/Mazel, 1970.

Baumrind, D. Current patterns of parental authority. *Developmental psychology monographs*, 1971, *4*, (No. 4, Part 2).

Bayley, N., & Oden, M. H. The maintenance of intellectual ability in gifted adults. *Journal of Gerontology*, 1955, *10*, 91–107.

Bearison, D. J. The construct of regression: A Piagetian approach. *Merrill Palmer Quarterly*, 1974, *20*, 21–30.

Bernstein, B. Social class and linguistic development: A theory of social learning: In A. H. Halsey, J. Floud, and A. Anderson, *Economy Education and Society*, New York: Harcourt, 1961.

Bishop, D. W., & Chace, C. A. Parental conceptual systems, home play environment, and potential creativity in children. *Journal of Experimental Child Psychology*, 1971, *12*, 318–338.

Block, J., Block, J. H., & Harrington, D. M. Some misgivings about the Matching Familiar Figures test as a measure of reflection-impulsivity. *Developmental Psychology*, 1974, *10*, 611–632.

Block, J., Block, J. H., & Harrington, D. M. Comment on the Kagan-Messer reply. *Developmental Psychology*, 1975, *11*, 249–252.

Block, J., & Block, J. H. Ego development and the provenance of thought. National Institute of Mental Health: Progress Report (Grant No. M. H. 16080), University of California, Berkeley, 1973.

Brodzinsky, D. M. The role of conceptual tempo and stimulus characteristics in children's humor development. *Developmental Psychology*, 1975, *11*, 843–850.

Brodzinsky, D. M. Children's comprehension and appreciation of verbal jokes in relation to conceptual tempo. Paper presented at the International Conference on Humor and Laughter, Cardiff, Wales, July, 1976.

Brodzinsky, D. M., & Feuer, V. Reflection-impulsivity and children's spatial perspective-taking. Paper presented at the meeting of the Piaget Society, Philadelphia, June, 1976.

Brodzinsky, D. M., Feuer, V., & Owens, J. Detection of linguistic ambiguity by reflective, impulsive, fast-accurate, and slow-inaccurate children. Unpublished manuscript, 1975.

Brodzinsky, D. M., & Rightmyer, J. Pleasure associated with cognitive mastery as related to conceptual tempo. *Child Development, 1976, 47,* 881–884.

Bruner, J. S., Olver, R. R., & Greenfield, P. M. *Studies in cognitive growth.* New York: Wiley, 1966.

Buss, A., & Plomin, R. *A temperamental theory of personality development.* New York: Wiley-Interscience, 1975.

Coates, S. *Preschool Embedded Figures Test.* Palo Alto, California: Consulting Psychologists Press, 1972.

Coates, S. Sex differences in field independence among preschool children. In R. C. Friedman, R. M. Richart, and R. L. Vande Wiele (Eds.), *Sex differences in behavior.* New York: Wiley, 1974.

Coates, S. Field independence and intellectual functioning in preschool children. *Perceptual and Motor Skills, 1975, 41,* 251–254.

Coates, S., & Bromberg, P. M. The factorial structure of the WPPSI between the ages of 4 and 6-1/2. *Journal of Consulting and Clinical Psychology, 1973, 40,* 365–370.

Cole, M., & Scribner, S. *Culture and thought: A psychological introduction.* New York: Wiley, 1974.

Crandall, V. J., & Sinkelman, C. Children's dependent and achievement behaviors in social situations and their perceptual field dependence. *Journal of Personality, 1964, 32,* 1–22.

Denny, N. W. Evidence for development changes in categorization criteria for children and adults. *Human Development, 1974, 17,* 41–53.

Denny, N. W., & Acito, M. A. Classification training in two- and three-year-old children. *Journal of Experimental Child Psychology, 1974, 17,* 37–48.

Dermen, D., & Meissner, J. A. Preschool Embedded Figures Test. In V. C. Shipman (Ed.), *Disadvantaged children and their first school experience.* Princeton, New Jersey: Educational Testing Service, 1972.

Donovan, A. Parent-child interaction and the development of representational skills in young children. Unpublished doctoral dissertation, SUNY at Buffalo, 1975.

Durrett, M. E., & Henman, J. Concurrent validity of the Peabody Picture Vocabulary Test, Draw-A-Man, and Children's Embedded Figures Test with four-year-old children. *Educational and Psychological Measurement, 1972, 32,* 1089–1093.

Dyk, R. B., & Witkin, H. A. Family experiences related to the development of differentiation in children. *Child Development, 1965, 30,* 21–55.

Egelund, B., & Weinberg, R. A. The Matching Familiar Figures Test: A look at its psychometric credibility. *Child Development, 1976, 47,* 483–491.

Elkind, D. Piagetian and psychometric conceptions of intelligence. In Discussion: How much can we boost IQ and scholastic achievement? *Harvard Educational Review, 1969, 39,* 319–337.

Faterson, H. F., & Witkin, H. A. Longitudinal study of development of the body concept. *Developmental Psychology, 1970, 2,* 429–438.

Fuqua, R. W., Bartsch, T. W., & Phye, G. D. An investigation of the relationship between cognitive tempo and creativity in preschool-age children. *Child Development, 1975, 46,* 779–782.

Gallagher, J. J. (Ed.), The application of child development research to exceptional children. Reston, Virginia: The Council for Exceptional Children, 1975.

Gardner, R. W., Holzman, P. S., Klein, G. S., Linton, B., & Spence, D. P. Cognitive control: A study of individual consistencies in cognitive behavior. *Psychological Issues, 1959, 1,* No. 4.

Goodenough, D. R. The Role of Individual differences in field dependence as a factor in learning and memory. *Psychological Bulletin, 1976, 83,* 675–694.

Goodenough, D. R., & Eagle, C. J. A modification of the Embedded Figures test for use with young children. *Journal of Genetic Psychology, 1963, 103,* 67–74.

Goodenough, D. R., & Karp, S. A. Field dependence and intellectual functioning. *Journal of Abnormal and Social Psychology*, 1961, *63*, 241–246.

Hess, R. D., & Shipman, V. C. Cognitive elements in maternal behavior. In J. P. Hill (Ed.), *Minnesota symposium on child psychology* (Vol. 1). Minneapolis: University of Minnesota Press, 1967.

Hunt, J. McV. *Intelligence and experience*. New York: Ronald Press, 1961.

Hunt, J. McV. Has compensory education failed? Has it been attempted? In Discussion: How much can we boost IQ and scholastic achievement? *Harvard Educational Review*, 1969, *39*, 278–299.

Inhelder, B. *The diagnosis of reasoning in the mentally retarded*. New York: The John Day Company, 1968.

Inhelder, B., & Piaget, J. *The early growth of logic in the child*. New York: Harper and Row, 1964.

Jensen, A. R. How much can we boost IQ and scholastic achievement? *Harvard Educational Review*, 1969, *39*, 1–123.

Kagan, J. Reflection-impulsivity and reading ability in primary grade children. *Child Development*, 1965, *36*, 609–628.

Kagan, J. Reflection-impulsivity: The generality and dynamics of conceptual tempo. *Journal of Abnormal Psychology*, 1966, *71*, 17–24.

Kagan, J. Inadequate evidence and illogical conclusions. In Discussion: How much can we boost IQ and scholastic achievement? *Harvard Educational Review*, 1969, *39*, 274–277.

Kagan, J., & Kogan, N. Individual variation in cognitive processes. In P. Mussen (Ed.), *Carmichael's manual of child psychology* (Vol. 1). New York: Wiley, 1970.

Kagan, J., & Messer, S. B. A reply to "Some misgivings about the Matching Familiar Figures Test as a measure of reflection-impulsivity." *Developmental Psychology*, 1975, *11*, 244–248.

Kagan, J., & Moss, H. A. *Birth to maturity: A study in psychological development*. New York: Wiley, 1962.

Kagan, J., Moss, H. A., & Sigel, I. E. Psychological significance of styles of conceptualization. In J. C. Wright and J. Kagan (Eds.), Basic cognitive processes in children. *Monographs of the Society for Research in Child Development*, 1963, *28*(2, Serial No. 86), 73–112.

Kagan, J., Pearson, L., & Welch, L. Conceptual impulsivity and inductive reasoning. *Child Development*, 1966, *37*, 583–594.

Kagan, J., Rosman, B. L., Day, D., Albert, J., & Phillips, W. Information processing in the child: Significance of analytic and reflective attitudes. *Psychological Monographs*, 1964, *78*(1, Whole No. 578).

Kamin, L. J. *The science and politics of IQ*. New York: Wiley, 1974.

Karp, S. A., & Konstadt, N. L. *Manual for the Children's Embedded Figures Test*. Brooklyn, New York: Cognitive Tests, 1963.

Keogh, B. K., Welles, M. F., & Weiss, A. L. *Field indepdnence-dependence, reflection-impulsivity, and problem-solving styles of preschool children*. (Technical Report SERP 1972-A1). University of California, Los Angeles, 1972.

Klein, G. S. Cognitive control and motivation. In G. Lindzey (Ed.), *Assessment of human motives*. New York: Rinehart, 1958.

Kogan, N. Educational implications of cognitive styles. In G. S. Lesser (Ed.), *Psychology and educational practice*. Glenview, Illinois: Scott, Foresman & Co., 1971.

Kogan, N. Creativity and cognitive style: A life span perspective. In P. B. Baltes and K. W. Schaie (Eds.), *Life span developmental psychology: Personality and socialization*. New York: Academic Press, 1973.

Kogan, N. *Cognitive styles in infancy and early childhood*. New York: Halsted Press, 1976.

Konstadt, N., & Forman, E. Field dependence and external directedness. *Journal of Personality and Social Psychology*, 1965, *1*, 490–493.

Lewis, M., Rausch, M., Goldberg, S., & Dodd, C. Error, response time, and IQ: Sex differences in the cognitive style of preschool children. *Perceptual and Motor Skills,* 1968, *26,* 563–568.

Lindstrom, D. R., & Shipman, V. C. Sigel Object Categorization Test. In V. C. Shipman (Ed.), *Disadvantaged children and their first school experiences.* Princeton, New Jersey: Educational Testing Service, 1972.

Lowentin, R. C. The fallacy of biological determinism. *The Sciences,* 1976, *16,* 6–10.

McCluskey, K. A., & Wright, J. C. Age and reflection-impulsivity as determinants of selective and relevant observing behavior. Paper presented at the meeting of the Society for Research in Child Development, Philadelphia, March, 1973.

Meichenbaum, D. H., & Goodman, J. Training impulsive children to talk to themselves: A means of developing self-control. *Journal of Abnormal Psychology,* 1971, *77,* 115–126.

Messer, S. B. The effect of anxiety over intellectual performance on reflection-impulsivity in children. *Child Development,* 1970, *41,* 723–735.

Messer, S. B. Reflection-impulsivity: A review. *Psychological Bulletin,* 1976, *83,* 1026–1052.

Neimark, E. D. Longitudinal development of formal operations thought. *Genetic Psychology Monographs,* 1975, *91,* 171–225.

Oltman, P. K. A portable rod-and-frame apparatus. *Perceptual and Motor Skills,* 1968, *26,* 503–506.

Owens, W. A. Age and mental abilities: A longitudinal study. *Genetic Psychology Monographs,* 1953, *48,* 3–54.

Papalia, D. E., & Bielby, D. D. V. Cognitive functioning in middle and old age. *Human Development,* 1974, *17,* 424–443.

Plomin, R., & Willerman, L. A cotwin control study and a twin study of reflection-impulsivity in children. *Journal of Educational Psychology,* 1975, *67,* 537–543.

Read, M. S. The biological bases: Malnutrition and behavioral development. In I. J. Gordon (Ed.), *Early childhood education.* Chicago: University of Chicago Press, 1972.

Ricciuti, H. N. Object grouping and selective ordering behavior in infants 12- to 24-months old. *Merrill-Palmer Quarterly,* 1965, *11,* 129–148.

Sarason, S. B., Davidson, K. S., Lighthall, F. F., Waite, R. R., & Ruebush, B. K. *Anxiety in elementary school children. A report of research.* New York: Wiley, 1960.

Scarr-Salapatek, S. Race, social class, and IQ. *Science,* 1971, *174,* 1285–1292.

Scarr-Salapatek, S. Genetics and the development of intelligence. In F. D. Horowitz (Ed.), *Review of child development research* (Vol. 4). Chicago: University of Chicago Press, 1975.

Siegel, A. W., Kirasic, K. C., & Kilburg, R. R. Recognition memory in reflective and impulsive preschool children. *Child Development,* 1973, *44,* 651–656.

Sigel, I. E. Developmental trends in the abstraction ability of children. *Child Development,* 1953, *24,* 131–144.

Sigel, I. E. How Intelligence tests limit understanding of intelligence. *Merrill-Palmer Quarterly,* 1963, *9,* 39–56.

Sigel, I. E. Styles of categorization in elementary school children: The role of sex differences and anxiety level. Paper presented at the meeting of the Society for Research in Child Development, Minneapolis, March, 1965.

Sigel, I. E. The distancing hypothesis: A causal hypothesis for the acquisition of representational thought. In M. R. Jones (Ed.), *Miami symposium on the prediction of behavior, 1968: Effects of early experience.* Coral Gables, Florida: The University of Miami Press, 1970.

Sigel, I. E. Concept formation. In J. J. Gallagher (Ed.), *The application of child development research to exceptional children.* Reston, Virginia: The Council for Exceptional Children, 1975.

Sigel, I. E., Anderson, L. M., & Shapiro, H. Categorization behavior of lower- and middle-class Negro preschool children: Differences in dealing with representation of familiar objects. *Journal of Negro Education,* 1966, *35*(3), 218–229.

Sigel, I. E., & Cocking, R. R. Cognition and communication: A dialectic paradigm for development. In M. Lewis and L. Rosenblum (Eds.), *Communication and language: The origins of behavior* (Vol. V). New York: Wiley, 1977.

Sigel, I. E., Jarman, P., & Hanesian, H. Styles of categorization and their intellectual and personality correlates in young children. *Human Development*, 1967, *10*, 1–17.

Sigel, I. E., & McBane, B. Cognitive competence and level of symbolization among five-year-old children. In J. Hellmuth (Ed.), *The disadvantaged child* (Vol. 1). New York: Brunner/Mazel, 1967.

Sigel, I. E., & Olmsted, P. Modification of cognitive skills among lower-class black children. In J. Hellmuth (Ed.), *The disadvantaged child* (Vol. 3). New York: Brunner/Mazel, 1970.

Sigel, I. E., Secrist, A., & Forman, G. Psycho-educational intervention beginning at age two: Reflections and outcomes. In J. C. Stanley (Ed.), *Compensatory education for children, ages two to eight: Recent studies of educational intervention.* Baltimore, Maryland: Johns Hopkins University Press, 1973.

Vaught, G. M., Pittman, M. D., & Roodin, P. A. Developmental curves for the portable rod-and-frame test. *Bulletin of the Psychonomic Society*, 1975, *5*, 151–152.

Ward, W. C. Reflection-impulsivity in kindergarten children. *Child Development*, 1968, *39*, 867–874.

Witkin, H. A. Social influences in the development of cognitive style. In D. A. Goslin (Ed.), *Handbook of socialization theory and research.* Chicago: Rand McNally, 1969.

Witkin, H. A. The role of cognitive style in academic performance and in teacher-student relations. Princeton, New Jersey: Educational Testing Service, 1973.

Witkin, H. A., Dyk, R. B., Faterson, H. F., Goodenough, D. R., & Karp, S. A. *Psychological differentiation.* New York: Wiley, 1962.

Witkin, H. A., Goodenough, D. R., & Karp, S. A. Stability of cognitive style from childhood to young adulthood. *Journal of Personality and Social Psychology*, 1967, *7*, 291–300.

Wright, J. C. Reflection-impulsivity and associated observing behavior in pre-school children. Paper presented at the meeting of the Society for Research in Child Development, Minneapolis, April, 1971.

Wright, J. C. The KRISP: A technical report. Unpublished manuscript, 1973.

Zigler, E. A. A measure in research of a theory. *Contemporary Psychology*, 1963, *8*, 133–135. (a)

Zigler, E. A. Zigler stands firm. *Contemporary Psychology*, 1963, *8*, 459–461. (b)